Technician Unit 11

DRAFTING FINANCIAL STATEMENTS
(ACCOUNTING PRACTICE, INDUSTRY AND COMMERCE)

For assessments in December 2004
and June 2005

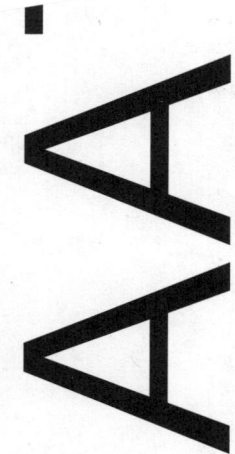

Interactive Text

In this May 2004 edition

- For assessments under the **new standards**
- Clear language and presentation
- Lots of diagrams and flowcharts
- Activities checklist to tie in each activity to specific knowledge and understanding, performance criteria and/or range statement
- Thorough reliable updating of material to 1 April 2004

FOR DECEMBER 2004 AND JUNE 2005 EXAMS

First edition May 2003
Second edition May 2004

ISBN 0 7517 1602 2 (Previous ISBN 0 7517 1133 0)

British Library Cataloguing-in-Publication Data
A catalogue record for this book
is available from the British Library

Published by

BPP Professional Education
Aldine House, Aldine Place
London W12 8AW

www.bpp.com

Printed in Great Britain by Ashford Colour Press Ltd
Unit 600
Fareham Reach
Fareham Road
Gosport
Hampshire
PO13 0FW

All our rights reserved. No part of this publication may be reproduced, stored in a retrieval system or transmitted, in any form or by any means, electronic, mechanical, photocopying, recording or otherwise, without the prior written permission of BPP Professional Education.

We are grateful to the Lead Body for Accounting for permission to reproduce extracts from the Standards of Competence for Accounting, and to the AAT for permission to reproduce extracts from the mapping and Guidance Notes.

BPP Professional Education
2004

Contents

Introduction

How to use this Interactive Text – Technician qualification structure –
Unit 11 Standards of competence – Exam based assessment technique – Assessment strategy

		Page	Answers to activities

PART A — Introducing limited company financial statements

1	Introducing limited company financial statements	3	311
2	Accounting conventions	25	314

PART B — Limited company accounts

3	The basics	43	315
4	The regulatory framework	73	318
5	Fixed assets and stocks	91	320
6	Taxation in company accounts	127	323
7	Provisions, contingencies and post balance sheet events	137	324
8	Reporting financial performance	153	326
9	Sundry standards in overview	171	331

PART C — Interpretation of accounts

10	Cash flow statements	197	342
11	Ratio analysis	223	351

CONTENTS

	Page	Answers to activities

PART D Simple consolidated accounts

		Page	Answers to activities
12	Introduction to group accounts	255	354
13	The consolidated balance sheet	267	355
14	Further aspects of group accounting	291	364

Answers to activities 311

Index 373

Order form

Review form & free prize draw

How to use this Interactive Text

Aims of this Interactive Text

> To provide the knowledge and practice to help you succeed in the assessment for Technician Unit 11 *Drafting Financial Statements*.

To pass the exam successfully you need a thorough understanding in all areas covered by the standards of competence.

> To tie in with the other components of the BPP Effective Study Package to ensure you have the best possible chance of success.

Interactive Text

This covers all you need to know for the exam based assessment for Unit 11 *Drafting Financial Statements*. Numerous activities throughout the text help you practise what you have just learnt.

Assessment Kit

When you have understood and practised the material in the Interactive Text, you will have the knowledge and experience to tackle the Assessment Kit for Unit 11 *Drafting Financial Statements*. This aims to get you through the exam.

Passcards

These short memorable notes are focused on key topics for the Technician Units, designed to remind you of what the Interactive Text has taught you.

Recommended approach to this Interactive Text

(a) To achieve competence in Unit 11 (and all the other units), you need to be able to do **everything** specified by the standards. Study the Interactive Text carefully and do not skip any of it.

(b) Learning is an **active** process. Do **all** the activities as you work through the Interactive Text so you can be sure you really understand what you have read. There is a checklist at the end of each chapter to show which knowledge and understanding, performance criteria and/or range statement is covered by each activity.

(c) After you have covered the material in the Interactive Text, work through the **Assessment Kit**.

(d) Before you take the assessment, check that you still remember the material using the following quick revision plan for each chapter.

   (i) Read and learn the **key learning points**, which are a summary of the chapter. This includes key terms and shows the sort of things likely to come up in an assessment.

   (ii) Do the **quick quiz** again. If you know what you're doing, it shouldn't take long.

   (iii) Go through the **Passcards** as often as you can in the weeks leading up to your assessment.

This approach is only a suggestion. Your college may well adapt it to suit your needs.

Quick quizzes

These include multiple choice questions, true/false and other formats not used by the AAT. However, these types of questions are usually very familiar to students and are used to help students adjust to otherwise unfamiliar material.

Remember this is a **practical** course.

(a) Try to relate the material to your experience in the workplace or any other work experience you may have had.

(b) Try to make as many links as you can to your study of the other Units at Technician level.

(c) Keep this text, (hopefully) you will find it invaluable in your everyday work too!

Technician qualification structure

The competence-based Education and Training Scheme of the Association of Accounting Technicians is based on an analysis of the work of accounting staff in a wide range of industries and types of organisation. The Standards of Competence for Accounting which students are expected to meet are based on this analysis.

The AAT issued new standards of competence in 2002, which take effect from 1 July 2003. This Text reflects the **new standards.**

The Standards identify the key purpose of the accounting occupation, which is to operate, maintain and improve systems to record, plan, monitor and report on the financial activities of an organisation, and a number of key roles of the occupation. Each key role is subdivided into units of competence, which are further divided into elements of competences. By successfully completing assessments in specified units of competence, students can gain qualifications at NVQ/SVQ levels 2, 3 and 4, which correspond to the AAT Foundation, Intermediate and Technician stages of competence respectively.

Whether you are competent in a Unit is demonstrated by means of:

- *Either* an Exam Based Assessment (set and marked by AAT assessors)
- *Or* a Skills Based Assessment (where competence is judged by an Approved Assessment Centre to whom responsibility for this is devolved)
- Or *both* Exam *and* Skills Based Assessment

Below we set out the overall structure of the Foundation (NVQ/SVQ Level 4) stage, indicating how competence in each Unit is assessed. In the next section there is more detail about the Exam Based Assessment for Unit 11.

INTRODUCTION

NVQ/SVQ Level 4

Group 1 Core Units – All units are mandatory.

Unit 8 Contributing to the Management of Performance and the Enhancement of Value	Element 8.1 Collect, analyse and disseminate information about costs
	Element 8.2 Make recommendations and make recommendations to enhance value

Unit 9 Contributing to the Planning and Control of Resources	Element 9.1 Prepare forecasts of income and expenditure
	Element 9.2 Produce draft budget proposals
	Element 9.3 Monitor the performance of responsibility centres against budgets

Unit 10 Managing Systems and People in the Accounting Environment	Element 10.1 Manage people within the accounting environment
	Element 10.2 Identify opportunities for improving the effectiveness of an accounting system

Unit 22 Contribute to the Maintenance of a Healthy, Safe and Productive Working Environment	Element 22.1 Monitor and maintain a safe, healthy and secure working environment
	Element 22.2 Monitor and maintain an effective and efficient working environment

NVQ/SVQ Level 4, continued

Group 2 Optional Units – Choose **one** of the following **four** units.

Unit 11 Drafting Financial Statements (Accounting Practice, Industry and Commerce)	Element 11.1 Draft limited company financial statements
	Element 11.2 Interpret limited company financial statements

Unit 12 Drafting Financial Statements (Central Government)	Element 12.1 Draft Central Government financial statements
	Element 12.2 Interpret Central Government financial statements

Unit 13 Drafting Financial Statements (Local Government)	Element 13.1 Draft Local Authority financial statements
	Element 13.2 Interpret Local Authority financial statements

Unit 14 Drafting Financial Statements (National Health Service)	Element 14.1 Draft NHS accounting statements and returns
	Element 14.2 Interpret financial statements of the NHS

INTRODUCTION

NVQ/SVQ Level 4, continued

Group 3 Optional Units – Choose **two** of the following **four** units.

Unit 15 Operating a Cash Management and Credit Control System	Element 15.1	Monitor and control cash receipts and payments
	Element 15.2	Manage cash balances
	Element 15.3	Grant credit
	Element 15.4	Monitor and control the collection of debts

Unit 17 Implementing Audit Procedures	Element 17.1	Contribute to the planning of an audit assignment
	Element 17.2	Contribute to the conduct of an audit assignment
	Element 17.3	Prepare related draft reports

Unit 18 Preparing Business Taxation Computations	Element 18.1	Prepare capital allowances computations
	Element 18.2	Compute assessable business income
	Element 18.3	Prepare capital gains computations
	Element 18.4	Prepare Corporation Tax computations

Unit 19 Preparing Personal Taxation Computations	Element 19.1	Calculate income from employment
	Element 19.2	Calculate property and investment income
	Element 19.3	Prepare Income Tax computations
	Element 19.4	Prepare Capital Gains Tax computations

Unit 11 Standards of competence

The structure of the Standards for Unit 11

The Unit commences with a statement of the **knowledge and understanding** which underpin competence in the Unit's elements.

The Unit of Competence is then divided into **elements of competence** describing activities which the individual should be able to perform.

Each element includes:

(a) A set of **performance criteria.** This defines what constitutes competent performance.

(b) A **range statement.** This defines the situations, contexts, methods etc in which competence should be displayed.

The elements of competence for Unit 11: *Drafting Financial Statements* are set out below. Knowledge and understanding required for the Unit as a whole are listed first, followed by the performance criteria and range statements for each element. Performance criteria are cross-referenced below to chapters in the Unit 11 *Drafting Financial Statements* Interactive Text.

Unit 11: Drafting financial statements

What is the Unit about?

This unit is about drafting and interpreting financial statements of limited companies. The first element in this unit is about drafting limited company year-end financial statements from a trial balance. You are responsible for ensuring that the financial statements comply with any relevant domestic legislation and *either* the relevant UK standards (Statements of Standard Accounting Practice, Financial Reporting Standards and other relevant pronouncements) *or* the International Accounting Standards. You also need to show that you ensure that confidentiality procedures are followed. The second element requires you to interpret the financial statements of companies and the relationships between the elements using ratio analysis.

Elements contained within this unit are:

Element 11.1   Draft limited company financial statements
Element 11.2   Interpret limited company financial statements

INTRODUCTION

Knowledge and understanding

The business environment

1. The elements and purposes of financial statements of limited companies as set out in the conceptual framework for financial reporting (Element 11.2)

2. The general legal framework of limited companies and the obligations of Directors in respect of the financial statements (Element 11.1)

3. The statutory form of accounting statements and disclosure requirements (Element 11.1)

4. The UK regulatory framework for financial reporting and the main requirements of relevant Financial Reporting Standards

    or

    The relevant requirements of the International Accounting Standards (Element 11.1)

5. The forms of equity and loan capital (Element 11.1)

6. The presentation of Corporation Tax in financial statements (Element 11.1)

Accounting techniques

7. Preparing financial statements in proper form (Element 11.1)

8. Analysing and interpreting the information contained in financial statements (Element 11.2)

9. Computing and interpreting accounting ratios (Element 11.2)

Accounting principles and theory

10. Generally accepted accounting principles and concepts (Elements 11.1)

11. The general principles of consolidation (Element 11.1)

The organisation

12. How the accounting systems of an organisation are affected by its roles, organisational structure, its administrative systems and procedures and the nature of its business transactions (Elements 11.1 & 11.2)

Element 11.1 Draft limited company financial statements

	Performance criteria	Chapters in this Text
A	Draft **limited company financial statements** from the appropriate information	3-9, 12-14
B	Correctly identify and implement subsequent adjustments and ensure that discrepancies, unusual features or queries are identified and either resolved or referred to the appropriate person	3, 5-7, 9, 12-14
C	Ensure that **limited company financial statements** comply with **relevant accounting standards** and **domestic legislation** and with the organisation's policies, regulations and procedures	2, 4-9, 12-14
D	Prepare and interpret a limited company cash flow statement	10
E	Ensure that confidentiality procedures are followed at all times	Throughout

Range statement

1	**Limited company financial statements:** Income statement; Balance sheet; Cash flow statement (not consolidated); Statement of total recognised gains and losses; The supplementary notes required by statute; Unitary; Consolidated	2-10, 12-14
2	**Domestic legislation:** Companies Act	2, 5, 9, 12-14
3	**Relevant accounting standards:** Relevant Statements of Standard Accounting Practice, Financial Reporting Standards and other relevant pronouncements; **or** International Accounting Standards	

INTRODUCTION

Element 11.2 Interpret limited company financial statements

Performance criteria		Chapters in this Text
A	Identify the general purpose of **financial statements** used in limited companies	1
B	Identify the **elements** of financial statements used in limited companies	1
C	Identify the **relationships between the elements** within financial statements of limited companies	1
D	Interpret the relationship between elements of limited company financial statements using ratio analysis	11
E	Identify unusual features or significant issues within financial statements of limited companies	11
F	Draw valid conclusions from the information contained within financial statements of limited companies	11
G	Present issues, interpretations and conclusions clearly to the appropriate people	11
Range statement		
1	**Financial statements:** Balance sheet; Income statement	1, 11
2	**Elements:** Assets; Liabilities; Ownership interest; Gains; Losses; Contributions from owners; Distributions to owners	1, 11
3	**Relationship between elements:** Profitability; Liquidity; Efficient use of resources; Financial position	1, 11

Exam Based Assessment technique

Completing exam based assessments successfully at this level is half about having the knowledge, and half about doing yourself full justice on the day. You must have the right **technique**.

The day of the exam based assessment

1. Set at least one **alarm** (or get an alarm call) for a morning exam.

2. Have **something to eat** but beware of eating too much; you may feel sleepy if your system is digesting a large meal.

3. Allow plenty of **time to get to where you are sitting the exam**; have your route worked out in advance and listen to news bulletins to check for potential travel problems.

4. **Don't forget** pens, pencils, rulers, erasers.

5. Put **new batteries** into your calculator and take a spare set (or a spare calculator).

6. **Avoid discussion** about the exam assessment with other candidates outside the venue.

Technique in the exam based assessment

1. **Read the instructions (the 'rubric') on the front of the assessment carefully**

   Check that the format hasn't changed. It is surprising how often assessors' reports remark on the number of students who do not attempt all the tasks.

2. **Read the paper twice**

   Read through the paper twice - don't forget that you are given 15 minutes' reading time. Check carefully that you have got the right end of the stick before putting pen to paper. Use your 15 minutes' reading time wisely.

3. **Check the time allocation for each section of the exam**

   Time allocations are given for each section of the exam. When the time for a section is up, you should go on to the next section.

4. **Read the task carefully and plan your answer**

   Read through the task again very carefully when you come to answer it. Plan your answer to ensure that you **keep to the point**. Two minutes of planning plus eight minutes of writing is virtually certain to produce a better answer than ten minutes of writing. Planning will also help you answer the assessment efficiently, for example by identifying workings that can be used for more than one task.

5. **Produce relevant answers**

   Particularly with written answers, make sure you **answer what has been set**, and not what you would have preferred to have been set. Do not, for example, answer a question on **why** something is done with an explanation of **how** it is done.

6. **Work your way steadily through the exam**

   Don't get bogged down in one task. If you are having problems with something, the chances are that everyone else is too.

INTRODUCTION

7 Produce an answer in the correct format

The assessor will state **in the requirements** the format which should be used, for example in a report or memorandum.

8 Do what the assessor wants

You should ask yourself what the assessor is expecting in an answer; many tasks will demand a combination of technical knowledge and business commonsense. Be careful if you are required to give a decision or make a recommendation; you cannot just list the criteria you will use, but you will also have to say whether those criteria have been fulfilled.

9 Lay out your numerical computations and use workings correctly

Make sure the layout is in a style the assessor likes.

Show all your **workings** clearly and explain what they mean. Cross reference them to your answer. This will help the assessor to follow your method (this is of particular importance where there may be several possible answers).

10 Present a tidy paper

You are a professional, and it should show in the **presentation of your work**. You should make sure that you write legibly, label diagrams clearly and lay out your work neatly.

11 Stay until the end of the exam

Use any spare time **checking and rechecking** your script. Check that you have answered all the requirements of the task and that you have clearly labelled your work. Consider also whether your answer appears reasonable in the light of the information given in the question.

12 Don't worry if you feel you have performed badly in the exam

It is more than likely that the other candidates will have found the exam difficult too. As soon as you get up to leave the venue, **forget** that exam and think about the next - or, if it is the last one, celebrate!

13 Don't discuss an exam with other candidates

This is particularly the case if you **still have other exams to sit**. Even if you have finished, you should put it out of your mind until the day of the results. Forget about exams and relax!

Assessment strategy

This Unit is assessed by **exam based assessment** only.

Exam based assessment

An exam based assessment is a means of collecting evidence that you have the **essential knowledge and understanding** which underpins competence. It is also a means of collecting evidence across the **range of contexts** for the standards, and of your ability to **transfer skills**, knowledge and understanding to different situations. Thus, although central assessments contain practical tests linked to the performance criteria, they also focus on the underpinning knowledge and understanding. You should, in addition, expect each central assessment to contain tasks taken from across a broad range of the standards.

Format of exam

There will be a three hour exam in two sections.

Section 1:   Element 11.1 (70% of the assessment)
Section 2:   Elements 11.2 (30% of the assessment)

There will be an additional 15 minutes reading time.

Guidance on the time allocation of tasks will be given in the exam.

The tasks are generally of a practical nature, designed to provide evidence that the performance criteria have been met and to ensure that the relevant knowledge and understanding is present.

Further guidance

The Standard is divided into two elements. Element 11.1 is called 'Draft limited company financial statements' and Element 11.2 is called 'Interpret limited company financial statements'.

Element 11.1 requires that the financial statements be drafted from appropriate information. This might include:

- A trial balance or an extended trial balance
- Other information about balances or transactions relating to the period under consideration

Students may be asked to draft financial statements for single companies or consolidated group accounts. Performance Criteria D makes it clear that the drafting of cash flow statements is also included in this Element. These may be drafted from the other financial statements of a company in conjunction with further relevant information.

In drafting financial statements the knowledge and understanding required is set out in the Standards. Students will need to know and understand the general legal framework of limited companies and the obligations of directors in respect of the financial statements. This includes a grasp of the Companies Act accounting and reporting requirements. The student must thus be aware of the statutory form of accounting statements and disclosure requirements in order that they can prepare the financial statements in proper form. This includes an understanding of the content and form of published accounts of limited companies. The Companies Act Format 1 for profit and loss accounts and balance sheets are used in the pro-formas provided in exams. Items required to be disclosed in notes to the accounts by the Companies Act Schedule 4 Part III, the disclosure of Directors' emoluments under Schedule 6 Part I and the requirements for disclosure of auditor's remuneration under Section 390A of the Companies Act must be grasped. The additional requirements of FRS 3 for profit and loss accounts and STRGL must also be understood and applied where required. Cash flow statements are to be drafted in accordance with the requirements of FRS 1 (Revised).

INTRODUCTION

There must be an understanding of the UK regulatory framework of financial reporting. This includes a grasp of which bodies are involved in the standard-setting process, the process by which standards are promulgated, the structure of regulation and the roles of the bodies involved and the process of enforcing standards. Drafting financial statements involves a grasp of generally accepted accounting principles and concepts as well as detailed knowledge of the main requirements of relevant Statements of Standard Accounting Practice, Financial Reporting Standards and other relevant pronouncements or, where applicable, the requirements of relevant International Accounting Standards (IAS) (from June 2006 at the earliest).

Drafting consolidated financial statements involves a grasp of the general principles of consolidation. Only simple consolidations will be assessed. This will involve minority interests and pre-acquisition profits. However, the consolidation of sub-subsidiaries or acquisitions where shares in subsidiary undertakings are acquired at different times will not be assessable. Simple equity accounting for associated companies is assessable. The forms of equity and loan capital and the presentation of corporation tax in financial statements must be understood for all companies.

Performance criteria for Element 11.2

This element requires students to understand the general purposes of limited company financial statements. The Range Statement makes clear that the financial statements in question are the balance sheet and income statement. The objective of financial statements is set out in Chapter 1 of the UK's conceptual framework The *Statement of Principles for Financial Reporting* (SOP). A knowledge of the purposes of financial statements as set out in this document is required by the knowledge and understanding of this Unit. The users of financial statements and the purposes for which they use financial statements are set out in the SOP.

The elements of financial statements are set out in the Range Statement. This follows the identification of elements given in the SOP. The elements are assets, liabilities, ownership interest, gains, losses, contributions from owners and distributions to owners and each of these are explained in the SOP. Students need to understand how these elements relate to each other within financial statements. This involves a grasp of which financial statement they appear in and how they are related to each other within the statements. In the balance sheet the relationship between assets, liabilities and ownership interest need to be understood using the accounting equation. The effect of contributions from owners and distributions to owners on the balance of ownership interest needs to be grasped. How gains and losses are reflected in the income statement must be understood and how the income statement articulates with the balance sheet must be grasped.

Students must also be able to interpret the relationship between elements of limited company financial statements using ratio analysis. This involves computing and interpreting accounting ratios relating to profitability, liquidity, efficient use of resources and financial position. Unusual features or significant issues raised by the analysis should be identified. Valid conclusions should be drawn from this information and the issues, interpretations and conclusions should be clearly presented to appropriate people.

Typical tasks in the first section

- Preparing a consolidated profit and loss account for a limited company
- Preparing a consolidated balance sheet for a limited company
- Calculating the goodwill on acquisition and/or minority interest for a limited company
- Calculating the amount at which an interest in an associate is to be included in consolidated financial statements
- Making adjustments to the balances in a trial balance or extended trial balance of a company in accordance with the requirements of company law, accounting concepts and accounting standards
- Explaining the UK regulatory framework of financial reporting including the bodies involved and their respective roles

INTRODUCTION

- Explaining the reason for the adjustments by reference to company law, accounting concepts and accounting standards
- Drafting a profit and loss account and/or a balance sheet from a trial balance or extended trial balance in accordance with the format and requirements of company law and accounting standards
- Explaining the requirements for the accounting treatment of items in company financial statements by reference to the requirements of accounting standards
- Drafting notes to the accounts as required by company law and accounting standards
- Explaining the general legal framework of limited companies and the obligations of directors in respect of the financial statements
- Drafting a reconciliation of movements in shareholders' funds and a note of historical cost profits and losses for a limited company
- Drafting a statement of total recognised gains and losses for a limited company
- Drafting a cash flow statement and/or a reconciliation between operating profit and cash flow from operating activities from the financial statements of a limited company
- Interpreting a cash flow statement

Typical tasks in the second section

- Setting out the general purposes of financial statements and illustrating these in relation to users and their needs
- Identifying and explaining the elements of financial statements
- Explaining what is meant by the balance sheet equation and how the elements fit into the equation
- Explaining the articulation of the balance sheet with the profit and loss account and STRGL
- Demonstrating the effect of contributions from owners and distributions to owners on ownership interest
- Calculating ratios for limited companies
- Interpreting the meaning of the ratios and of changes in the ratios of limited companies
- Comparing ratios of limited companies with industry averages
- Setting out the results of the computation and analysis of ratios in report format or in a letter and clearly setting out conclusions of the analysis therein

What is the Chief Assessor looking for?

What is expected of competent students in this Unit and some typical areas of weakness are set out below.

Section 1

(a) Students need to have a clear grasp what is involved in drafting consolidated financial statements. This involves a clear understanding of when there is a parent/subsidiary undertaking relationship. The student must grasp the principles behind consolidated accounts and demonstrate a clear grasp of the techniques of producing consolidated profit and loss accounts and balance sheets. The lack of a clear technique often lies behind the failure to demonstrate competence in these tasks.

(b) In order to show competence in the tasks of adjusting balances a clear grasp of the accounts affected by transactions or the requirements of company law, accounting concepts and accounting standards is required as

INTRODUCTION

well as a grasp of the mechanics of journal entries. Failure in this area would result from a lack of precision in identifying the accounts affected and through confusions as to when an account is debited or credited.

(c) Students need to be able to draft financial statements in accordance with the requirements of the Companies Act and accounting standards. This involves an ability to enter the balances and transactions correctly onto the pro-formas provided. Students who are not sufficiently familiar with the accounts that form part of the financial statement balances may encounter problems. The lack of knowledge of certain accounting standards may be reflected in uncertainty as to the treatment of certain accounting items. undermines efforts to answer the tasks that require an explanation of adjustments to account balances or an explanation of accounting treatment of certain items in the financial statements of companies.

(d) The drafting of financial statements in accordance with FRS 3, including the STRGL, may have caused problems for students. An adequate familiarity with the requirements of this accounting standard is required.

(e) Tasks which require the drafting of notes to the accounts may suffer from an occasional gap in knowledge. Once again, reference to the guidance given by the AAT on the assessable notes should be made to ensue adequate coverage.

(f) Knowledge of the standard-setting process and the bodies involved in the promulgation and policing of accounting standards is required by the Unit. A lack of precise knowledge of the bodies involved and their particular roles may result in a lack of competence in tasks in this area.

(g) The drafting of cash flow statements and the reconciliation and notes required by FRS 1 (Revised) is required by this Unit. A clear grasp of the technique of drafting such a statement and reconciliation may prove problematic for some students. The interpretation of such statements may also present particular problems for students. It is important to try and relate the information presented in cash flow statements into a coherent whole. Part of the problem with such tasks is the potential failure of students to be explicit in stating what information the cash flow statement and the reconciliation are giving about the company. Figures may be left to speak for themselves and hence there would appear to be little in the way of interpretation of the information.

Section 2

(a) Students must demonstrate an awareness of the overall purpose of financial statements and of the particular purposes of individual users of financial statements. Students may not be competent on these tasks because they do not pay sufficient attention to the requirements of the task. Students need to be able to distinguish external and internal users of financial information as well as appreciating the difference between the use of financial statements for the purposes of stewardship and other economic decisions.

(b) The student must be able to identify the elements of financial statements and give appropriate definitions. Some students may not be competent because they do not set out definitions of the elements with sufficient precision. They might fail to adequately explain the elements in terms of the SOP definitions and give examples of elements rather than explanations of the sort of thing that they are.

(c) Student must have a clear grasp of the accounting equation and be able to show how the equation reflects the equation through a numerical example. The articulation of the profit and loss account with the balance sheet needs to be grasped and students should be prepared to show how the profit for the year and any other gains shown in the STRGL changes the ownership interest.

(d) The calculation of the various ratios that show profitability, liquidity, efficient use of resources and financial position is required by the Unit. This involves a grasp of the formulas. In general, students must demonstrate a grasp of the meaning of the ratios, the import of changes in the ratios from one year to the next or of the differences in ratios between two companies and/or the industry averages. The results of the analysis should be clearly set out and relevant conclusions drawn. Students may not demonstrate competence because their analysis is superficial and does not demonstrate a clear understanding of the ratios and the information they convey. Sometimes the ratios may be left to speak for themselves and little more is said than that the ratio went

INTRODUCTION

up or down without any indication of the effect that this has on the company. Conclusions may be inadequately supported or not derived from a consideration of the preceding analysis. The presentation of answers to some of the tasks may not be in accordance with the requirements of the task. Credit for presentation would be accordingly lost.

Guidance on FRSs, SSAPs and legislation

Guidance on the FRSs, SSAPs and legislation that are assessable under this unit, and the extent to which they will be assessed, is set out below.

FRS 1 (revised)	–	all aspects
FRS 2, 6 and 7	–	restricted to identifying parent/subsidiary undertakings, the criteria for treating a business combination as an acquisition or a merger, preparing a simple consolidated balance sheet and profit and loss account (pre- and post-acquisition profits, minority interests, fair value adjustments, calculation and treatment of goodwill, elimination of inter-company profit)
	–	preparation of merger accounts or determining fair value in acquisition accounting is excluded
FRS 3	–	all aspects
FRS 4	–	definition of 'capital instrument' only
FRS 5	–	appreciation of the importance of recognising the substance of transactions, but no detailed questions requiring determination of the substance of a transaction or the disclosures required will be set
FRS 8	–	only the definition of 'related party' and the fact that transactions between related parties need to be disclosed
FRS 9	–	an understanding of the definition of associates and the application of equity accounting to simple examples. Accounting for joint ventures is not assessed
FRS 10	–	all aspects
FRS 11	–	limited to an understanding of the notion of an impairment review of fixed assets and goodwill, and the principles of recognition and measurement of impairment losses (including definitions of net reliable value and value in use)
	–	only the principles of calculation of impairment losses (excluding the principles of calculation in relation to income-generating units) will be assessed
	–	calculation of impairment losses will not be assessed
	–	subsequent monitoring of cash flows, reversal of past impairments and impairment losses on revalued fixed assets will not be assessed
FRS 12	–	all aspects except application of detailed rules on onerous contracts or restructuring
	–	no calculation of present value of expenditures expected to settle an obligation
FRS 13	–	not assessable
FRS 14	–	only the definition of EPS and simple calculations of basic EPS (diluted EPS excluded)
FRS 15	–	all aspects assessable, but emphasis on discursive rather than computational tasks
FRS 16	–	limited to disclosure of current tax in profit and loss account, balance sheet and statement of total recognised gains and losses and the measurement rule (paragraph 14)

INTRODUCTION

FRS 17	–	restricted to an understanding of the FRS and the difference between a defined contribution scheme and a defined benefit scheme. There will be no detailed assessment of the accounting treatment of retirement benefits or of the computation that relate to this.
FRS 18	–	all aspects of this FRS are assessable. It may be helpful to consider the requirements of the standard in conjunction with the *Statement of Principles* which contains further discussion of matters relevant to an understanding of this FRS.
FRS 19	–	understanding of deferred tax and the general requirements for recognition of deferred tax assets and liabilities
	–	no computations or detailed accounting treatment assessed
FRSSE	–	limited to an awareness of the objective of the standard and its scope. There will be no assessment of the detailed accounting requirements of the standard or of the differences or similarities between the requirements of the FRSSE and those of other accounting standards applicable to entities that do not fall within the scope of the FRSSE
SSAP 4	–	all aspects
SSAP 5	–	standard accounting practice of excluding VAT in turnover only
	–	no detailed computations of VAT or treatment of irrecoverable VAT will be assessed
SSAP 9	–	all aspects, excluding accounting treatment of long-term contracts
SSAP 13	–	all aspects
SSAP 17	–	all aspects
SSAP 19	–	all aspects
SSAP 20	–	appreciation of the need to account for foreign currency transactions for individual companies and for foreign enterprises in consolidated financial statements
	–	no assessment of methods of accounting
SSAP 21	–	appreciation of difference between finance and operating leases and overview of difference in accounting treatment, but no detailed computational questions
SSAP 25	–	appreciation of the need to provide segmental information in financial statements, but no computation of disclosures

Other pronouncements

Statement of Principles for Financial Reporting:

- objective of financial reporting
- qualitative characteristics of financial information
- elements of financial statements
- recognition criteria
- components of financial statements
- reporting entities

Exclude: urgent issues, SORPs, Accounting Standards Board statements.

Legislation

Companies Acts – general accounting and reporting requirements
- formats and understanding of items disclosed
- items to be disclosed in notes to accounts
- contents of directors' report
- filing exemptions for small and medium-sized companies

INTRODUCTION

Although all of the requirements for notes to the accounts under the Companies Act Schedule 4 Part III are assessable under this Unit, students should concentrate on understanding the content of, and from information given be able to produce, the following notes to the accounts:

- Disclosure of accounting policies
- Details of authorised and allotted share capital
- Movement on fixed assets
- Details of listed investments including information on market value where different from carrying value
- Movements on reserves and provisions
- Provision for deferred tax
- Analysis of indebtedness
- Details of charges and contingent liabilities
- Details of interest or similar charges on loans and overdrafts
- Basis of computation of UK corporation tax and details of tax charge

Under Schedule 6 of the Companies Act the following information required to be disclosed by way of notes to the accounts should also be covered:

- Directors' emoluments including Chairman's emoluments where necessary.

Under s 390A of the Companies Act 1985 the following note should be covered:

- Auditors' remuneration.

INTRODUCTION

PART A

Introducing limited company financial statements

chapter 1

Introducing limited company financial statements

Contents

1 The problem
2 The solution
3 Why do we need accounting information?
4 The accounting equation
5 The main financial statements
6 ASB *Statement of Principles*

Performance criteria

11.2.A Identify the general purpose of **financial statements** used in limited companies
11.2.B Identify the **elements** of financial statements used in limited companies
11.2.C Identify the **relationships between the elements** within financial statements of limited companies

Range statement

11.2.1 Financial statements: balance sheet; income statement
11.2.2 Elements: assets; liabilities; ownership interest; gains; losses; contributions from owners; distributions to owners
11.2.3 Relationship between elements: profitability; liquidity; efficient use of resources; financial position

Knowledge and understanding

1 The elements and purposes of financial statements of limited companies as set out in the conceptual framework for financial reporting (Element 11.2)
10 Generally accepted accounting principles and concepts (Elements 11.1)
12 How the accounting systems of an organisation are affected by its roles, organisational structure, its administrative systems and procedures and the nature of its business transactions (Elements 11.1 & 11.2)

1 The problem

So far in your studies, you've learnt how to prepare accounts for sole traders and partnerships (in Unit 5 at Intermediate Level). So what's so special about limited companies?

2 The solution

You may remember, from your Unit 5 studies, that limited companies have advantages over sole traders and partnerships because of **limited liability**. We will look at this in detail in Chapter 3.

However, limited liability means that the assets and liabilities of the limited company are **legally** separate from the owners. Therefore, the owners are not responsible for the company's liabilities.

Due to this advantage, limited companies are highly regulated.

- Companies Act
- Accounting standards

We will look at the affect of these later in this Text.

This chapter revises business basics and introduces some new ideas applicable to limited companies.

3 Why do we need accounting information?

3.1 What is a business?

You should know by now what a business is. There are a number of different ways of looking at it. Some ideas are listed below.

(a) A business is a **commercial or industrial concern** which deals in the manufacture, re-sale or supply of goods and services.

(b) It is an **organisation which uses economic resources** to create goods or services which customers will buy.

(c) It is an **organisation providing jobs** for people.

(d) It **invests money in resources** (for example it buys buildings, machinery and so on, it pays employees) in order to make even more money for its owners.

Businesses vary in character, size and complexity. They range from very small businesses (the local shopkeeper or plumber) to very large ones (ICI). But they have one important thing in common.

1: INTRODUCING LIMITED COMPANY FINANCIAL STATEMENTS

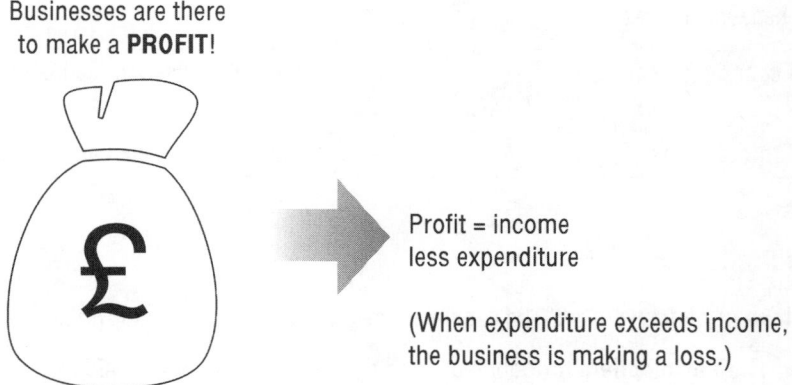

One of the jobs of an accountant is to measure income and expenditure and so profit. It is not such a straightforward problem as it may seem and in later chapters we will look at some of the theoretical and practical difficulties involved.

3.2 Assets and liabilities

An asset is something valuable which a business owns or has the use of. A **liability** is something which is owed to somebody else. 'Liabilities' is the accounting term for the debts of a business.

3.2.1 Examples of assets

Examples include office buildings, warehouses, delivery vans, lorries, plant and machinery, computer equipment, office furniture, cash and also goods held in store awaiting sale to customers, and raw materials and components held in store by a manufacturing business for use in production.

Some assets are **held and used** in operations **for a long time**. An office building might be occupied by administrative staff for years. A machine might have a productive life of many years before it wears out. These are **fixed assets**.

Other assets are held for only a **short time**. The owner of a newsagent shop, for example, will have to sell his newspapers on the same day that he gets them, and weekly newspapers and monthly magazines also have a short shelf life. These are **current** assets.

The more quickly a business can sell the goods it has in stock, the more profit it is likely to make, provided of course, that the goods are sold at a higher price than what it cost the business to acquire them.

3.2.2 A new definition of assets

You have come across assets in your earlier studies. Now consider a more formal definition, taken from an important document, the Accounting Standard Board's *Statement of Principles*.

> **Assets** are **rights** or other access to **future economic benefits** as a result of past transactions or events.

A machine is an asset because it gives:

Rights to future economic benefits	The machine will be used in the business to make products and earn revenue.
Because of past transactions	The machine was purchased at some time in the past.

3.2.3 Examples of liabilities

(a) A **bank loan** or bank *overdraft*. The liability is the amount which must eventually be repaid to the bank.

(b) **Amounts owed to suppliers** for goods on credit purchased but not yet paid for.

(c) **Taxation** owed to the government. A business pays tax on its profits but there is a gap in time between when a company declares its profits and becomes liable to pay tax and the time when the tax bill must eventually be paid.

(d) **Amounts invested in a business by its shareholders or owners**. This is explained in detail later.

3.2.4 A new definition of liabilities

The *Statement of Principles* also defines a liability.

> A **liability** is an obligation of an entity to transfer economic benefits as a result of past transactions or events.

A bank loan is a liability because it gives:

An obligation to transfer economic benefits	The loan must be repaid.
Because of a past transaction	The loan was taken out in the past.

The *Statement of Principles* is covered in more detail in Section 6.

3.3 The business as a separate entity

Many businesses are carried on in the form of **limited companies**. The owners of a limited company are its shareholders, who may be few in number (as with a small, family-owned company) or very numerous (for example in the case of a large public company whose shares are quoted on the Stock Exchange).

The law recognises a **company** as a **legal entity, quite separate from its owners**. A company may, in its own name, acquire assets, incur debts, and enter into contracts. If a company's assets became insufficient to meet its liabilities, the company as a separate entity might become 'bankrupt', but the owners of the company could not usually be required to pay the debts from their own private resources: the debts are not debts of the shareholders, but of the company.

Contrast this with the case of sole traders and partnerships, where **the law** sees no difference between the business and the owners.

Remember **in accounting**, the business is always treated as a **separate entity** from its owners, regardless of whether it is a sole trader, partnership or limited company.

3.4 The need for accounts

Why do businesses need to produce accounts? If a business is being run efficiently, why should it have to go through all the bother of accounting procedures in order to produce financial information?

The answer is simple. A business should produce information about its activities because there are **various groups** of people who **want or need to know** that information. This sounds rather vague: to make it clearer, we should look more closely at the classes of people who might need information about a business. We need also to think about what information in particular is of interest to the members of each class.

Because large businesses are usually of interest to a greater variety of people than small businesses we will consider the case of a large public company whose shares can be purchased and sold on the Stock Exchange.

3.5 Users of accounting information

The people who might be interested in financial information about a large public company may be classified as follows.

(a) **Employees of the company**. These should have a right to information about the company's financial situation, because their future careers and the size of their wages and salaries depend on it.

(b) **Lenders**. These might include a bank which permits the company to operate an overdraft, or provides longer-term finance by granting a loan. The bank will want to ensure that the company is able to keep up with interest payments, and eventually to repay the amounts advanced.

(c) **Suppliers and other creditors** will want to know about the company's ability to pay its debts.

(d) **Customers** need to know that the company is a secure source of supply and is in no danger of having to close down.

(e) **Government and their agencies.** Governments and their agencies are interested in the allocation of resources and therefore in the activities of enterprises. They also require information in order to provide a basis for national statistics.

(f) **The public**. Enterprises affect members of the public in a variety of ways. For example, enterprises may make a substantial contribution to a local economy by providing employment and using local suppliers. Another important factor is the effect of an enterprise on the environment, for example as regards pollution.

(g) **Shareholders of the company**, ie the company's owners. These will want to assess how effectively management is performing its stewardship function. They will want to know how profitably management is running the company's operations and how much profit they can afford to withdraw from the business for their own use.

(h) **The Inland Revenue**, who will want to know about business profits in order to assess the tax payable by the company, and also the **Customs and Excise**.

(i) **Managers of the company**. These are people appointed by the company's owners to supervise the day-to-day activities of the company. They need information about the company's financial situation as it is currently and as it is expected to be in the future. This is to enable them to manage the business efficiently and to take effective control and planning decisions.

(j) **Financial analysts and advisers**, who need information for their clients or audience. For example, stockbrokers will need information to advise investors in stocks and shares; credit agencies will want information to advise potential suppliers of goods to the company; and journalists need information for their reading public.

Users (a) – (f) are also specified in the *Statement of Principles*.

Accounting information is prepared in financial statements to satisfy the **information needs** of these different groups. Not all will be equally satisfied.

Managers of a business need the most information, to help them take their planning and control decisions; and they obviously have 'special' access to information about the business, because they can get people to give them the types of statements they want. When managers want a large amount of information about the costs and profitability of individual products, or different parts of their business, they can arrange to obtain it through a system of cost and management accounting.

In addition to management information, financial statements are prepared and perhaps published for the benefit of other user groups.

(a) The **law** provides for the provision of some information. The Companies Acts require every company to publish accounting information for its shareholders; and companies must also file a copy of their accounts with the Registrar of Companies, so that any member of the public who so wishes can go and look at them.

(b) The **Inland Revenue** authorities will receive the information they need to make tax assessments.

(c) A **bank** might demand a forecast of a company's expected future cash flows as a pre-condition of granting an overdraft.

(d) The **professional accountancy bodies** have been jointly responsible for issuing **accounting standards** and some standards require companies to publish certain additional information. Accountants, as members of these professional bodies, are placed under a strong obligation to ensure that company accounts conform to the requirements of the standards.

(e) Some companies provide, voluntarily, specially prepared financial information for issue to their employees. These statements are known as **employee reports**.

Activity 1.1

It is easy to see how 'internal' people get hold of accounting information. A manager, for example, can just go along to the accounts department and ask the staff there to prepare whatever accounting statements he needs. But external users of accounts cannot do this. How, in practice, can a business contact or a financial analyst access accounting information about a company?

4 The accounting equation

Signpost

This section is mainly revision. By now you should understand the accounting equation. Just read though this section to make sure you remember it and to learn some new terminology.

We will use an example to illustrate the 'accounting equation', ie the rule that the assets of a business will at all times equal its liabilities. This is also known as the **balance sheet equation**.

$$\boxed{\text{Assets}} = \boxed{\text{Liabilities}}$$

4.1 Starting the business

Liza Doolittle starts a business selling flowers. She puts in £2,500. The business begins by **owning** the cash that Liza has put into it, £2,500. The business is a separate entity in accounting terms and so it owes the money to Liza as **capital**.

In accounting, **capital** is an investment with the intention of earning a return. A business proprietor invests capital with the intention of earning profit. As long as that money is invested, accountants will treat the capital as money owed to the proprietor by the business. So capital is a form of liability so:

$$\boxed{\text{Assets}} = \boxed{\text{Capital}} + \boxed{\text{Liabilities}}$$

Capital is also called **ownership interest**. This is the term used in the *Statement of Principles*.

Ownership interest is the residual amount found by deducting all of the entity's liabilities from the entity's assets.

$$\boxed{\text{Assets}} - \boxed{\text{Liabilities}} = \boxed{\text{Capital (ownership interest)}}$$

When Liza Doolittle sets up her business:

Capital invested = £2,500
Cash = £2,500

Assets – Liabilities = Capital (ownership interest)

For Liza Doolittle, as at 1 July 20X6:

£2,500 (cash) – £0 = £2,500

4.2 Buying fixed assets and stock

Liza Doolittle purchases a market stall from Len Turnip, who is retiring from his fruit and vegetables business. The cost of the stall is £1,800.

She also purchases some flowers and potted plants from a trader in the wholesale market, at a cost of £650.

This leaves £50 in cash, after paying for the stall and goods for resale, out of the original £2,500. Liza kept £30 in the bank and drew out £20 in small change. She was now ready for her first day of market trading on 3 July 20X6.

The assets and liabilities of the business have now altered, and at 3 July before trading begins, the state of her business is as follows.

Assets	£	–	Liabilities	=	Ownership interest
Stall	1,800	–	£0	=	£2,500
Flower and plants	650				
Cash at bank	30				
Cash in hand	20				
	2,500				

The stall and the flowers and plants are physical items, but they must be given a money value. This money value is usually what they cost the business (called **historical cost** in accounting terms).

4.3 Profit introduced into the accounting equation

On 3 July Liza has a very successful day. She sells all of her flowers and plants for £900 cash.

Since Liza has sold goods costing £650 to earn revenue of £900, we can say that she has **earned a profit of £250 on the day's trading.**

Profits belong to the owners of a business. In this case, the £250 belongs to Liza Doolittle. However, so long as the business retains the profits and does not pay anything out to its owners, the **retained profits** are accounted for as an addition to the ownership interest.

Assets	£	–	Liabilities	=	Ownership interest	£
Stall	1,800				Original investment	2,500
Flower and plants	0					
Cash in hand and at bank						
(30+20+900)	950				Retained profit	
					(900 –650)	250
	2,750	–	£0			2,750

Assets less liabilities are often called **net assets**.

Net Assets = Ownership interest

At the beginning and end of 3 July 20X6, Liza Doolittle's financial position was as follows.

		Net assets	Ownership interest
(a)	At the beginning of the day:	£(2,500 – 0) = £2,500 =	£2,500
(b)	At the end of the day:	£(2,750 – 0) = £2,750 =	£2,750

There has been an increase of £250 in net assets, which is the amount of profits earned during the day.

Activity 1.2

Fill in the missing words. (Don't cheat!)

.... less .... = ownership interest

5 The main financial statements

In this section we look briefly at the two principal financial statements drawn up by accountants: the **balance sheet** and the **profit and loss account**.

5.1 What is a balance sheet?

The **balance sheet** is simply a list of all the assets owned by a business and all the liabilities owed by a business as at a particular date. It is a snapshot of the financial position of the business at a particular moment.

Assets are the business's **resources** which it uses in its operations. Additionally, it may have bank balances, cash and amounts of money owed to it. These provide the **funds** it needs to carry out its operations, and are also assets. On the other hand, it may **owe money** to the bank or to suppliers. These are **liabilities**.

5.2 What is a profit and loss account?

A **profit and loss account** is a record of income generated and expenditure incurred over a given period. The profit and loss account shows whether the business has had more income than expenditure (a profit) or vice versa (a loss).

The period chosen will depend on the purpose for which the statement is produced. The profit and loss account which forms part of the published annual accounts of a **limited company** will be made up for the period of a **year**, commencing from the date of the previous year's accounts. On the other hand, **management** might want to keep a closer eye on a company's profitability by making up **quarterly or monthly** profit and loss accounts.

5.3 Accruals basis

It is very important to grasp the principle, which is applied in nearly all business accounts, that financial statements are not prepared on a cash basis but on an **accruals** (or earnings) basis. That is, a sale or purchase is dealt with in the year in which it is made, even if cash changes hands in a later year.

This is important because most businesses, even if they do not sell on credit, make purchases on credit. If cash accounting is used, then accounts do not present a true picture of the activities in any given period. Accountants call this convention an application of the **accruals concept**. This is discussed in more detail in Chapter 2 of this Interactive Text, but in the meantime is explained briefly by means of the example below.

Example: accruals concept

Emma has a business printing and selling T-shirts. In May 20X7 she makes the following purchases and sales.

Invoice date	Numbers bought/sold	Amount	Date paid
Purchases		£	
7.5.X7	20	100	1.6.X7
Sales			
8.5.X7	4	40	1.6.X7
12.5.X7	6	60	1.6.X7
23.5.X7	10	100	1.7.X7

What is Emma's profit for May?

Emma's profit and loss account for May 20X7:

	£
Cash basis	
Sales	0
Purchases	0
Profit/loss	0
Accruals basis	
Sales (£40 + £60 + £100)	200
Purchases	100
Profit	100

Obviously, the accruals basis gives a truer picture than the cash basis. Emma has no cash to show for her efforts until June but her customers are legally bound to pay her and she is legally bound to pay for her purchases.

Her balance sheet as at 31 May 20X7 would therefore show her assets and liabilities as follows.

	£
Assets	
Debtors (£40 + £60 + £100)	200
Liabilities	
Creditors	100
Net assets	100
Proprietor's capital (ownership interest)	100

5.4 Capital

Capital is a special form of liability, representing the amount owed by the business to its proprietor(s). In Emma's case it represents the profit earned in May, which she, as sole proprietor of the business, is entitled to in full. Usually, however, capital will also include the proprietor's initial capital, introduced as cash and perhaps equipment or other assets.

For example, if Emma had begun her business on 30 April 20X7 by opening a business bank account and paying in £100, her balance sheet immediately after this transaction would look like this.

	£
Assets	
Bank	100
Proprietor's capital	100

On 31 May 20X7 the balance sheet would look like this.

	£
Assets	
Debtors	200
Bank	100
	300
Liabilities	
Creditors	100
Net assets	200
Proprietor's capital	
Brought forward	100
Profit for the period	100
Carried forward	200

This simple example shows that both the balance sheet and the profit and loss account are summaries of a great many transactions.

Accountancy textbooks often write 20X3 or 20X4 and so on for dates instead of 2003 etc. You will find both conventions in this Interactive Text, but in the Exam only 'real dates' (2003 etc) will be used.

5.5 Articulation of the profit and loss account and the balance sheet

At the end of the accounting period, the profit for the year is added to the profit brought forward in the balance sheet to arrive at the profit carried forward in the balance sheet. You can see this in the example of Emma above.

Look at the example below. This is another illustration of the link (articulation) between the profit and loss account and the balance sheet.

PROFIT AND LOSS ACCOUNT		BALANCE SHEET	
Sales	100	Assets	200
Cost of sales	(60)	Liability	(100)
Gross profit	40	Net assets	100
Expenses	(10)	Capital	30
Net profit	30	Profits brought forward	40
		Profit for the year	30
			100

6 ASB Statement of Principles

6.1 What is it?

The Accounting Standards Board (ASB) published (in December 1999) its *Statement of Principles for Financial Reporting*. You have met some of its definitions earlier, but this section sets them in context. The statement consists of eight chapters.

(1) The objective of financial statements
(2) The reporting entity
(3) The qualitative characteristics of financial information
(4) The elements of financial statements
(5) Recognition in financial statements
(6) Measurement in financial statements
(7) Presentation of financial information
(8) Accounting for interests in other entities

6.2 Purpose of the Statement of Principles

Here are the main reasons why the Accounting Standards Board (ASB) developed the *Statement of Principles*.

(a) To assist the ASB by providing a basis for **reducing** the **number of alternative** accounting treatments permitted by accounting standards and company law

(b) To provide a **framework** for the future development of accounting standards

(c) To **assist auditors** in forming an opinion as to whether financial statements conform with accounting standards

(d) To **assist users** of accounts in interpreting the information contained in them

1: INTRODUCING LIMITED COMPANY FINANCIAL STATEMENTS

(e) To provide **guidance in applying accounting standards**

(f) To give **guidance** on **areas** which are **not yet covered by accounting standards**

(g) To **inform interested parties** of the approach taken by the ASB in formulating accounting standards

The role of the *Statement* can thus be summed up as being to provide **consistency, clarity and information**.

6.3 Chapter 1 The objective of financial statements

6.3.1 Main points

(a) 'The objective of financial statements is to provide information about the **financial position, performance** and **financial adaptability** of an enterprise that is useful to a wide range of users for assessing the stewardship of management and for making economic decisions.'

(b) It is acknowledged that while not all the information needs of users can be met by financial statements, there are needs that are common to all users. Financial statements that meet the needs of providers of risk capital to the enterprise will also meet most of the needs of other users that financial statements can satisfy.

Users of financial statements other than present and potential investors include:

(i) Employees
(ii) Lenders
(iii) Suppliers and other creditors
(iv) Customers
(v) Government and their agencies
(vi) The public

(c) The **limitations** of financial statements are emphasised as well as the strengths.

(d) All of the **components** of financial statements (balance sheet, profit and loss account, cash flow statement) are **interrelated** because they reflect different aspects of the same transactions.

(e) The *Statement* emphasises the ways financial statements provide information about the financial position of an enterprise. The main elements which affect the position of the company are:

(i) The economic resources it controls

(ii) Its financial structure

(iii) Its liquidity and solvency

(iv) Its capacity to adapt to changes in the environment in which it operates (called **financial adaptability**)

The *Statement* discusses the importance of each of these elements and how they are **disclosed** in the financial statements.

6.3.2 Stewardship

A limited liability company is not usually run by its owners (unless it is a small family run company). Therefore the owners will appoint managers to run the business for them.

These managers are responsible for the safekeeping of the company's assets and for their 'proper, efficient and profitable use'. This is called the managers' **stewardship role**.

Financial statements show whether the business has made a profit or loss and the assets (and liabilities) still held at the balance sheet date. Therefore, they provide useful information for seeing how well managers have performed their stewardship duties.

6.4 Chapter 2 The reporting entity

It is important that entities that ought to prepare financial statements, in fact do so. The entity must be a **cohesive economic unit**. It has a **determinable boundary** and is held to account for all the things it **can control**.

6.5 Chapter 3 Qualitative characteristics of financial information

The *Statement* gives a diagrammatic representation of the discussion, shown below.

(a) Qualitative characteristics that relate to **content** are **relevance** and **reliability**.
(b) Qualitative characteristics that relate to **presentation** are **comparability** and **understandability**.

The diagram shown here is reasonably explanatory.

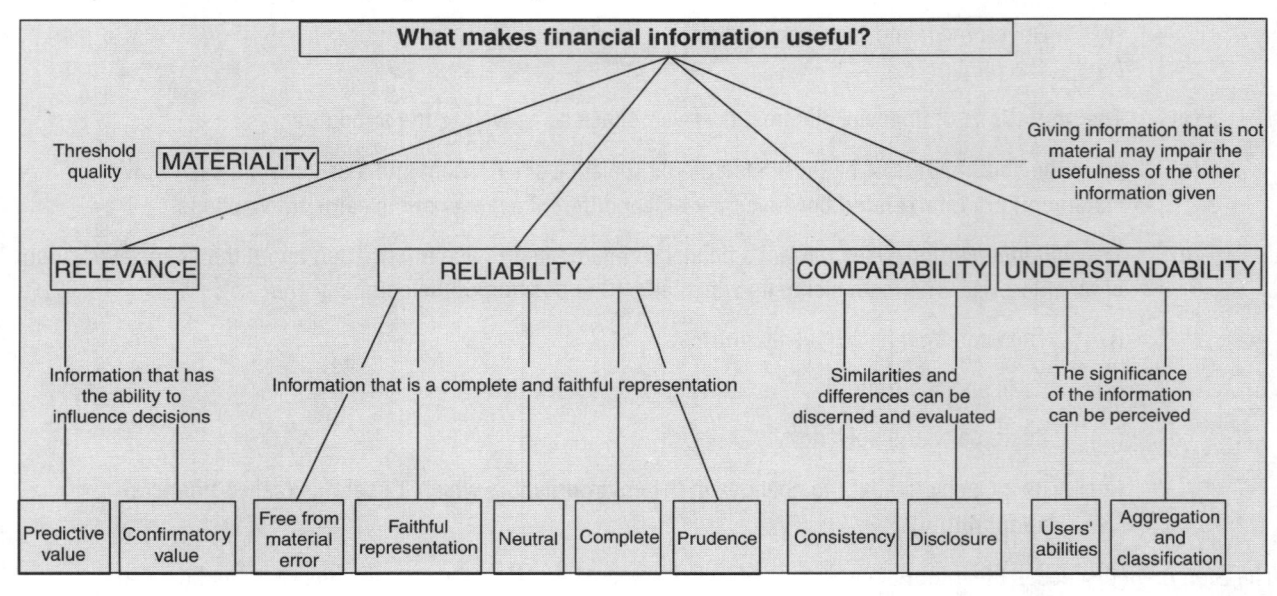

```
                    What makes financial information useful?
                                      |
   Threshold      MATERIALITY                          Giving information that is not
   quality                                             material may impair the
                                                      usefulness of the other
                                                      information given

   RELEVANCE         RELIABILITY          COMPARABILITY      UNDERSTANDABILITY

Information that has   Information that is a complete    Similarities and       The significance
the ability to         and faithful representation       differences can be     of the information
influence decisions                                      discerned and evaluated can be perceived

Predictive  Confirmatory   Free from   Faithful      Neutral  Complete  Prudence   Consistency  Disclosure   Users'      Aggregation
value       value          material    representation                                                        abilities   and
                           error                                                                                         classification
```

We will look at these characteristics again when considering prudence and consistancy in Chapter 2 of this Interactive text.

1: INTRODUCING LIMITED COMPANY FINANCIAL STATEMENTS

6.6 Chapter 4 Elements of financial statements

These are:

- Assets
- Liabilities
- Ownership interest
- Gains
- Losses
- Contributions from owners
- Distributions to owners

Any item that does not fall within one of the definitions of elements should not be included in financial statements. The definitions are as follows.

(a) **Assets** are rights or other access to future economic benefits controlled by an entity as a result of past transactions or events.

(b) **Liabilities** are obligations of an entity to transfer economic benefits as a result of past transactions or events.

(c) **Ownership interest** is the residual amount found by deducting all of the entity's liabilities from all of the entity's assets.

(d) **Gains** are increases in ownership interest, other than those relating to contributions from owners.

(e) **Losses** are decreases in ownership interest, other than those relating to distributions to owners.

(f) **Contributions from owners** are increases in ownership interest resulting from investments made by owners in their capacity as owners.

(g) **Distributions to owners** are decreases in ownership interest resulting from transfers made to owners in their capacity as owners.

> **Problems**
>
> The Chief Assessor has identified three problems which candidates have regarding the *Statement's* elements.
>
> - Some students only gave examples of specific elements (eg 'stock') rather than explaining the meaning.
> - A number of students did not know the **Statement of Principles** definitions.
> - Other explanations are acceptable, but the *Statement* is an authoritative source which should not be ignored.

6.7 Chapter 5 Recognition in financial statements

This chapter explains what is meant by recognition and discusses the three stages of recognition of assets and liabilities.

- Initial recognition
- Subsequent remeasurement
- Derecognition

The chapter goes on to describe the criteria which determine each of these stages.

(a) **Initial recognition**. An element should be recognised if there is sufficient evidence that the change in assets or liabilities is inherent in the element has occurred, including, where appropriate, evidence that a future inflow or outflow of benefit will occur, and it can be measured at a monetary amount with sufficient reliability.

(b) **Subsequent remeasurement**. A change in the amount at which an asset or liability is recorded should be recognised if there is sufficient evidence that the amount of an asset or liability has changed and the new amount of the asset or liability can be measured with sufficient reliability.

(c) **Derecognition**. An asset or liability should cease to be recognised if there is no longer sufficient evidence that the entity has access to future economic benefits or an obligation to transfer economic benefit (including, where appropriate, evidence that a future inflow or outflow of benefit will occur).

In practice, entities operate in an uncertain environment and this **uncertainty** may sometimes make it necessary to delay the recognition process. The uncertainty is twofold.

- **Element uncertainty** – does the item exist and meet the definition of elements?
- **Measurement uncertainty** – at what monetary amount should the item be recognised?

Activity 1.3

Consider the following situations. In each case, do we have an asset or liability within the definitions given by the *Statement of Principles?* Give reasons for your answer.

(a) Pat Ltd has purchased a patent for £20,000. The patent gives the company sole use of a particular manufacturing process which will save £3,000 a year for the next five years.

(b) Baldwin Ltd paid Don Brennan £10,000 to set up a car repair shop, on condition that priority treatment is given to cars from the company's fleet.

(c) Deals on Wheels Ltd provides a warranty with every car sold.

(d) Monty Ltd has signed a contract with a human resources consultant. The terms of the contract are that the consultant is to stay for six months and be paid £3,000 per month.

(e) Rachmann Ltd owns a building which for many years it had let out to students. The building has been declared unsafe by the local council. Not only is it unfit for human habitation, but on more than one occasion slates have fallen off the roof, nearly killing passers-by. To rectify all the damage would cost £300,000; to eliminate the danger to the public would cost £200,000. The building could then be sold for £100,000.

6.8 Chapter 6 Measurement in financial statements

This chapter, with its emphasis on current values, is fairly radical and controversial. The following approach is taken.

(a) **Initially**, when an asset is purchased or a liability incurred, the asset/liability is recorded at the **transaction cost**, that is historical cost, which at that time is equal to current replacement cost.

(b) An asset/liability may subsequently be '**remeasured**'. In a historical cost system, this can involve writing down an asset to its recoverable amount. For a liability, the corresponding treatment would be amendment of the monetary amount to the amount ultimately expected to be paid.

(c) Such re-measurements will, however, only be recognised if there is **sufficient evidence** that the monetary amount of the asset/liability has changed and the new amount can be reliably measured.

6.9 Chapter 7 Presentation of financial information

Aspects of this chapter have also given rise to some **controversy**. The chapter begins by making the general point that financial information is presented in the form of a structured set of financial statements comprising primary statements and supporting notes and, in some cases, supplementary information.

6.9.1 Components of financial statements

The primary financial statements are as follows.

(a) Profit and loss account
(b) Statement of total recognised gains and losses
(c) Balance sheet
(d) Cash flow statement

(a) and (b) are the 'statements of financial performance'.

The notes to the financial statements 'amplify and explore' the primary statements; together they form an 'integrated whole'. Disclosure in the notes does not correct or justify non-disclosure or misrepresentation in the primary financial statements.

'Supplementary information' embraces voluntary disclosures and information which is too subjective for disclosure in the primary financial statement and the notes.

We will be looking at items (a) to (d) in detail later in this Interactive Text.

6.10 Chapter 8 Accounting for interests in other entities

Financial statements need to reflect the effect on the reporting entity's financial performance and financial position of its interests in other entities. This involves various measurement, presentation and consolidation issues which are dealt with in this chapter of the *Statement*.

6.11 To sum up

The *Statement of Principles* will not have direct effect. It is **not an accounting standard** with which companies have to comply. Having said that, it may well be **influential**, especially where there is no specific standard dealing with an issue. There is still a great deal of controversy surrounding this document.

PART A   INTRODUCING LIMITED COMPANY FINANCIAL STATEMENTS

Activity 1.4

What is the purpose of the ASB's *Statement of Principles*?

> **TYPICAL EXAM TASKS**
>
> - Set out the general purpose of financial statements and illustrate this by identifying the users of financial statements in various organisations and their needs.
> - Identify and explain the nature of the elements of financial statements.
> - Explain the balance sheet equation and how the elements fit into it.
> - Explain the articulation of the balance sheet with the profit and loss account (ie the link between the two statements).
> - Demonstrate the effect of contributions from owners and distributions to owners.
>
> You should come back to this chapter after you have worked through the rest of this text and check that you feel happy about tackling any of the above.

Try the activity below. It is from a past exam and is typical of the sort of task you are likely to face.

Activity 1.5

(a) For a limited company:

    (i) Give an example of an external user of the financial statements.

    (ii) Describe one type of decision which would be made by the users with the assistance of the financial statements of the organisation.

(b) The accounting equation is often expressed as:

ASSETS – LIABILITIES = OWNERSHIP INTEREST

Explain what each of the terms 'assets', 'liabilities' and 'ownership interest' means.

Key learning points

- Businesses of whatever size or nature exist to make a **profit.**
- An **asset** is something which a business owns. A **liability** is something which a business owes.
- A business is a **separate entity** from its owner (for accounting purposes).
- There are various groups of people who need information about the activities of a business. You should be fully aware of these different **user groups** and their varying needs.
- The main financial statements of a business are the **balance sheet** and the **profit and loss account**.
  - The balance sheet is a 'snapshot' of the business position at a given point in time.
  - The profit and loss account is a record of income and expenditure over a period
- Both financial statements are prepared on an **accruals basis**, not a cash basis.
- The ASB's **Statement of Principles** should provide the backbone of the conceptual framework in the UK.
- Key elements in the *Statement* are as follows.
  - Financial statements should give financial information useful for assessing stewardship of management and for making economic decisions.
  - Financial information should be relevant, reliable, comparable and understandable.
  - The elements of financial statements are assets; liabilities; ownership interest; gains, losses; contributions from owners; and distributions to owners.
  - An element should be recognised if: there is sufficient evidence of its existence; and it can be measured at a monetary amount with sufficient reliability.

Quick quiz

1. What is an asset? Give three examples.
2. What is a liability? Give three examples
3. Identify seven user groups who need accounting information.
4. What are the two main financial statements drawn up by accountants?
5. At the end of the accounting year the profit for the year is added to the ………………….. to arrive at the ……………. in the balance sheet.
6. How does the *Statement of Principles* define 'gains' and 'losses'?
7. Which of the following are chapters in the Statement?

    A   Subsidiaries, associates and joint ventures
    B   Profit measurement in financial statements
    C   The objective of financial statements
    D   Accounting for interests in other entities
    E   Recognition in financial statements
    F   Presentation of financial statements
    G   Substance of transactions in financial statements
    H   The qualitative characteristics of financial information
    I   The quantitative characteristics of financial information
    J   Measurement in financial statements
    K   The reporting entity
    L   The elements of financial statements

8. A **gain** as defined by the *Statement of Principles* is an increase in the net assets of the entity.

    True ☐

    False ☐

Answers to quick quiz

1. An asset is something which a business owns or has the use of, eg a factory, a delivery van or a piece of machinery.
2. A liability is something which is owed to somebody else, eg a bank overdraft, amounts owed to suppliers or taxation owed to the government.
3. Seven from: Managers; shareholders; trade contacts; providers of finance; the Inland Revenue; employees; financial analysts and advisers; the public.
4. The balance sheet and the profit and loss account.
5. Profit brought forward. Profit carried forward.

1: INTRODUCING LIMITED COMPANY FINANCIAL STATEMENTS

6   (a) Gains are increases in ownership interest other than those relating to contributions from owners.
    (b) Losses are decreases in ownership interest other than those relating to distributions to owners.

7   C, D, E, F, H, J, K and L

8   False, see 6(a) above.

Activity checklist

This checklist shows which performance criteria, range statement or knowledge and understanding point is covered by each activity in this chapter. Tick off each activity as you complete it.

Activity

1.1 ☐ This activity deals with Knowledge and Understanding point 12: roles, structure, procedures and business transactions.

1.2 ☐ This activity deals with Performance Criteria 11.2.C: relationships between elements of financial statements.

1.3 ☐ This activity deals with Knowledge and Understanding point 1: elements of financial statements as set out in the conceptual framework.

1.4 ☐ This activity deals with Knowledge and Understanding point 1: conceptual framework for financial reporting.

1.5 ☐ This activity deals with Performance Criteria 11.2.B: elements of financial statements.

PART A INTRODUCING LIMITED COMPANY FINANCIAL STATEMENTS

chapter 2

Accounting conventions

Contents

1 The problem
2 The solution
3 'Bedrock' concepts
4 Other concepts and conventions
5 Accounting policies

Performance criteria
11.1.C Ensure that limited company financial statements comply with relevant accounting standards and domestic legislation and with the organisation's policies, regulations and procedures

Range statement
11.1.1 Limited company financial statements: income statement; balance sheet
11.1.3 Relevant accounting standards: FRS 18

Knowledge and understanding
4 The UK regulatory framework for financial reporting and the main requirements of relevant Financial Reporting Standards (Element 11.1)
10 Generally accepted accounting principles and concepts (Element 11.1)

PART A   INTRODUCING LIMITED COMPANY FINANCIAL STATEMENTS

1 The problem

Accounting practice has developed gradually over a matter of centuries. Many of its procedures are operated automatically by people who have never questioned whether alternative methods exist which are just as valid. However, the procedures in common use imply the acceptance of certain concepts which are by no means self-evident; nor are they the only possible **concepts**. These concepts could be used to build up an accounting framework.

2 The solution

Our next step is to look at some of the more important concepts which are taken for granted in preparing accounts. Originally, a statement of standard accounting practice (SSAP 2 *Disclosure of accounting policies*) described four concepts as *fundamental accounting concepts*: they were **going concern**, **prudence**, **accruals** and **consistency**.

In December 2000 FRS 18 *Accounting policies* replaced SSAP 2. FRS 18 emphasises the importance of **going concern** and **accruals** calling them the **bedrock** of financial statements. **Prudence** and **consistency** have been relegated to **'desirable'** elements of financial statements.

In this chapter we shall single out the following concepts for discussion.

(a) The **going concern** concept
(b) The **accruals** or matching concept
(c) The **prudence** concept
(d) The **consistency** concept
(e) The **entity** concept
(f) The **separate valuation** principle
(g) The **materiality** concept
(h) The **historical cost** convention
(i) The **objectivity** concept
(j) **Substance over form**

You have already met the going concern, accruals, prudence, consistency, entity and materiality concepts in your Unit 5 studies.

3 'Bedrock' concepts

Below are discussed the two 'bedrocks' of financial statements as identified by FRS 18 *Accounting policies*.

3.1 The going concern concept

> The **going concern concept** implies that the business will continue in operational existence for the foreseeable future, and that there is no intention to put the company into liquidation or to make drastic cutbacks to the scale of operations.

FRS 18 states that the financial statements **must** be prepared under the going concern basis unless the entity is being (or is going to be) liquidated or if it has ceased (or is about to cease) trading. The directors of a company must also disclose any significant doubts about the company's future if and when they arise.

The main significance of the going concern concept is that the assets of the business should not be valued at their 'break-up' value, which is the amount that they would sell for if they were sold off piecemeal and the business were thus broken up.

Example: going concern concept

Suppose, for example, that Emma acquires a T-shirt making machine at a cost of £60,000. The asset has an estimated life of six years, and it is normal to write off the cost of the asset to the profit and loss account over this time. In this case a depreciation cost of £10,000 per annum will be charged.

Using the going concern concept, it is presumed that the business will continue its operations and so the asset will live out its full six years in use. A depreciation charge of £10,000 will be made each year, and the value of the asset in the balance sheet will be its cost less the accumulated amount of depreciation charged to date. After one year, the **net book value** of the asset would therefore be £(60,000 – 10,000) = £50,000, after two years it would be £40,000, after three years £30,000 etc, until it has been written down to a value of 0 after 6 years.

Now suppose that this asset has no other operational use outside the business, and in a forced sale it would only sell for scrap. After one year of operation, its scrap value might be, say, £8,000.

The net book value of the asset, applying the going concern concept, is £50,000 after one year, but its immediate sell-off value only £8,000. It can be argued that the asset is over-valued at £50,000 and that it should be written down to its break-up value (ie in the balance sheet it should be shown at £8,000 and the balance of its cost should be treated as an expense). However, provided that the going concern concept is valid, so that the asset will continue to be used in the business and not sold, it is appropriate to value the asset at its net book value (£50,000).

Activity 2.1

Now try this example yourself.

A retailer commences business on 1 January and buys a stock of 20 washing machines, each costing £100. During the year he sells 17 machines at £150 each. How should the remaining machines be valued at 31 December if:

(a) He is forced to close down his business at the end of the year and the remaining machines will realise only £60 each in a forced sale?

(b) He intends to continue his business into the next year?

Entities are required to consider going concern and disclose the following.

(a) **Material uncertainties**. Conditions or events which present significant doubts about the entity's ability to continue as a going concern.

(b) **Foreseeable future**. Where the future of the trade is restricted to less than one year from the approval of the financial statements.

(c) **Going concern**. Where the financial statements are **not prepared** on a **going concern basis**, the reason for this and the method under which they have been prepared.

3.2 The accruals concept or matching concept

FRS 18 also stipulates that financial statements must be prepared under the accruals concept. This concept is a cornerstone of present day financial statements, so work through this section carefully so that you understand how it is applied during the preparation of accounts.

> The **accruals concept** states that revenue and costs must be recognised as they are earned or incurred, not as money is received or paid. They must be matched with one another so far as their relationship can be established or justifiably assumed, and dealt with in the profit and loss account of the period to which they relate.

This is illustrated in the example of Emma introduced in Chapter 1; profit of £100 was computed by matching the revenue (£200) earned from the sale of 20 T-shirts against the cost (£100) of acquiring them.

If, however, Emma had only sold eighteen T-shirts, it would have been incorrect to charge her profit and loss account with the cost of twenty T-shirts, as she still has two T-shirts in stock. If she intends to sell them in June she is likely to make a profit on the sale. Therefore, only the purchase cost of eighteen T-shirts (£90) should be matched with her sales revenue (£180), leaving her with a profit of £90.

Her balance sheet would therefore look like this.

	£
Assets	
Stock (at cost, ie 2 x £5)	10
Debtors (18 x £10)	180
	190
Liabilities	
Creditors	100
	90
Proprietor's capital (profit for the period)	90

In this example, the concepts of going concern and matching are linked. Because the business is assumed to be a going concern it is possible to carry forward the cost of the unsold T-shirts as a charge against profits of the next period.

Essentially, the accruals concept states that, in computing profit, revenue earned must be matched against the expenditure incurred in earning it.

4 Other concepts and conventions

4.1 The prudence concept

> The **prudence concept** states that where alternative procedures, or alternative valuations, are possible, the one selected should be the one which gives the most cautious presentation of the business's financial position or results.

The importance of **prudence** has diminished over time. Prudence is a **desirable quality** of financial statements but **not** a bedrock. The key reason for this change of perspective is that some firms have been over pessimistic and **over stated provisions** in times of high profits, they then release the over-provision in times of low profit, in order to 'profit-smooth'.

You should bear this in mind as you read through the explanation of prudence. On the one hand assets and profits should never be overstated, but a balance is needed to prevent the material overstatement of liabilities or losses.

You may have wondered why the three washing machines in Activity 2.1 were included in the balance sheet at cost (£100 each) rather than selling price (£150 each). This is an example of the prudence concept: to value the machines at £150 takes account of a profit before the profit is made.

The other aspect of prudence occurs where a **loss** is foreseen. It is taken into account immediately. If a business purchases stock for £1,200 but, because of a sudden slump in the market, it is likely to sell for only £900 prudence dictates that the stock is valued at £900. It is not enough to wait until the stock is sold, and then recognise the £300 loss; it must be recognised as soon as it is foreseen.

A profit is a **realised profit** when it is in the form of:

- Cash
- Another asset which has a reasonably certain cash value.

This includes amounts owing from debtors, provided that there is a reasonable certainty that the debtors will eventually pay up what they owe.

You may find the following description of prudence helpful.

> 'Revenue and profits are not anticipated, but are recognised by inclusion in the profit and loss account only when realised ....; provision is made for all known ... expenses and losses whether the amount of these is known with certainty or is a best estimate in the light of the information available.'
>
> SSAP 2

Examples: prudence concept

The following examples will help to explain the prudence concept.

(a) A company begins trading on 1 January 20X5 and sells goods worth £100,000 during the year to 31 December. At 31 December there are debts outstanding of £15,000. Of these, the company is now doubtful whether £6,000 will ever be paid.

The company should make a **provision for doubtful debts** of £6,000. Sales for 20X5 will be shown in the profit and loss account at their full value of £100,000, but the provision for doubtful debts would be a charge of £6,000. Because there is some uncertainty that the sales will be realised in the form of cash, the prudence concept dictates that the £6,000 should not be included in the profit for the year. The balance sheet will show debtors of £9,000 (£15,000 − £6,000).

(b) Samson Feeble trades as a carpenter. He makes a range of kitchen furniture for a customer at an agreed price of £1,000. At the end of Samson's accounting year the job is unfinished (being two thirds complete) and the following data has been assembled:

	£
Costs incurred in making the furniture to date	800
Further estimated costs to completion of the job	400
Total cost	1,200

The incomplete job represents *work in progress* at the end of the year which is an asset, like stock. Its cost to date is £800, but by the time the job is completed Samson will have made a loss of £200.

The full £200 loss should be charged against profits of the current year. The value of work in progress at the year end should be the lower of cost and *net realisable value*. The net realisable value can be calculated in either of two ways:

(i)	£	(ii)	£
Eventual sales value	1,000	Work in progress at cost	800
Less further costs to completion in order to make the sale	400	Less loss foreseen	200
Net realisable value	600		600

4.2 The consistency concept

Accounting is not an exact science. Judgement is used to attribute money values to many items appearing in accounts. Over the years certain procedures and principles have come to be recognised as good accounting practice, but there are often various acceptable methods of accounting for similar items.

> The **consistency concept** states that similar items should be accorded similar accounting treatments.

(a) Similar items within a single set of accounts should be given similar accounting treatment.

(b) The same treatment should be applied from one period to another in accounting for similar items. This enables valid comparisons to be made from one period to the next.

FRS 18 is designed to sit alongside the *Statement of Principles* framework. This helps explain the downplaying of the previously important prudence and consistency concepts.

From Chapter 3 *Qualitive characteristics of financial information*, the preparers of financial statements must now consider:

- Relevance
- Reliability
- Comparability
- Understandability

There is an assumption that by following these objectives, **prudence and consistency will be achieved** anyway. The objectives need to be weighed against each other and a course of action taken which **best fits all four.**

By fulfilling the reliability and comparability objectives, an accounting policy is likely to fulfil the consistency concept. If a policy provides information which is relevant and reliable, then it is likely that amounts are not overstated and so the prudence concept is fulfilled.

4.3 The entity concept

This concept has already been discussed in Chapter 1. Briefly, the concept is that accountants regard a business as a separate entity, distinct from its owners or managers. The concept applies whether the business is a limited company (and so recognised in law as a separate entity) or a sole proprietorship or partnership (in which case the business is not recognised as separate in law).

4.4 The separate valuation principle

> The **separate valuation principle** states that, in determining the amount to be attributed to an asset or liability in the balance sheet, each component item of the asset or liability must be determined separately.

These separate valuations are then added together to arrive at the balance sheet figure. For example, if a company's stock comprises 50 separate items, a valuation must (in theory) be made for each item separately; the 50 figures are then added up and the total is the stock figure in the balance sheet.

4.5 The materiality concept

> The **materiality concept**. Only items material in amount or in their nature will affect the accounts.

An error which is too trivial to affect anyone's understanding of the accounts is referred to as **immaterial**. In preparing accounts it is important to assess what is material and what is not, so that time and money are not wasted in the pursuit of excessive detail.

Determining whether or not an item is material is a **very subjective exercise**. There is no absolute measure of materiality. It is common to apply a convenient rule of thumb (for example to define material items as those with a value greater than 5% of the net profit disclosed by the accounts).

Some items disclosed in accounts are regarded as particularly sensitive and even a very small misstatement is regarded as a material error. An example in the accounts of a limited company is the amount of remuneration paid to the directors.

Whether an item is material or immaterial will affect its treatment in the accounts. For example, the profit and loss account of a business shows the expenses incurred grouped under suitable headings (heating and lighting expenses, rent and rates expenses etc). In the case of very small expenses it is appropriate to lump them together under 'sundry expenses', because a more detailed breakdown is inappropriate for such immaterial amounts.

IMPORTANT!

In assessing whether or not an item is material, it is not only the amount of the item which needs to be considered. The context is also important.

Example: materiality

(a) A balance sheet shows fixed assets of £2 million and stocks of £30,000. An error of £20,000 in the depreciation calculations might not be regarded as material, whereas an error of £20,000 in the stock valuation probably would be. In other words, you need to consider the effect on each item in the accounts.

(b) A business has a bank loan of £50,000 and a £55,000 balance on bank deposit account. It might well be regarded as a material misstatement if these two amounts were displayed on the balance sheet as 'cash at bank £5,000'. In other words, incorrect presentation may amount to material misstatement even if there is no monetary error.

Activity 2.2

Would you capitalise the following items in the accounts of a company?

(a) A box file costing £1.50
(b) A computer costing £1,500.00
(c) A plastic display stand costing £150.00

4.6 The historical cost convention

A basic principle of accounting is that items are normally stated in accounts at historical cost, ie at the amount which the business paid to acquire them. An important advantage of this procedure is that there is usually documentary evidence to prove the amount paid to purchase an asset or pay an expense.

> **Historical cost** means transactions are recorded at the cost when they occurred.

In general, accountants prefer to deal with costs, rather than with 'values'. This is because valuations tend to be subjective and to vary according to what the valuation is for. For example, suppose that a company acquires a machine to manufacture its products. The machine has an expected useful life of four years. At the end of two years the company is preparing a balance sheet and has to decide what monetary amount to attribute to the asset.

Numerous possibilities might be considered:

- The original cost (historical cost) of the machine
- Half of the historical cost, on the ground that half of its useful life has expired
- The amount the machine might fetch on the secondhand market
- The amount it would cost to replace the machine with an identical machine
- The amount it would cost to replace the machine with a more modern machine incorporating the technological advances of the previous two years
- The machine's economic value, ie the amount of the profits it is expected to generate for the company during its remaining life

All of these valuations have something to commend them, but the great advantage of the first two is that they are based on a figure (the machine's historical cost) which is objectively verifiable. The subjective judgement involved in the other valuations, particularly the last, is so great as to lessen the reliability of any accounts in which they are used.

4.7 Objectivity (neutrality)

> **Objectivity** means that accountants must be free from bias. They must adopt a neutral stance when analysing accounting data.

The result of this should be that any number of accountants will give the same answer independently of each other.

In practice, objectivity is difficult. Two accountants faced with the same accounting data may come to different conclusions as to the correct treatment. It was to combat subjectivity that accounting standards were developed.

4.8 Substance over form

> **Substance over form** means that transactions should be accounted for and presented in accordance with their economic substance, not their legal form.

An example of an application of substance over form is that of assets acquired on hire purchase. Legally the purchaser does not own the asset until the final instalment has been paid. However, the accounting treatment required is to record a fixed asset in the accounts at the start of the hire purchase agreement. The substance of the transaction is that the business owns the asset. The same could be said of fixed assets acquired under long-term leases.

5 Accounting policies

FRS 18 requires the **regular consideration of the company's accounting policies**. The **best** accounting policy should be adopted at all times. This is the major reason for downplaying consistency (and to a lesser extent prudence). A company **cannot retain** an accounting policy merely because it was used last year or because it gives a prudent view.

However, the company should consider how a **change** in accounting policy may affect **comparability**. Essentially a **balance** must be struck between selecting the **most appropriate policies** and presenting **coherent and useful** financial statements. The overriding guidance is that the financial statements should give a **true and fair view** of the entity's business. Chopping and changing accounting policies year on year is likely to jeopardise the true and fair view but so too is retaining accounting policies which do not present the most useful information to the users of the accounts.

5.1 Disclosure

FRS 18 requires the disclosure of

- A **description of each accounting policy** which is material to the company's financial statements
- A description of any significant estimation technique
- **Changes** to accounting policies
- The effects of any material change to an estimation technique

5.1.1 Estimation techniques

An estimation technique is material **only where a large range** of monetary values may be arrived at. The company should vary the assumptions it uses, to assess how sensitive monetary values are under that technique. In most cases the range of values will be relatively narrow (consider the useful life of motor vehicles for example).

5.1.2 Changes to accounting policies

The disclosure of new accounting policies also requires

- An explanation of the **reason for change**
- The **effects of a prior period adjustment** on the previous years results (in accordance with FRS 3)
- The **effects of the change in policy** on the previous year's results

If it is **not possible** to disclose the last two points then the **reason** for this should be disclosed instead.

5.2 FRS 18 in the exam

You need to be confident about the application of FRS 18. Make sure that you can **identify** a change in accounting policy and the **reason** that it is a change in accounting policy as opposed to a change in estimation technique. You will have to **discuss** the decision you have reached **and justify** your conclusions.

The most complex aspect to FRS 18 is the **application of the terms and definitions** within the standard.

5.3 Definitions

It is essential that you **learn the following definitions**. However, once you have read them you should **apply them** to the activities later in this section to make sure that you understand them.

> **Accounting policies**. The principles, conventions, rules and practices applied by an entity that prescribe how transactions and other events are to be reflected in its financial statements.

Accounting policies are **not** estimation techniques.

> An accounting policy includes the
>
> - Recognition
> - Presentation
> - And measurement basis
>
> Of assets, liabilities, gains, losses and changes to shareholders funds.

> **Estimation technique**. The methods used by an entity to establish the estimated monetary amounts associated with the measurement bases selected for assets, liabilities, gains, losses and changes to shareholder's funds.

Estimation techniques are used to **implement the measurement basis** of an accounting policy. The accounting policy specifies the measurement basis and the estimation technique is used when there is an uncertainty over this amount.

The **method of depreciation is an estimation technique**. The accounting policy is to spread the cost of the asset over its useful economic life. Depreciation is the measurement basis. The estimation technique would be the use of, say, straight line depreciation as opposed to reducing balance.

A change of estimation technique should **not** be accounted for as a prior period adjustment unless the following apply.

- It is the correction of a fundamental error
- The Companies Act, an accounting standard or a UITF Abstract **requires the change to be accounted** for as a prior period adjustment.

5.4 Application of FRS 18

FRS 18 gives a number of examples of its application in an appendix to the standard. When a change is required to an accounting policy then **three criteria** must be **considered** to ensure that the change is affecting the accounting policy and not an estimation technique.

1. Recognition
2. Presentation
3. Measurement basis

If **any one of the criteria apply** then a change has been made to the accounting policy. If they do **not** apply then a change to an estimation technique has taken place.

You should note that where an **accounting standard gives a choice** of treatments (ie SSAP 9 states that stock can be recognised on a FIFO or weighted average cost basis) then adopting the alternative treatment is a **change of accounting policy.** Also note that FRS 15 states that a **change in depreciation method is not** a change in accounting policy.

Example	Change to			Change of Accounting Policy
	Recognition	Presentation	Measurement basis?	
1. Changing from capitalisation of finance costs associated with the construction of fixed assets to charging them through the profit and loss	Yes	Yes	No	Yes
2. A reassessment of an entity's cost centres means that all three will have production overheads allocated to them instead of just two	No	No	No	No
3. Overheads are reclassified from distribution to cost of sales	No	Yes	No	Yes
4. Change from straight-line depreciation to machine hours	No	No	No	No
5. Reallocate depreciation from administration to cost of sales	No	Yes	No	Yes

Activity 2.3

The board of Beezlebub plc decide to change the depreciation method they use on their plant and machinery from 30% reducing balance to 20% straight line to better reflect the way the assets are used within the business. Is this a change of accounting policy?

Activity 2.4

The board of Beezlebub plc also decide to change their stock valuation. They replace their FIFO valuation method for an AVCO method to better reflect the way that stock is used within the business. Is this a change in accounting policy?

Activity 2.5

The board of Beezlebub plc decide in the following year that the development costs the business incurs should not be capitalised and presented on the balance sheet. Instead they agree that all development expenditure should be charged as an expense in the profit and loss account. Is this an accounting policy change?

Activity 2.6

Beezlebub plc's board are also considering reallocating the depreciation charges made on its large fleet of company cars to administration expenses, they were previously shown in cost of sales. Is this an accounting policy change?

Key learning points

- In preparing financial statements, certain **fundamental concepts** are adopted as a framework.
- Two such concepts are identified by FRS 18 *Accounting policies* as the bedrock of accounting.
  - The **going concern concept**. Unless there is evidence to the contrary, it is assumed that a business will continue to trade normally for the foreseeable future.
  - The **accruals or matching concept**. Revenue earned must be matched against expenditure incurred in earning it.
- A number of other concepts may be regarded as fundamental.
  - The **prudence concept**. Where alternative accounting procedures are acceptable, choose the one which gives the less optimistic view of profitability and asset values.
  - The **consistency concept**. Similar items should be accorded similar accounting treatments.
  - The **entity concept**. A business is an entity distinct from its owner(s).
  - The **separate valuation principle**. Each component of an asset or liability must be valued separately.
  - The **materiality concept**. Only items material in amount or in their nature will affect the true and fair view given by a set of accounts.
  - The **historical cost convention**. Transactions are recorded at the cost when they occurred.
  - **Objectivity**. Accountants must be free from bias.
  - **Substance over form**. Transactions must be presented and accounted for in accordance with their substance and financial reality and not merely with their legal form.
- **Accounting policies** are selected from the choices provided by accounting standards to provide a true and fair view.
- Accounting estimates are the application of judgement to allocate monetary values using the criteria provided by an accounting policy.
- FRS 18 requires an entity to conduct a review on an annual basis in order to ensure that it is using the most appropriate accounting policies.

  The objectives of
  - Reliability
  - Relevance
  - Comparability
  - Understandability

  Must be fulfilled by the accounting policies adopted. This requirement helps prevent entities from changing accounting policies too often.
- The three criteria
  - Recognition
  - Presentation
  - Measurement basis

  are considered in order to establish whether there has been a change of accounting policy or merely a change of estimation technique.

Quick quiz

1. List five important accounting concepts.
2. What is the prudence concept?
3. What is meant by an accounting policy?
4. Per FRS 18 the objectives of

    R ....

    R ....

    C ....

    U ....

    must be fulfilled by the accounting policies adopted.

5. Which of the following assumptions are included in FRS 18?

    A   Money measurement
    B   Objectivity
    C   Going concern
    D   Business entity

Answers to quick quiz

1. (a) Going concern
    (b) Accruals
    (c) Prudence
    (d) Consistency
    (e) Materiality

    These are the most important, but you could have mentioned entity, separate valuation, historical cost, objectivity and substance over form.

2. Where alternative procedures or alternative valuations are possible, the one selected should be the one which gives the most cautious presentation of the business's financial position or results.

3. Accounting policies are selected from the choices provided by accounting standards to provide a true and fair view.

4. Reliability
    Relevance
    Comparability
    Understandability

5. C   Of these, only going concern is included in FRS 18. The others are assumptions and concepts generally used in accounting, but not mentioned in FRS 18.

PART A INTRODUCING LIMITED COMPANY FINANCIAL STATEMENTS

Activity checklist

This checklist shows which performance criteria, range statement or knowledge and understanding point is covered by each activity in this chapter. Tick off each activity as you complete it.

Activity

2.1	☐	This activity deals with Performance Criteria 11.1.C: compliance with accounting standards.
2.2	☐	This activity deals with Knowledge and Understanding point 4: requirements of FRS.
2.3	☐	This activity deals with Performance Criteria 11.1.C: compliance with accounting standards.
2.4	☐	This activity deals with Performance Criteria 11.1.C: compliance with accounting standards.
2.5	☐	This activity deals with Performance Criteria 11.1.C: compliance with accounting standards.
2.6	☐	This activity deals with Performance Criteria 11.1.C: compliance with accounting standards.

PART B

Limited company accounts

chapter 3

The basics

Contents

1 The problem
2 The solution
3 What are limited companies?
4 The accounting records of limited companies
5 The board of directors
6 The capital of limited companies
7 Ordinary shares and preference shares
8 Dividends
9 The final accounts of limited companies: internal use
10 Fixed assets
11 Current liabilities
12 Debenture loans
13 Taxation
14 Ledger accounts and limited companies
15 Share capital and reserves
16 Example: company accounts

Performance criteria
11.1.A Draft limited company financial statements from the appropriate information
11.1.B Correctly identify and implement subsequent adjustments and ensure that discrepancies, unusual features or queries are identified and either resolved or referred to the appropriate person

Range statement
11.1.1 Limited company financial statements: income statement; balance sheet

Knowledge and understanding
2 The general legal framework of limited companies and the obligations of directors in respect of the financial statements (Element 11.1)
5 The forms of equity and loan capital (Element 11.1)
6 The presentation of corporation tax in financial statements (Element 11.1)
12 How the accounting systems of an organisation are affected by its roles, organisational structure, its administrative systems and procedures and the nature of its business transactions (Elements 11.1 and 11.2)

PART B   LIMITED COMPANY ACCOUNTS

1 The problem

From your earlier studies of Unit 5 at Intermediate Level, you will be aware of the format of accounts for sole traders and partnerships.

However, the format for limited companies is controlled by legislation (the Companies Act) and accounting standards. What information needs to be included in limited company accounts? How do they differ from those for sole traders and partnerships?

2 The solution

As we should expect, the accounting rules and conventions for recording the business transactions of limited companies and then preparing their final accounts are much the same as for sole traders. For example, companies will have a cash book, sales day book, purchase day book, journal, sales ledger, purchase ledger and main ledger. They will also prepare a profit and loss account annually and a balance sheet at the end of the accounting year.

However there are some major **differences** in the accounts of limited companies.

The **legislation** governing the activities of limited companies is very extensive. Amongst other things, the Companies Acts define certain minimum accounting records which must be maintained by companies. They specify that the **annual accounts** of a company must be filed with the Registrar of Companies and so available for public inspection. They also contain detailed requirements on the **minimum information** which must be disclosed in a company's accounts. Businesses which are not limited companies (non-incorporated businesses) enjoy comparative freedom from statutory regulation.

The owners of a company (its **members** or **shareholders**) may be very numerous. Their capital is shown differently from that of a sole trader; and similarly the 'appropriation account' of a company is different.

As you saw in Chapter 1, there are various users of company financial statements. In this chapter, we will consider the format of accounts for **internal use**, ie by the managers of the company, which do not need to comply with the Companies Act.

In Chapter 4, we will look at the format for **external users**, which will need to comply with the Companies Act format.

However, there are various items unique to limited company accounts (whether for internal or external use) and we will introduce you to these items in this chapter.

3 What are limited companies?

3.1 Limited liability

Unlimited liability means that if the business runs up debts that it is unable to pay, the proprietors will become personally liable for the unpaid debts.

3: THE BASICS

Sole traders and partnerships are, with some significant exceptions, generally fairly small concerns. The amount of capital involved may be modest and the proprietors of the business usually participate in managing it. Their liability for the debts of the business is unlimited. For example, a sole trader has a business which owes £40,000 but which it cannot repay. The trader might have to sell his house to raise the money to pay off his business debts.

Limited companies offer limited liability to their owners.

> **Limited liability** means that the maximum amount that an owner stands to lose in the event that the company becomes insolvent and cannot pay off its debts, is his share of the capital in the business.

Limited liability is a major advantage of turning a business into a limited company. However, in practice, banks will normally seek personal guarantees from the owners or managers before making loans or granting an overdraft facility to a small owner managed business.

There are **other disadvantages** too. In comparison with sole traders and partnerships, there is a significantly increased administrative and financial burden.

As a business grows, it needs more capital to finance its operations, and significantly more than the people currently managing the business can provide themselves. One way of obtaining more capital is to invite **investors from outside** the business to invest in the ownership or equity of the business. These new co-owners would not usually be expected to help with managing the business. To such investors, **limited liability is very attractive**.

Investments are always risky undertakings, but with limited liability the investor knows the maximum amount that he stands to lose when he puts some capital into a company.

3.2 Public and private companies

There are two classes of limited company.

(a) **Private companies**. These have the word 'limited' at the end of their name. Being private, they cannot invite members of the public to invest in their equity (ownership).

(b) **Public companies**. These are much fewer in number than private companies, but are generally much larger in size. They have the words 'public limited company' – shortened to PLC or plc (or the Welsh language equivalent) at the end of their name. Public limited companies can invite members of the general public to invest in their equity, and the 'shares' of these companies may be traded on The Stock Exchange if the necessary approval has been obtained (see Chapter 4).

Activity 3.1

Limited liability means that the directors do not have to account for their mistakes. True or false?

4 The accounting records of limited companies

There is a legal requirement for companies in the UK to keep **accounting records** which are sufficient to show and explain the company's transactions. This means, in theory, that the preparation of a company's accounts is not an 'incomplete records' problem. However, books can be destroyed, eg in a fire, and so accounts may need to be reconstructed.

4.1 Registers: the statutory books

A company must also keep a number of registers. These include:

- Register of members
- Register of shareholders' 3 per cent interests
- Register of charges and a register of debenture holders
- Register of directors and company secretaries
- Register of directors' interests (in shares or debentures of the company)

These registers are known collectively as the non-accounting **statutory books** of the company.

5 The board of directors

The owners (or shareholders) delegate authority for the day-to-day management of the company to its **directors**, who are directly responsible to the shareholders for what they do. (In some companies, the directors of the company and its shareholders might be the same people.) There must also be a company secretary. Company policy is decided at regular meetings of the board of directors.

> **IMPORTANT!**
>
> Whereas the salary of a sole trader or a partner is not a charge in the profit and loss account, but is an appropriation of profit, the salary of a director is a profit and loss account expense, even when the director is also a shareholder of the company.

It would be wrong to give the impression that all companies are large-scale with many shareholders. The vast majority of UK companies are in fact small and family-owned.

Example

There are many good reasons why a sole trader, say Alfred Newbegin Tools might choose to set up his own company (Newbegin Tools Ltd). These include limited personal liability and various tax advantages. Such a company would typically have one director (Alf) and his wife (Mabel) would be the company secretary. There would be two shareholders (Alf and Mabel) and board meetings would tend to be held during the commercial breaks on television or over breakfast. In this case it would be true to say that the providers of capital would also be running the business (as is normal with a sole trader) but Alf and Mabel as individuals would now be distinct from the business, because a company is a 'person' in its own right in the eyes of the law. Alf's salary, formerly an appropriation of profit, would now be a charge against company profits.

6 The capital of limited companies

The proprietors' capital in a limited company consists of **share capital**. When a company is set up for the first time, it issues shares, which are paid for by investors, who then become **shareholders** of the company. Shares are denominated in units of 25 pence, 50 pence, £1 or whatever seems appropriate. The 'face value' of the shares is called their **nominal value**.

For example, when a company is set up with a share capital of, say, £100,000, it may be decided to issue:

- (a) 100,000 shares of £1 each nominal value, or
- (b) 200,000 shares of 50p each, or
- (c) 400,000 shares of 25p each, or
- (d) 250,000 shares of 40p each etc

The amount to be paid may exceed the nominal value. For example, a company might issue 100,000 £1 shares at a price of £1.20 each. Subscribers will then pay a total of £120,000. The issued share capital of the company would be shown in its accounts at nominal value, £100,000; the excess of £20,000 is described not as share capital, but as **share premium**.

6.1 Authorised, issued, called-up and paid-up share capital

A distinction must be made between authorised, issued, called-up and paid-up share capital.

- (a) **Authorised (or nominal) capital** is the maximum amount of share capital that a company is empowered to issue. The amount of authorised share capital varies from company to company, and can change by agreement.

    For example, a company's authorised share capital might be 5,000,000 ordinary shares of £1 each. This would then be the maximum number of shares it could issue, unless the maximum were to be changed by agreement.

- (b) **Issued capital** is the nominal amount of share capital that has been issued to shareholders. The amount of issued capital cannot exceed the amount of authorised capital.

    Continuing the example above, the company with authorised share capital of 5,000,000 ordinary shares of £1 might have issued 4,000,000 shares. This would leave it the option to issue 1,000,000 more shares at some time in the future.

    When share capital is issued, shares are allotted to shareholders. The term 'allotted' share capital means the same thing as issued share capital.

- (c) **Called-up capital**. When shares are issued or allotted, a company does not always expect to be paid the full amount for the shares at once. It might instead call up only a part of the issue price, and wait until a later time before it calls up the remainder. There may be several 'calls' or instalments.

For example, if a company allots 400,000 ordinary shares of £1, it might call up only, say, 75 pence per share. The issued share capital would be £400,000, but the called up share capital would only be £300,000.

(d) **Paid-up capital**. Like everyone else, investors are not always prompt or reliable payers. When capital is called up, some shareholders might delay their payment (or even default on payment). Paid-up capital is the amount of called-up capital that has been paid.

For example, if a company issues 400,000 ordinary shares of £1 each, calls up 75 pence per share, and receives payments of £290,000, we would have:

	£
Allotted or issued capital	400,000
Called-up capital	300,000
Paid-up capital	290,000
Called-up capital not paid	10,000

The balance sheet of the company would then include called up capital not paid on the assets side, as a debtor.

	£
Called-up capital not paid	10,000
Cash (called-up capital paid)	290,000
	300,000
Called-up share capital	
400,000 ordinary shares of £1, with 75p per share called up.	300,000

7 Ordinary shares and preference shares

At this stage it is relevant to distinguish between the two types of shares most often encountered, **preference shares** and **ordinary shares**.

7.1 Preference shares

Preference shares are shares which confer certain preferential rights on their holder.

Preference shares carry the right to a final dividend which is expressed as a percentage of their nominal value: eg a 6% £1 preference share carries a right to an annual dividend of 6p. Preference dividends have priority over ordinary dividends; in other words, if the directors of a company wish to pay a dividend (which they are not obliged to do) they must pay any preference dividend first. Otherwise, no ordinary dividend may be paid.

The rights attaching to preference shares are set out in the company's constitution. They may vary from company to company, but typically:

(a) Preference shareholders have a **priority right** over ordinary shareholders to a **return of their capital** if the company goes into liquidation.

(b) Preference shares do **not carry a right to vote**.

(c) If the preference shares are **cumulative**, it means that before a company can pay an ordinary dividend it must not only pay the current year's preference dividend, but must also make good any arrears of preference dividends unpaid in previous years.

7.2 Ordinary shares

Ordinary shares are by far the most common. They carry no right to a fixed dividend but are entitled to all profits left after payment of any preference dividend. Generally however, only a part of such remaining profits is distributed, the rest being kept in reserve (see section 5 of this chapter).

The amount of ordinary dividends fluctuates although there is a general expectation that it will increase from year to year. Should the company be wound up, any surplus not distributed is shared between the ordinary shareholders. Ordinary shares normally carry voting rights.

Ordinary shareholders are the effective owners of a company. They own the 'equity' of the business, and any reserves of the business (described later) belong to them. Ordinary shareholders are sometimes referred to as **equity shareholders**. Preference shareholders are in many ways more like creditors (although legally they are members, not creditors).

It should be emphasised however that the precise rights attached to preference and ordinary shares vary from company to company; the distinctions noted above are generalisations.

Example: dividends, ordinary shares and preference shares

Garden Gloves Ltd has issued 50,000 ordinary shares of 50 pence each and 20,000 7% preference shares of £1 each. Its profits after taxation for the year to 30 September 20X5 were £8,400. The board of directors has decided to pay an ordinary dividend (ie a dividend on ordinary shares) which is 50% of profits after tax and the preference dividend.

Task

Show the amount in total of dividends and of retained profits, and calculate the dividend per share on ordinary shares.

Solution

Profits after tax and preference dividend are called *earnings*, and an important measure of company performance is the *earnings per share*. Although not required by the problem, the earnings per share (EPS) is also shown below.

	£
Profit after tax	8,400
Preference dividend (7% of £1 × 20,000)	1,400
Earnings (profit after tax and preference dividend)	7,000
Earnings per share (÷ 50,000) 14 pence	
Ordinary dividend (50% of earnings)	3,500
Retained profit (also 50% of earnings)	3,500

The ordinary dividend is 7 pence per share (£3,500 ÷ 50,000 ordinary shares).

The appropriation of profit would be shown as follows:

	£	£
Profit after tax		8,400
Dividends: preference	1,400	
ordinary	3,500	
		4,900
Retained profit		3,500

7.3 The market value of shares

The nominal value of shares will be different from their market value, which is the price at which someone is prepared to purchase shares in the company from an existing shareholder. If Mr A owns 1,000 £1 shares in Z Ltd he may sell them to B for £1.60 each.

This transfer of existing shares does not affect Z Ltd's own financial position in any way whatsoever, and apart from changing the register of members, Z Ltd does not have to bother with the sale by Mr A to Mr B at all.

Shares in private companies do not change hands very often, hence their market value is often hard to estimate. Public companies are usually (not always) quoted; a quoted company is one whose shares are traded on The Stock Exchange and it is the market value of the shares which is quoted.

8 Dividends

8.1 Paying dividends

Dividends are appropriations of profit after tax.

A company might pay dividends in **two stages** during the course of their accounting year.

(a) In mid year, after the half-year financial results are known, the company might pay an **interim dividend**.
(b) At the end of the year, the company might pay a further **final dividend**.

The **total dividend** for the year is the **sum of the interim and the final dividend.** (Not all companies by any means pay an interim dividend. Interim dividends are, however, commonly paid out by public limited companies.)

At the end of an accounting year, a company's directors will have **proposed a final dividend** payment, but this will not yet have been paid. This means that the **final dividend** should be appropriated out of profits and shown as a **current liability** in the balance sheet.

8.2 Terminology

The terminology of dividend payments can be confusing, since they may be expressed either in the form, as **'x pence per share'** or as **'y per cent'**. In the latter case, the meaning is always 'y per cent of the nominal value of the shares in issue'. For example, suppose a company's issued share capital consists of 100,000 50p ordinary shares which were issued at a premium of 10p per share. The company's balance sheet would include:

			£
Called up share capital:	100,000 50p ordinary shares		50,000
Share premium account	(100,000 × 10p)		10,000

If the directors wish to pay a dividend of £5,000, they may propose either:

(a) a dividend of 5p per share (100,000 × 5p = £5,000); or
(b) a dividend of 10% (10% × £50,000 = £5,000).

8.3 Profits re-invested

Not all profits are distributed as dividends; some will be retained in the business to finance future projects. The 'market value' of the share should, all other things being equal, be increased if these projects are profitable.

Activity 3.2

A company has authorised share capital of 1,000,000 50p ordinary shares and an issued share capital of 800,000 50p ordinary shares. If an ordinary dividend of 5% is declared, what is the amount payable to shareholders?

9 The final accounts of limited companies: internal use

The preparation and publication of the final accounts of limited companies in the UK are governed by the Companies Act 1985 as amended by the Companies Act 1989. At this stage we are concerned with the preparation of limited company accounts for *internal use*. If you are asked to produce such a set of final accounts, you need not follow the detailed regulations laid down by the Act. However, the general format of the balance sheet and profit and loss account of a limited company is shown below, in order to introduce certain assets and liabilities which we have not come across before in earlier chapters of this Interactive Text.

PART B   LIMITED COMPANY ACCOUNTS

9.1 Format of a limited company balance sheet

TYPICAL COMPANY LIMITED BALANCE SHEET
AS AT....

	£	£	£
Fixed assets			
Intangible assets			
Development costs		X	
Concessions, patents, licences, trademarks		X	
Goodwill		X	
			X
Tangible assets			
Land and buildings		X	
Plant and machinery		X	
Fixtures, fittings, tools and equipment		X	
Motor vehicles		X	
			X
Investments			X
			X
Current assets			
Stocks		X	
Debtors and prepayments		X	
Investments		X	
Cash at bank and in hand		X	
		X	
Creditors: amounts falling due within one year (ie current liabilities)			
Debenture loans (nearing their redemption date)	X		
Bank overdraft and loans	X		
Trade creditors	X		
Bills of exchange payable	X		
Taxation	X		
Accruals	X		
Proposed dividend	X		
	(X)		
Net current assets			X
Total assets less current liabilities			X
Creditors: amounts falling due after more than one year (ie long term liabilities)			
Debenture loans		X	
Taxation		X	
			(X)
Provisions for liabilities and charges			(X)
			A

	£	£

Capital and reserves
Called up share capital
Ordinary shares — X
Preference shares — X
                                                    X

Reserves
Share premium account — X
Revaluation reserve — X
Other reserves — X
Profit and loss account (retained profits) — X
                                                    X
                                                    A

9.2 Format of a limited company profit and loss account

TYPICAL COMPANY LIMITED
PROFIT AND LOSS ACCOUNT FOR THE YEAR ENDED...

	£	£
Turnover		X
Cost of sales		(X)
Gross profit		X
Distribution costs	X	
Administrative expenses	X	
		(X)
		X
Other operating income	X	
Income from fixed asset investments	X	
Other interest receivable and similar income	X	
		X
		X
Interest payable		(X)
Profit before taxation		X
Tax		(X)
Profit after tax		X
Dividends: preference	X	
ordinary	X	
		(X)
Retained profit for the year		X
Profit and loss account as at the beginning of the year		X
Profit and loss account as at the end of the year		X

You may be asked to produce a set of accounts for **external use**, in which case you will have to follow the statutory format in all respects. This is covered in Chapter 4.

10 Fixed assets

10.1 Intangible fixed assets

Intangible fixed assets represent amounts of money paid by a business to acquire benefits of a long-term nature.

For example, if a company purchases some **patent rights**, or a concession from another business, or the right to use a trademark, the cost of the purchase can be accounted for as the purchase of an intangible fixed asset. These assets must then be **amortised** (depreciated) over their economic life.

Other types of intangible asset include **goodwill**, and **deferred development expenditure**. These will be discussed in detail in a later chapter.

10.2 Tangible fixed assets

Tangible fixed assets (literally items that can be touched) are shown in the balance sheet at their net book value (ie at cost less provision for depreciation). Sometimes, a fixed asset, such as a building, might be revalued to a current market value. Depreciation would then be based on the revalued amount, and the balance sheet value of the asset would be the revalued amount less provision for depreciation on the revalued amount.

10.3 Investments

Investments are fixed assets if the company intends to hold on to them for a long time, and current assets if they are only likely to be held for a short time before being sold.

11 Current liabilities

The term **'creditors: amounts falling due within one year'** is used in the Companies Act 1985 as an alternative phrase meaning 'current liabilities'. Similarly **'creditors: amounts falling due after more than one year'** means 'long-term liabilities'.

12 Debenture loans

Limited companies may issue **debenture stock** (debentures) or loan stock. These are **long-term liabilities**, also called **loan capital**. They are different from share capital in the following ways.

(a) Shareholders are members of a company, while providers of loan capital are creditors.

(b) Shareholders receive dividends (appropriations of profit) whereas the holders of loan capital are entitled to a fixed rate of interest (an expense charged against revenue).

(c) Loan capital holders can take legal action against a company if their interest is not paid when due, whereas shareholders cannot enforce the payment of dividends.

(d) **Debentures** or loan stock are often **secured on company assets**, whereas shares are not.

The holder of loan capital is generally in a less risky position than the shareholder. He has greater security, although his income is fixed and cannot grow, unlike ordinary dividends. As remarked earlier, preference shares are in practice very similar to loan capital, not least because the preference dividend is normally fixed.

Interest is calculated on the nominal value of loan capital, regardless of its market value. If a company has £700,000 (nominal value) 12% debentures in issue, interest of £84,000 will be charged in the profit and loss account per year. Interest is usually paid half-yearly; examination questions often require an accrual to be made for interest due at the year-end.

For example, if a company has £700,000 of 12% debentures in issue, pays interest on 30 June and 31 December each year, and ends its accounting year on 30 September, there would be an accrual of three months' unpaid interest (3/12 × £84,000) = £21,000 at the end of each accounting year that the debentures are still in issue.

13 Taxation

Companies pay **corporation tax** on the profits they earn. Currently (2004), small companies pay tax at the rate of 19% on their taxable profits, and large companies pay 30%. Note that because a company has a separate legal personality, its tax is included in its accounts. An unincorporated business would not show income tax in its accounts, as it would not be a business expense but the personal affair of the proprietors.

(a) The **charge** for corporation tax on profits for the year is shown as a **deduction** from **net profit**, before appropriations.

(b) In the balance sheet, **tax payable** to the government is generally shown as a **current liability** as it is usually due nine months after the year end.

(c) For various reasons (discussed in Chapter 6), the tax on profits in the P & L account and the tax payable in the balance sheet are not usually the same amount.

14 Ledger accounts and limited companies

Limited companies keep ledger accounts, and the only difference between the ledger accounts of companies and sole traders is the nature of some of the transactions, assets and liabilities for which accounts need to be kept.

14.1 Taxation

(a) Tax charged against profits will be accounted for by:

DEBIT   Profit and loss account
CREDIT   Taxation account

(b) The outstanding balance on the taxation account will be a liability in the balance sheet, until eventually paid, when the accounting entry would be:

DEBIT   Taxation account
CREDIT   Cash

PART B   LIMITED COMPANY ACCOUNTS

14.2 Dividends

A separate account will be kept for the dividends for each different class of shares (eg preference, ordinary).

(a) Dividends declared out of profits will be accounted for by

DEBIT   Profit and loss appropriation account
CREDIT   Dividends payable account

Dividends payable (but not yet paid) are a current liability.

(b) When dividends are paid, we then have

DEBIT   Dividends payable account
CREDIT   Cash

14.3 Debenture loans

Debenture loans being a long-term liability will be shown as a credit balance in a debenture loan account, (debit cash).

Interest payable on such loans is not credited to the loan account, but is credited to a separate creditors' account for interest until it is eventually paid: ie

DEBIT   Interest account (an expense, chargeable against profits)
CREDIT   Interest payable (creditors, and a current liability until eventually paid)

14.4 Share capital and reserves

There will be a separate account for:

(a) each different class of share capital (always a credit balance b/f);
(b) each different type of reserve (nearly always a credit balance b/f).

We shall now turn our attention to these items in more detail.

15 Share capital and reserves

15.1 Shareholders' capital

The net assets of a company are 'financed' by the shareholders' capital.

Shareholders' capital consists of

- the nominal value of called up share capital
- reserves

The share capital itself might consist of both ordinary shares and preference shares. All reserves, however, are owned by the ordinary shareholders, who own the 'equity' in the company.

15.2 Reserves

In the case of a sole trader, the proprietor's interest = net assets of the business, and in the case of a partnership, partners' funds = net assets. For a company the equation is:

> Shareholders' funds = net assets

Furthermore:

> Shareholders' funds = share capital and reserves

A company's share capital will remain fixed from year to year, unless new shares are issued. The total amount of reserves in a company varies, according to changes in the net assets of the business.

The typical balance sheet in Section 9 lists a number of reserves, although the list is not comprehensive.

Statutory reserves are required to be set up by law, and are not available for the distribution of dividends.

Non-statutory reserves are reserves set up from profits, which are distributable as dividends if the company so wishes.

15.3 Profit and loss reserve (retained profits)

The most significant **non-statutory reserve** is variously described as:

- Revenue reserve
- Retained profits
- Retained earnings
- Undistributed profits
- Profit and loss account
- Unappropriated profits

These are **profits** earned by the company and **not appropriated** by dividends, taxation or transfer to another reserve account.

Provided that a company is earning profits, this reserve generally increases from year to year, as most companies do not distribute all their profits as dividends. Dividends can be paid from it: even if a loss is made in one particular year, a dividend can be paid from previous years' retained profits.

For example, if a company makes a loss of £100,000 in one year, yet has unappropriated profits from previous years totalling £250,000, it can pay a dividend not exceeding £150,000. One reason for retaining some profit each year is to enable the company to pay dividends even when profits are low (or non-existent). Another reason is usually shortage of cash.

Very occasionally, you might come across a debit balance on the profit and loss account. This indicates that the company has accumulated losses.

15.4 Other non-statutory reserves

The company directors may choose to set up other reserves. These may have a specific purpose (eg plant and machinery replacement reserve) or not (eg general reserve). The creation of these reserves usually indicates an intention not to distribute the profits involved at any future date, although legally any such reserves (being non-statutory) remain available for the payment of dividends.

15.4.1 Appropriation of profit

Profits are transferred to these reserves by making an appropriation out of profits, usually profits for the year. Typically, you might come across the following:

	£	£
Profit after taxation		100,000
Appropriations of profit		
Dividend	60,000	
Transfer to general reserve	10,000	
		70,000
Retained profits for the year		30,000
Profit and loss reserve b/f		250,000
Profit and loss reserve c/f		280,000

15.5 The share premium account

There are a number of statutory (or capital) reserves, the most important at this stage is the **share premium account**. Section 130 of the Companies Act 1985 states that 'where a company issues shares at a premium, whether for cash or otherwise, a sum equal to.... the premiums on those shares shall be transferred to the share premium account'.

By **'premium'** is meant the difference between the issue price of the share and its nominal value. When a company is first incorporated (set up) the issue price of its shares will probably be the same as their nominal value and so there would be no share premium. If the company does well the market value of its shares will increase, but not the nominal value. The price of any new shares issued will be approximately their market value.

The difference between cash received by the company and the nominal value of the new shares issued is transferred to the share premium account. For example, if X Ltd issues 1,000 £1 ordinary shares at £2.60 each the book entry will be:

		£	£
DEBIT	Cash	2,600	
CREDIT	Ordinary share capital (nominal value 1,000 × £1)		1,000
	Share premium account (1,000 × £1.60)		1,600

A **share premium account** is an account into which sums received as payment for shares in excess of their nominal value must be placed.

Once established, the share premium account constitutes capital of the company which cannot be paid out in dividends. The share premium account will increase in value if and when new shares are issued at a price above their nominal value.

The share premium account can be 'used' – and so decrease in value – only in certain very limited ways. One use of the share premium account, however, is to 'finance' the issue of bonus shares, which are described later in this section.

> **IMPORTANT!**
> The share premium account cannot be distributed as dividend under any circumstances.

The reason for creating statutory reserves is to **maintain the capital** of the company. This capital 'base' provides some security for the company's creditors, bearing in mind that the liability of shareholders is limited in the event that the company cannot repay its debts. It would be most unjust – and illegal – for a company to pay its shareholders a dividend out of its base capital when it is not even able to pay back its debts.

Activity 3.3

What are the ledger entries needed to record the issue of 200,000 £1 ordinary shares at a premium of 30p and paid for by cheque in full.

15.6 Distinction between reserves and provisions

A **reserve** is an appropriation of distributable profits for a specific purpose (eg plant replacement) while a **provision** is an amount charged against revenue as an expense.

A **provision** relates either to a diminution in the value of an asset (eg doubtful debtors) or a known liability (eg audit fees).

Provisions (for depreciation, doubtful debts etc) are dealt with in company accounts in the same way as in the accounts of other types of business.

15.7 Bonus issues

A company may wish to increase its share capital without needing to raise additional finance by issuing new shares. For example, a profitable company might expand from modest beginnings over a number of years. Its profitability would be reflected in large balances on its reserves, while its original share capital might look like that of a much smaller business.

It is open to such a company to **re-classify some of its reserves as share capital**. This is purely a paper exercise which raises no funds. Any reserve may be re-classified in this way, including a share premium account or other statutory reserve. Such a re-classification increases the capital base of the company and gives creditors greater protection.

Example: bonus issue

BUBBLES LIMITED
BALANCE SHEET (EXTRACT)

	£'000	£'000
Funds employed		
Share capital		
£1 ordinary shares (fully paid)		1,000
Reserves		
Share premium	500	
Undistributed profit	2,000	
Shareholders' funds		2,500
		3,500

Bubbles decided to make a '3 for 2' bonus issue (ie 3 new shares for every 2 already held). Therefore 1,500,000 new bonus shares are issued.

	£'000	£'000
The double entry is		
DEBIT Share premium	500	
Undistributed profit	1,000	
CREDIT Ordinary share capital		1,500

	£'000
After the issue the balance sheet is as follows	
Share capital	
£1 ordinary shares (fully paid)	2,500
Reserves	
Undistributed profit	1,000
Shareholders' funds	3,500

The new ('bonus') shares are issued to existing shareholders, so that if Mr X previously held 20,000 shares he will now hold 50,000. The total value of his holding will remain the same however, since the net assets of the company remain unchanged and his share of those net assets remains at 2% (ie 50,000/2,500,000; previously 20,000/1,000,000).

15.8 Rights issues

A rights issue (unlike a bonus issue) is an issue of shares for cash. The 'rights' are offered to existing shareholders, who can sell them if they wish.

Example: rights issue

Bubbles Ltd decides to make a rights issue, shortly after the bonus issue. The terms are '1 for 5 @ £1.20' (ie one new share for every five already held, at a price of £1.20). Assuming that all shareholders take up their rights (which they are not obliged to) the double entry is:

		£'000	£'000
DEBIT	Cash (2,500,000 ÷ 5 × £1.20)	600	
CREDIT	Ordinary share capital		500
	Share premium		100

Mr X who previously held 50,000 shares will now hold 60,000, and the value of his holding should increase (all other things being equal) because the net assets of the company will increase. The new balance sheet will show:

	£'000	£'000
Share capital		
£1 ordinary shares		3,000
Reserves		
Share premium	100	
Undistributed profit	1,000	
		1,100
Shareholders' funds		4,100

The increase in funds of £600,000 represents the cash raised from the issue of 500,000 new shares at a price of £1.20 each.

Rights issues are a popular way of raising cash by issuing shares as they are cheap to administer. In addition, shareholders retain control of the business as their holding is not diluted.

16 Example: company accounts

We can now try to draw together several of the items described in this chapter into an illustrative example. Study it carefully, as it also acts as revision of items, such as accruals and prepayments, studied at Foundation and Intermediate Levels.

The accountant (unqualified) of Megatec Ltd has prepared the following trial balance as at 31 December 20X7.

	£'000
50p ordinary shares (fully paid)	350
7% £1 preference shares (fully paid)	100
10% debentures (secured)	200
Retained profit 1.1.X7	242
General reserve 1.1.X7	171
Freehold land and buildings 1.1.X7 (cost)	430
Plant and machinery 1.1.X7 (cost)	830
Provision for depreciation:	
Freehold buildings 1.1.X7	20
Plant and machinery 1.1.X7	222
Stock 1.1.X7	190
Sales	2,695
Purchases	2,152
Preference dividend	7
Ordinary dividend (interim)	8
Debenture interest	10
Wages and salaries	254
Light and heat	31
Sundry expenses	113
Suspense account	135
Debtors	179
Creditors	195
Cash	126

PART B LIMITED COMPANY ACCOUNTS

Notes

1. Sundry expenses include £9,000 paid in respect of insurance for the year ending 1 September 20X8. Light and heat does not include an invoice of £3,000 for electricity for the three months ending 2 January 20X8, which was paid in February 20X8. Light and heat also includes £20,000 relating to salesmen's commission.

2. The suspense account is in respect of the following items:

	£'000
Proceeds from the issue of 100,000 ordinary shares	120
Proceeds from the sale of plant	300
	420
Less purchase of plant	285
	135

3. The freehold property was acquired some years ago. The buildings element of the cost was estimated at £100,000 and the estimated useful life of the assets was fifty years at the time of purchase. As at 31 December 20X7 the property is to be revalued at £800,000.

4. The plant which was sold had cost £350,000 and had a net book value of £274,000 as on 1.1.X7. £36,000 depreciation is to be charged on plant and machinery for 20X7.

5. The debentures have been in issue for some years. The 50p ordinary shares all rank for dividends at the end of the year.

6. The directors wish to provide for:

    (a) Debenture interest due
    (b) A final ordinary dividend of 2p per share
    (c) A transfer to general reserve of £16,000
    (d) Audit fees of £4,000

7. Stock as at 31 December 20X7 was valued at £220,000 (cost).

8. Taxation is to be ignored.

Task

Prepare the final accounts of Megatec Ltd in a form suitable for internal purposes.

Approach and suggested solution

(a) Normal adjustments are needed for accruals and prepayments (insurance, light and heat, debenture interest and audit fees). The debenture interest accrued is calculated as follows:

	£'000
Charge needed in profit and loss account (10% × £200,000)	20
Amount paid so far, as shown in trial balance	10
Accrual – presumably six months' interest now payable	10

The accrued expenses shown in the balance sheet comprise:

	£'000
Debenture interest	10
Light and heat	3
Audit fee	4
	17

Prepayment comprises:

	£'000
Insurance ($^8/_{12}$ × £9,000)	6

(b) The misposting of £20,000 to light and heat is also adjusted, by reducing the light and heat expense, but charging £20,000 to salesmen's commission.

(c) Depreciation on the freehold building is calculated as $\frac{£100,000}{50}$ = £2,000 pa.

The NBV of the freehold property is then £430,000 – £20,000 – £2,000 = £408,000 at the end of the year.

(d) The profit on disposal of plant is calculated as proceeds £300,000 (per suspense account) less NBV £274,000, ie £26,000. The cost of the remaining plant is calculated at £830,000 – £350,000 = £480,000. Add cost of new plant £285,000 and cost carried forward is £765,000. The depreciation provision at the year end is:

	£'000
Balance 1.1.X7	222
Charge for 20X7	36
Less depreciation on disposals (350 – 274)	(76)
	182

(e) The other item in the suspense account is dealt with as follows:

	£'000
Proceeds of issue of 100,000 ordinary shares	120
Less nominal value 100,000 × 50p	50
Excess of consideration over nominal value (= share premium)	70

(f) Appropriations of profit must be considered. The final ordinary dividend, shown as a current liability in the balance sheet, is

(700,000 + 100,000 ordinary shares) × 2p = £16,000

(g) The transfer to general reserve increases that reserve to £171,000 + £16,000 = £187,000.

PART B   LIMITED COMPANY ACCOUNTS

MEGATEC LIMITED
TRADING AND PROFIT AND LOSS ACCOUNT
FOR THE YEAR ENDED 31 DECEMBER 20X7

	£'000	£'000	£'000
Turnover			2,695
Cost of sales			
Opening stock		190	
Purchases		2,152	
		2,342	
Less closing stock		220	
			2,122
Gross profit			573
Profit on disposal of plant			26
			599
Administrative expenses			
Wages, salaries and commission		274	
Sundry expenses		107	
Light and heat		14	
Depreciation: freehold buildings		2	
plant		36	
Audit fees		4	
Debenture interest		20	
			457
Net profit			142
Appropriations			
Transfer to general reserve		16	
Dividends: preference (paid)	7		
ordinary: interim (paid)	8		
final (proposed)	16		
		31	
			47
Retained profit for the year			95
Retained profit brought forward			242
Retained profit carried forward			337

MEGATEC LIMITED
BALANCE SHEET AS AT 31 DECEMBER 20X7

	Cost/val'n £'000	Dep'n £'000	£'000
Fixed assets			
Tangible assets			
Freehold property	430	22	408
Plant and machinery	765	182	583
	1,195	204	
			991
Current assets			
Stock		220	
Debtors		179	
Prepayment		6	
Cash		126	
		531	
Creditors: amounts falling due within one year			
Creditors	195		
Accrued expenses	17		
Proposed dividend	16		
		228	
Net current assets			303
Total assets less current liabilities			1,294
Creditors: amounts falling due after more than one year			
10% debentures (secured)			(200)
			1,094
Capital and reserves			
Called up share capital			
50p ordinary shares		400	
7% £1 preference shares		100	
			500
Reserves			
Share premium		70	
General reserve		187	
Profit and loss account		337	
			594
			1,094

Activity 3.4

You are the assistant to the financial controller of Hanoi Ltd, a manufacturing company. The company's year end is 31 March 20X4. The following balances have been extracted as at 1 April 20X3.

	£'000
Freehold land	200
Freehold premises: cost	150
accumulated amortisation	6
Plant and equipment: cost	120
accumulated depreciation	48
Trade debtors	100
Provision for doubtful debts	2
Trade creditors	76
Operating expenses accrual	10
Stocks	62
Bank balance (positive)	20
10% debentures	110
8% preference shares	100
Share capital (ordinary £1 shares)	200
Profit and loss account	100

The following information is also available.

(a) During the year, a boring machine was found to be past its best. It was decided to write down the machine from its net book value of £20,000 to its scrap value of £5,000. The original cost of the machine was £40,000.

(b) On 31 March 20X4 the preference dividend for the year was paid. Debenture interest was also all paid on 31 March 20X4.

(c) On 30 April 20X3 50,000 £1 ordinary shares were issued at a premium of 50p per share.

(d) An ordinary dividend of 10p per share was paid on 31 March 20X4.

(e) In the year ended 31 March 20X4, the following transactions took place.

	£
Sales	305,000
Purchases	108,000
Contras between debtors and creditors accounts	25,000
Operating expenses paid	58,000
Bad debts written off	12,000

(f) The freehold premises are depreciated over fifty years. Plant and equipment is depreciated at 20% pa on the straight line basis.

(g) Stock at 31 March 20X4 amounted to £45,000.

(h) The following balances were available as at 31 March 20X4.

	£
Accrued operating expenses	15,000
Trade creditors	58,000
Trade debtors	96,000

Task

Prepare the profit and loss account of Hanoi Ltd for the year ended 31 March 20X4 and a balance sheet at that date.

Note. While you are not required to comply with all statutory disclosure requirements, your financial statements should be clearly and informatively presented and be in accordance with generally accepted principles.

PART B   LIMITED COMPANY ACCOUNTS

Key learning points

- ☑ Limited companies have limited liability, which means that their members' liability in the event of insolvency is limited to the amount of capital they put in.
- ☑ You should be able to distinguish:
    - Private companies
    - Public companies
- ☑ Limited companies must keep accounting records.
- ☑ Limited companies have a share capital. Distinguish:
    - Authorised share capital
    - Issued share capital
    - Called up share capital
    - Paid up share capital
- ☑ Dividends are appropriations of profit.
- ☑ Ordinary shares are different from preference shares, mainly because they carry no right to a fixed dividend.
- ☑ Revenue reserves are available for distribution. Capital reserves are not.
- ☑ Debentures are long term liabilities, not capital. Unlike dividends, debenture interest must be paid.
- ☑ Companies pay corporation tax on their profits.

Quick quiz

1. What is the meaning of limited liability?
2. List four of the statutory books which companies must maintain.
3. What is the difference between issued capital and called-up capital?
4. What are the differences between ordinary shares and preference shares?
5. What are the differences between debentures and share capital?
6. How does a share premium account arise?
7. Distinguish between a bonus issue and a rights issue.
8. Companies pay .... on the profits they earn.
9. A company issues 50,000 £1 shares at a price of £1.25 per share. How much should be posted to the share premium account?

    A   £50,000
    B   £12,500
    C   £62,500
    D   £60,000

PART B   LIMITED COMPANY ACCOUNTS

Answers to quick quiz

1   The maximum an owner stands to lose if the company becomes insolvent is his share of the capital in the business.

2   Register of members; register of charges; register of directors and secretaries; register of directors' interests.

3   Issued capital is the nominal amount of share capital that has been issued to shareholders. Only part of the issue price may be called up.

4   Preference shares are shares which confer certain preferential rights on their owner. Preference dividends have priority over ordinary dividends. Ordinary shares are more common and carry no such rights.

5   (a)   Shareholders are members; debenture holders are creditors.
    (b)   Shareholders receive dividends; debenture holders receive interest, to which they are legally entitled.
    (c)   Debentures are often secured on company assets. Shares are not.

6   The share premium is the difference between the issue price of a share and its nominal value. It must be credited to a share premium account.

7   A bonus issue is a way of re-classifying reserves as share capital. A rights issue is an issue of shares for cash to existing shareholders.

8   Corporation tax.

9   B (50,000 × 25p)

Activity checklist

This checklist shows which performance criteria, range statement or knowledge and understanding point is covered by each activity in this chapter. Tick off each activity as you complete it.

Activity

3.1 ☐ This activity deals with Knowledge & Understanding point 2: general legal framework of limited companies.

3.2 ☐ This activity deals with Performance criteria 11.1.B regarding the identification of adjustments.

3.3 ☐ This activity deals with Knowledge & Understanding point 5: forms of equity and loan capital.

3.4 ☐ This activity deals with Performance Criteria 11.1.A and 11.1.B regarding drafting of financial statements and making adjustments.

PART B LIMITED COMPANY ACCOUNTS

chapter 4

The regulatory framework

Contents

1. Introduction
2. The standard setting process
3. UK Accounting Standards
4. Published accounts
5. Small and medium sized companies
6. The role of the Stock Exchange
7. Generally accepted accounting practice (GAAP)

Performance criteria
11.1.A Draft limited company financial statements from the appropriate information
11.1.C Ensure that limited company financial statements comply with relevant accounting standards and domestic legislation and with the organisation's policies, regulations and procedures

Range statement
11.1.1 Limited company financial statements: income statement; balance sheet; cash flow statement; statement of total recognised gains and losses
11.1.2 Domestic legislation: Companies Act

Knowledge and understanding
2. The general legal framework of limited companies and the obligations of Directors in respect of the financial statements (Element 11.1)
3. The statutory form of accounting statements and disclosure requirements (Element 11.1)
4. The UK regulatory framework for financial reporting and the main requirements of relevant Financial Reporting Standards (Element 11.1)
7. Preparing financial statements in proper form (Element 11.1)
12. How the accounting systems of an organisation are affected by its roles, organisational structure, its administrative systems and procedures and the nature of its business transactions (Elements 11.1 & 11.2)

PART B   LIMITED COMPANY ACCOUNTS

1 Introduction

Limited companies are required by law (the Companies Act 1985 or CA 1985) to **prepare** and **publish accounts annually**. The form and content of the accounts are regulated primarily by CA 1985, but must also comply with **accounting standards**.

The regulatory framework over company accounts is therefore based on several sources.

- **Company law**
- **Accounting standards** and other related pronouncements
- **International accounting standards** (and the influence of other national standard setting bodies)
- The requirements of the **Stock Exchange**

2 The standard setting process

2.1 Company law

The Companies Act 1985 (CA 1985) consolidated the bulk of previous company legislation. This was substantially amended by the **Companies Act 1989** (CA 1989). All references in this text are to CA 1985 as amended by CA 1989.

2.2 The European Union

Since the United Kingdom became a member of the **European Union** (EU) it has been obliged to comply with legal requirements decided on by the EU. It does this by enacting UK laws to implement EU directives. For example, the CA 1989 was enacted in part to implement the provisions of the seventh and eighth EU directives, which deal with consolidated accounts and auditors.

> Although Unit 11 does not require you to be an expert on EU procedure, you should be aware that the form and content of company accounts can be influenced by international developments.

2.3 Accounting standards

> An **accounting standard** is a rule or set of rules which prescribes the method (or methods) by which accounts should be prepared and presented.

These 'working regulations' are issued by a national or international body of the accountancy profession.

In the UK, such standards were called Statements of Standard Accounting Practice (SSAPs) and were until 31 July 1990 formulated by the Accounting Standards Committee (ASC). SSAPs have nearly all been replaced by Financial Reporting Standards (FRSs) produced by the successor to the ASC, the Accounting Standards Board (ASB).

2.4 The standard-setting process in the UK

In 1987 the Consultative Committee of Accountancy Bodies (CCAB) established a review committee (the Dearing committee) and its report was published in September 1988. Its conclusions were, in essence, that the arrangements then in operation, where 21 unpaid ASC members met for a half-day once a month to discuss new standards, were no longer adequate to produce timely and authoritative pronouncements. On 1 August 1990 the ASC was disbanded and the following regime took its place.

2.4.1 Financial Reporting Council (FRC)

The FRC was created to cover a wide constituency of interests at a high level. It guides the standard setting body on policy and sees that its work is properly financed. It also funds and oversees the Review Panel (see below). It has about 25 members drawn from users, preparers and auditors of accounts.

2.4.2 Accounting Standards Board (ASB)

The task of devising accounting standards is now carried out by the ASB, with a full-time chairman and technical director. A majority of two thirds of the Board is required to approve a new standard. Previously, each new standard had to be approved by the Councils of each of the six CCAB bodies separately before it could be published. The new ASB now issues standards itself on its own authority. The ASB can produce standards more quickly than the ASC and it has the great advantage of legal backing (see below).

2.4.3 Urgent Issues Task Force (UITF)

An offshoot of the ASB is the **UITF**, whose function is:

> 'to tackle urgent matters not covered by existing standards, and for which, given the urgency, the normal standard-setting process would not be practicable.'
>
> (Sir Ron Dearing)

The UITF pronouncements, which are called 'abstracts', are intended to come into effect quickly. They therefore tend to become effective within approximately one month of publication date. The UITF abstracts **will not be examined**.

2.4.4 Review Panel

The **Financial Reporting Review Panel**, often known as the Review Panel, is chaired by a barrister and is concerned with the examination and questioning of departures from accounting standards by large companies. It has about 15 members from which smaller panels are formed to tackle cases as they arise. The Review Panel is alerted to most cases for investigation by the results of the new CA 1985 requirement that companies must include in the **notes to the accounts** a statement that they have been **prepared in accordance with applicable accounting standards** or, failing that, give details of **material departures** from those standards, with reasons.

Although it is expected that most referrals would be resolved by discussion, the Panel (and the Secretary of State for Trade and Industry) have the power to apply to the court for revision of the accounts, with all costs potentially payable (if the court action is successful) by the company's directors. The auditors may also be disciplined if the audit report on the defective accounts was not qualified with respect to the departure from standards. **Revised accounts**, whether prepared voluntarily or under duress, will have to be **circulated** to all persons likely to rely on the previous accounts.

Because of the Review Panel, listed companies and their auditors are becoming far more cautious in their attempts to break or bend the rules laid out by both the Companies Act and accounting standards.

2.4.5 Summary

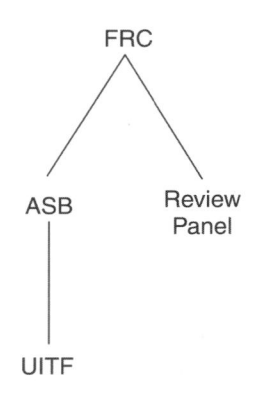

```
            FRC
           /   \
         ASB   Review
          |    Panel
          |
         UITF
```

2.5 International Accounting Standards

International Accounting Standards (IASs) are produced by the International Accounting Standards Board (IASB).

IASs have helped to both **improve** and **harmonise** financial reporting around the world. The standards are used:

- As national requirements, often after a national process
- As the basis for all or some national requirements
- As an international benchmark for those countries which develop their own requirements
- By regulatory authorities for domestic and foreign companies
- By companies themselves

Although the Unit 11 standards include IAS, the assessor has indicated that individual IASs will not be examined until June 2006 at the earliest.

2.6 The Stock Exchange

In the UK there are two different markets on which it is possible for a company to have its securities quoted:

- The **Stock Exchange**
- The **Alternative Investment Market** (AIM)

Shares quoted on the main market, the Stock Exchange, are said to be **'listed'** or to have obtained a 'listing'. In order to receive a listing for its securities, a company must conform with Stock Exchange regulations contained in the **Listing Rules** or **Yellow Book** issued by the Council of The Stock Exchange. The company commits itself to certain procedures and standards, including matters concerning the disclosure of accounting information, which are more extensive than the disclosure requirements of the Companies Acts. The requirements of the AIM are **less stringent** than the main Stock Exchange. It is aimed at new, higher risk or smaller companies.

Many requirements of the Yellow Book do not have the backing of law, but the ultimate sanction which can be imposed on a listed company which fails to abide by them is the **withdrawal** of its securities from the Stock Exchange List: the company's shares would no longer be traded on the market.

3 UK Accounting standards

3.1 The Accounting Standards Board and FRSs

The ASB's consultative process leads to the setting of **Financial Reporting Standards** (**FRSs**). To produce an FRS, first a working Draft for Discussion (DD) is published to get feedback from people closely involved with or with a direct interest in the standard setting process. The DD, as a result of this process, is converted into a Financial Reporting Exposure Draft (FRED). The FRED (which is a draft version of the proposed new FRS) is then published and feedback is obtained from interested parties. Finally, the FRS is issued.

The standard-setting process can be summarised as follows.

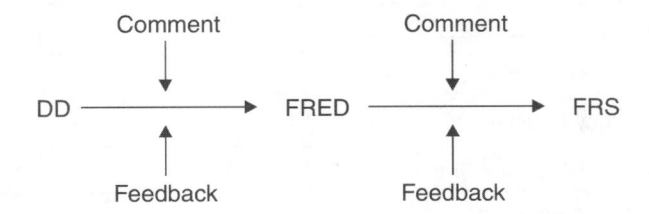

```
        Comment              Comment
           ↓                    ↓
DD ──────────────→ FRED ──────────────→ FRS
           ↑                    ↑
        Feedback             Feedback
```

3.2 UK accounting standards

Title		Issue date
	Foreword to accounting standards	Jun 93
FRS 1	Cash flow statements (revised Oct 96)	Sep 91
FRS 2	Accounting for subsidiary undertakings	July 92
FRS 3	Reporting financial performance	Oct 92
FRS 4	Capital instruments	Dec 93
FRS 5	Reporting the substance of transactions	Apr 94
FRS 6	Acquisitions and mergers	Sep 94
FRS 7	Fair values in acquisition accounting	Sep 94
FRS 8	Related party disclosures	Oct 95
FRS 9	Associates and joint ventures	Nov 97
FRS 10	Goodwill and intangible assets	Dec 97

PART B LIMITED COMPANY ACCOUNTS

Title		Issue date
FRS 11	Impairment of fixed assets and goodwill	July 98
FRS 12	Provisions, contingent liabilities and contingent assets	Sept 98
FRS 13	Derivatives and other financial instruments: disclosures	Sept 98
FRS 14	Earnings per share	Oct 98
FRS 15	Tangible fixed assets	Feb 99
FRS 16	Current tax	Dec 99
FRS 17	Retirement benefits	Dec 00
FRS 18	Accounting policies	Dec 00
FRS 19	Deferred tax	Dec 00
SSAP 4	Accounting for government grants	Jul 90
SSAP 5	Accounting for value added tax	Apr 74
SSAP 9	Stocks and long-term contracts	Sep 88
SSAP 13	Accounting for research and development	Jan 89
SSAP 17	Accounting for post balance sheet events	Aug 80
SSAP 19	Accounting for investment properties	Nov 81
SSAP 20	Foreign currency translation	Apr 83
SSAP 21	Accounting for leases and hire purchase contracts	Aug 84
SSAP 25	Segmental reporting	Jun 90
	Financial Reporting Standard for Smaller Entities (FRSSE)	Dec 99

Notes

FREDs are not examinable. The *Statement of Principles for Financial Reporting*, which is covered in Chapter 1, is assessable. The *Statement* was published in December 1999.

See roman pages (xxi to xxii) for details of which standards are assessable.

4 Published accounts

4.1 Statutory accounts

Statutory accounts are accounts which limited companies are obliged by law to publish in a particular form.

Statutory accounts are part of the price to be paid for the benefits of limited liability. Limited companies must produce such accounts annually and they must appoint an independent person to audit and report on them. Once prepared, a copy of the accounts must be sent to the Registrar of Companies, who maintains a separate file for every company. The Registrar's files may be inspected for a nominal fee, by any member of the public. This is why the statutory accounts are often referred to as **published accounts**.

It is the responsibility of the company's directors to produce accounts which show a **true and fair view** of the company's results for the period and its financial position at the end of the period. The board evidence their approval of the accounts by the signature of one director on the balance sheet. Once this has been done, and the auditors have completed their report, the accounts are laid before the members of the company in general meeting. When the members have adopted the accounts they are sent to the Registrar for filing.

The requirement that the accounts show a true and fair view is paramount.

> **IMPORTANT!**
>
> Although statute lays down numerous rules on the information to be included in the published accounts and the format of its presentation, any such rule may be **overridden** if compliance with it would prevent the accounts from showing a **true and fair view**.

The documents which must be included by law in the accounts laid before a general meeting of the members are:

(a) A **profit and loss account** (or an income and expenditure account in the case of a non-trading company)
(b) A **balance sheet** as at the date to which the profit and loss account is made up
(c) A **directors' report** (see below)
(d) An **auditors' report** addressed to the members (not to the directors) of the company
(e) The **group accounts** in the case of a company which has subsidiaries at the year end date (see Part D of this text)

FRS 1 requires the inclusion of a **cash flow statement**. This statement is discussed in Chapter 10; here we will look at the legally required accounting statements, the profit and loss account and balance sheet.

The following example shows a *pro forma* profit and loss account and balance sheet with selected notes.

STANDARD PLC
PROFIT AND LOSS ACCOUNT FOR THE YEAR ENDED 31 DECEMBER 20X5

	Notes	£'000	£'000
Turnover			X
Cost of sales			X
Gross profit			X
Distribution costs			X
Administrative expenses			X
Operating profit	1		X
Income from fixed asset investments			X
			X
Interest payable and similar charges			X
Profit on ordinary activities before taxation			X
Tax on profit on ordinary activities			X
Profit on ordinary activities after taxation			X
Dividend paid and proposed		X	
Transfer to general reserve		X	
			X
Retained profit for the financial year			X

STANDARD PLC
BALANCE SHEET AS AT 31 DECEMBER 20X5

	Notes	£'000	£'000
Fixed assets			
Intangible assets	2		X
Tangible assets	3		X
Fixed asset investments			X
			X
Current assets			
Stocks		X	
Debtors		X	
Cash at bank and in hand		X	
		X	
Creditors: amounts falling due within one year		X	
Net current assets			X
Total assets less current liabilities			X
Creditors: amounts falling due after more than one year			X
Accruals and deferred income			X
			X
Capital and reserves			
Called up share capital			X
Share premium account	4		X
Revaluation reserve	4		X
General reserve	4		X
Profit and loss account	4		X
			X

Approved by the board on ....

.... Director

The notes on pages XX to XX form part of these accounts.

It is very unlikely that published accounts questions will require anything more complicated than the above proforma.

NOTES TO THE ACCOUNTS

1   *Operating profit*

   Operating profit is stated after charging:

	£'000
Depreciation (see Chapter 5)	X
Amortisation	X
Auditors' remuneration	X
Exceptional items (see Chapter 8)	X
Directors' emoluments	X
Staff costs	X
Research and development (see Chapter 5)	X

   Note. Separate totals are required to be disclosed for:

   (a)   audit fees and expenses; and

(b) fees paid to auditors for non-audit work.

This disclosure is not **required** for small or medium-sized companies.

Activity 4.1

Arco Ltd receives an invoice in respect of the current year from its auditors made up as follows.

	£
Audit of accounts	10,000
Taxation computation and advice	1,500
Travelling expenses: audit	1,100
Consultancy fees charged by another firm of accountants	1,600
	14,200

What figure should be disclosed as auditors' remuneration in the notes to the profit and loss account?

---

2   *Intangible fixed assets*

	Development expenditure £'000
Cost	
At 1 January 20X5	X
Expenditure	X
At 31 December 20X5	X
Amortisation	
At 1 January 20X5	X
Charge for year	X
At 31 December 20X5	X
Net book value at 31 December 20X5	X
Net book value 31 December 20X4	X

Note. The above disclosure should be given for each intangible asset.

PART B LIMITED COMPANY ACCOUNTS

3   Tangible fixed assets

	Freehold land and buildings £'000	Leasehold land and buildings		Plant and machinery £'000	Fixtures and fittings £'000	Total £'000
		Long leases £'000	Short leases £'000			
Cost (or valuation)						
At 1 Jan 20X5	X	X	X	X	X	X
Additions	X	–	X	–	X	X
Revaluation	X	–	–	–	–	X
Disposals	(X)	–	–	(X)	(X)	(X)
At 31 Dec 20X5	X	X	X	X	X	X
Depreciation						
At 1 Jan 20X5	X	X	X	X	X	X
Charge for year	X	X	X	X	X	X
Revaluation	(X)	–	–	–	–	(X)
Disposals	(X)	–	–	(X)	(X)	(X)
At 31 Dec 20X5	X	X	X	X	X	X
Net book value						
At 31 Dec 20X5	X	X	X	X	X	X
At 31 Dec 20X4	X	X	X	X	X	X

Notes

(a) Long leases are $\geq$ 50 years unexpired at balance sheet date.

(b) Classification by asset type represents arabic numbers from formats.

(c) Motor vehicles (unless material) are usually included within plant and machinery.

(d) Revaluations in the year: state for each asset revalued:

   (i)   method of valuation;
   (ii) date of valuation; and
   (iii) the historical cost equivalent of the above information as if the asset had not been revalued.

4   Reserves

	Share premium £'000	Revaluation £'000	General £'000	Profit and loss £'000
At 1 January 20X5	X	X	X	X
Retained profit for the year	–	–	–	X
Revaluation	–	X	–	–
Transfers	–	–	X	X
At 31 December 20X5	X	X	X	X

Activity 4.2

The best way to learn the format and content of published accounts and notes is to practise questions. However, you must start somewhere, so try to learn the above formats, then close this text and write out on a piece of paper:

(a) A standard layout for a balance sheet and profit and loss account
(b) A standard layout for the notes to these accounts specified above

4.2 Directors' report

Attached to every balance sheet there must be a **directors' report** (s 234 CA 1985). (The Companies Act 1985 allows small companies exemption from delivering a copy of the directors' report to the registrar of companies.)

The directors' report is largely a **narrative report**, but certain figures must be included in it. The purpose of the report is to give the users of accounts a more complete picture of the state of affairs of the company. Narrative descriptions should help to 'put flesh on' the skeleton of details provided by the figures of the accounts themselves. However, in practice the directors' report is often a rather dry and uninformative document, perhaps because it must be verified by the company's external auditors, whereas the chairman's report need not be.

The directors' report is expected to contain:

> 'a **fair review of the development of the business** of the company and its subsidiary undertakings during that year and of their position at the end of it...'

No guidance is given on the form of the review, nor the amount of detail it should go into.

S 234 CA 1985 also requires the report to show the amount, if any, recommended for **dividend**.

Other disclosure requirements in the directors' report are as follows.

(a) The **principal activities** of the company and its subsidiaries in the course of the financial year, and any significant changes in those activities during the year.

(b) Where significant, an estimate should be provided of the **difference** between the **book value** of land held as fixed assets and its realistic **market value**.

(c) Information about the company's policy for the employment of **disabled persons.**

  (i) The policy for giving fair consideration to applications for jobs from disabled persons
  (ii) The policy for continuing to employ (and train) people who have become disabled whilst employed by the company
  (iii) The policy for the training, career development and promotion of disabled employees.

  (Companies with fewer than 250 employees are exempt from (c).)

(d) The names of persons who were **directors** at any time during the financial year.

(e) For those persons who were directors at the year end, the **interests** of each (or of their spouse or infant children) in shares or debentures of the company or subsidiaries:

If a director has no such interests at either date, this fact must be disclosed. (This information in (e) may be shown as a note to the accounts instead of in the directors' report.)

(f) **Political and charitable contributions** made, if these together exceeded more than £200 in the year.

(g) Particulars of any **important events** affecting the company or any of its subsidiaries which have occurred since the end of the financial year (significant 'post-balance sheet events').

(h) An indication of likely **future developments** in the business of the company and of its subsidiaries.

(i) An indication of the **activities** (if any) of the company and its subsidiaries in the field of **research and development**.

(j) Particulars of **purchases** (if any) **of its own shares** by the company during the year, including reasons for the purchase.

(k) Particulars of **other acquisitions of its own shares** during the year (perhaps because shares were forfeited or surrendered, or because its shares were acquired by the company's nominee or with its financial assistance).

(l) Details of **important post balance** sheet events.

(m) **Creditor payment policy**.

5 Small and medium sized companies

Small and medium sized companies are allowed certain **filing exemptions**: the accounts they lodge with the registrar of companies, and which are available for public inspection, need not contain all the information which must be published by large companies. This concession allows small and medium-sized companies to reduce the amount of information about themselves available to, say, trading rivals. It does not relieve them of their obligation to prepare full statutory accounts, because all companies, regardless of their size, must prepare full accounts for approval by the shareholders.

Small and medium-sized companies must therefore balance the expense of preparing two different sets of accounts against the advantage of publishing as little information about themselves as possible. Many such companies may decide that the risk of assisting their competitors is preferable to the expense of preparing accounts twice over, and will therefore not take advantage of the filing exemptions.

5.1 Small companies

A company qualifies as a **small company** in a particular financial year if, for that year, two or more of the following conditions are satisfied.

(a) The amount of its turnover for the year should not exceed £2.8 million. This amount must be adjusted proportionately in the case of an accounting period greater or less than twelve months.

(b) Its balance sheet total should not exceed £1.4 million. Balance sheet total means total assets before deduction of any liabilities.

(c) Its average number of employees should not exceed 50.

5.2 Medium sized companies

For a **medium-sized company**, the corresponding conditions are:

(a) Turnover not more than £11.2 million
(b) Balance sheet total not more than £5.6 million
(c) Average number of employees not more than 250

Again, a minimum of two of these conditions must be satisfied.

5.3 Exemptions

Public companies can **never be entitled to the filing exemptions whatever their size**; nor can banking and insurance companies; nor can companies which are authorised persons under the Financial Services Act 1986; nor can members of groups containing any of these exceptions.

6 The role of the Stock Exchange

The Stock Exchange is a market for stocks and shares, and a company whose securities are traded on the main market is known as being 'quoted' as a 'listed' company.

When a share is granted a quotation on The Stock Exchange, it appears on the *Official List* which is published in London for each business day. The Official List shows the 'official quotation' or price for the share for that particular day; it is drawn up by the Quotations Department of The Stock Exchange, which derives its prices from those actually ruling in this market. In practice, the buying and selling prices used by member firms will be within the prices quoted on the Official List.

In order to receive a listing for its securities, a company must conform with Stock Exchange regulations contained in the **Listing Rules** issued by the Council of The Stock Exchange. The company commits itself to certain procedures and standards, including matters concerning the disclosure of accounting information, which are more extensive than the disclosure requirements of the Companies Acts.

Activity 4.3

To ensure you understand which regulations apply to which type of business, fill in the table below with a 'yes' where compliance is required and 'no' where it is not.

Type of Business	Companies Act	FRSs/ SSAPs	IASs	Stock Exchange Listing Rules
Public Listed Company				
Private Limited Company				
Sole Tradership				

7 Generally Accepted Accounting Practice (GAAP)

This term signifies all the rules, from whatever source, which govern accounting. In the UK this is seen primarily as a combination of:

(a) **Company law** (mainly CA 1985)
(b) Accounting standards
(c) Stock Exchange requirements

Although those sources are the basis for **UK GAAP**, the concept also includes the effects of non-mandatory sources such as

(a) International accounting standards
(b) Statutory requirements in other countries, particularly the US

In the UK, GAAP does not have any statutory or regulatory authority or definition (unlike other countries, such as the US). The term is mentioned rarely in legislation, and only then in fairly limited terms.

GAAP is in fact a **dynamic concept**: it changes constantly as circumstances alter through new legislation, standards and practice. This idea that GAAP is constantly changing is recognised by the ASB in its *Statement of Aims* where it states that it expects to issue new standards and amend old ones in response to 'evolving business practices, new economic developments and deficiencies identified in current practice.' The emphasis has shifted from 'principles' to 'practice' in UK GAAP.

The problem of what is 'generally accepted' is not easy to settle, because new practices will obviously not be generally adopted yet. The criteria for a practice being 'generally accepted' will depend on factors such as whether the practice is addressed by UK accounting standards or legislation, or their international equivalents, and whether other companies have adopted the practice. Most importantly perhaps, the question should be whether the practice is **consistent with the needs of users** and the objectives of financial reporting and whether it is consistent with the 'true and fair' concept.

7.1 Big GAAP/little GAAP

Most UK companies are small companies. They are generally owned and managed by one person or a family. The owners have invested their own money in the business and there are no outside shareholders to protect. Large companies, by contrast, particularly public limited companies may have shareholders who have invested their money, possibly through a pension fund, with no knowledge whatever of the company. These shareholders need protection and the regulations for such companies need to be more stringent.

It could therefore be argued that company accounts should be of two types: 'simple' ones for small companies with fewer regulations and disclosure requirements and 'complicated' ones for larger companies with extensive and detailed requirements. This is the '**big GAAP/little GAAP**' divide.

7.2 The FRSSE

In November 1997 the ASB published the *Financial Reporting Standard for Smaller Entities* (FRSSE). This represents a major simplification of financial reporting for smaller entities. It is revised regularly to take account of changes in financial reporting. The latest version was published in December 1999.

At present preparers and auditors of small entities' accounts need to refer to the complete range of accounting standards, many of whose provisions are not relevant to smaller entities. The FRSSE provides preparers and auditors with a single reference point, a **single comprehensive accounting standard** containing the measurement and disclosure requirements most relevant to their circumstances.

The FRSSE is examinable only to the extent of awareness of its objective and scope.

The FRSSE is applicable to all companies that satisfy the definition of a small company in companies legislation and would also be available to other entities that would meet that definition if they were companies. A company that chooses to comply with the FRSSE is then exempt from all other accounting standards and UITF Abstracts. The FRSSE **contains in a simplified form the requirements from existing accounting standards that are relevant to the majority of smaller entities**.

In order to keep the FRSSE as user-friendly as possible some of the requirements in accounting standards relating to more complex transactions have not been included in the FRSSE, as they do not affect most smaller entities. Where guidance is needed on a matter not contained in the FRSSE, regard should be paid to existing practice as set out in the relevant accounting standards.

7.2.1 Measurement

The measurement bases in the FRSSE are the same as, or a simplification of, those in existing accounting standards.

7.2.2 Disclosure requirements

One of the many ways in which the FRSSE should reduce the burden for preparers of smaller entities' financial statements is likely to be its *reduced* disclosure requirements. For example, the FRSSE does not require an analysis of turnover and profits into continuing operations, acquisitions and discontinued operations, nor a reconciliation of movements in shareholders' funds.

7.2.3 Related parties

The disclosure requirements for related party transactions in the FRSSE represent a useful dispensation for smaller entities compared with those in FRS 8 *Related party disclosures*. Under FRS 8, related party transactions that are material to the related party, where that related party is an individual, are required to be disclosed in the accounts of the reporting entity even if the transaction is not material to the entity. This is not so for smaller entities adopting the FRSSE, as they need disclose only those related party transactions that are material in relation to the reporting entity.

7.2.4 Cash flow statement

Since small entities are already exempt from the requirements of FRS 1 *Cash flow statements* the FRSSE does not include a requirement for a cash flow statement. The ASB nevertheless believes that a cash flow statement is an important aid to the understanding of an entity's financial position and performance and the FRSSE therefore includes a 'voluntary disclosures' section, recommending that smaller entities present a simplified cash flow statement using the indirect method (ie starting with operating profit and reconciling it to the total cash generated (or utilised) in the period).

7.2.5 Future developments

With the assistance of its advisory committee, the Committee on Accounting for Smaller Entities, the ASB will update and revise the FRSSE periodically to reflect future developments in financial reporting. Any changes to the FRSSE, for example as a result of new accounting standards and UITF Abstracts, will be the subject of public consultation.

The FRSSE attempts to balance the conflicting views of those who commented on the proposals, ranging from those who believe small companies should be exempt from all accounting standards to those who favour retaining virtually the status quo. Given this divergence of views, the ASB believes that it is particularly important that, going forward, the FRSSE is carefully monitored.

Activity 4.4

'The going concern concept is fundamental to the preparation of financial statements. If a company cannot be assumed to be a going concern, the effect on those statements is dramatic.'

Discuss and illustrate your arguments with an example.

4: THE REGULATORY FRAMEWORK

Key learning points

- ☑ In this chapter we have looked at the **legal and professional** framework governing the preparation of limited companies' **published accounts**. We also considered the role of the **Stock Exchange**, **GAAP** and the **conceptual framework** of accounting.

- ☑ Accounting standards were formerly published by the **Accounting Standards Committee** and called **SSAPs** (statements of standard accounting practice). In future, they will be published by the **Accounting Standards Board** and called **FRSs** (financial reporting standards). Make sure you know the differences between the old system and the new.

- ☑ You should also be able to discuss the role of the **Urgent Issues Task Force** and the **Review Panel**.

- ☑ All companies must prepare full **statutory accounts** for approval by their shareholders. For large companies, a copy of these accounts must also be made available to the public by filing with the registrar of companies.

- ☑ **Small and medium-sized companies** may, if they wish, prepare an additional set of accounts for publication disclosing less information.

- ☑ Listed companies must comply with **Stock Exchange regulations** contained in the *Listing Rules*. The requirements are more stringent than for non-listed companies.

- ☑ You should ensure that you understand what is meant by **GAAP**.

- ☑ There is a case for having separate regulations for smaller companies. To this end, the FRSSE was issued.

Quick quiz

1. What body currently produces accounting standards?
2. What is the relationship between accounting standards and the Companies Act requirement to show a true and fair view?
3. What are 'filing exemptions'? Which companies can benefit from them?
4. What do you understand by GAAP?
5. The 'Big GAAP/Little GAAP' debate led to the publication of the ………………………………… .

Answers to quick quiz

1. The Accounting Standards Board
2. Compliance with accounting standards is likely to be held necessary in order to meet the statutory 'true and fair' requirement.
3. The accounts lodged with the Registrar of Companies need not contain all the information required by large companies. The exemptions are available to 'small' and 'medium sized' companies as defined by the Companies Act.
4. Rules governing accounting deriving principally from:
    (a) Company law
    (b) Accounting standards
    (c) Stock Exchange requirements
5. FRSSE

Activity checklist

This checklist shows which performance criteria, range statement or knowledge and understanding point is covered by each activity in this chapter. Tick off each activity as you complete it.

Activity

4.1		This activity deals with Knowledge & Understanding point 3: statutory form of accounting statements and disclosure requirements.
4.2		This activity deals with Knowledge & Understanding point 3: statutory form of accounting statements and disclosure requirements.
4.3		This activity deals with Performance Criteria 11.1.C: ensure that limited company financial statements comply with accounting standards and domestic legislation.
4.4		This activity deals with Knowledge & Understanding point 2: obligations of directors.

chapter 5

Fixed assets and stocks

Contents

1. Introduction
2. Fixed assets: statutory requirements
3. FRS 15 *Tangible fixed assets*
4. Revaluations
5. SSAP 19 *Accounting for investment properties*
6. SSAP 4 *Accounting for government grants*
7. SSAP 13 *Accounting for research and development*
8. Goodwill and intangible assets
9. Investments
10. Stock valuation: revision

Performance criteria

- 11.1.A Draft limited company financial statements from the appropriate information
- 11.1.B Correctly identify and implement subsequent adjustments and ensure that discrepancies, unusual features or queries are identified and either resolved or referred to the appropriate person
- 11.1.C Ensure that limited company financial statements comply with relevant accounting standards and domestic legislation and with the organisation's policies, regulations and procedures

Range statement

- 11.1.1 Limited company financial statements: income statement; balance sheet, statement of total recognised gains and losses, notes
- 11.1.2 Limited company financial statements: domestic legislation – Companies Act
- 11.1.3 Relevant accounting standards - FRS

Knowledge and understanding

1. The elements and purposes of financial statements of limited companies as set out in the conceptual framework for financial reporting (Element 11.2)
2. The general legal framework of limited companies and the obligations of directors in respect of the financial statements (Element 11.1)

Knowledge and understanding (cont'd)

3   The statutory form of accounting statements and disclosure requirements (Element 11.1)
4   The UK regulatory framework for financial reporting and the main requirements of relevant Financial Reporting Standards
7   Preparing financial statements in proper form (Element 11.1)

1 Introduction

From your Intermediate studies you will have a good idea of the basics of fixed assets. However, you will not have covered fixed assets in the context of limited company accounts or the disclosures required. Also, you will not have covered intangible fixed assets in more than outline.

The good news is that the work you did at Intermediate Level is directly relevant to this topic. The principles are the same for tangibles, and intangibles are largely common sense.

This chapter also revises stock valuation from your earlier studies, since you are required to know the SSAP 9 requirements in full apart from long-term contracts.

2 Fixed assets: statutory requirements

This section acts as both revision and as an introduction to the Companies Act requirements for all fixed assets.

2.1 Statutory provisions relating to all fixed assets

The standard balance sheet format of CA 1985 divides fixed assets into three categories:

(a)   Intangible assets
(b)   Tangible assets
(c)   Investments

Companies Act requirements in regard to fixed assets may be considered under two headings.

(a)   **Valuation:** the amounts at which fixed assets should be stated in the balance sheet; and
(b)   **Disclosure:** the information which should be disclosed in the accounts as to valuation of fixed assets and as to movements on fixed asset accounts during the year.

2.2 Valuation of fixed assets

Where an asset is **purchased**, its cost is simply the **purchase price plus any expenses incidental to its acquisition**.

Where an asset is **produced by a company for its own use**, its 'production cost' **must** include the cost of **raw materials, consumables** and **other attributable direct costs** (such as labour). Production cost may additionally include a reasonable proportion of indirect costs, together with the interest on any capital borrowed to finance production of the asset.

The 'cost' of any fixed asset having a limited economic life, whether purchase price or production cost, must be reduced by provisions for depreciation calculated to write off the cost, less any residual value, systematically over the period of the asset's useful life. This very general requirement is supplemented by the more detailed provisions of FRS 15 *Tangible fixed assets* (see Section 3 of this chapter).

Provision for a permanent reduction in value ('impairment') of a fixed asset must be made in the profit and loss account and the asset should be disclosed at the reduced amount in the balance sheet. Any such provision should be disclosed on the face of the profit and loss account or by way of note. Where a provision becomes no longer necessary, because the conditions giving rise to it have altered, it should be written back, and again disclosure should be made.

2.3 Fixed assets valuation: alternative accounting rules

Although the Companies Act 1985 maintains historical cost principles as the normal basis for the preparation of accounts, **alternative bases** allowing for revaluations and current cost accounting are permitted provided that:

(a) the **items affected** and the **basis of valuation** are **disclosed** in a note to the accounts;

(b) the **historical cost** in the current and previous years is **separately disclosed** in the balance sheet or in a note to the accounts. Alternatively, the difference between the revalued amount and historical cost may be disclosed.

Using the **alternative accounting rules** the appropriate value of any fixed asset (its current cost or market value), rather than its purchase price or production cost, may be included in the balance sheet.

2.4 Revaluation reserve

Where the value of any fixed asset is determined by using the alternative accounting rules the amount of profit or loss arising must be credited or debited to a separate reserve, the revaluation reserve. This is a statutory reserve. The calculation of the relevant amounts should be based on the written down values of the assets prior to revaluation.

The revaluation reserve must be reduced to the extent that the amounts standing to the credit of the reserves are, in the opinion of the directors of the company, no longer necessary for the purposes of the accounting policies adopted by the company. However, an amount may only be transferred from the reserve to the profit and loss account if either:

(a) The amount in question was previously charged to that account, or
(b) It represents realised profit (for example on disposal of a fixed asset)

The only other transfer possible from the revaluation reserve is on capitalisation, that is, when a bonus issue is made. Previously, some companies had written off goodwill arising on consolidation against the revaluation reserve. This is no longer permissible.

The amount of a revaluation reserve must be shown under a separate sub-heading on the balance sheet. However, the reserve need not necessarily be called a 'revaluation reserve'. Revaluation will be dealt with in detail in Section 4 of this chapter.

PART B   LIMITED COMPANY ACCOUNTS

2.5 Fixed assets: disclosure

Notes to the accounts must show, for each class of fixed assets, an analysis of the movements on both costs and depreciation provisions.

The following format (with notional figures) is commonly used to disclose fixed asset movements.

	Total £	Land and buildings £	Plant and machinery £
Cost or valuation			
At 1 January 20X4	50,000	40,000	10,000
Revaluation surplus	12,000	12,000	–
Additions in year	4,000	–	4,000
Disposals in year	(1,000)	–	(1,000)
At 31 December 20X4	65,000	52,000	13,000
Depreciation			
At 1 January 20X4	16,000	10,000	6,000
Charge for year	4,000	1,000	3,000
Elimination on revaluation	–	(10,000)	–
Eliminated on disposals	(500)	–	(500)
At 31 December 20X4	9,500	1,000	8,500
Net book value			
At 31 December 20X4	55,500	51,000	4,500
At 1 January 20X4	34,000	30,000	4,000

Where any fixed assets of a company (other than listed investments) are included in the accounts at an alternative accounting valuation, the following information must also be given.

(a) The years (so far as they are known to the directors) in which the assets were severally valued and the several values

(b) In the case of assets that have been valued during the financial period, the names of the persons who valued them or particulars of their qualifications for doing so and (whichever is stated) the bases of valuation used by them.

A note to the accounts must classify land and buildings under the headings of:

(a) Freehold property

(b) Leasehold property, distinguishing between:

(i) Long leaseholds, in which the unexpired term of the lease at the balance sheet date is not less than 50 years

(ii) Short leaseholds which are all leaseholds other than long leaseholds

3 FRS 15 *Tangible fixed assets*

FRS 15 *Tangible fixed assets* was published in February 1999. It goes into a lot more detail than the Companies Act.

FRS 15 does not cover investment properties, which are still accounted for in accordance with SSAP 19 (see Section 5).

3.1 Objective

FRS 15 deals with accounting for the initial measurement, valuation and depreciation of tangible fixed assets. It also sets out the information that should be disclosed to enable readers to understand the impact of the accounting policies adopted in relation to these issues.

3.2 Initial measurement

A tangible fixed asset should **initially be measured at cost**.

> **Cost** is purchase price and any costs directly attributable to bringing the asset into working condition for its intended use.

Examples of directly attributable costs are:

- **Acquisition costs**, eg stamp duty, import duties
- Cost of **site preparation** and clearance
- Initial **delivery and handling** costs
- **Installation** costs
- **Professional fees** eg legal fees
- The estimated cost of **dismantling and removing** the asset and restoring the site, to the extent that it is recognised as a provision under FRS 12 *Provisions, contingent liabilities and contingent assets* (discussed in Chapter 7).

Any abnormal costs, such as those arising from design error, industrial disputes or idle capacity are not directly attributable costs and therefore should not be capitalised as part of the cost of the asset.

3.2.1 Finance costs

The **capitalisation of finance costs**, including interest, is **optional**. However, if a company does capitalise finance costs it must do so **consistently**.

All finance costs that are **directly attributable** to the construction of a tangible fixed asset should be capitalised as part of the cost of the asset.

> **Directly attributable finance costs** are those that would have been avoided if there had been no expenditure on the asset.

PART B   LIMITED COMPANY ACCOUNTS

If finance costs are capitalised, capitalisation should start when:

- Finance costs are being incurred
- Expenditure on the asset is being incurred
- Activities necessary to get the asset ready for use are in progress

Capitalisation of finance costs should cease when the asset is ready for use.

3.3 Subsequent expenditure

Subsequent expenditure on a tangible fixed asset should only be capitalised in the following three circumstances.

(a) It enhances the economic benefits over and above those previously estimated. An example might be modifications made to a piece of machinery that increases its capacity or useful life.

(b) A component of an asset that has been treated separately for depreciation purposes (because it has a substantially different useful economic life from the rest of the asset) has been restored or replaced.

(c) It relates to a major inspection or overhaul that restores economic benefits that have been consumed and reflected in the depreciation charge.

Activity 5.1

Can you think of examples for (b) and (c) above?

3.4 Valuation

FRS 15 supplements and clarifies the rules on revaluation of fixed assets which the Companies Act allows. Revaluation is discussed in the next section.

3.5 Depreciation

As noted earlier, the Companies Act 1985 requires that all fixed assets having a limited economic life should be depreciated. FRS 15 gives a useful discussion of the purpose of depreciation and supplements the statutory requirements in important ways.

> **Depreciation** is defined in FRS 15 as the measure of the cost or revalued amount of the economic benefits of the tangible fixed asset that have been consumed during the period. Consumption includes the wearing out, using up or other reduction in the useful economic life of a tangible fixed asset, whether arising from use, effluxion of time or obsolescence through either changes in technology or demand for the goods and services produced by the asset.

This definition covers the amortisation of assets with a pre-determined life, such as a leasehold, and the depletion of wasting assets such as mines.

The need to depreciate fixed assets arises from the accruals concept. If money is used in purchasing an asset then the amount paid must at some time be charged against profits. If the asset is one which contributes to a company's income over a number of accounting periods it would be inappropriate to charge any single period (for example the period in which the asset was acquired) with the whole of the expenditure. Instead, some method must be found of spreading the cost of the asset over its useful economic life.

This view of depreciation as a process of **allocation** of the cost of an asset over several accounting periods is the view adopted by FRS 15. It is worth mentioning here two common **misconceptions** about the purpose and effects of depreciation.

It is sometimes thought that the net book value (NBV) of an asset is equal to its net realisable value and that the object of charging depreciation is to reflect the fall in value of an asset over its life. This misconception is the basis of a common, but incorrect, argument which says that freehold properties need not be depreciated in times when property values are rising. It is true that historical cost balance sheets often give a misleading impression when a property's NBV is much below its market value, but in such a case it is open to a business to incorporate a revaluation into its books. This is a separate problem from that of allocating the property's cost over successive accounting periods.

Another misconception is that depreciation is provided so that an asset can be replaced at the end of its useful life. This is not the case.

(a) If there is no intention of replacing the asset, it could then be argued that there is no need to provide for any depreciation at all.

(b) If prices are rising, the replacement cost of the asset will exceed the amount of depreciation provided.

FRS 15 contains **no detailed guidance** on the calculation of depreciation or the suitability of the various depreciation methods.

We will therefore consider first the factors affecting depreciation and then proceed to an analysis of the main depreciation methods available.

3.6 Factors affecting depreciation

FRS 15 states that the following factors need to be considered in determining the useful economic life, residual value and depreciation method of an asset.

(a) The **expected usage** of the asset by the entity, assessed by reference to the asset's expected capacity or physical output

(b) The **expected physical deterioration** of the asset through use or effluxion of time; this will depend upon the repair and maintenance programme of the entity both when the asset is in use and when it is idle

(c) **Economic or technological obsolescence**, for example arising from changes or improvements in production, or a change in the market demand for the product or service output of that asset

(d) **Legal or similar limits** on the use of the asset, such as the expiry dates of related leases

If it becomes clear that the **original estimate** of an asset's useful life was **incorrect**, it should be **revised**. Normally, no adjustment should be made in respect of the depreciation charged in previous years; instead the remaining net book value of the asset should be depreciated over the new estimate of its remaining useful life. But if future results could be materially distorted, the adjustment to accumulated depreciation should be recognised in the accounts in accordance with FRS 3 (usually as an exceptional item). FRS 3 is discussed in a later chapter of this Interactive Text.

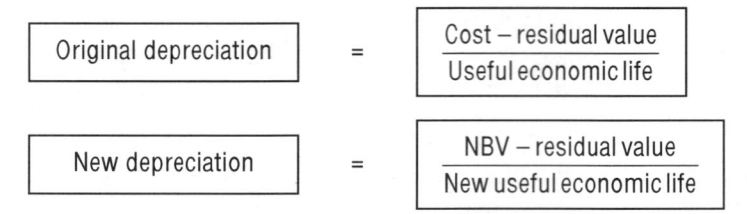

$$\text{Original depreciation} = \frac{\text{Cost} - \text{residual value}}{\text{Useful economic life}}$$

$$\text{New depreciation} = \frac{\text{NBV} - \text{residual value}}{\text{New useful economic life}}$$

3.7 Methods of depreciation

3.7.1 Depreciable amount

The **cost of an asset less its residual value is known as the depreciable amount** of the asset. For example, some plant has anticipated capital costs of:

	£
Purchase cost	19,000
Delivery	1,500
Installation by own employees	2,700
	23,200

The residual value is expected to be £3,200 and so the depreciable amount is £20,000.

However, if major improvements are made to an asset, thereby increasing its expected life, the depreciable amount should be adjusted. For example, if at the beginning of year 3, £11,000 was spent on technological improvements to the plant so prolonging its expected life from five to eight years (with a residual value of £1,200), the depreciable amount would be adjusted.

	£
Original depreciable amount	20,000
Less amount already depreciated (say 2 × £4,000)	8,000
	12,000
Add fall in residual value £(3,200 − 1,200)	2,000
	14,000
Add further capital expenditure	11,000
New depreciable amount	25,000

The new depreciable amount would be written off over the remaining useful life of the asset, 6 years.

3.7.2 Depreciation

There are a number of different methods of calculating the depreciation charge for an accounting period, each giving a different result. The most common are:

- Straight line method
- Reducing balance method

- Sum of digits method
- Machine hour method
- Revaluation

The **straight line method** is the simplest and the most commonly used in practice. The **reducing balance** and **sum of digits** methods are accelerated methods which lead to a higher charge in earlier years. Since repair and maintenance costs tend to increase as assets grow older these methods lead to a more even allocation of total fixed asset costs (depreciation plus maintenance).

The **machine hour method** is suited to assets which depreciate primarily through use rather than through passing of time. Such assets might include mines and quarries, which are subject to gradual exhaustion of the minerals that they contain, and also delivery lorries, which may be argued to depreciate in accordance with the number of miles travelled.

Neither the CA nor FRS 15 prescribes which method should be used. **Management** must **exercise its judgement**. Furthermore, FRS 15 states:

> 'The useful economic life of a tangible fixed asset should be **reviewed at the end of each reporting period** and revised if expectations are significantly different from previous estimates. If a useful economic life is revised, the carrying amount of the tangible fixed asset at the date of revision should be **depreciated over the revised remaining useful economic life.**'

3.7.3 Changes in method

FRS 15 also states that a **change from one method** of providing depreciation **to another** is permissible only on the grounds that the new method will give a **fairer presentation** of the results and of the financial position. Such a change does **not**, however, constitute a **change of accounting policy**; the carrying amount of the tangible fixed asset is depreciated using the revised method over the remaining useful economic life, beginning in the period in which the change is made.

3.7.4 Impairment

Tangible fixed assets other than non depreciable land, should be **reviewed for impairment** at the end of the reporting period where:

- No depreciation is charged on the grounds that it would be immaterial, or
- The estimated remaining useful economic life exceeds 50 years

The review should be in accordance with FRS 11 *Impairment of fixed assets and goodwill,* discussed later in this chapter (Section 8).

3.7.5 Miscellaneous topics

Many companies carry fixed assets in their balance sheets at revalued amounts, particularly in the case of freehold buildings. When this is done, the **depreciation charge** should be calculated **on the basis of the revalued amount** (not the original cost).

Where the tangible fixed asset comprises two or more major components with substantially different useful economic lives, each component should be accounted for separately for depreciation purposes and depreciated over its individual useful economic life.

You still need to charge depreciation if there is subsequent expenditure on a tangible fixed asset that maintains or enhances the previously assessed standard of performance of the asset.

3.8 Disclosure requirements of FRS 15

The following information should be disclosed separately in the financial statements for each class of tangible fixed assets.

(a) The depreciation methods used

(b) The useful economic lives or the depreciation rates used

(c) Total depreciation charged for the period

(d) Where material, the financial effect of a change during the period in either the estimate of useful economic lives or the estimate of residual values

(e) The cost or revalued amount at the beginning of the financial period and at the balance sheet date

(f) The cumulative amount of provisions for depreciation or impairment at the beginning of the financial period and at the balance sheet date

(g) A reconciliation of the movements, separately disclosing additions, disposals, revaluations, transfers, depreciation, impairment losses, and reversals of past impairment losses written back in the financial period

(h) The net carrying amount at the beginning of the financial period and at the balance sheet date

Where there has been a change in the depreciation method used, the effect, if material, should be disclosed in the period of change. The reason for the change should also be disclosed.

4 Revaluations

4.1 Freehold revaluations

You won't have come across revaluations before. But you know from experience that the market value of a building is often greater than the cost.

For freehold property which is in operational use, the principle laid down in FRS 15 is that since **buildings have a finite useful life**, a part of their **cost must be charged against profit each year,** in order to be consistent with the accruals concept.

Where there is a freehold property this means that the land element in its cost will not be depreciated, but the building element of cost must be depreciated. When a property is revalued, depreciation should be charged so as to write off the new valuation over the estimated remaining useful life of the building.

5: FIXED ASSETS AND STOCKS

Example: revaluation of a freehold building

A freehold building is purchased on 1 January 20X4 for £20,000. Its estimated useful life is 20 years and it is depreciated at the rate of £1,000 per annum in each of the years ending 31 December 20X4 and 20X5. On 1 January 20X6 a professional valuer estimates the value of the building at £54,000.

On the assumption that the revaluation is to be incorporated into the books of account, and that the original estimate of useful life was correct, show the relevant ledger accounts for the period 1 January 20X4 to 31 December 20X6.

Solution

FREEHOLD BUILDING AT COST

			£				£
1.1.X4	Purchase		20,000	31.12.X4	Balance c/d		20,000
1.1.X5	Balance b/d		20,000	31.12.X5	Balance c/d		20,000
1.1.X6	Balance b/d		0,000				
	Revaluation		34,000	31.12.X6	Balance c/d		54,000
			54,000				54,000

DEPRECIATION ON FREEHOLD BUILDINGS

		£			£
31.12.X4	Balance c/d	1,000	31.12.X4	Profit and loss account	1,000
			1.1.X5	Balance b/d	1,000
31.12.X5	Balance c/d	2,000	31.12.X5	Profit and loss account	1,000
		2,000			2,000
1.1.X6	Revaluation	2,000	1.1.X6	Balance b/d	2,000
			31.12.X6	Profit and loss account	
31.12.X6	Balance c/d	3,000		(£54,000/18 years)	3,000
		5,000			5,000

REVALUATION RESERVE

		£			£
31.12.X6	Balance c/d	36,000	1.1.X6	Freehold building	34,000
				Dep'n on freehold	2,000
		36,000			36,000

Note that the revaluation surplus is the difference between valuation (£54,000) and net book value at the time of revaluation (£20,000 – £2,000 = £18,000). The revalued amount, £54,000, must then be depreciated over the asset's remaining estimated useful life of 18 years.

PART B LIMITED COMPANY ACCOUNTS

Activity 5.2

Beelzebub plc has a property with a net book value of £125,000. The valuers estimate that the property is now worth £250,000. The remaining useful life is 25 years.

(a) Calculate the revaluation reserve
(b) Calculate the revised annual depreciation

5: FIXED ASSETS AND STOCKS

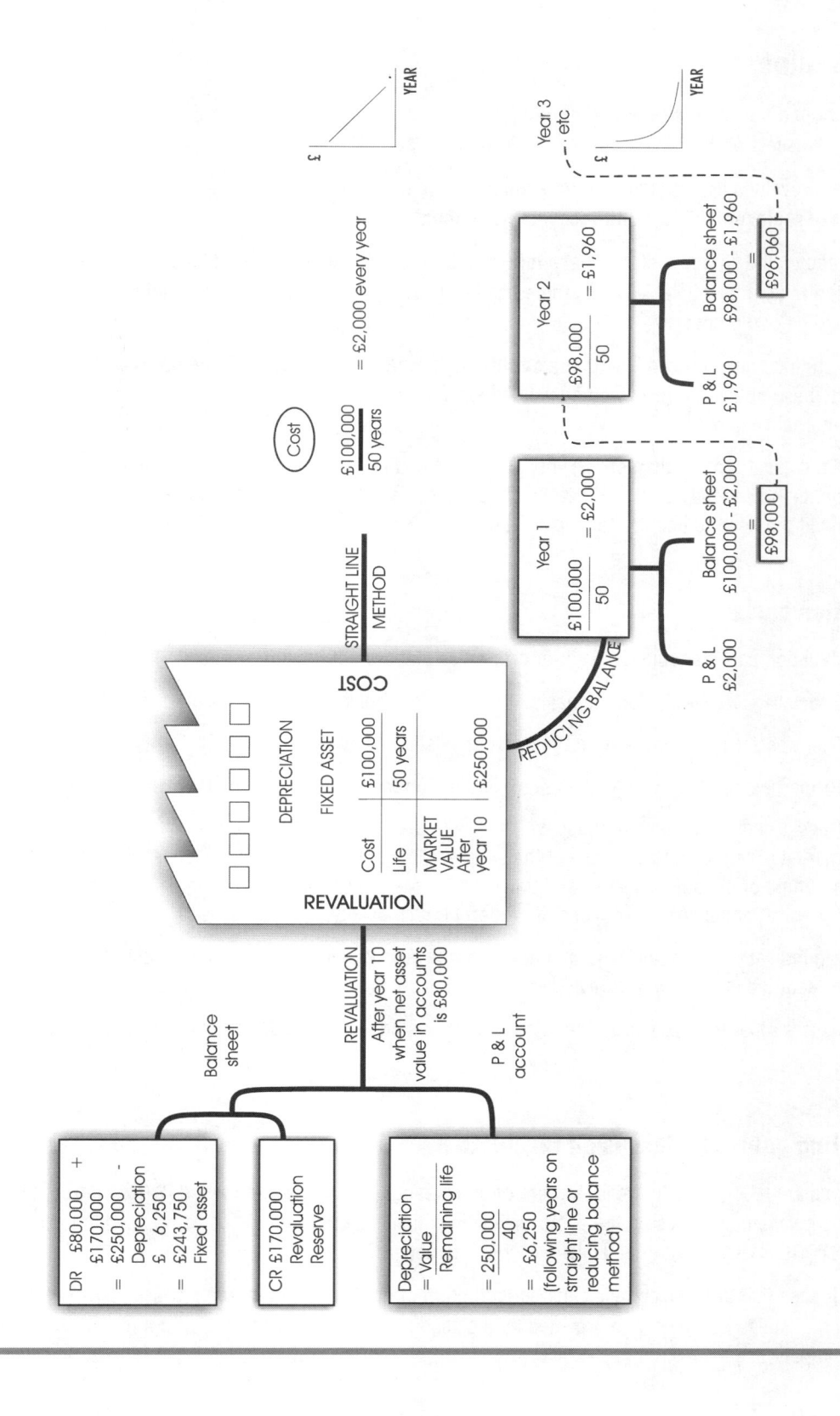

FIXED ASSET

Cost	£100,000
Life	50 years
MARKET VALUE After year 10	£250,000

DEPRECIATION

STRAIGHT LINE METHOD

$$\frac{\text{Cost £100,000}}{50 \text{ years}} = £2,000 \text{ every year}$$

Year 1
$$\frac{£100,000}{50} = £2,000$$

P & L £2,000

Balance sheet £100,000 − £2,000 = £98,000

Year 2
$$\frac{£98,000}{50} = £1,960$$

P & L £1,960

Balance sheet £98,000 − £1,960 = £96,060

Year 3 etc.

REDUCING BALANCE

(graphs: Year axis)

REVALUATION

After year 10 when net asset value in accounts is £80,000

Balance sheet

DR £80,000 +
 £170,000
 = £250,000 −
 Depreciation
 £ 6,250
 = £243,750
 = Fixed asset

CR £170,000 Revaluation Reserve

P & L account

Depreciation
 = Value / Remaining life
 = 250,000 / 40
 = £6,250
 (following years on straight line or reducing balance method)

4.2 FRS 15 rules

An entity may adopt a policy of **revaluing tangible fixed assets**. Where this policy is adopted **it must be applied consistently** to all assets of the same class, eg all freehold properties.

Where an asset is revalued its carrying amount should be its **current value** as at the balance sheet date, current value being the **lower of replacement cost and recoverable amount**.

To achieve the above, the standard states that a **full valuation** should be carried out **at least every five years** with an **interim valuation in year 3**. If it is likely that there has been a material change in value, interim valuations in years 1, 2 and 4 should also be carried out.

A full valuation should be conducted by either a **qualified external valuer** or a **qualified internal valuer**, provided that the valuation has been subject to review by a qualified external valuer. An interim valuation may be carried out by either an external or internal valuer.

For certain types of assets (other than properties) eg company cars, there may be an active second hand market for the asset or appropriate indices may exist, so that the directors can establish the asset's value with reasonable reliability and therefore avoid the need to use the services of a qualified valuer.

4.2.1 Valuation basis

The following valuation bases should be used for properties that are not impaired.

- Specialised properties on the basis of depreciated replacement cost
- Non-specialised properties on the basis of existing use value (EUV)
- Properties surplus to an entity's requirements on the basis of open market value (OMV).

    Specialised properties are those which, due to their specialised nature, are rarely, if ever, sold on the open market except as part of a sale of the business in occupation. Eg oil refineries, chemical works, power stations, or schools, colleges and universities where there is no competing market demand from other organisations using these types of property in the locality.

Where there is an indication of impairment, an impairment review should be carried out in accordance with FRS 11. The asset should be recorded at the lower of revalued amount (as above) and recoverable amount.

Tangible fixed assets other than properties should be valued using market value or, if not obtainable, depreciated replacement cost.

4.2.2 Reporting gains and losses on revaluation

Revaluation **gains** are recognised in the **statement of total recognised gains and losses (STRGL)** except to the extent that they reverse revaluation losses on the same assets, in which case they should be recognised in the profit and loss account. (The STRGL is discussed in detail later in this Interactive Text.)

All revaluation **losses** that are caused by a clear consumption of economic benefit (eg physical damage or a deterioration in the quality of the service provided by the asset) are recognised in the **profit and loss account**, ie the asset is clearly impaired.

Other losses are recognised in the **STRGL until the carrying amount reaches depreciated historical cost** and **thereafter in the profit and loss account**. However, if it can be demonstrated that the recoverable amount of the asset is more than its revalued amount, the loss will be recognised in the STRGL to the extent that the recoverable amount exceeds the revalued amount. This is because the difference between recoverable amount and revalued amount is not an impairment and should therefore be recognised in the STRGL as a valuation adjustment, rather than the profit and loss account.

Example: accounting for revaluation losses

The following details are available in relation to a non specialised property.

Carrying value (NBV)	£960,000
Depreciated historic cost	£800,000
Recoverable amount	£760,000
Existing use value	£700,000

How should the revaluation loss be treated?

Note. The property has been revalued, which is why the carrying value (or the amount shown in the books) is more than depreciated historic cost.

Solution

(a) The revaluation loss on the property is £260,000 (ie carrying value of £960,000 compared with EUV of £700,000).

(b) The fall in value from carrying value (£960,000) to depreciated historic cost (£800,000) of £160,000 is recognised in the STRGL.

(c) The fall in value from depreciated historic cost (£800,000) to recoverable amount (£760,000) of £40,000 is recognised in the profit and loss account.

(d) The difference between recoverable amount (£760,000) and EUV (£700,000) is recognised in the STRGL.

5 SSAP 19 *Accounting for investment properties*

The requirement that all fixed assets including freehold buildings (though not freehold land) should be depreciated, caused a stir amongst property investment companies who feared that their reported profits would be severely reduced. The lobby was sufficiently strong to gain a respite from the standard-setters and investment properties were temporarily excluded from the scope of SSAP 12, the forerunner of FRS 15. Eventually, the ASC's deliberations resulted in the publication of a separate standard for such properties.

The main provisions of SSAP 19 *Accounting for investment properties* follow, but first it is worth noting the conceptual difference which the ASC identified between investment properties and other fixed assets.

> **Investment properties** are held: '.... not for consumption in the business operations but as investments, the disposal of which would not materially affect any manufacturing or trading operations of the enterprise.'

Contrast this with the concept underlying the FRS 15 definition of depreciation.

5.1 Definition of investment properties

SSAP 19 defines an investment property as an interest in land and/or buildings:

(a) in respect of which construction work and development have been completed; and
(b) which is held for its investment potential, any rental income being negotiated at arm's length.

The following are exceptions from the definition:

(a) a property which is owned and occupied by a company for its own purposes is not an investment property;
(b) a property let to and occupied by another group company is not an investment property for the purposes of its own accounts or the group accounts.'

You should bear in mind that a group company is a company's parent, subsidiary or fellow subsidiary company. An associated company is not a group company (see Chapter 14).

5.2 Accounting treatment of investment properties

The provisions of SSAP 19 are based on the principle that the item of prime importance is the current value of the investment properties and changes in their current value, rather than a calculation of systematic annual depreciation.

This leads to the following accounting treatment. Investment properties are included in the balance sheet at their open market value. Investment properties are not depreciated unless they are short leaseholds. Short leaseholds of 20 years or less, should be depreciated over the period.

The explanatory note to the standard suggests that the valuation need not be made by a qualified independent valuer, except that in cases where a major enterprise holds a substantial portfolio of investment properties, then an external valuation ought to be made at least once every five years. The name of the valuer or his qualifications must be disclosed together with the basis of valuation used. If a person making a valuation is an employee or officer of the company or group which owns the property this fact should be disclosed.

Changes in the value of an investment property should not be taken to the profit and loss account. In other words a company cannot claim profit on the unrealised gains of such properties. The revaluation should be disclosed as a movement on an 'investment revaluation reserve'. (However, should this reserve show a debit balance (a loss) the full amount of the balance should be removed by charging it to the profit and loss account.)

The investment revaluation reserve should be disclosed prominently in the accounts. Investment properties can be owned by ordinary trading companies as well as property investment companies, and if the assets of a company consist wholly or mainly of investment properties, this fact should also be disclosed.

Further points to note about SSAP 19 are as follows.

(a) It is recognised in SSAP 19 that exemption from depreciation for investment property is contrary to the depreciation rules in the Companies Act 1985. This departure is considered permissible because the Act states that compliance with the rules is a subordinate requirement to the 'overriding purpose of giving a true and fair view'.

(b) SSAP 19 does not apply to immaterial items.

5.3 Disposals

SSAP 19 does not deal with the problem of accounting for the disposal of investment properties. However, FRS 3 *Reporting financial performance* states the following in relation to the disposal of any revalued fixed assets.

(a) The profit or loss on disposal of an asset should be accounted for as the difference between the sale proceeds and the net carrying amount.

(b) Any revaluation surplus remaining is now realised, so FRS 3 requires this to be transferred to the profit and loss reserve.

5.4 Diminution in value: amendment to SSAP 19

At the time that SSAP 19 was originally issued, any *deficit* on the IRR had to be taken to the profit and loss account. In other words, where the value of one or more investment property fell so far that the total IRR was insufficient to cover the deficit, then the excess was taken to the profit and loss account. SSAP 19 was later amended as follows.

(a) Any diminution in value which is considered *permanent* should be charged to the profit and loss account.

(b) Where diminution is temporary, a temporary IRR deficit is allowed.

Activity 5.3

With reference to SSAP 19, explain why a building owned for its investment potential should be accounted for differently from one which is occupied by its owners.

6 SSAP 4 *Accounting for government grants*

One further aspect of accounting for fixed assets concerns the accounting treatment of **government grants** which may be available to assist in the purchase of assets.

In the UK, the government provides grants to companies which invest in assisted areas (such as development areas or special development areas). These grants may be:

(a) **Revenue grants** to cover some of the costs of certain categories of revenue expenditure

(b) **Capital grants**, which are cash grants to cover a proportion of the costs of certain items of capital expenditure (buildings, plant and machinery and so on)

Companies receiving such grants must account for them. No particular problem arises in respect of revenue grants as they can be credited to revenue in the same period in which the revenue expenditure to which they relate is charged. However, capital grants may be treated in a number of ways.

6.1 Capital grants

On receipt, should a company credit the full amount of the capital grant to either the **profit and loss account** or **non-distributable reserve** (such as a Government grant reserve) in the balance sheet?

In the first case there is an immediate effect on earnings and in the second there is none, and in both cases the concept of matching costs and revenues is not applied. The grant, like the depreciation cost of fixed assets, applies to the full life of the assets and so should be spread over that period of time.

SSAP 4 states that **grants relating to fixed assets should be credited to revenue over the expected useful life of the assets** and this can be done in one of two ways:

(a) By reducing the acquisition cost of the fixed asset by the amount of the grant, and providing depreciation on the reduced amount

(b) By treating the amount of the grant as a **deferred credit** and transferring a portion of it to revenue annually

Example: accounting for government grants

A company receives a 20% grant towards the cost of a new item of machinery, which cost £100,000. The machinery has an expected life of four years and a nil residual value. The expected profits of the company, before accounting for depreciation on the new machine or the grant, amount to £50,000 per annum in each year of the machinery's life.

Task

Show how the results of the company would be affected by treating the grant under each of the methods discussed above.

Solution

The results of the company for the four years of the plant's life would be as follows.

(a) Reducing the cost of the asset

	Year 1 £	Year 2 £	Year 3 £	Year 4 £	Total £
Profits					
Profit before depreciation	50,000	50,000	50,000	50,000	200,000
Depreciation*	20,000	20,000	20,000	20,000	80,000
Profit	30,000	30,000	30,000	30,000	120,000

*The depreciation charge on a straight line basis, for each year, is ¼ of £(100,000 – 20,000) = £20,000.

Balance sheet at year end (extract)

	£	£	£	£
Fixed asset at cost	80,000	80,000	80,000	80,000
Depreciation	20,000	40,000	60,000	80,000
Net book value	60,000	40,000	20,000	–

(b) Treating the grant as a deferred credit

Profits	Year 1 £	Year 2 £	Year 3 £	Year 4 £	Total £
Profit before grant and depreciation	50,000	50,000	50,000	50,000	200,000
Depreciation	(25,000)	(25,000)	(25,000)	(25,000)	(100,000)
Grant	5,000	5,000	5,000	5,000	20,000
Profit	30,000	30,000	30,000	30,000	120,000

Balance sheet at year end (extract)

Profits	Year 1 £	Year 2 £	Year 3 £	Year 4 £
Fixed asset at cost	100,000	100,000	100,000	100,000
Depreciation	(25,000)	(50,000)	(75,000)	(100,000)
Net book value	75,000	50,000	25,000	–
Deferred income				
Government grant deferred credit	15,000	10,000	5,000	–

The annual profits under both methods are the same, and both methods apply the matching concept in arriving at the profit figure. Reducing the cost of the asset is simpler since, by reducing the depreciation charge, the amount of the grant is automatically credited to revenue over the life of the asset. However, the **deferred credit method** has the advantage of recording fixed assets at their actual cost, which allows for comparability and is independent of government policy. In addition, the former method may be in conflict with the Companies Act 1985 in that the asset would no longer be carried at its purchase price or production cost.

The application of SSAP 4 is limited to grants made for the purchase of fixed assets in the UK and the Republic of Ireland and permits the use of either of the methods described above. However, because of the possible legal problem with the 'netting' method the deferred credit method is to be preferred and the amount of the deferred credit, if material, should be shown separately in the balance sheet.

6.2 SSAP 4 disclosures

(a) The accounting policy adopted for government grants

(b) The effect of government grants on the company's profits in the period and/or on its financial position generally

(c) Any potential liability to repay grants

(d) The nature of government aid other than grants which has materially affected profits in the period and an estimate of the effects, where possible

Activity 5.4

Newtrade Ltd, a manufacturing company, has prepared draft accounts as on 31 March 20X3 for the purpose of producing its first year's financial statements.

Included in assets is a balance on the suspense account of £170,036 made up as follows.

Purchases	£	Grants received	£
Plant and machinery	148,732	On cost of plant and machinery	25,316
Motor lorries	49,961	For employment of local labour	15,600
Motor cars	12,259	Balance	170,036
	210,952		210,952

All the amounts shown for the purchase of assets include VAT at 17.5%.

The directors wish to deal with capital grants on the deferred credit method and to depreciate all fixed assets at 20% per annum.

Task

Prepare journal entries to incorporate the various items in the suspense account into the draft accounts.

Note. You should know all about journal entries from your Intermediate studies. You need to be aware that the Assessor often asks for journal entries in the Unit 11 exam.

7 SSAP 13 *Accounting for research and development*

7.1 Introduction

Large companies may spend significant amounts of money on **research and development** (R & D) activities. Obviously, these amounts must be credited to cash and debited to an account for research and development expenditure. The accounting problem is how to treat the debit balance on R & D account at the balance sheet date.

There are two possibilities.

(a) The debit balance may be classified as an **expense** and transferred to the profit and loss account. This is referred to as 'writing off' the expenditure.

(b) The debit balance may be classified as an **asset** and included in the balance sheet. This is referred to as 'capitalising' or 'carrying forward' or 'deferring' the expenditure.

The argument for writing off R & D expenditure is that it is an expense just like heating or wages and its accounting treatment should be the same.

The argument for carrying forward R & D expenditure is based on the accruals concept. If R & D activity eventually leads to new or improved products which generate revenue, the costs should be carried forward to be matched against that revenue in future accounting periods.

R & D expenditure is the subject of an accounting standard, SSAP 13 *Accounting for research and development*. SSAP 13 defines research and development expenditure as falling into one or more of the following categories.

(a) **Pure research** is original research to obtain new scientific or technical knowledge or understanding. There is no clear commercial end in view and such research work does not have a practical application. Companies and other business entities might carry out this type of research in the hope that it will provide new knowledge which can subsequently be exploited.

(b) **Applied research** is original research work which also seeks to obtain new scientific or technical knowledge, but which has a specific practical aim or application (eg research on improvements in the effectiveness of toothpastes or medicines etc). Applied research may develop from 'pioneering' pure research, but many companies have full-time research teams working on applied research projects.

(c) **Development** is the use of existing scientific and technical knowledge to produce new (or substantially improved) products or systems, prior to starting commercial production operations.

7.2 How do we distinguish these categories?

The dividing line between each of these categories will often be indistinct in practice, and some expenditure might be classified as research or as development. It may be even more difficult to distinguish development costs from production costs. For example, if a prototype model of a new product is developed and then sold to a customer, the costs of the prototype will include both development and production expenditure.

SSAP 13 states that although there may be practical difficulties in isolating research costs and development costs, there is a difference of principle in the method of accounting for each type of expenditure.

(a) (i) Expenditure on pure and applied research is usually a continuing operation which is necessary to ensure a company's survival.

(ii) One accounting period does not gain more than any other from such work, and it is therefore appropriate that research costs should be written off as they are incurred (ie in the year of expenditure).

(iii) This conforms with CA 1985, which seems not to envisage the capitalisation of research expenditure in any circumstances.

(b) (i) The development of new and improved products is different, because development expenditure is incurred with a particular commercial aim in view and in the reasonable expectation of earning profits or reducing costs.

(ii) In these circumstances it is appropriate that development costs should be deferred (capitalised) and matched against the future revenues.

Deferred development costs are intangible fixed assets.

> **Signpost**
> If you are in a hurry, or revising, read the SECTOR mnemonic below.

SSAP 13 attempts to restrict indiscriminate deferrals of development expenditure and states that development costs may only be deferred to future periods, when the following criteria are met.

(a) There must be a **clearly defined development project**, and the related expenditure on this project is separately identifiable.

(b) The **expected outcome** of the project must have been assessed, and there should be **reasonable certainty** that:

(i) It is technically feasible

(ii) It is commercially viable, having regard to market conditions, competition, public opinion and consumer and environmental legislation

(c) The **eventual profits** from the developed product or system should reasonably be expected to **cover the past and future development costs.**

(d) The company should have **adequate resources to complete** the development project.

If *any* of these conditions are not satisfied the development costs should be written off in the year of expenditure.

The following mnemonic may be helpful. Remember: SECTOR.

S   Separately defined project
E   Expenditure separately identifiable
C   Commercially viable
T   Technically feasible
O   Overall profit expected
R   Resources exist to complete project

Where development expenditure is deferred to future periods, its **amortisation should begin with the commencement of production**, and should then be written off over the period in which the product is expected to be sold. Amortisation is the name for depreciation of intangible fixed assets.

Deferred development expenditure should be reviewed at the end of every accounting period. If the conditions which justified the deferral of the expenditure no longer apply or are considered doubtful, the deferred expenditure, to the extent that it is now considered to be irrecoverable, should be written off.

Development expenditure once written off can now be reinstated, if the uncertainties which had led to its being written off no longer apply. This was not permitted by the original SSAP 13, but has been amended because the CA 1985 does permit the reinstatement of costs previously written off.

7.3 Examples of R & D items

Examples given by SSAP 13 (revised) of activities that would normally be **included** in R & D are:

(a) Experimental, theoretical or other work aimed at the discovery of new knowledge or the advancement of existing knowledge.

(b) Searching for applications of that knowledge.

(c) Formulation and design of possible applications for such work.

(d) Testing in search for, or evaluation of, product, service or process alternatives.

(e) Design, construction and testing of pre-production prototypes and models and development batches.

(f) Design of products, services, processes or systems involving new technology or substantially improving those already produced or installed.

(g) Construction and operation of pilot plants.

7.4 Examples of non R & D items

Examples of activities that would normally be **excluded** from research and development include:

(a) Testing and analysis either of equipment or product for purposes of quality or quantity control.

(b) Periodic alterations to existing products, services or processes even though these may represent some improvement.

(c) Operational research not tied to a specific research and development activity.

(d) Cost of corrective action in connection with break-downs during commercial production.

(e) Legal and administrative work in connection with patent applications, records and litigation and the sale or licensing of patents.

(f) Activity, including design and construction engineering, relating to the construction, relocation, rearrangement or start-up of facilities or equipment other than facilities or equipment whose sole use is for a particular research and development project.

(g) Market research.

Under the revised SSAP 13, a company can still defer the expenditure under the accruals concept (if it is prudent so to do) but it must be disclosed entirely separately from deferred development expenditure.

7.5 Examples of items excluded from SSAP 13

The above provisions of SSAP 13 do not extend to the following cases.

(a) Expenditure on tangible fixed assets acquired or constructed to provide facilities for research and/or development activities should be capitalised and depreciated over their useful lives in the usual way. However, the depreciation may be capitalised as part of deferred development expenditure if the development work for which the assets are used meets the criteria given above.

(b) Expenditure incurred in locating mineral deposits in extractive industries is outside the scope of SSAP 13.

(c) Expenditure incurred where there is a firm contract to:

(i) carry out development work on behalf of third parties on such terms that the related expenditure is to be fully reimbursed; or

(ii) develop and manufacture at an agreed price which has been calculated to reimburse expenditure on development as well as on manufacture

is not to be treated as deferred development expenditure.

Any such expenditure which has not been reimbursed at the balance sheet date should be included in work in progress.

Activity 5.5

Tank Top Ltd has purchased a tank for £50,000. The purpose of the tank is to investigate the possibility of growing food under water. What would be the appropriate accounting treatment for this item as per SSAP 13?

7.6 Disclosure requirements

The Companies Act 1985 does not require disclosure of the total amount of R & D expenditure during an accounting period, but SSAP 13 (revised) requires that all large companies (defined below) should disclose this total, distinguishing between current year expenditure and amortisation of deferred development expenditure.

SSAP 13 (revised) requires the following companies to disclose R & D expenditure.

(a) All public companies
(b) All special category companies (ie banking and insurance companies)
(c) All holding companies with a plc or special category company as a subsidiary
(d) All companies who satisfy the criteria, multiplied by 10, for defining a medium-sized company

This means that, currently, a private company will be exempted if it is not itself (and does not control) a special category company and it meets two of the following criteria:

- Turnover ≤ £112 million
- Total assets (*before* deduction of current or long-term liabilities) ≤ £56 million
- ≤ 2,500 employees

Where deferred development costs are included in a company's balance sheet the following information must be given in the notes to the accounts:

(a) Movements on deferred development expenditure, and the amount brought forward and carried forward at the beginning and end of the period.

(b) The accounting policy used to account for R & D expenditure should be clearly explained.

Activity 5.6

Y Ltd is a research company which specialises in developing new materials and manufacturing processes for the furniture industry. The company receives payments from a variety of manufacturers, which pay for the right to use the company's patented fabrics and processes.

Research and development costs for the year ended 30 September 20X5 can be analysed as follows.

	£
Expenditure on continuing research projects	1,420,000
Amortisation of development expenditure capitalised in earlier years	240,000
New projects started during the year:	
Project A	280,000

New flame-proof padding. Expected to cost a total of £800,000 to develop. Expected total revenue £2,000,000 once work completed - probably late 20X6

Project B   150,000

New colour-fast dye. Expected to cost a total of £3,000,000 to complete. Future revenues are likely to exceed £5,000,000. The completion date is uncertain because external funding will have to be obtained before research work can be completed.

Project C   110,000

Investigation of new adhesive recently developed in aerospace industry. If this proves effective then Y Ltd may well generate significant income because it will be used in place of existing adhesives.

                                                                                                                       2,200,000

The company has a policy of capitalising all development expenditure where permitted by SSAP 13.

Explain how the three research projects A, B and C will be dealt with in Y Ltd's profit and loss account and balance sheet.

In each case, explain your proposed treatment in terms of SSAP 13 and, where relevant, in terms of the fundamental accounting assumptions of going concern and accruals, and the prudence concept.

8 Goodwill and intangible assets

8.1 What is goodwill?

It is usual for the value of a business as a going concern to differ from the aggregate value of its net assets. The difference, which may be positive or negative, is described as goodwill. By definition, goodwill is an asset which cannot be realised separately from the business as a whole.

There are many factors which may explain why goodwill arises. Examples are a skilled management team, good labour relations and a strategic location. These factors are intangible and it is difficult to place a money value on them. For this reason, it is not usual to show goodwill as an asset in the balance sheet; any amount at which it was valued would be arbitrary and subject to fluctuations.

8.2 Inherent goodwill and purchased goodwill

It is generally agreed that goodwill of a kind exists in every business. However, the only time when goodwill is valued and may be disclosed as an asset in the balance sheet is when one business acquires another as a going concern. This is because there is then a positive indication available of the value of goodwill acquired.

For example, suppose that Mountain acquires the business of Pinhead for £120,000 in cash at a time when the balance sheets of the two businesses are:

	Mountain £	Pinhead £
Tangible fixed assets	500,000	66,000
Net current assets	220,000	33,000
Capital and reserves	720,000	99,000

Assuming that the book values of Pinhead's assets equate to their market values it is clear that Mountain values Pinhead's goodwill at £21,000 since he is willing to pay £120,000 for assets which separately have a value of £99,000. Mountain's balance sheet after the acquisition might appear as follows:

	£
Purchased goodwill	21,000
Tangible fixed assets	566,000
Net current assets £(220,000 + 33,000 – 120,000)	133,000
Capital and reserves	720,000

The goodwill acquired from Pinhead is described as *purchased goodwill* because Mountain paid cash for it in buying the business of Pinhead as a going concern. It is likely that Mountain's business also has goodwill, but because its value has not been evidenced in a purchase transaction it would be unacceptable, under existing accounting conventions, to disclose it as an asset in Mountain's balance sheet. Goodwill which is presumed to exist, but which has not been evidenced in a purchase transaction, is called *non-purchased* or *inherent goodwill*.

FRS 10 *Goodwill and intangible assets* was issued in December 1997. Its provisions are summarised here.

8.3 Provisions of FRS 10

(a) Both positive purchased goodwill and purchased intangible assets should initially be capitalised and classed as an asset at cost.

(b) Inherent (non-purchased) goodwill should not be capitalised.

(c) When intangible assets are acquired as part of a takeover they should be capitalised separately from goodwill if their fair value can be reliably measured. If this is not possible, then they should be subsumed into goodwill.

(d) If, after stringently testing the fair values of the assets for impairment, **negative goodwill** arises this should be shown on the balance sheet separately and immediately below positive goodwill.

(e) Goodwill and intangible assets should be amortised on a systematic basis over their useful economic lives. If it is considered that the economic life is infinite no amortisation is needed.

(f) The standard **presumes** that intangibles (including goodwill) have a life of **less than 20 years** but accepts that this is rebuttable. This, however, puts the responsibility on the reporting entity to demonstrate that not only does the asset have an extended life but that its value is capable of an **annual impairment review**.

(g) In all cases the economic life should be **reviewed annually**.

8.3.1 Disclosures

There are few disclosures other than those normally required for any type of fixed asset. Significant additional disclosure requirements include requirements to explain:

- The bases of valuation of intangible assets
- The grounds for believing a useful economic life to exceed 20 years or to be indefinite
- The treatment adopted for negative goodwill

8.3.2 Negative goodwill

Negative goodwill arises when the price paid for a business is less than the fair value of the separate net assets acquired. This might happen, for example, if the vendor needed the cash quickly and was forced to sell at a bargain price.

FRS 10 requires that negative goodwill should be shown on the balance sheet separately and immediately below positive goodwill.

8.4 FRS 11 *Impairment of fixed assets and goodwill*

FRS 11 *Impairment of fixed assets and goodwill,* was published in July 1998. It sets out the principles and methodology for accounting for impairments of fixed assets and goodwill.

It would be unnecessarily onerous for all fixed assets and goodwill to be tested for impairment every year. In general, fixed assets and goodwill need be **reviewed for impairment only if there is some indication that impairment has occurred**.

Where possible, **individual assets** should be tested for impairment. However, impairment can often be tested only for groups of assets because the cash flows upon which the calculation is based do not arise from the use of a single asset. In these cases, impairment is measured for the smallest group of assets (the **income-generating unit**) that produces a largely independent income stream, subject to constraints of practicality and materiality. You do not need to know about income generating units for the exam.

Impairment is measured by **comparing the carrying value of the fixed asset with its recoverable amount**. The recoverable amount is the higher of the amounts that can be obtained from selling the fixed asset (net realisable value) or using the fixed asset (value in use).

Net realisable value is the expected proceeds of selling the fixed asset or less any direct selling costs. **Value in use** is calculated by discounting the expected cash flows arising from the use of fixed asset at the rate of return that the market would expect from an equally risky investment.

In some cases a detailed calculation of value in use will not be necessary. A simple estimate may be sufficient to demonstrate that either value in use is higher than carrying value or value in use is lower than net realisable value, in which case impairment is measured by reference to net realisable value.

The **reversal** of past impairment losses is recognised when the recoverable amount of a **tangible fixed asset** or investment in a subsidiary, an associate or a joint venture has **increased because of a change in economic conditions** or in the expected use of the asset. Increases in the recoverable amount of **goodwill and intangible assets** are recognised **only** when an **external event** caused the recognition of the impairment loss in previous periods, and subsequent external events clearly and **demonstrably reverse** the effects of that event in a way that was not foreseen in the original impairment calculations.

Impairment losses are recognised in the **profit and loss account**, unless they arise on a previously revalued fixed asset. Impairment losses on **revalued fixed assets** are recognised in the **statement of total recognised gains and losses** until the carrying value of the asset falls below depreciated historical cost unless the impairment is clearly caused by a consumption of economic benefits, in which case the loss is recognised in the profit and loss account. **Impairments below depreciated historical cost** are recognised in the **profit and loss account**.

9 Investments

The provisions relating to fixed assets in general, embrace investments which are held as fixed assets. **But investments will not normally have a limited economic life, so that the requirement of systematic depreciation does not apply.**

The **alternative accounting rules** allow the following bases of valuation, other than cost, for **fixed asset investments**.

(a) **Market value**: if this is higher than the stock exchange value, the latter should also be disclosed
(b) **Directors' valuation**

As always when advantage is taken of alternative accounting rules, disclosure must be made of the items affected, the basis of valuation adopted and the comparable amounts determined according to the historical cost convention.

Current asset investments should be shown, in accordance with the **prudence** concept, at the lower of purchase price and net realisable value.

10 Stock valuation: revision

10.1 Valuation rule

This area should be familiar to you from your Intermediate studies.

The AAT's Guidance for Unit 11 states that SSAP 9 *Stocks and long-term contracts* is assessable but that long-term contracts will not be assessed.

There are **several methods** which, in theory, might be used for the valuation of stock items.

- **Expected selling price**
- Expected selling price, less any costs still to be incurred in getting them ready for sale and then selling them (**Net Realisable Value** (NRV))
- **Historical cost** (the cost at which they were originally bought)
- Cost to replace them (**current replacement cost**)

Current replacement costs are not used in the type of accounts dealt with in this Interactive Text, and so are not considered further.

The use of selling prices in stock valuation is ruled out because this would create a profit for the business before the stock has been sold.

A simple example might help to explain this. Suppose that a trader buys two items of stock, each costing £100. He can sell them for £140 each, but in the accounting period we shall consider, he has only sold one of them. The other is closing stock in hand.

Since only one item has been sold, you might think it is common sense that profit ought to be £40. But if closing stock is valued at selling price, profit would be £80 as profit would be taken on the closing stock as well.

	£	£
Sales		140
Opening stock	–	
Purchases (2 × 100)	200	
	200	
Less closing stock (at selling price)	140	
Cost of sale		60
Profit		80

This would contradict the accounting concept of prudence, as it involves claiming a profit before the item has actually been sold.

The same objection *usually* applies to the use of NRV in stock valuation. Say that the item purchased for £100 requires £5 of further expenditure in getting it ready for sale and then selling it (for example, £5 of processing costs and distribution costs). If its expected selling price is £140, its NRV is £(140 – 5) = £135. To value it at £135 in the balance sheet would still be to anticipate a profit of £35.

We are left with historical cost as the normal basis of stock valuation. The only times when historical cost is not used is in the exceptional cases when the prudence concept requires a lower value to be used.

Staying with the example above, suppose that the market in this kind of product suddenly slumps and the item's expected selling price is only £90. The item's NRV is then £(90 – 5) = £85 and the business has in effect made a loss of £15 (£100 – £85). The prudence concept requires that losses should be recognised as soon as they are foreseen. This can be achieved by valuing the stock item in the balance sheet at its NRV of £85.

> **Rule to remember**
>
> SSAP 9 *Stocks and long-term contracts* states that **stock should be valued at the lower of cost and net realisable value**

Cost is that expenditure which has been incurred in the normal course of business in bringing the product or service to its present location and condition. This expenditure should include:

(a) Cost of purchase (including import duties, transport and handling costs and any other directly attributable costs, less trade discounts, rebates and subsidies)

(b) Any costs of conversion appropriate to that location and condition (including direct labour and expenses, and attributable production overheads)

Net realisable value is the actual or estimated selling price (net of trade but before settlement discounts) less:

(a) All further costs to completion; and
(b) All costs to be incurred in marketing, selling and distributing

10.2 Applying the basic valuation rule

If a business has many stock items on hand, the comparison of cost and NRV should theoretically be carried out for each item separately. It is not sufficient to compare the total cost of all stock items with their total NRV. An example will show why.

Suppose a company has four items of stock on hand at the end of its accounting period. Their cost and NRVs are as follows.

Stock item	Cost	NRV	Lower of cost/NRV
	£	£	£
1	27	32	27
2	14	8	8
3	43	55	43
4	29	40	29
	113	135	107

It would be incorrect to compare total costs (£113) with total NRV (£135) and to state stocks at £113 in the balance sheet. The company can foresee a loss of £6 on item 2 and this should be recognised. If the four items are taken together in total the loss on item 2 is masked by the anticipated profits on the other items. By performing the cost/NRV comparison for each item separately, the prudent valuation of £107 can be derived. This is the value which should appear in the balance sheet. This is an example of the fifth accounting principle introduced by CA 1985 and mentioned in Chapter 2: the **separate valuation principle**.

However, for a company with large amounts of stock this procedure may be impracticable. In this case it is acceptable to group similar items into categories and perform the comparison of cost and NRV category by category, rather than item by item.

So have we now solved the problem of how a business should value its stocks? It seems that all the business has to do is to choose the lower of cost and net realisable value. This is true as far as it goes, but there is one further problem, perhaps not so easy to foresee: for a given item of stock, what was the cost?

10.3 Determining the purchase cost

Stock may be raw materials or components bought from suppliers, finished goods which have been made by the business but not yet sold, or work in the process of production, but only part-completed (this type of stock is called **work in progress** or WIP). It will simplify matters, however, if we think about the historical cost of purchased raw materials and components, which ought to be their purchase price.

A business may be continually purchasing consignments of a particular component. As each consignment is received from suppliers it is stored in the appropriate bin or on the appropriate shelf or pallet, where it will be mingled with previous consignments. When the storekeeper issues components to production he will simply pull out from the bin the nearest components to hand, which may have arrived in the latest consignment or in an earlier consignment or in several different consignments. Our concern is to devise a pricing technique, a rule of thumb which we can use to attribute a cost to each of the components issued from stores.

There are several techniques which are used in practice.

(a) **FIFO (first in, first out).** Using this technique, we assume that components are used in the order in which they are received from suppliers. The components issued are deemed to have formed part of the oldest consignment still unused and are costed accordingly.

(b) **LIFO (last in, first out).** This involves the opposite assumption, that components issued to production originally formed part of the most recent delivery, while older consignments lie in the bin undisturbed.

(c) **Average cost**. As purchase prices change with each new consignment, the average price of components in the bin is constantly changed. Each component in the bin at any moment is assumed to have been purchased at the average price of all components in the bin at that moment.

(d) **Standard cost**. A pre-determined standard cost is applied to all stock items. If this standard price differs from prices actually paid during the period it will be necessary to write off the difference as a 'variance' in the profit and loss account.

(e) **Replacement cost**. The arbitrary assumption is made that the cost at which a stock unit was purchased is the amount it would cost to replace it. This is often (but not necessarily) the unit cost of stocks purchased in the next consignment *following* the issue of the component to production. For this reason, a method which produces similar results to replacement costs is called NIFO (next in, first out).

Any or all of these methods might provide a suitable basis for valuing stocks. But it is worth mentioning here that if you are preparing financial accounts you would normally expect to use FIFO or average cost for the balance sheet valuation

PART B LIMITED COMPANY ACCOUNTS

of stock. SSAP 9 specifically discourages the use of LIFO and replacement costs. Nevertheless, you should know about all of the methods so that you can discuss the differences between them.

One particular little known aspect of SSAP 9 recently appeared in an AAT exam.

> 'No reduction falls to be made when the realisable value of material stocks is less than the purchase price, provided that the goods in which they are to be incorporated can still be sold at a profit after incorporating the goods at cost price.'

Key learning points

- ☑ A number of accounting regulations on the valuation and disclosure of fixed assets are contained in the Companies Act 1985. In the case of tangible fixed assets, these regulations are supplemented by the provisions of FRS 15 on tangible fixed assets and SSAP 4 on the accounting treatment of government grants.

- ☑ Remember that Section 1 of this chapter lists the statutory requirements applying to all fixed assets, including the intangible assets and investments.

- ☑ SSAP 19 conflicts with the statutory requirement to depreciate all fixed assets with a limited economic life by stating that investment properties need not ordinarily be depreciated. Companies taking advantage of this provision will need to justify their departure from statute as being necessary to provide a true and fair view.

- ☑ SSAP 13 is a standard which is generally accepted and well understood. You should ensure that you are very familiar with its provisions. Don't forget to learn the disclosure requirements.

- ☑ FRS 10 *Goodwill and intangible assets* was issued to deal with a complex and controversial area. You must ensure that you can discuss the accounting treatment of positive and negative goodwill.

- ☑ SSAP 9 requires that stock be valued at the lower of cost and net realisable value.

PART B   LIMITED COMPANY ACCOUNTS

Quick quiz

1   What elements of expenditure are included in the production cost of a fixed asset?

2   What disclosures are required when a fixed asset is valued according to the alternative valuation rules?

3   In what circumstances may an amount be transferred from revaluation reserve to the credit of profit and loss account?

4   Define 'depreciation'.

5   What accounting treatment is required if the estimated useful life of a fixed asset is revised?

6   Give the SSAP 19 definition of investment properties.

7   What is the required accounting treatment in respect of government grants?

8   Development expenditure must always be written off. True or false?

9   Development expenditure written off may be reinstated if the uncertainties which led to the write-off no longer apply. True or false?

10 Bob buys Elba's business for £28,000. The business assets are a car valued at £6,000, stocks valued at £15,000 and debtors of £4,000. How much is goodwill valued at?

11 What accounting treatments are prescribed by FRS 10 in respect of purchased goodwill?

12 How should negative goodwill be accounted for under FRS 10?

13 What methods of valuing investments are permitted under the alternative accounting rules?

14 An item of stock was purchased for £10. However, due to a fall in demand, its selling price will be only £8. In addition further costs will be incurred prior to sale of £1. What is the net realisable value?

　　A   £7
　　B   £8
　　C   £10
　　D   £11

15 Which stock costing methods are permissible under SSAP 9?

　　A   FIFO, LIFO, average cost, unit cost
　　B   Unit cost, job cost, batch cost, LIFO
　　C   Process costing, unit cost, LIFO, average cost
　　D   Job costing, average cost, FIFO, unit cost

16 Which of the following statements regarding fixed asset accounting is correct?

　　A   All fixed assets should be revalued each year.

　　B   Fixed assets may be revalued at the discretion of management. Once revaluation has occurred it must be repeatedly regularly for all fixed assets in a class.

　　C   Management can choose which fixed assets in a class of fixed assets should be revalued.

　　D   Fixed assets should be revalued to reflect rising price.

17 Which of the following statements regarding depreciation is correct?

   A   All fixed assets must be depreciated.
   B   Straight line depreciation is usually the most appropriate method of depreciation.
   C   A change in the chosen depreciation method is a change in accounting policy which should be disclosed.
   D   Depreciation charges must be based upon the depreciable amount.

18 A fixed asset (cost £10,000, depreciation £7,500) is given in part exchange for a new asset costing £20,500. The agreed trade-in value was £3,500. The profit and loss account will include:

   A   A loss on disposal £1,000
   B   A profit on disposal £1,000
   C   A loss on purchase of a new asset £3,500
   D   A profit on disposal £3,500

Answers to quick quiz

1   Raw materials, consumables and other attributable direct costs such as labour.

2   The items affected and basis of valuation and the historical cost in the current and previous years.

3   If the amount in question was previously charged to the profit and loss account or if it represents profit, for example on disposal of a fixed asset.

4   The measure of the cost or revalued amount of the economic benefits of the tangible fixed asset that have been consumed during the period.

5   Depreciate the remaining net book value of the asset over the new estimate of its remaining useful life.

6   An interest in land and/or buildings:

   (a)   In respect of which construction work and development have been completed
   (b)   Which is held for its investment potential, any rental income being negotiated at arm's length

7   Treat the amount of the grant as a deferred credit and transfer a portion of it to revenue annually.

8   False. It may be capitalised provided certain strict criteria are met.

9   True

10 £28,000 – £(6,000 + 15,000 + 4,000) = £3,000.

11 (a)   Goodwill and intangible assets should be amortised on a systematic basis over their useful economic lives.

   (b)   If it is considered that the economic life is infinite, no amortisation is needed.

   (c)   The economic life should be reviewed annually.

12 It should be shown on the balance sheet separately and immediately below positive goodwill.

13 Market value or directors' valuation

14 A   A net realisable value is selling price (£8) less further costs to sale (£1), ie £7.

PART B LIMITED COMPANY ACCOUNTS

15 D LIFO is not an acceptable costing method.

16 B Correct
   A Fixed assets may be revalued; there is no requirement to do so in FRS 15.
   C Incorrect; all fixed assets in a class must be revalued.
   D Incorrect; fixed assets may be reduced in value as well as being increased.

17 D Correct.
   A Incorrect; some fixed assets are not depreciated, eg land.
   B Incorrect; management should choose the most appropriate method.
   C Incorrect; a method change is not a change in accounting policy.

18 B
	£
Net book value at disposal	2,500
Trade-in allowance	3,500
Profit	1,000

Activity checklist

This checklist shows which performance criteria, range statement or knowledge and understanding point is covered by each activity in this chapter. Tick off each activity as you complete it.

Activity

5.1	☐	This activity deals with Range Statement 11.1.3: relevant accounting standards.
5.2	☐	This activity deals with Range Statement 11.1.2 domestic legislation
5.3	☐	This activity deals with Knowledge & Understanding point 4: main requirements of FRS.
5.4	☐	This activity deals with Knowledge & Understanding point 7: preparing financial statements in proper form.
5.5	☐	This activity deals with Knowledge & Understanding point 4: main requirements of FRS.
5.6	☐	This activity deals with Performance Criteria 11.1.C: compliance with accounting standards.

chapter 6

Taxation in company accounts

Contents

1 Introduction
2 SSAP 5 *Accounting for value added tax*
3 Corporation tax
4 FRS 19 *Deferred tax*
5 Taxation in company accounts

Performance criteria

11.1.A Draft limited company financial statements from the appropriate information
11.1.B Correctly identify and implement subsequent adjustments and ensure that discrepancies, unusual features or queries are identified and either resolved or referred to the appropriate person
11.1.C Ensure that limited company financial statements comply with relevant accounting standards and domestic legislation and with the organisation's policies, regulations and procedures

Range statement

11.1.1 Limited company financial statements: income statement; balance sheet

Knowledge and understanding

4 The UK regulatory framework for financial reporting and the main requirements of relevant Financial Reporting Standards (Element 11.1)
6 The presentation of corporation tax in financial statements (Element 11.1)

PART B   LIMITED COMPANY ACCOUNTS

1 Introduction

You'll have come across **VAT** in your earlier studies. Calculating VAT to go on an invoice, working out the VAT on a VAT inclusive amount and working out how much to pay to HM Customs and Excise is familiar territory. What will be new to you, however, is the **treatment of VAT in the accounts of limited companies**. This is the subject of **SSAP 5**.

Corporation tax is just the equivalent of **income tax for limited companies**. You don't need to know the details for this Unit, just **presentation issues**.

Deferred tax is a way of accounting for **timing differences**, which arise when certain items are included in the accounts of a different period from that used for taxation purposes.

2 SSAP 5 *Accounting for value added tax*

VAT is a tax on the **supply of goods and services**. The tax authority responsible for collecting VAT is HM Customs & Excise. Tax is collected at each transfer point in the chain from prime producer to final consumer. Eventually, the consumer bears the tax in full and any tax paid earlier in the chain can be recovered by the trader who paid it.

Example: VAT

A manufacturing company, A Ltd, purchases raw materials at a cost of £1,000 plus VAT at 17½%. From the raw materials A Ltd makes finished products which it sells to a retail outlet, B Ltd, for £1,600 plus VAT. B Ltd sells the products to customers at a total price of £2,000 plus VAT. How much VAT is paid to Customs & Excise at each stage in the chain?

Solution

	Value of goods sold £	VAT at 17½% £
Supplier of raw materials	1,000	175
Value added by A Ltd	600	105
Sale to B Ltd	1,600	280
Value added by B Ltd	400	70
Sales to 'consumers'	2,000	350

2.1 How is VAT collected?

Although it is the final consumer who eventually bears the full tax of £350, the sum is **collected and paid over to Customs & Excise by the traders who make up the chain.** Each trader must assume that his customer is the final consumer and must collect and pay over VAT at the appropriate rate on the full sales value of the goods sold. He is entitled to reclaim VAT paid on his own purchases (inputs) and so makes a net payment to Customs & Excise equal to the tax on value added by himself.

In the example above, the supplier of raw materials collects from A Ltd VAT of £175, all of which he pays over to Customs & Excise. When A Ltd sells goods to B Ltd VAT is charged at the rate of 17½% on £1,600 = £280. Only £105, however, is paid by A Ltd to Customs & Excise because the company is entitled to deduct VAT of £175 suffered on its own purchases. Similarly, B Ltd must charge its customers £350 in VAT but need only pay over the net amount of £70 after deducting the £280 VAT suffered on its purchase from A Ltd.

2.2 Registered and non-registered persons

Traders whose sales (outputs) are below a certain minimum need not register for VAT. Such traders neither charge VAT on their outputs nor are entitled to reclaim VAT on their inputs. They are in the same position as a final consumer.

All outputs of registered traders are either **taxable** or **exempt**. Traders carrying on exempt activities (such as banks) cannot charge VAT on their outputs and consequently cannot reclaim VAT paid on their inputs.

Taxable outputs are chargeable at one of **three rates.**

   (a)   Zero per cent (**zero-rated items**)
   (b)   5% (lower rated items)
   (c)   17½% (standard-rated items)

Customs & Excise publish lists of supplies falling into each category. Persons carrying on taxable activities (even activities taxable at zero per cent) are entitled to reclaim VAT paid on their inputs.

Some traders carry on a mixture of taxable and exempt activities. Such traders need to apportion the VAT suffered on inputs and can only reclaim the proportion relating to taxable outputs.

2.3 Accounting for VAT

As a general principle the treatment of VAT in the accounts of a trader should reflect his role as a collector of the tax and **VAT should not be included in income or in expenditure whether of a capital or of a revenue nature.**

Where the **trader bears the VAT** himself, as in the following cases, this should be reflected in the accounts.

   (a)   **Persons not registered** for VAT will suffer VAT on inputs. This will effectively increase the cost of their consumable materials and their fixed assets and must be so reflected, ie shown **inclusive of VAT.**

   (b)   **Registered persons** who also carry on **exempted** activities will have a residue of VAT which falls directly on them. In this situation the costs to which this residue applies will be inflated by the **irrecoverable VAT**.

   (c)   **Non-deductible inputs will be borne** by all traders (examples are tax on cars bought which are not for resale, entertaining expenses and provision of domestic accommodation for a company's directors).

2.4 Further points

VAT is charged on the price **net of any discount** and this general principle is carried to the extent that where a cash discount is offered, VAT is charged on the net amount even where the discount is not taken up.

Most VAT registered persons are obliged to record VAT when a supply is received or made (effectively when a credit sales invoice is raised or a purchase invoice recorded). This has the effect that the net VAT liability has on occasion to be paid to Customs & Excise before all output tax has been paid by customers. If a debt is subsequently written off, the VAT element may not be recovered from Customs & Excise for six months from the date of sale, even if the customer becomes insolvent.

Some small businesses can join the **cash accounting scheme** whereby VAT is only paid to Customs & Excise after it is received from customers. This delays recovery of input tax but improves cash flow overall, although it may involve extra record keeping. Bad debt relief is automatic under this scheme since if VAT is not paid by the customer it is not due to Customs & Excise.

2.5 Requirements of SSAP 5

SSAP 5 requires the following accounting rules to be followed.

(a) **Turnover** shown in the profit and loss account should **exclude VAT** on taxable outputs. If gross turnover must be shown then the VAT in that figure must also be shown as a deduction in arriving at the turnover exclusive of VAT.

(b) **Irrecoverable VAT** allocated to fixed assets and other items separately disclosed should be **included in their cost** where material and practical.

(c) The **net amount due to (or from) Customs & Excise** should be included in the **total for creditors** (or **debtors**), and need not be separately disclosed.

Note that the CA 1985 also requires disclosure of the cost of sales figure in the published accounts. This amount should exclude VAT on taxable inputs.

3 Corporation tax

Companies are required to pay **corporation tax** on their taxable profits. The **taxable profits** of a company are essentially its net profit before dividends, adjusted for certain items where the tax treatment differs from the accounts treatment.

The rate at which companies are charged to corporation tax depends on the level of their profits. Companies with small profits currently (2004) pay corporation tax at a rate of 19%; other companies at a rate of 30%.

The amount of tax to which a company is assessed on its profit for an accounting period is called its **tax liability** for that period. In general, a company must pay its tax liability nine months after the end of the relevant accounting period.

IMPORTANT!
You will not be required to calculate corporation tax.

4 FRS 19 *Deferred tax*

4.1 What is deferred tax?

You may already be aware that accounting profits and taxable profits are not the same. There are several reasons for this but they may conveniently be considered under two headings.

(a) **Permanent differences** arise because certain expenditure, such as entertainment of UK customers, is not allowed as a deduction for tax purposes although it is quite properly deducted in arriving at accounting profit. Similarly, certain income (such as franked investment income) is not subject to corporation tax, although it forms part of accounting profit.

(b) **Timing differences** arise because certain items are included in the accounts of a period different from that in which they are dealt with for taxation purposes.

FRS 19 identifies the main categories in which timing differences can occur. The two most important are explained below.

(a) **Short-term timing differences.** These arise because taxable profits are calculated on a receipts and payments basis, whereas accounting profits are calculated on an accruals basis. Examples include the following.

   (i) Interest receivable at the end of one year will be credited to the accounting profit of the year but taxed only when it is received in the next year.

   (ii) Pension contributions payable at the end of one year will be accrued in the accounts but not allowed for tax purposes until they are actually paid.

(b) **Accelerated capital allowances.** Depreciation cannot be deducted from profits in arriving at taxable profits (and so it must be 'added back'). Instead, when new assets are purchased, capital allowances may be available to deduct from taxable profits and may exceed the amount of depreciation chargeable on the assets in the financial accounts. This used to be a major cause of timing differences because 100% capital allowances in the year of acquisition were available on many assets. First year allowances have now been phased out and for the time being it is likely that capital allowances for tax purposes will not differ greatly from depreciation charged in the accounts. There are still timing differences, but they are not so large in amount. A change in government policy could increase the significance of deferred tax again.

> **Deferred taxation** is a means of ironing out the tax inequalities arising from timing differences. In years when corporation tax is saved by timing differences such as accelerated capital allowances, a charge for deferred taxation is made in the profit and loss account and a provision set up in the balance sheet; in years when timing differences reverse, because the depreciation charge exceeds the capital allowances available, a deferred tax credit is made in the profit and loss account and the balance sheet provision is reduced.

You should be clear in your mind that the tax actually payable to the Inland Revenue is the corporation tax liability. The credit balance on the deferred taxation account represents an estimate of tax saved because of timing differences but expected ultimately to become payable when those differences reverse.

4.2 Deferred tax – a simple example of differences

Corporation tax is payable on a company's profits, but these profits are 'taxable' profits, not 'accounting' profits, as revealed by the profit and loss account. The Inland Revenue will not accept certain expenditure (eg hospitality and depreciation), but replaces depreciation with its own national system of capital allowances.

This may give rise to the following position, assuming a 30% rate of corporation tax.

	£		£
Accounting profits	150,000	Tax @ 30%	45,000
Add back non acceptable expenditures	20,000		
	170,000		
Less capital allowances	50,000		
Taxable profits	120,000	Tax @ 30%	36,000
		Tax 'deferred'	9,000

This tax 'saving' must be credited to a deferred tax provision in the balance sheet, as it will need to be applied to a future position when accounting profits exceed taxable profits.

> **IMPORTANT!**
> The assessment of FRS 19 is restricted to understanding 'deferred tax' and the general requirements for regulation of deferred tax assets and liabilities. There will be no detailed assessment of the treatment of deferred tax or the computations that relate to this.

5 Taxation in company accounts

We have now looked at the 'ingredients' of taxation in company accounts. There are two aspects to be learned.

- Taxation on profits in the profit and loss account
- Taxation payments due, shown as a liability in the balance sheet

5.1 Taxation in the profit and loss account

The tax on profit on ordinary activities is calculated by **aggregating**:

- **Corporation tax** on taxable profits
- Transfers to or from deferred taxation
- Any under provision or overprovision of corporation tax on profits of previous years

When corporation tax on profits is calculated for the profit and loss account, the calculation is only an estimate of what the company thinks its tax liability will be. In subsequent dealings with the Inland Revenue, a different corporation tax charge might eventually be agreed.

The difference between the estimated tax on profits for one year and the actual tax charge finally agreed for the year is made as an adjustment to taxation on profits in the following year, resulting in the disclosure of either an **underprovision** of tax or an **overprovision** of tax.

Activity 6.1

In the accounting year to 31 December 20X3, Ben Nevis Ltd made an operating profit before investment income and taxation of £110,000.

Corporation tax on the operating profit has been estimated as £45,000.

In the previous year (20X2) corporation tax on 20X2 profits had been estimated as £38,000 but it was subsequently agreed at £40,500 with the Inland Revenue.

A transfer to the deferred taxation account of £16,000 will be made in 20X3.

Task

Calculate the tax on profits for 20X3 for disclosure in the accounts.

5.2 Taxation in the balance sheet

It may already be apparent that the corporation tax charge in the profit and loss account will not be the same as the corporation tax liability in the balance sheet.

In the balance sheet, there are several items which we might expect to find.

(a) **Income tax may be payable** in respect of (say) interest payments paid in the last accounting return period of the year, or accrued.

(b) If no corporation tax is payable (or very little), then there might be an **income tax recoverable asset** disclosed in current assets (income tax is normally recovered by offset against the tax liability for the year).

(c) There will usually be a **liability for mainstream corporation tax**, possibly including the amounts due in respect of previous years but not yet paid.

(d) We may also find a **liability on the deferred taxation account**. Deferred taxation is shown under 'provisions for liabilities and charges' in the balance sheet.

Activity 6.2

Take the facts as given in activity 6.1. The tax for 20X2 was paid on 1 October 20X3. The balances bought forward at 1 January 20X3 were:

Corporation Tax   38,000 credits
Deferred tax   12,000 credits

Task

Calculate the balance sheet figures for corporation tax and deferred tax for 20X3 for disclosure in the accounts.

Key learning points

- A trader generally collects **VAT** on behalf of HM Customs & Excise.
    - VAT is charged on sales (outputs).
    - VAT is paid on purchases (inputs).
    - The difference is paid over to or collected from HM Customs & Excise every quarter.
- **VAT** should **not be included** in either income or expenditure.
- Companies pay **corporation tax** on profits.
- Accounting profits are not the same as taxable profits, partly because of **timing differences**. **Deferred tax** is the tax attributable to timing differences.
- You should be aware of the way in which taxation is disclosed in the profit and loss account and the balance sheet.

Quick quiz

1. Who bears the cost of VAT?
2. VAT should be included in turnover (per SSAP 5). True or false?
3. What are timing differences?
4. How is the tax charge in the profit and loss account made up?

Answers to quick quiz

1. The final customer
2. False
3. Differences which arise because certain items are included in the accounts of a period different from that in which they are dealt with for tax purposes.
4. - Corporation tax on taxable profits, *plus*
   - Transfers to or from deferred taxation, *plus*
   - Any over or under provision from previous years

Activity checklist

This checklist shows which performance criteria, range statement or knowledge and understanding point is covered by each activity in this chapter. Tick off each activity as you complete it.

Activity

6.1		This activity deals with Knowledge & Understanding point 6: presentation of corporation tax.
6.2		This activity deals with Knowledge & Understanding point 6: presentation of corporation tax.

PART B LIMITED COMPANY ACCOUNTS

chapter 7

Provisions, contingencies and post balance sheet events

Contents

1. The problem
2. The solution
3. Post balance sheet events
4. Provisions, contingent liabilities and contingent assets

Performance criteria

11.1.A Draft limited company financial statements from the appropriate information
11.1.B Correctly identify and implement subsequent adjustments and ensure that discrepancies, unusual features or queries are identified and either resolved or referred to the appropriate person
11.1.C Ensure that limited company financial statements comply with relevant accounting standards and domestic legislation and with the organisation's policies, regulations and procedures

Range statement

11.1.1 Limited company financial statements: income statement; balance sheet; supplementary notes
11.2.2 Elements: Assets; liabilities

Knowledge and understanding

1. The elements and purposes of financial statements of limited companies as set out in the conceptual framework for financial reporting (Element 11.2)
2. The general legal framework of limited companies and the obligations of directors in respect of the financial statements (Element 11.1)
3. The statutory form of accounting statements and disclosure requirements (Element 11.1)

PART B LIMITED COMPANY ACCOUNTS

Knowledge and understanding (cont'd)

4   The UK regulatory framework for financial reporting and the main requirements of relevant Financial Reporting Standards
5   The forms of equity and loan capital (Element 11.1)
10 Generally accepted accounting principles and concepts (Elements 11.1)

1 The problem

The financial statements are significant indicators of a company's success or failure. It is important, therefore, that they include **all the information necessary for an understanding of the company's position**.

The problem is, however, that events may occur **after the balance sheet date** which affect the position at the balance sheet date. Furthermore there may be issues which remain **uncertain at the balance sheet date**.

2 The solution

SSAP 17 *Accounting for post balance sheet events* and FRS 12 *Provisions, contingent liabilities and contingent assets* both require the provision of **additional information** in order to help the user understand the position. SSAP 17 deals with events after the balance sheet date which may affect the position at the balance sheet date. FRS 12 deals with matters which are uncertain at the balance sheet date.

3 Post balance sheet events

3.1 What are post balance sheet events?

SSAP 17 *Accounting for post balance sheet events* deals with events **after** the balance sheet date which may **affect the position** at the balance sheet date.

> **Post balance sheet events** are those events, both favourable and unfavourable, which occur between the balance sheet date and the date on which the financial statements are approved by the board of directors.
> *(SSAP 17)*

SSAP 17 also explains the **rationale** behind the proposed accounting treatment of such events.

> '1. Events arising after the balance sheet date need to be reflected in financial statements if they provide additional evidence of conditions that existed at the balance sheet date and materially affect the amounts to be included.'

Even events which do not provide such evidence may need to be **disclosed** if a true appreciation is to be made of a company's state of affairs and profit or loss.

7: PROVISIONS, CONTINGENCIES AND POST BALANCE SHEET EVENTS

> '2. To prevent financial statements from being misleading, disclosure needs to be made by way of notes of other material events arising after the balance sheet date which provide evidence of conditions not existing at the balance sheet date. Disclosure is required where this information is necessary for a proper understanding of the financial position.'

The circumstances described above correspond to the distinction made in SSAP 17 between 'adjusting events' and 'non-adjusting events'.

3.2 Adjusting events

SSAP 17 defines adjusting events.

> **Adjusting events** are post balance sheet events which provide additional evidence of conditions existing at the balance sheet date. They include events which because of statutory or conventional requirements are reflected in financial statements.
> *(SSAP 17)*

The second sentence of this definition refers to such events as:

(a) Resolutions relating to proposed dividends and amounts appropriated to reserves

(b) The effects of changes in taxation rates

(c) The declaration, by subsidiaries or associated companies, of dividends relating to periods prior to the balance sheet date of the holding company

3.3 Examples of adjusting events

An appendix to SSAP 17 cites a number of post balance sheet events which normally should be classified as adjusting events.

(a) The subsequent determination of the purchase price or of sale proceeds of assets purchased or sold before the year end

(b) The valuation of a property which provides evidence of impairment in value

(c) The receipt of a copy of the financial statements or other information in respect of an unlisted company which provides evidence of impairment in the value of a long-term investment

(d) The receipt of proceeds of sale or other evidence after the balance sheet date concerning the net realisable value of stock

(e) The receipt of evidence that the previous estimate of accrued profit on a long term contract was materially inaccurate

(f) The renegotiation of amounts owing by debtors, or the insolvency of a debtor

(g) Amounts received or receivable in respect of insurance claims which were in the course of negotiation at the balance sheet date

(h) The discovery of errors or frauds which show that the financial statements were incorrect

Some events occurring after the balance sheet date, such as a deterioration in the company's operating results and in its financial position, may indicate a need to consider whether it is appropriate to use the going concern concept in the preparation of financial statements. Consequently such events may fall to be treated as adjusting events.

3.4 Non-adjusting events

> **Non-adjusting events** are events which arise after the balance sheet date and concern conditions which did not exist at that time. Consequently they do not result in changes in amounts in financial statements. They may, however, be of such materiality that their disclosure is required by way of notes to ensure that financial statements are not misleading.
> *(SSAP 17)*

3.5 Examples of non-adjusting events

Again, a number of examples are given in the appendix including the following.

- (a) Issues of shares and debentures
- (b) Purchases and sales of fixed assets and investments
- (c) Losses of fixed assets or stocks as a result of a catastrophe such as fire or flood
- (d) Opening new trading activities or extending existing trading activities
- (e) Closing a significant part of the trading activities if this was not anticipated at the year end
- (f) Decline in the value of property and investments held as fixed assets, if it can be demonstrated that the decline occurred after the year end
- (g) Government action, such as nationalisation
- (h) Strikes and other labour disputes

In exceptional circumstances, to accord with the prudence concept, an adverse event which would normally be classified as non-adjusting may need to be reclassified as adjusting. In such circumstances full disclosure of the adjustment would be required.

3.6 'Window dressing'

Although 'window dressing' is not a precise term, and SSAP 17 does not attempt to define it, disclosure is required of the reversal or maturity after the year end of transactions entered into before the year end, the substance of which was primarily to alter the appearance of the company's balance sheet. Any 'window dressing' which may encompass fraud is, of course, unlawful and unacceptable.

3.7 Disclosure requirements

Financial statements should be prepared on the basis of **conditions existing** at the **balance sheet** date and should also disclose the date on which they were approved by the board of directors (so that users can establish the duration of the 'post balance sheet events period'). The standard is not intended to apply to events occurring after the date of board approval, but recommends that if such events are material the directors should consider publishing the relevant information so that users of financial statements are not misled.

SSAP 17 states that a material post balance sheet event requires **changes** in the amounts to be included in financial statements where:

(a) it is an **adjusting event**; or

(b) it indicates that application of the **going concern** concept to the whole or a material part of the company is **not appropriate**.

Separate disclosure of adjusting events is not normally required as they do no more than provide additional evidence in support of items in financial statements. However in exceptional circumstances, where a non-adjusting event is reclassified as an adjusting event, full disclosure of the adjustment is required.

The CA 1985 requires that all liabilities and losses which have arisen or are likely to arise in respect of the financial year to which the accounts relate (or a previous financial year) shall be taken into account, including those that only become apparent between the balance sheet date and the date on which it is signed on behalf of the board of directors.

The Act therefore gives some statutory enforcement to the provisions in SSAP 17 in respect of adjusting post balance sheet events, but refers to 'liabilities and losses' only, and not to 'gains'.

SSAP 17 also requires that a material post balance sheet event should be **disclosed:**

(a) Where it is a **non-adjusting event** of such materiality that its non-disclosure would affect the ability of the users of financial statements to reach a proper understanding of the financial position

(b) Where it is the reversal or maturity after the year end of a transaction entered into before the year end, the substance of which was primarily to alter the appearance of the company's balance sheet (reversal of window dressing)

In determining which non-adjusting events are of sufficient materiality to require disclosure regard should be had to all matters which are necessary to enable users of financial statements to assess the financial position.

In respect of each post balance sheet event which is required to be disclosed, the following information should also be given

(a) The nature of the event

(b) An estimate of the financial effect, or a statement that it is not practicable to make such an estimate. (*Note.* The estimate of the financial effect should be disclosed before taking account of taxation and the taxation implications should be explained where necessary for a proper understanding of the financial position.)

The CA 1985 requires that the directors' report should contain particulars of any important events affecting the company (or its subsidiaries) which have occurred since the end of the year.

Although this gives some statutory backing to the provisions of SSAP 17 in respect of non-adjusting post balance sheet events, it suggests the information be given in the directors' report rather than the notes to the accounts (as required by SSAP 17).

3.8 SSAP 17 key points summarised

```
POST BALANCE SHEET EVENTS occur between the balance
sheet date and the date on which the financial statements
are approved by the board of directors.
```

ADJUSTING EVENTS
Provide additional evidence of conditions existing at the balance sheet date.

NON-ADJUSTING EVENTS
Concern conditions which did not exist at the balance sheet date.

STANDARD ACCOUNTING
Change the figures in the financial statements if the post balance sheet event is material and either it's an adjusting event or the going concern concept is no longer appropriate.

STANDARD ACCOUNTING
Disclose a post balance sheet event in a note if it is material and either it's a non-adjusting event or it was window dressing.

EVENTS AFTER THE DATE OF APPROVAL OF THE ACCOUNTS
The directors should consider publishing these if material.

Activity 7.1

State whether the following post balance sheet events are adjusting or non-adjusting:

(a) Purchase of an investment
(b) A change in the rate of corporation tax, applicable to the previous year
(c) An increase in pension benefits
(d) Losses due to fire
(e) A bad debt suddenly being paid
(f) The receipt of proceeds of sales or other evidence concerning the net realisable value of stock
(g) A sudden decline in the value of property held as a fixed asset
(h) A merger

Activity 7.2

(a) The directors of Duck plc, a large quoted company, are currently drafting its financial statements for the year ended 30 November 20X8.

Quack, a former director, is suing the company after being summarily dismissed by the Chairman on 1 December 20X8. Beak, the company's solicitor, thinks that Quack will win punitive damages (about £500,000 – this would be material for the company).

Is this:

- A A contingent loss, which should be accrued
- B A contingent liability, which should be disclosed in a note
- C A non-adjusting post balance sheet event
- D An adjusting post balance sheet event

(b) Betrayed Ltd has discovered since its year end (31 March 20X8) that its longest serving employee, Ann Dinthetill, has systematically stolen £1m from the company over her forty years of service in the purchase ledger department. Material errors have thus been made in its accounts over many years. There is no hope of recovery as Ann anonymously donated the money to a dogs' home.

In addition, the government announced on 1 April 20X8 that it intends compulsorily to purchase Betrayed Ltd's headquarters building. The purchase price will be below book value.

In accordance with SSAP 17, how should each discovery be treated in Betrayed Ltd's financial statements?

	Theft	Compulsory purchase
A	Adjust accounts	Adjust accounts
B	Adjust accounts	Disclose in a note
C	Disclose in a note	Adjust accounts
D	Disclose in a note	Disclose in a note

Activity 7.3

Fabricators Ltd, an engineering company, makes up its financial statements to 31 March in each year. The financial statements for the year ended 31 March 20X1 showed a turnover of £3m and trading profit of £400,000.

Before approval of the financial statements by the board of directors on 30 June 20X1 the following events took place.

(a) The financial statements of Patchup Ltd for the year ended 28 February 20X1 were received which indicated a permanent decline in that company's financial position. Fabricators Ltd had bought shares in Patchup Ltd some years ago and this purchase was included in unquoted investments at its cost of £100,000. The financial statements received indicated that this investment was now worth only £50,000.

(b) There was a fire at the company's warehouse on 30 April 20X1 when stock to the value of £500,000 was destroyed. It transpired that the stock in the warehouse was under-insured by some 50%.

(c) It was announced on 1 June 20X1 that the company's design for tank cleaning equipment had been approved by the major oil companies and this could result in an increase in the annual turnover of some £1m with a relative effect on profits.

4 Provisions, contingent liabilities and contingent assets

As we have seen with regard to post balance sheet events, financial statements must include **all the information necessary for an understanding of the company's financial position**. Provisions, contingent liabilities and contingent assets are 'uncertainties' that must be accounted for consistently if are to achieve this understanding.

FRS 12 *Provisions, contingent liabilities and contingent assets* aims to ensure that appropriate **recognition criteria** and **measurement bases** are applied to provisions, contingent liabilities and contingent assets and that **sufficient information** is disclosed in the **notes** to the financial statements to enable users to understand their nature, timing and amount.

4.1 Provisions

You will be familiar with provisions for depreciation and doubtful debts from your earlier studies. The sorts of provisions addressed by FRS 12 are, however, rather different.

Before FRS 12, there was no accounting standard dealing with provisions. Companies wanting to show their results in the most favourable light used to make large **'one off' provisions** in years where a high level of underlying profits was generated. These provisions, often known as **'big bath'** provisions, were then available to shield expenditure in future years when perhaps the underlying profits were not as good.

In other words, **provisions were used for profit smoothing**. Profit smoothing is misleading.

> **Signpost**
> The key aim of FRS 12 is to ensure that **provisions are made only where there are valid grounds for them**.

FRS 12 views a provision as a **liability**.

> A **provision** is a **liability** of uncertain timing or amount.
>
> A **liability** is an obligation of an entity to transfer economic benefits as a result of past transactions or events.
>
> *(FRS 12)*

The FRS distinguishes provisions from other liabilities such as trade creditors and accruals. This is on the basis that for a provision there is **uncertainty** about the timing or amount of the future expenditure. Whilst uncertainty is clearly present in the case of certain accruals the uncertainty is generally much less than for provisions.

7: PROVISIONS, CONTINGENCIES AND POST BALANCE SHEET EVENTS

4.2 Recognition

FRS 12 states that a provision should be **recognised** as a liability in the financial statements when:

- An entity has a **present obligation** (legal or constructive) as a result of a past event
- It is probable that a **transfer of economic benefits** will be required to settle the obligation
- A **reliable estimate** can be made of the obligation

In other words, a provision should only be recognised where an entity has a liability as defined by the *Statement of Principles*.

4.3 Meaning of obligation

It is fairly clear what a legal obligation is. However, you may not know what a **constructive obligation** is.

> FRS 12 defines a constructive obligation as
>
> 'An obligation that derives from an entity's actions where:
>
> - by an established pattern of past practice, published policies or a sufficiently specific current statement the entity has indicated to other parties that it will accept certain responsibilities; and
>
> - as a result, the entity has created a valid expectation on the part of those other parties that it will discharge those responsibilities.

Activity 7.4

In which of the following circumstances might a provision be recognised?

(a) On 13 December 20X9 the board of an entity decided to close down a division. The accounting date of the company is 31 December. Before 31 December 20X9 the decision was not communicated to any of those affected and no other steps were taken to implement the decision.

(b) The board agreed a detailed closure plan on 20 December 20X9 and details were given to customers and employees.

(c) A company is obliged to incur clean up costs for environmental damage (that has already been caused).

(d) A company intends to carry out future expenditure to operate in a particular way in the future.

4.4 Probable transfer of economic benefits

For the purpose of the FRS, a transfer of economic benefits is regarded as **'probable'** if the event is **more likely than not** to occur. This appears to indicate a probability of more than 50%. However, the standard makes it clear that where there is a number of similar obligations the probability should be based on considering the population as a whole, rather than one single item.

Example: transfer of economic benefits

If a company has entered into a warranty obligation then the probability of transfer of economic benefits may well be extremely small in respect of one specific item. However, when considering the population as a whole the probability of some transfer of economic benefits is quite likely to be much higher. If there is a **greater than 50% probability** of some transfer of economic benefits then a **provision** should be made for the **expected amount**.

4.5 Measurement of provisions

The amount recognised as a provision should be the best estimate of the expenditure required to settle the present obligation at the balance sheet date.

The estimates will be determined by the **judgement** of the entity's management supplemented by the experience of similar transactions.

Allowance is made for **uncertainty**.

Where the effect of the **time value of money** is material, the amount of a provision should be the **present value** of the expenditure required to settle the obligation. An appropriate **discount** rate should be used.

4.6 Provisions for restructuring

One of the main purposes of FRS 12 was to target abuses of provisions for restructuring. Accordingly, FRS 12 lays down **strict criteria** to determine when such a provision can be made.

> FRS 12 defines a **restructuring** as:
>
> A programme that is planned and is controlled by management and materially changes either:
>
> - the scope of a business undertaken by an entity; or
> - the manner in which that business is conducted.

The FRS gives the following **examples** of events that may fall under the definition of restructuring.

- The **sale or termination** of a line of business
- The **closure of business locations** in a country or region or the **relocation** of business activities from one country region to another
- **Changes in management structure**, for example, the elimination of a layer of management
- **Fundamental reorganisations** that have a material effect on the **nature and focus** of the entity's operations

7: PROVISIONS, CONTINGENCIES AND POST BALANCE SHEET EVENTS

The question is whether or not an entity has an obligation – legal or constructive – at the balance sheet date.

- An entity must have a **detailed formal plan** for the restructuring.
- It must have **raised a valid expectation** in those affected that it will carry out the restructuring by starting to implement that plan or announcing its main features to those affected by it

> **IMPORTANT!**
> **A mere management decision is not normally sufficient.** Management decisions may sometimes trigger off recognition, but only if earlier events such as negotiations with employee representatives and other interested parties have been concluded subject only to management approval.

Where the restructuring involves the **sale of an operation** then FRS 12 states that no obligation arises until the entity has entered into a **binding sale agreement**. This is because until this has occurred the entity will be able to change its mind and withdraw from the sale even if its intentions have been announced publicly.

4.6.1 Costs to be included within a restructuring provision

The FRS states that a restructuring provision should include only the **direct expenditures** arising from the restructuring, which are those that are both:

- **Necessarily entailed** by the restructuring
- Not associated with the **ongoing activities** of the entity

The following costs should specifically **not** be included within a restructuring provision.

- **Retraining** or relocating continuing staff
- Marketing
- Investment in new systems and distribution networks

4.7 Disclosure

Disclosures for provisions fall into two parts.

- Disclosure of details of the **change in carrying value** of a provision from the beginning to the end of the year
- Disclosure of the **background** to the making of the provision and the uncertainties affecting its outcome

4.8 Contingent liabilities

Now you understand provisions it will be easier to understand contingent assets and liabilities.

> FRS 12 defines a **contingent liability** as:
>
> - A possible obligation that arises from past events and whose existence will be confirmed only by the occurrence or non-occurrence of one or more uncertain future events not wholly within the entity's control; or
> - A present obligation that arises from past events but is not recognised because:-
>   - It is not probable that a transfer of economic benefits will be required to settle the obligation; or
>   - The amount of the obligation cannot be measured with sufficient reliability.

As a rule of thumb, probable means more than 50% likely. **If an obligation is probable, it is not a contingent liability –** instead, a **provision is needed**.

4.8.1 Treatment of contingent liabilities

Contingent liabilities **should not be recognised in financial statements** but they **should be disclosed**. The required disclosures are:

- A brief description of the nature of the contingent liability
- An estimate of its financial effect
- An indication of the uncertainties that exist
- The possibility of any reimbursement

4.9 Contingent assets

> FRS 12 defines a **contingent asset** as:
>
> A possible asset that arises from past events and whose existence will be confirmed by the occurrence of one or more uncertain future events not wholly within the entity's control.

A contingent asset must not be recognised. Only when the realisation of the related economic benefits is **virtually certain** should recognition take place. At that point, **the asset is no longer a contingent asset**!

Before trying Activity 7.5, study the flow chart, taken from FRS 12, which is a good summary of the requirements of the standard.

7: PROVISIONS, CONTINGENCIES AND POST BALANCE SHEET EVENTS

4.10 Learn this flow chart!

If you learn this flow chart you should be able to deal with most tasks you are likely to meet in an exam.

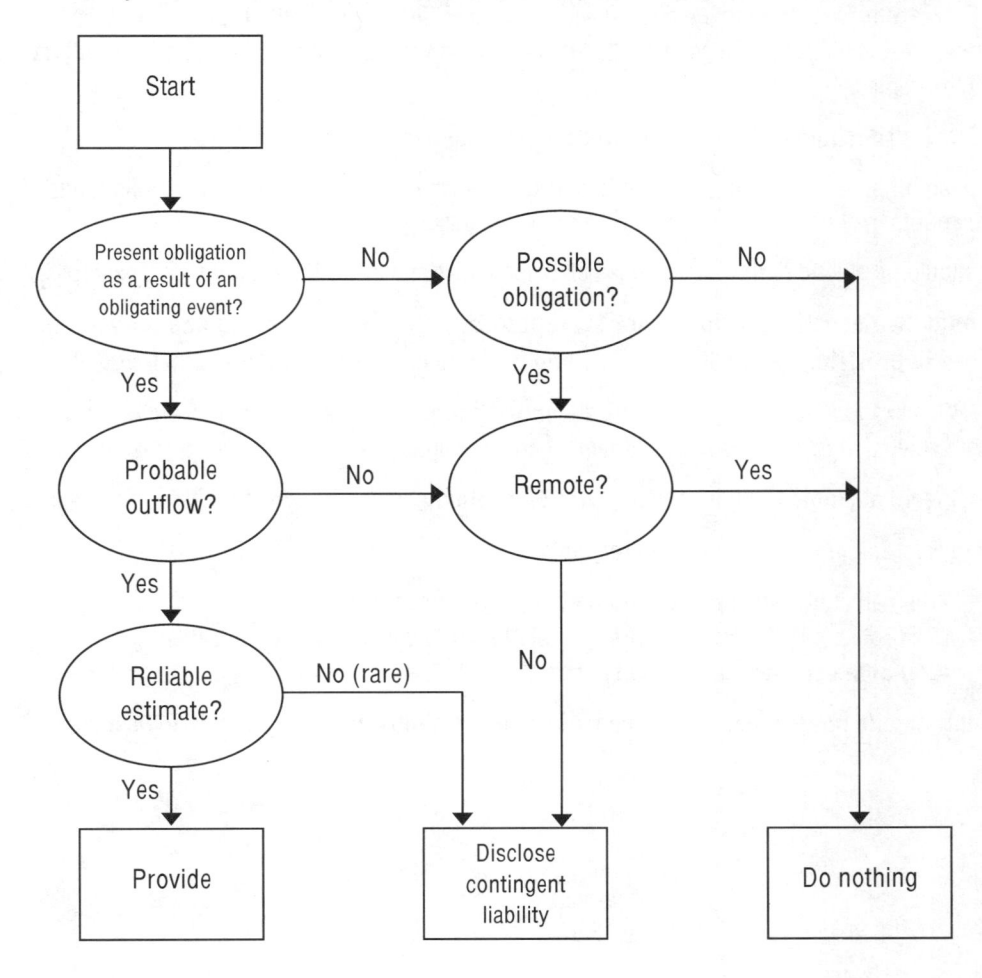

```
Start
  │
  ▼
Present obligation as a result of an obligating event? ──No──▶ Possible obligation? ──No──────────────┐
  │                                                              │                                    │
  Yes                                                             Yes                                  │
  ▼                                                              ▼                                    │
Probable outflow? ──No──────────────────────────────▶ Remote? ──Yes──▶                               │
  │                                                              │                                    │
  Yes                                                             No                                   │
  ▼                                                              ▼                                    ▼
Reliable estimate? ──No (rare)──▶                        Disclose contingent liability         Do nothing
  │
  Yes
  ▼
Provide
```

Activity 7.5

During 20X1 Smack Ltd gives a guarantee of certain borrowings of Pony Ltd, whose financial condition at that time is sound. During 20X2, the financial condition of Pony Ltd deteriorates and at 30 June 20X2 Pony Ltd files for protection from its creditors.

What accounting treatment is required?

(a) At 31 December 20X1
(b) At 31 December 20X2?

PART B LIMITED COMPANY ACCOUNTS

Key learning points

- SSAP 17 *Accounting for post balance sheet events* amplifies the CA 1985 requirement to take account of post balance sheet liabilities and losses by distinguishing between **adjusting events** and **non-adjusting events** and giving examples.

- The SSAP also requires disclosure of **window dressing** transactions.

- Where an otherwise non-adjusting event indicates that the going concern concept is no longer appropriate then the accounts may have to be restated on a break-up basis.

- You should be able to define and discuss all these terms and apply them to practical examples.

- **The objective of FRS 12 is to ensure that** appropriate recognition criteria **and measurement bases are applied to** provisions and contingencies **and that** sufficient information **is disclosed.**

- The FRS seeks to ensure that provisions are **only recognised** when a **measurable obligation** exists. It includes detailed rules that can be used to ascertain when an obligation exists and how to measure the obligation.

- The standard attempts to **eliminate** the **'profit smoothing'** which has gone on before it was issued.

- Under FRS 12, a **provision** should be recognised
    - When an entity has a **present obligation**, legal or constructive
    - It is probable that a **transfer of economic benefits** will be required to settle it
    - A **reliable estimate** can be made of its amount

- An entity **should not recognise a contingent asset or liability**, but they **should be disclosed**.

Quick quiz

1. Distinguish between adjusting events and non-adjusting events.
2. What is window-dressing?
3. When does a post balance sheet event require changes to the financial statements?
4. A contingent liability should be disclosed if a transfer of economic benefits is probable. True or false?
5. A property is valued and an impairment in value is identified.

    Adjusting event □

    Non-adjusting event □

6. Stocks are lost in a fire.

    Adjusting event □

    Non-adjusting event □

7. A provision is a ……………………….. of ……………………….. timing or amount.

Answers to quick quiz

1. Adjusting events are post balance sheet events which provide additional evidence of conditions existing at the balance sheet date. Non adjusting events are events which arise after the balance sheet date and concern conditions which did not exist at that time.
2. Transactions entered into before the year end, the substance of which was primarily to alter the appearance of the company's balance sheet.
3. When it is an adjusting event, or when it indicates that the application of the going concern concept is not appropriate.
4. False. If such a transfer is probable, we are dealing with a provision, not a contingent liability. However, if the transfer is only *possible* a contingent liability should be *disclosed*.
5. Adjusting
6. Non-adjusting
7. **Liability** of **uncertain** timing or amount.

PART B LIMITED COMPANY ACCOUNTS

Activity checklist

This checklist shows which performance criteria, range statement or knowledge and understanding point is covered by each activity in this chapter. Tick off each activity as you complete it.

Activity

7.1	☐	This activity deals with Performance Criteria 11.1.B: correctly implement adjustments.
7.2	☐	This activity deals with Performance Criteria 11.1.B: correctly implement adjustments.
7.3	☐	This activity deals with Performance Criteria 11.1.B: correctly implement adjustments.
7.4	☐	This activity deals with Knowledge & Understanding point 4: requirements of Financial Reporting Standards.
7.5	☐	This activity deals with Knowledge & Understanding point 4: requirements of Financial Reporting Standards.

chapter 8

Reporting financial performance

Contents

1. Introduction
2. Exceptional and extraordinary items
3. Structure of the profit and loss account
4. FRS 3 statements and notes
5. Earnings Per Share (EPS)
6. Prior period adjustments

Performance criteria

11.1.A Draft limited company financial statements from the appropriate information

11.1.C Ensure that limited company financial statements comply with relevant accounting standards and domestic legislation and with the organisation's policies, regulations and procedures

Range statement

11.1.1 Limited company financial statements: income statement; balance sheet; statement of total recognised gains and losses; supplementary notes

11.2.2 Elements: assets; liabilities; ownership interest; gains; losses; contributions from owners; distributions to owners

Knowledge and understanding

1 The elements and purposes of financial statements of limited companies as set out in the conceptual framework for financial reporting (Element 11.2)

4 The UK regulatory framework for financial reporting and the main requirements of relevant Financial Reporting Standards (Element 11.1)

7 Preparing financial statements in proper form (Element 11.1)

9 Computing accounting ratios (Element 11.2)

PART B   LIMITED COMPANY ACCOUNTS

> **Signpost**
> All aspects of FRS 3 are assessable.

1 Introduction

The introduction of FRS 3 *Reporting financial performance* has meant significant changes to company published accounts. All the changes were intended to improve the quality of information provided to shareholders.

Before we launch into the details of FRS 3, it is worth considering briefly why the changes were necessary. In other words, what was wrong with the profit and loss account before FRS 3?

1.1 Comparisons

Before FRS 3, it was difficult to make comparisons between one year and another because there was no information about the turnover and profit drawn from activities that ceased during the year (and so will not continue next year) and new activities that did not exist last year.

To try to deal with this problem, FRS 3 requires an analysis of the profit and loss account as far as the figure of profit on ordinary activities before interest into three elements.

(a) **Continuing operations**
(b) **New acquisitions**
(c) **Discontinued operations**

This is discussed in more detail in Section 3 below.

Someone needing to make comparisons between this year's and last year's turnover and profit, will thus be **comparing like with like**. Similarly, someone needing to forecast next year's turnover and profit can now see how much of this year's operations will continue into the future.

To facilitate the comparison with previous years, FRS 3 requires the comparative figures for the previous year (which have to be disclosed alongside those for the current year in published accounts) to be **restated** so as to show as continuing activities only those which are still continuing in the current year.

1.2 Manipulation

Another reason for introducing FRS 3 was to put an end to the **manipulation** of the profit and loss account by means of **exceptional and extraordinary items**. These, and the changes introduced in FRS 3 are discussed in more detail in Section 2 of this chapter, but here we just look briefly at the problem which FRS 3 needed to remedy.

1.2.1 Effect on profit after tax

The forerunner to FRS 3, SSAP 6 *Extraordinary items and prior year adjustments* recognised that large and unusual 'one-off' items in a profit and loss account could distort results and make year-on-year comparisons difficult. It identified two such items, defined informally here, and prescribed two kinds of accounting treatment for the items in question.

(a) **Exceptional items**. These are part of the normal course of a company's business, but hardly ever happen. They were to be disclosed separately but *included* in the calculation of profit on *ordinary* activities before tax.

(b) **Extraordinary items**. These hardly ever happen and are *not* part of a company's ordinary activities. They are to be disclosed separately and *excluded* from the calculation of profit on ordinary activities before, and hence after, tax.

On occasions there was a fine line between extraordinary and exceptional items. An obvious temptation was to show 'plus points' as exceptional and 'minus points' as extraordinary. Thus good news appeared above the line and bad news below it.

1.2.2 Effect on earnings per share

Earnings per share is a way of calculating the return on each ordinary share in the year. It is basically earnings (profit after tax and preference dividends) divided by number of shares. Users of accounts place a great deal of faith in this figure. There is an incentive to make it appear as high as possible.

Because in pre-FRS 3 times 'earnings' excluded extraordinary items but included exceptional items, there was again an incentive to make 'bad news' extraordinary and 'good news' exceptional, so the earnings per share figure was as high as possible.

By defining exceptional items very precisely and all **but outlawing extraordinary items** (see Section 3), it was hoped to deal with the above abuse, both as regards the profit and loss account, and as regards earnings per share. It was hoped, furthermore, that earnings per share would decline in importance as an indicator of financial performance.

1.3 Main elements of FRS 3

The main elements of FRS 3 are as follows.

(a) Exceptional and extraordinary items
(b) Structure of the profit and loss account
(c) Additional statements
(d) Earnings per share
(e) Prior period adjustment

2 Exceptional and extraordinary items

FRS 3 lays down the rules for dealing with 'out of the ordinary' items and how they are shown in the P & L account. FRS 3 restricts the way companies could manipulate the figures.

2.1 Exceptional items

> **Exceptional items**: Material items which derive from events or transactions that fall within the ordinary activities of the reporting entity and which individually or, if of a similar type, in aggregate, need to be disclosed by virtue of their *size or incidence* if the financial statements are to give a true and fair view. *(FRS 3)*

The definition of ordinary activities is important.

> 'Any activities which are undertaken by a reporting entity as part of its business and such related activities in which the reporting entity engages in furtherance of, incidental to, or arising from these activities. Ordinary activities include the effects on the reporting entity of any event in the various environments in which it operates including the political, regulatory, economic and geographical environments irrespective of the frequency or unusual nature of the event.'

There are two types of exceptional item and their accounting treatment is as follows.

(a) Firstly, there are **three categories** of exceptional items which must be **shown separately** on the face of the profit and loss account after operating profit and before interest and allocated appropriately to discontinued and continued activities.

  (i) Profit or loss on the sale or termination of an operation.

  (ii) Costs of a fundamental reorganisation or restructuring that has a material effect on the nature and focus of the reporting entity's operations.

  (iii) Profit or loss on disposal of fixed assets.

  For both items (i) and (iii) profit and losses may not be offset within categories.

(b) **Other items** should be allocated to the **appropriate statutory format heading** and attributed to continuing or discounted operations as appropriate. If the item is sufficiently material that it is needed to show a true and fair view it must be disclosed on the face of the profit and loss account.

In both (a) and (b) an adequate description must be given in the notes to the accounts.

FRS 3 does not give examples of the type of transaction which is likely to be treated as exceptional. However, its predecessor on the subject, SSAP 6, gave a useful list of examples of items which if of a sufficient size might normally be treated as exceptional.

(a) Abnormal charges for bad debts and write-offs of stock and work in progress.
(b) Abnormal provisions for losses on long-term contracts.
(c) Settlement of insurance claims.

2.2 Extraordinary items

The term extraordinary item was once one of great significance. However, the ASB publicly stated that it does not envisage such items to appear on a company's profit and loss account. Its decline in importance has been achieved by tightening of the definition of an extraordinary item.

> **Extraordinary items** are defined as material items possessing a high degree of abnormality which arise from events or transactions that fall outside the ordinary activities of the reporting entity and which are not expected to recur.
> *(FRS 3)*

Extraordinary items should be shown on the face of profit and loss account before dividends. Tax on the extraordinary item should be shown separately. A description of the extraordinary items should be given in the notes to the accounts.

3 Structure of the profit and loss account

3.1 Overview and example

All statutory headings from turnover to operating profit must be subdivided between that arising from continuing operations and that arising from discontinued operations. In addition, turnover and operating profit must be further analysed between that from existing and that from newly acquired operations. This analysis is generally known as layering. Only figures for turnover and operating profit need be shown on the face of the P & L account; all additional information regarding costs may be relegated to a note. The example below is a simplified version of the example in FRS 3.

PART B LIMITED COMPANY ACCOUNTS

PROFIT AND LOSS EXAMPLE 1

	20X3 £m	20X3 £m	20X2 as restated £m
Turnover			
Continuing operations	550		500
Acquisitions	50		
	600		
Discontinued operations	175		190
		775	690
Cost of sales		(620)	(555)
Gross profit		155	135
Net operating expenses		(104)	(83)
Operating profit			
Continuing operations	50		40
Acquisitions	6		
	56		
Discontinued operations	(15)		12
Less 20X2 provision	10		
		51	52
Profit on sale of properties in continuing operations		9	6
Provision for loss on operations to be discontinued			(30)
Loss on disposal of discontinued operations	(17)		
Less 20X2 provision	20		
		3	—
Profit on ordinary activities before interest		63	28
Interest payable		(18)	(15)
Profit on ordinary activities before taxation		45	13
Tax on profit on ordinary activities		(16)	(6)
Profit on ordinary activities after taxation		29	7
Extraordinary items – (included only to show positioning)		–	–
Profit for the financial year		29	7
Dividends		(8)	(1)
Retained profit for the financial year		21	6
Earnings per share		39p	10p

PROFIT AND LOSS ACCOUNT EXAMPLE 2 (to operating profit line)

	Continuing operations 20X3 £m	Acquisitions 20X3 £m	Discontinued of operations 20X3 £m	Total 20X3 £m	Total 20X2 as restated £m
Turnover	550	50	175	775	690
Cost of sales	(415)	(40)	(165)	(620)	(555)
Gross profit	135	10	10	155	135
Net operating expenses	(85)	(4)	(25)	(114)	(83)
Less 20X2 provision			10	10	
Operating profit	50	6	(5)	51	52
Profit on sale of properties	9			9	6
Provision for loss on operations to be discontinued					(30)
Loss on disposal of the discontinued operations			(17)	(17)	
Less 20X2 provision			20	20	
Profit on ordinary activities before interest	59	6	(2)	63	28

Thereafter example 2 is the same as example 1.

A note to the profit and loss account will give the analysis of distribution and administrative expenses between continuing and discontinued operations.

Examples 1 and 2 give slightly different information. It would be difficult to combine the two without producing a profit and loss account so complicated that nobody would understand it.

3.2 Discontinued operations

A discontinued operation is one which meets four conditions.

(a) The sale or termination must have been **completed** before the earlier of **3 months after the year end** or the date the financial statements are approved. (Terminations not completed by this date may be disclosed in the notes.)

(b) Former activity must have **ceased permanently**.

(c) The sale or termination has a **material effect on the nature and focus of the entity's operations** and represents a material reduction in its operating facilities resulting either from one of two things.

  (i) Its withdrawal from a particular market (class of business or geographical)
  (ii) A material reduction in turnover in its continuing markets.

(d) The assets, liabilities, results of operations and activities are **clearly distinguishable**, physically, operationally and for financial reporting purposes.

PART B LIMITED COMPANY ACCOUNTS

3.2.1 Accounting for the discontinuation

(a) **Results**. The results of the discontinued operation up to the date of sale or termination or the balance sheet date should be shown under each of the relevant profit and loss account headings.

(b) **Profit/loss on discontinuation**. The profit or loss on discontinuation or costs of discontinuation should be disclosed separately as an exceptional item after operating profit and before interest.

(c) **Comparative figures**. Figures for the previous year must be adjusted for any activities which have become discontinued in the current year.

Activity 8.1

B&C plc's profit and loss account for the year ended 31 December 20X2, with comparatives, is as follows.

	20X2	20X1
	£'000	£'000
Turnover	200,000	180,000
Cost of sales	(60,000)	(80,000)
Gross profit	140,000	100,000
Distribution costs	(25,000)	(20,000)
Administration expenses	(50,000)	(45,000)
Operating profit	65,000	35,000

During the year the company sold a material business operation with all activities ceasing on 14 February 20X3. The loss on the sale of the operation amounted to £2m included in admin expenses. The results of the operation for 20X1 and 20X2 were as follows.

	20X2	20X1
	£'000	£'000
Turnover	22,000	26,000
Profit/(loss)	(7,000)	(6,000)

In addition, the company acquired a business which contributed £7m to turnover and an operating profit of £1m.

Task

Prepare the profit and loss account for the year ended 31 December 20X2 complying with the requirements of FRS 3 as far as possible.

4 FRS 3 statements and notes

FRS 3 introduced a new statement and a variety of notes to expand the information required in published accounts which we saw in Chapter 4.

4.1 Statement of total recognised gains and losses

> The **statement of total recognised gains and losses** brings together the profit as shown in the profit and loss account and other gains or losses.

It is important to understand that the profit and loss account can only deal with *realised* profits. An example of realised profits might be profits resulting from the sale proceeds already received or about to be received.

A company can also make substantial **unrealised profits** and losses, for example through changes in the *value* of its fixed assets. These are **recognised**, in the case of asset revaluation, by increasing the value or the assets in the balance sheet, the double entry being to a revaluation reserve included in shareholders' funds.

Activity 8.2

Can you think of two other types of gains and losses which might be recognised during a period but which are not realised and do not pass through the profit and loss account?

Generally speaking, realised profits and losses have been recognised in the profit and loss account; unrealised profits and losses may be recognised in the balance sheet. FRS 3 argues that users of accounts need to know about the unrealised movements. The statement brings all the information together.

The ASB regards the statement of total recognised gains and losses as very important, and accords it the status of a **primary statement**. This means that it must be presented with the same prominence as the balance sheet, the profit and loss account and the cash flow statement. Below is a specimen statement.

STATEMENT OF TOTAL RECOGNISED GAINS AND LOSSES

	£m
Profit for the financial year (ie profit after tax and extraordinary items if any)	29
Unrealised surplus on revaluation of properties	4
Unrealised loss on trade investment	(3)
	30
Foreign currency translation differences	(2)
Total gains and losses recognised since last annual report	28

The statement is, as you can see, fairly brief, but it is useful in that it brings together information from different sources: the profit and loss account, the balance sheet and the supporting notes for the asset revaluations.

> **IMPORTANT!**
> The Chief Assessor has singled this statement out as an area where students have problems, so make sure you understand it.

PART B LIMITED COMPANY ACCOUNTS

4.2 Reconciliation of movements in shareholders' funds

This reconciliation is required by FRS 3 to be included in the notes to the accounts. What the statement aims to do is to clarify exactly what has caused shareholders' funds to change during the period. The statement will include anything which causes share capital or reserves to change, ie:

(a) the profit and loss account;

(b) other movements in shareholders' funds as determined by the statement of total recognised gains and losses; and

(c) all other changes in shareholders' funds not recognised in either of the above such as goodwill immediately written off to reserves, or a new issue of shares

The typical contents of the reconciliation would be as follows.

	£
Profit for the financial year	29
Dividends	(8)
	21
Other recognised gains and losses (per statement of total recognised gains and losses)	(1)
New share capital	20
Net addition to shareholders' funds	40
Opening shareholders' funds	365
Closing shareholders' funds	405

Activity 8.3

Extracts from Z Ltd's profit and loss account for the year ended 31 December 20X1 were as follows.

	£'000
Profit after tax	512
Dividend	(120)
Retained profit	392

During the year the following important events took place.

(a) Assets were revalued upward by £110,000.
(b) £300,000 share capital was issued during the year.
(c) Certain stock items were written down by £45,000.
(d) Opening shareholders' funds at 1 January 20X1 were £3,100,000.

Show how the events for the year would be shown in the statement of recognised gains and losses and the reconciliation of movements in shareholders funds.

8: REPORTING FINANCIAL PERFORMANCE

4.3 Note of historical cost profits and losses

If a company has adopted any of the alternative accounting rules as regards revaluation of assets then the reported profit figure per the profit and loss account may deviate from the historical cost profit figure. If this deviation is material then the financial statements must include a reconciliation statement after the statement of recognised gains and losses or the profit and loss account.

The profit figure to be reconciled is profit before tax; however, the retained profit for the year must also be restated.

The profit or loss based on historical cost will appear in the note of historical cost profits. This is the profit or loss calculated as if the revaluation had not taken place, and will be higher, because the carrying value to be compared with the sale proceeds is lower. Below is an example of a note of historical cost profits and losses.

NOTE OF HISTORICAL COST PROFITS AND LOSSES

	£m
Reported profit on ordinary activities before taxation	45
Realisation of property revaluation gains of previous years	9
Difference between historical cost depreciation charge and the actual depreciation charge of the period calculated on revalued amounts	5
Historical cost profit on ordinary activities before taxation	59

Activity 8.4

A Ltd reported a profit before tax of £162,000 for the year ended 31 December 20X1. During the year the following transactions in fixed assets took place.

(a) An asset with a book value of £40,000 was revalued to £75,000. The remaining useful life is estimated to be five years.

(b) An asset (with a five year useful life at the date of revaluation) was revalued by £20,000 (book value £30,000) was sold one year after revaluation for £48,000.

Show the reconciliation of reported profit to historical cost profit for the year ended 31 December 20X1.

5 Earnings Per Share (EPS)

Earnings per share (EPS) is widely used by investors as a measure of a company's performance and is of particular importance in:

(a) Comparing the results of a company over a period of time

(b) Comparing the performance of one company's equity shares against the performance of another company's equity, and also against the returns obtainable from loan stock and other forms of investment

PART B LIMITED COMPANY ACCOUNTS

The purpose of any earnings yardstick is to achieve as far as possible clarity of meaning, comparability between one company and another, one year and another, and attributability of profits to the equity shares. FRS 14 *Earnings per share* goes some way to ensuring that all these aims are achieved.

FRS 14 *Earnings per share* states the following with regard to **earnings per share**.

> 'Basic earnings per share should be calculated by dividing the net profit or loss for the period attributable to ordinary shareholders by the weighted average number of ordinary shares outstanding during the period.
>
> For the purpose of calculating basic earnings per share, the net profit or loss for the period attributable to ordinary shareholders should be the net profit or loss for the period after deducting dividends and other appropriations in respect of non-equity shares.'

Activity 8.5

Pulp plc has 100,000 ordinary shares of £1 each. Its profit and loss account for the year ended 30 June 20X7 was as follows,

	£	£
Gross profit		250,000
Less exceptional items		50,000
Profit on ordinary activities before tax		200,000
Tax on profit on ordinary activities		66,000
Profit on ordinary activities after tax		134,000
Extraordinary charges	50,000	
Tax on extraordinary charges	16,500	
		33,500
Profit for the financial year		100,500
Less dividends:		
Preference	2,000	
Ordinary	22,000	
		24,000
Retained profit		76,500

Task

Calculate earnings per share.

FRS 14 is a very complex standard. Most of it is outside the scope of your detailed AAT studies. The information given above and Activity 8.5 will suffice for your exam.

6 Prior period adjustments

When the financial statements of a company are compiled, certain items (eg accruals, provisions) represent best estimates at a point in time. Further evidence received in the following year may suggest that previous estimates were incorrect. In most cases the 'error' will not be significant in size and so as a result the difference should be dealt with in the current year's accounts.

There are two situations where a **prior period adjustment** is necessary:

(a) **Fundamental errors** – evidence is found to suggest last year's accounts were wrong and
(b) **A change in accounting policy**

The following accounting treatment should be used.

(a) Restate the prior year profit and loss account and balance sheet.
(b) Restate the opening reserves balance.
(c) Include the adjustment in the reconciliation of movements in shareholders' funds.
(d) Include a note at the foot of the statement of total recognised gains and losses of the current period.

> **Prior period adjustments** are therefore defined by FRS 3 as:
>
> 'Material adjustments applicable to prior periods arising from changes in accounting policy or from the correction of fundamental errors. They do not include normal recurring adjustments or corrections of accounting estimates made in prior periods.'

A **fundamental error** is an error which is so significant that the truth and fairness of the financial statements is not achieved.

A **change in accounting policy** requires a prior period adjustment based on the fundamental accounting concept of **consistency**. For users of the financial statements to make meaningful comparisons of a company's results it is important that the current year's and the last year's comparatives are prepared on the same basis. Therefore if for any reason a company changes its accounting policy they must go back and represent last year's accounts on the same basis.

Reasons for a change in accounting policy, then, are:

(a) To show a truer and fairer view, or
(b) Introduction of, or change to, standards or legislation.

Note that a change in depreciation is not accounted for as a prior year adjustment.

Activity 8.6

Wick Ltd was established on 1 January 20X0. In the first three years' accounts deferred development expenditure was carried forward as an asset in the balance sheet. During 20X3 the directors decided that for the current and future years, all development expenditure should be written off as it is incurred. This decision has not resulted from any change in the expected outcome of development projects on hand, but rather from a desire to favour the prudence concept. The following information is available.

PART B LIMITED COMPANY ACCOUNTS

(a) Movements on the deferred development account.

Year	Deferred development expenditure incurred during year £'000	Transfer from deferred development expenditure account to P & L account £'000
20X0	525	-
20X1	780	215
20X2	995	360

(b) The 20X2 accounts showed the following.

	£'000
Retained reserves b/f	2,955
Retained profit for the year	1,825
Retained profits carried forward	4,780

(c) The retained profit for 20X3 after charging the actual development expenditure for the year was £2,030,000.

Task

Show how the change in accounting policy should be reflected in the statement of reserves in the company's 20X3 accounts.

Ignore taxation.

Activity 8.7

Stud-U-Like Ltd is a publisher of Study Packs for various accountancy bodies. The packs are printed in-house and contained in ring binders which are made to a distinctive design in a small factory at the company's main site near Wormwood Scrubs, London. During the year ended 30 June 20X7, it was found necessary to shut down this factory and the workers were made redundant. The binders were to be bought in from an external supplier.

The following trial balance is available as at 30 June 20X7.

	£'000	£'000
Share capital – £1 ordinary shares		20
10% preference shares, 25p nominal value		20
Profit and loss account		38
Sales and purchases	85	300
Sales/purchase returns	4	8
Land and buildings (cost)	80	
Plant: cost/depn to 1 July 20X6	100	20
10% debentures		60
Opening stock	30	
Operating expenses	18	
Cost of factory closure (including redundancy)	75	
Sales/purchase ledger control	40	18
Provision for doubtful debts		2
Bank	54	
	486	486

In preparing the financial statements, the following information needs to be taken into account.

(a) No debenture interest has been accrued for.
(b) The provision for doubtful debts is to be 2½% of debtors.
(c) Depreciation at 10% on cost should be provided on plant.
(d) Sales returns of £2,000 were entered in the sales day book as if they were sales.
(e) Closing stock was valued at £35,000.
(f) The corporation tax charge for the year is £30,000.

Task

(a) Prepare a profit and loss account for the year ended 30 June 20X7. Your profit and loss account should be in good form, although it need not conform to the exact requirements of the Companies Act 1985. It must show clearly the items: gross profit, net operating profit, net profit before tax and profit for the year available to ordinary shareholders. Your workings should be set out clearly.

(b) 'FRS 3 *Reporting financial performance* aimed to improve the quality of financial information provided to shareholders.'

　　(i) How might FRS 3 be applied to the profit and loss account you prepared in part (a)?

　　(ii) What further information would you need in order to prepare the profit and loss account in accordance with FRS 3?

Key learning points

- FRS 3 *Reporting financial performance* has introduced radical changes to the profit and loss account of large and medium sized companies.

- You should be aware of the **FRS 3 definitions** of:
    - Extraordinary items
    - Exceptional items
    - Prior year adjustments
    - Discontinued operations
    - Total recognised gains and losses

- You should be aware of the format of the **statement of total recognised gains and losses**, the **reconciliation of movements in shareholders' funds** and the **note on historical cost profits and losses**, and understand their contents.

- **Earnings per share** is a measure of the amount of profits earned by a company for each ordinary share. Earnings are profits after tax, preference dividends and extraordinary items.

- **Prior period adjustments** will only occur in two types of situation: a change in accounting policy; a correction of a fundamental error. Make sure that you can account for a prior period adjustment.

Quick quiz

1 Which exceptional items must be shown on the face of the P & L account?
2 Define extraordinary items.
3 What components of financial performance should be shown in the profit and loss account according to FRS 3?
4 A discontinued operation is one where the sale or termination must have been completed within the accounting year. True or false?
5 How should the profit or loss on discontinued activities be shown?
6 What is shown in the statement of total recognised gains and losses?
7 What is shown in the reconciliation of movements in shareholders' funds?
8 When is a prior period adjustment necessary?
9 Which of the following occurrences would be treated as extraordinary under FRS 3?

    A   Restructuring
    B   Natural disasters
    C   Revaluation
    D   Discontinuing operations

Answers to quick quiz

1 (a) Profit or loss on sale or termination of an operation
  (b) Costs of a material fundamental reorganisation or restructuring
  (c) Profit or loss on disposal of fixed assets

2 Material items possessing a high degree of abnormality which arise from events or transactions that fall outside the ordinary activities of the reporting entity and which are not expected to recur.

3 All statutory headings from turnover to operating profit must be subdivided between that arising from continuing operations and that arising from discontinued operations. Turnover and operating profit must be further analysed between that from existing and that from newly acquired operations.

4 False. The sale or termination must have been completed before the earlier of three months after the year end or the date the financial statements are approved.

5 As an exceptional item after operating profit and before interest.

6 The statement brings together realised and unrealised gains and losses from both the profit and loss account and the balance sheet.

7 Anything which causes capital or reserves to change.

8 (a) Fundamental errors
  (b) Change in accounting policies

9 B The others are normal trading activities.

PART B   LIMITED COMPANY ACCOUNTS

Activity checklist

This checklist shows which performance criteria, range statement or knowledge and understanding point is covered by each activity in this chapter. Tick off each activity as you complete it.

Activity

8.1	☐	This activity deals with Performance Criteria 11.1.A regarding drafting of limited company financial statements.
8.2	☐	This activity deals with Knowledge & Understanding point 4: main requirements of relevant FRS.
8.3	☐	This activity deals with Performance Criteria 11.1.C regarding compliance with accounting standards.
8.4	☐	This activity deals with Performance Criteria 11.1.C regarding compliance with accounting standards.
8.5	☐	This activity deals with Knowledge & Understanding point 9: computing accounting ratios.
8.6	☐	This activity deals with Performance Criteria 11.1.A regarding drafting of limited company financial statements.
8.7	☐	This activity deals with Performance Criteria 11.1.A regarding drafting of limited company financial statements.

chapter 9

Sundry standards in overview

Contents

1 Introduction
2 SSAP 20 *Foreign currency translation*
3 SSAP 21 *Accounting for leases and hire purchase contracts*
4 FRS 17 *Retirement benefits*
5 FRS 5 *Reporting the substance of transactions*
6 FRS 8 *Related party disclosures*
7 SSAP 25 *Segmental reporting*
8 FRS 4 *Capital instruments*
9 Limited company accounts and the extended trial balance

Performance criteria

11.1.A Draft limited company financial statements from the appropriate information
11.1.B Correctly identify and implement subsequent adjustments and ensure that discrepancies, unusual features or queries are identified and either resolved or referred to the appropriate person
11.1.C Ensure that limited company financial statements comply with relevant accounting standards and domestic legislation and with the organisation's policies, regulations and procedures

Range statement

11.1.1 Limited company financial statements: income statement; balance sheet; statement of total recognised gains and losses
11.1.3 Relevant accounting standards: relevant SSAPs and FRSs

Knowledge and understanding

4 The UK regulatory framework for financial reporting and the main requirements of relevant Financial Reporting Standards
7 Preparing financial statements in proper form (Element 11.1)

PART B LIMITED COMPANY ACCOUNTS

1 Introduction

The Standards covered in this chapter are to be known in terms of their **general principles only**, rather than in detail. However, you should cover all of them, as any of them could come up in an exam.

2 SSAP 20 *Foreign currency translation*

2.1 The basics

Foreign currency translation is a topic of great practical importance as many companies, from large multi-nationals to the smallest of companies, will buy and sell goods overseas. For the purposes of your assessment, however, only a general understanding of the subject is required.

> **Signpost**
> You must understand the **need to account for foreign currency transactions** for individual companies and for foreign enterprises in consolidated financial statements. There will be no assessment of methods of accounting.

If a company trades overseas, it will buy or sell assets in foreign currencies; for example, a British company might buy materials from the United States, and pay for them in US dollars, and then sell its finished goods in West Germany, receiving payment in German marks, or perhaps in some other currency. If the company owes money in a foreign currency at the end of the accounting year, or holds assets which were bought in a foreign currency, those liabilities or assets must be translated into £ sterling, in order to be shown in the books of account.

A company might have a subsidiary abroad, and the subsidiary will trade in its own local currency. The subsidiary will keep books of account and prepare its annual accounts in its own currency. However, at the year end, the UK holding company must consolidate the results of the overseas subsidiary into its group accounts, so that somehow, the assets and liabilities and the annual profits of the subsidiary must be translated from the foreign currency into £ sterling.

If foreign currency exchange rates remained constant, there would be no accounting problem. As you will be aware, however, foreign exchange rates are continually changing; and it is not inconceivable for example, that the rate of exchange between the US dollar and the pound might be $1.40 to £1 at the start of the accounting year, and $1.05 to £1 at the end of the year (in this example, a 25% increase in the relative strength of the dollar).

There are two distinct types of foreign currency transaction, **conversion** and **translation**.

2.2 Conversion gains and losses

Conversion is the process of exchanging amounts of one foreign currency for another.

For example, suppose a company buys a large consignment of goods from a supplier in Sweden. The order is placed on 1 May and the agreed price is 124,250 Swedish Kroner. At the time of delivery the rate of foreign exchange was 3.50 Kr to £1. The UK company would record the creditor in its books as follows.

DEBIT	Purchases account (124,250 ÷ 3.5)	£35,500	
CREDIT	Creditors' account		£35,500

When the UK company comes to pay the supplier, it needs to obtain some foreign currency. By this time, however, if the rate of exchange has altered to 3.55 Kr to £1, the cost of raising 124,250 Kr would be (÷ 3.55) £ 35,000. The company would need to spend only £35,000 to settle a debt for stocks 'costing' £35,500. Since it would be administratively difficult to alter the value of the stocks in the company's books of account, it is more appropriate to record a profit on conversion of £500.

DEBIT	Creditors' account	£35,500	
CREDIT	Cash		£35,000
	Profit on conversion		£500

Profits (or losses) on conversion would be included in the profit and loss account for the year in which conversion (whether payment or receipt) takes place.

Suppose that another UK company sells goods to a Danish company, and it is agreed that payment should be made in Danish Kroner at a price of 116,000 Kroner. We will further assume that the exchange rate at the time of sale is 10.75 Kr to £1, but when the debt is eventually paid, the rate has altered to 10.8 Kr to £1. The company would record the sale as follows.

DEBIT	Debtor account (116,000 ÷ 10.75)	£10,800	
CREDIT	Sales account		£10,800

When the 116,000 Kroner are paid, the UK company will convert them into pounds, to obtain (÷ 10.8) £10,750. In this example, there has been a loss on conversion of £50 which will be written off to the profit and loss account:

CREDIT	Debtor account		£10,800
DEBIT	Cash	£10,750	
	Loss on conversion	£50	

There are no accounting difficulties concerned with foreign currency conversion gains or losses, and the procedures described above are uncontroversial.

2.3 Translation

Foreign currency **translation**, as distinct from conversion, does not involve the act of exchanging one currency for another. Translation is required at the end of an accounting period when a company still holds assets or liabilities in its balance sheet which were obtained or incurred in a foreign currency.

These assets or liabilities might consist of:

(a) An individual UK company holding individual assets or liabilities originating in a foreign currency 'deal'

(b) An individual UK company with a separate branch of the business operating abroad which keeps its own books of account in the local currency

(c) A UK company which wishes to consolidate the results of a foreign subsidiary

There has been great uncertainty about the method which should be used:

(a) To translate the value of assets and liabilities from a foreign currency into £ for the year end balance sheet

(b) To translate the profits reported by an independent foreign branch or foreign subsidiary into £ for the annual profit and loss account

Suppose, for example, that a Swiss subsidiary purchases a piece of property for 2,100,000 Swiss francs on 31 December in year 1. The rate of exchange at this time was 70 SFr to £1. During year 2, the subsidiary charged depreciation on the building of 16,800 Francs, so that at 31 December year 2, the subsidiary recorded the asset as follows.

	SFr
Property at cost	2,100,000
Less accumulated depreciation	16,800
Net book value	2,083,200

At this date, the rate of exchange has changed to 60 SFr. to £1.

The UK holding company must translate the asset's value into £s, but there is a choice of exchange rates:

(a) Should the rate of exchange for translation be the rate which existed at the date of purchase, which would give a net book value of 2,083,200 ÷ 70 = £29,760?

(b) Should the rate of exchange for translation be the rate existing at the end of year 2 (the closing rate of 60Fr to £1)? This would give a net book value of £34,720

Similarly, should depreciation be charged in the consolidated profit and loss account at the rate of 70 Francs to £1 (the historical rate), 60 Francs to £1 (the closing rate), or at an average rate for the year (say, 64 Francs to £1)?

In the accounting debate as to which method of translating foreign currencies was most appropriate, the major problems focused on the consolidation of the results of foreign subsidiaries, and two 'rival' methods emerged:

- The **temporal** (or 'historical') method
- The **closing rate** method, or closing rate/net investment method

It is beyond the scope of your exam to discuss these methods here. All you need to know is that SSAP 20 *Foreign currency translation* sets out clear rules and makes a distinction between accounting procedures by an individual company, and the accounting procedures for consolidation in group accounts.

3 SSAP 21 *Accounting for leases and hire purchase contracts*

Where goods are acquired other than on immediate cash terms, arrangements have to be made in respect of the future payments on those goods. In the simplest case of credit sales, the purchaser is allowed a period of time (say one month) to settle the outstanding amount and the normal accounting procedure in respect of debtors/creditors will be adopted. However, in recent years there has been considerable growth in hire purchase and leasing agreements. SSAP 21 *Accounting for leases and hire purchase contracts* was issued in 1984 to standardise the accounting treatment and disclosure of assets held under lease or hire purchase.

In a leasing transaction there is a contract between the lessor and the lessee for the hire of an asset. The lessor retains legal ownership but conveys to the lessee the right to use the asset for an agreed period of time in return for specified rentals. SSAP 21 recognises two types of lease.

> A **finance lease** transfers substantially all the risks and rewards of ownership to the lessee. Although strictly the leased asset remains the property of the lessor, in substance the lessee may be considered to have acquired the asset and to have financed the acquisition by obtaining a loan from the lessor.

> An **operating lease** is any lease which is not a finance lease. An operating lease has the character of a rental agreement with the lessor usually being responsible for repairs and maintenance of the asset. Often these are relatively short-term agreements with the same asset being leased, in succession, to different lessees.

A finance lease is presumed to exist if, at the start of a lease, the present value of the minimum lease payments is greater than or equal to 90% fair value of the leased asset. This arbitrary line has been criticised, and the ASB is considering reforming lease accounting.

For a **finance lease** the lessee **records an asset and liability** in respect of the payments the lease requires. This reflects the ownership interest in the leased property. The leased asset is depreciated.

For an **operating lease** the lessee **does not record an asset or liability**. Instead, **operating lease rentals are charged to the profit and loss account** and **information** about operating lease commitments is **disclosed** in the notes to the accounts.

Signpost

You will need to understand the difference between operating leases and finance leases and an overview of the accounting treatment. There will be no detailed computational questions.

4 FRS 17 *Retirement benefits*

An increasing number of companies are providing a pension as part of their employees' remuneration packages. In view of this trend, it is important to standardise the way in which pension costs are recognised, measured and disclosed in the accounts of sponsoring companies.

Accounting for different types of pension scheme will not be assessed in detail. However, it would be useful to understand the difference between a 'defined contribution' pension scheme and a 'defined benefit' scheme.

> Under a **defined contribution scheme**, the employer will normally discharge his obligation by making agreed contributions to a pension scheme. The amount of pension ultimately payable to the employee is not guaranteed: it depends on the investment earnings of the funds contributed. Under this kind of scheme the cost to the employer is easily measured. it is simply the amount of the contributions payable in the period.
>
> Under a **defined benefit scheme** the eventual benefit payable to the employee is a predetermined amount, usually depending on the employee's salary immediately prior to retirement. In these circumstances it is impossible to be sure in advance that the regular contributions will generate a fund sufficient to provide the benefits. The employer may be obliged for legal reasons, or in the interest of maintaining good employee relations, to make good any deficiency in funding. This means that the cost to the company is uncertain.

Signpost

No detailed computational questions will be set on FRS 17. You just need to know the objective of the FRS and the difference between a defined contribution scheme and a defined benefit scheme.

The **objective** of the FRS is to ensure that:

(a) Financial statements reflect at fair value the assets and liabilities arising from an employer's retirement benefit obligations and any related funding

(b) The operating costs of providing retirement benefits to employees are recognised in the accounting period(s) in which the benefits are earned by the employees, and the related finance costs and any other changes in value of the assets and liabilities are recognised in the accounting periods in which they arise

(c) The financial statements contain adequate disclosure of the cost of providing retirement benefits and the related gains, losses, assets and liabilities

Because, under FRS 17, companies are now required to show the extent of future liabilities, some companies are considering moving from defined benefit to defined contribution schemes. Arguably, FRS 17 does not change anything, it just exposes the reality of a company's obligation.

5 FRS 5 *Reporting the substance of transactions*

5.1 The problem of off balance sheet finance

Over the last decade the transactions undertaken by businesses have become more and more complex often resulting in the divorce of legal title from access to the transaction's economic benefits and risks. Accounting for their legal form often meant that such transactions were not reflected on the balance sheet. This resulted in misleading accounting results and ratios. The **creative accounting** which has emerged over recent years occurred for two main reasons.

(a) Complex schemes were deliberately engineered by companies to ensure transactions were not reflected on the balance sheet, largely to manipulate gearing (ie borrowing) ratios.

(b) There was a lack of guidance for transactions not covered by a specific standard. This allowed companies to adopt a variety of accounting treatments.

The development of the ASB's *Statement of Principles* (see Chapter 1) will help to provide guidance. FRS 5 reinforces the recognition principles embodied in the *Statement of Principles* in a specific standard.

5.2 FRS 5

FRS 5 aims to tackle the problem of off balance sheet finance.

It is a complex standard whose objective is to ensure that financial statements reflect the **commercial substance** of transactions and not just their legal form. The ASB felt that, rather than issue specific standards to deal with individual transactions, a general one was required to set out the principles of when commercial substance should apply.

The general principle of FRS 5 is that financial statements should reflect the commercial **substance** of transactions **rather than their legal form**. You should note that one of the best examples of placing substance over form is SSAP 21 – a finance lease is where, in substance if not in form, a company 'owns' an asset.

For the majority of transactions the legal form and the commercial substance will be identical. However, three main features can be identified of situations where FRS 5 is most likely to apply.

(a) Where the legal owner is not the person benefiting from the asset.

(b) Where the transaction is part of a series. It will be necessary to view the series as a whole to determine the substance.

(c) The inclusion of options and conditions which are likely to be exercised.

5.3 What do you need to know for your exam?

Your exam will not require you to determine the substance of transactions. However, you might like to bear in mind the following checklist of points to consider.

(a) FRS 5 'commercial substance over legal form'
(b) FRS 18 accruals and prudence
(c) Companies Act 1985 Schedule 4 fundamental principles
(d) Materiality
(e) Disclosure
(f) Truth and fairness
(g) Requirements of any relevant SSAP/FRS

The diagram below should also help.

PART B LIMITED COMPANY ACCOUNTS

Accounting treatment for the recognition of assets and liabilities

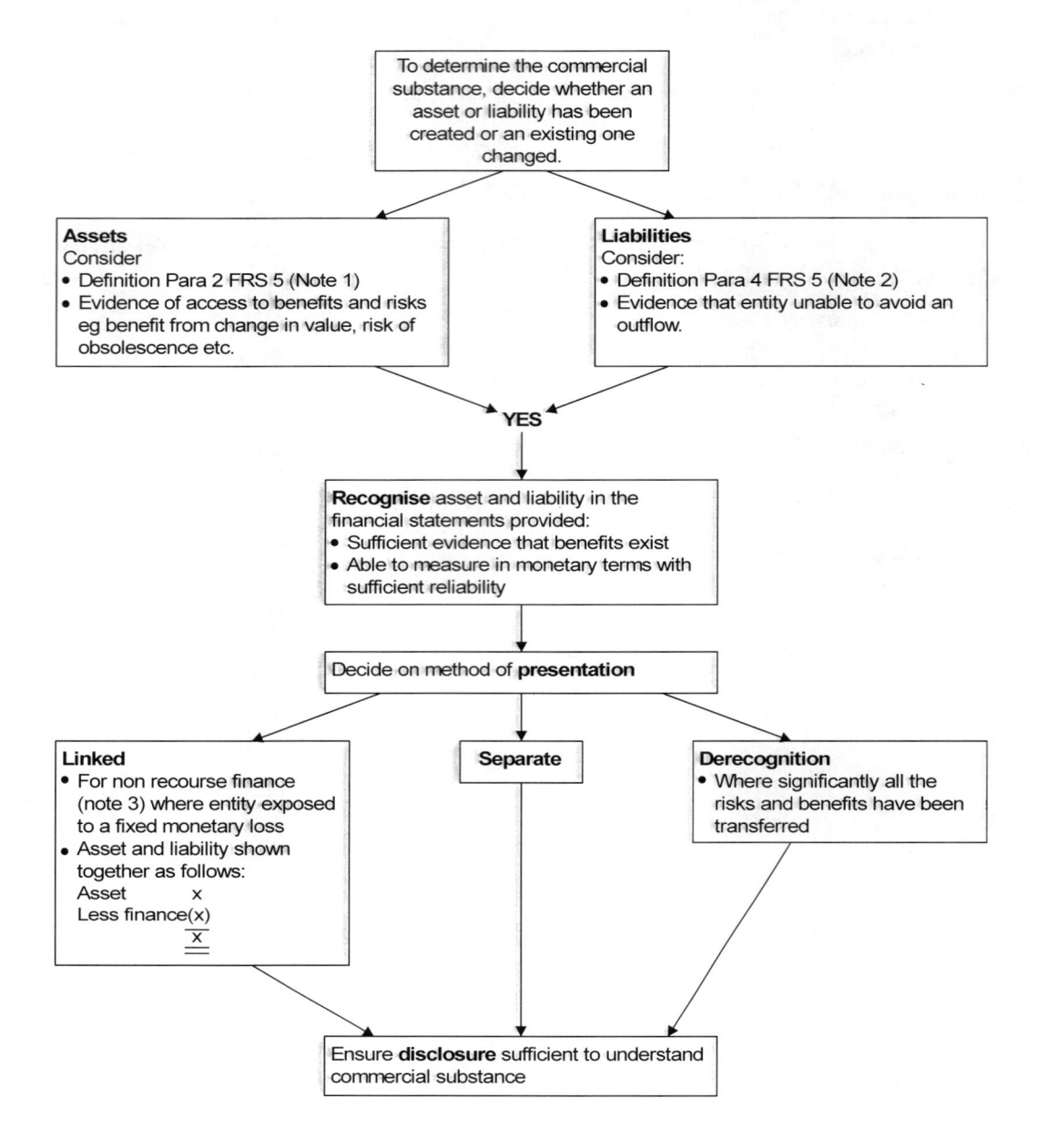

```
┌─────────────────────────────┐
│ To determine the commercial │
│ substance, decide whether an│
│ asset or liability has been │
│ created or an existing one  │
│ changed.                    │
└─────────────────────────────┘
```

Assets
Consider
- Definition Para 2 FRS 5 (Note 1)
- Evidence of access to benefits and risks eg benefit from change in value, risk of obsolescence etc.

Liabilities
Consider:
- Definition Para 4 FRS 5 (Note 2)
- Evidence that entity unable to avoid an outflow.

YES

Recognise asset and liability in the financial statements provided:
- Sufficient evidence that benefits exist
- Able to measure in monetary terms with sufficient reliability

Decide on method of **presentation**

Linked
- For non recourse finance (note 3) where entity exposed to a fixed monetary loss
- Asset and liability shown together as follows:
  Asset   x
  Less finance (x)
               $\underline{\underline{X}}$

Separate

Derecognition
- Where significantly all the risks and benefits have been transferred

Ensure **disclosure** sufficient to understand commercial substance

Notes

1 *Assets*: rights or other access to future economic benefits controlled by an entity as a result of past transactions or events.

2 *Liabilities*: an entity's obligations to transfer future economic benefits as a result of past transactions or events.

3 *Non-recourse finance*: there is no (or limited) recourse to the seller for losses.

5.4 Interaction with other standards

The recognition criteria contained in FRS 5 will determine which assets and liabilities appear in the balance sheet. It will therefore influence the accounting treatment in future standards. In particular accounting for intangibles will be affected.

It is possible that a transaction will be covered by both FRS 5 and a specific standard. Where this overlap occurs the more detailed provisions should be followed unless commercial substance would not be reflected. Users should be guided by the 'spirit' and not the 'letter' of FRS 5.

6 FRS 8 *Related party disclosures*

6.1 Why disclose related party transactions?

FRS 8 *Related party disclosures* makes it clear why a standard was required on related parties.

> 'In the absence of information to the contrary, it is assumed that a reporting entity has independent discretionary power over its resources and transactions and pursues its activities independently of the interests of its individual owners, managers and others. Transactions are presumed to have been undertaken on an arm's length basis, ie on terms such as could have obtained in a transaction with an external party, in which each side bargained knowledgeably and freely, unaffected by any relationship between them.
>
> These assumptions may not be justified when related party relationships exist, because the requisite conditions for competitive, free market dealings may not be present. Whilst the parties may endeavour to achieve arm's length bargaining the very nature of the relationship may preclude this occurring.'

Signpost

The AAT have stated that you only need to know the definition of related parties and the fact that transactions between related parties need to be disclosed.

The objective of FRS 8 is to ensure that financial statements contain the disclosures necessary to draw attention to the possibility that the reported financial position and results may have been affected by the existence of related parties and by material transactions with them. In other words, this is a standard which is primarily concerned with **disclosure.**

6.2 Who are related parties?

(a) Two or more parties are related parties when, at any time during the financial period any of the following apply.

   (i) One party has **direct or indirect control** of the other party ('control' is defined as the ability to direct the financial and operating policies of an entity with a view to gaining economic benefits from its activities).

   (ii) The parties are subject to **common control** from the same source.

   (iii) One party has **influence over the financial and operating policies** of the other party to an extent that that other party might be inhibited from pursuing at all times its own separate interests.

(iv) The parties, in entering a transaction, are subject to **influence from the same source** to such an extent that one of the parties to the transaction has subordinated its own separate interests.

(b) The following are related parties of the reporting entity.

(i) Its **ultimate and intermediate parent undertakings**, subsidiary undertakings, and fellow subsidiary undertakings

(ii) Its **associates and joint venturers**

(iii) The **investor or venturer** in respect of which the reporting entity is an associate or a joint venture

(iv) **Directors**, including shadow directors, of the reporting entity and the directors of its ultimate and intermediate parent undertakings

(v) **Pension funds** for the benefit of employees of the reporting entity or of any entity that is a related party of the reporting entity

Shadow directors are persons in accordance with whose directions or instructions the directors of the company are accustomed to act.

7 SSAP 25 *Segmental reporting*

7.1 SSAP 25

Signpost

The exam will require an appreciation of the need to provide segmental information in financial statements but no computation of disclosures.

If a company (or group of companies) engages in several **different activities or operates in several geographical markets**, then users of its accounts will find it helpful in judging the risk of investing in the company, to see how important each class of business and each market is. They can then see how vulnerable the company is to exchange rate fluctuations, political changes and recession in respect of any given market.

Example 1

A UK company with a high proportion of sales to the USA risks losing sales if the value of the pound sterling rises in proportion to the US dollar, as its prices will seem more expensive. It is also at risk if the US economy is in recession or if import controls are imposed.

Example 2

If a company has two main businesses, widget making and ice cream manufacture, it will be helpful to an investor to see how profitable, and how significant to the company as a whole, each one is.

SSAP 25 *Segmental reporting* requires companies to provide **limited segmental analyses**, as follows.

(a) Where a company has two or more classes of business, it must show in a note the amount of turnover and operating profit attributable to each class of business.

(b) Where a company operates in more than one geographical market, it must show in a note the amount of turnover attributable to each market.

Any or all of these analyses can be omitted on grounds of commercial sensitivity, but the directors must then state that these analyses would have been published but for these considerations.

A segment should normally be regarded as significant if third party turnover, results or net assets are greater than 10% of those of the whole company or group.

7.2 Arguments against reporting by segment

Those who argue against this form of disclosure generally emphasise the practical problems, which include:

(a) Identifying segments for reporting purposes

(b) Allocating common income and costs among the different segments

(c) Reporting inter-segment transactions

(d) Providing information in such a way as to eliminate misunderstanding by investors

(e) Avoiding any potential damage that may be done to the reporting entity by disclosing information about individual segments

8 FRS 4 *Capital instruments*

The ASB issued FRS 4 *Capital instruments* in December 1993.

> **Capital instruments** are instruments which are issued to raise finance. There are many different types. Common ones include bank loans, corporate bonds, convertible debt, ordinary shares, preference shares and options and warrants to subscribe for shares.

FRS 4 addresses how issuers should account for capital instruments. The standard covers all capital instruments except leases, options or warrants granted under employee share schemes and equity shares issues in a business combination accounted for as a merger.

Signpost
You only need to know the definition of capital instruments.

PART B LIMITED COMPANY ACCOUNTS

9 Limited company accounts and the extended trial balance

For your Intermediate Studies you learned how to prepare the final accounts of sole traders and partnerships from the extended trial balance.

Before you read this section, you should be aware that not all activities will involve preparing accounts from the ETB. Some may involve preparing accounts from the trial balance. Try the activity below.

Activity 9.1

Butthead Ltd is a small trading company. From the information below, you are required to prepare a trading, profit and loss account and a balance sheet in a form suitable for presentation to the directors. You should show all your workings and your financial statements should provide as much information as is helpful. Taxation is to be ignored.

(a) BUTTHEAD LIMITED
TRIAL BALANCE AS AT 31 DECEMBER 20X7

	£	£
Sales		160,800
Purchases	82,400	
Stock at 1 January 20X7	10,800	
Suspense account	2,800	
Freehold building	56,000	
Fixtures and fittings: cost	52,000	
depreciation 31.12.X7		18,800
Ordinary shares of 25p each		20,000
10% debentures		16,000
5% preference shares of 25p each		8,000
Profit and loss reserve at 1.1.X7		15,200
Cash at bank	1,200	
Cash in hand	1,200	
Sundry expenses*	37,600	
New issue account		12,000
Debtors control account	21,200	
Creditors control account		14,400
	265,200	265,200

*Note. This figure includes depreciation for the year.

(b) The following details relate to the company's bank reconciliation.

(i) The balance per the bank statement was £1,200 overdrawn.

(ii) A cheque for £2,000 had been accepted by the bank as being for £2,000, but had been entered in the cash book as £1,600.

(iii) Bank charges appear on the bank statement, but are not shown in the cash book.

(iv) On 31 December 20X7 there were unpresented cheques totalling £800, all of which cleared in the first week of the next accounting period.

(c) Stock at 31 December 20X7 was £13,600.

(d) In January 20X7 12,000 25p shares were issued at £1 each. The cash received was treated correctly, but the corresponding credit was made to a 'share issue account', as the bookkeeper was unsure of the correct treatment.

(e) As at 31 December 20X7, the building is to be revalued to £60,000.

(f) The directors propose a dividend on the ordinary share capital as at 31 December 20X7 of 20p per share. No dividends were paid during the year.

(g) Debenture interest for the six months to 30 June 20X7 has been paid and is included in the figure for sundry expenses.

(h) The debtors and creditors ledgers do not reconcile with the debtors and creditors control accounts. Balance totals are as follows.

Debtors ledger
Debit balances	£20,000
Credit balances	£1,200

Creditors ledger
Credit balances	£16,000
Debit balances	£800

In reconciling the accounts you discover the following errors.

(i) The total on the debtors control account should be £22,400, not £21,200.

(ii) Contras of £1,600 have been correctly entered in the individual ledger accounts but not in the control accounts.

(iii) The list of debit balances on the sales ledger has been understated by £400.

(iv) The balance owed to Beavis plc of £800 has not been included in the list of ledger balances.

(v) During the year, a credit note was issued for £800. This has been treated like an invoice in both the individual ledger account and the control account.

After adjusting for the above errors, any remaining differences should be dealt with by transferring from the control accounts to the suspense account. If there is still a balance on the suspense account, this must be transferred to sundry expenses.

PART B LIMITED COMPANY ACCOUNTS

Activity 9.2

Using the information below prepare the statement of recognised gains and losses, the reconciliation of movements in shareholders' funds and the reconciliation of profit to historical cost profit for Gains Ltd for the year ended 31 December 20X9.

(a) **Gains Ltd profit and loss account extract**

	£'000
Operating profit	792
Interest receivable	24
Interest payable	(10)
Profit before tax	806
Taxation	(240)
Profit after tax	566
Dividend	(200)
Retained profit	366

(b) **Note.** Any of the following items have (where appropriate) already passed through the profit and loss account.

Fixed assets

(i) Assets held at cost were written down by £25,000, the reduction in value was deemed to be permanent.

(ii) Freehold land and buildings were revalued to £500,000 (book value £375,000). The remaining life of the assets is 25 years.

(iii) A previously revalued asset was sold for £60,000.

Details of the revaluation and subsequent depreciation are as follows.

	£
Book value at revaluation	30,000
Revaluation	50,000
	80,000
Depreciation ((80,000/10) × 3)	24,000
	56,000

(iv) Details of investment properties are as follows.

	£
Cost	120,000
Investment revaluation reserve	40,000
Value at 1.1.20X9	160,000

The properties had a valuation on 31 December 20X9 of £100,000. This fall in value is expected to be temporary.

(c) **Share capital**

During the year the company had the following changes to its capital structure.

(i) An issue of £200,000 £1 ordinary bonus shares.
(ii) An issue of 400,000 £1 ordinary shares (issue price £1.50 per share)

(d) **Shareholders' funds**

The book value of shareholders' funds at the start of the year amounted to £6,820,000.

In many exams set so far candidates have been required to prepare financial statements from the extended trial balance. Questions often take the form of journal entries for adjustments, then the financial statements themselves, then a 'written' question usually on an accounting policy.

You should now have sufficient knowledge of limited company accounts to be able to draft financial statements from information in an extended trial balance, together with any post ETB adjustments. It is **essential** that you try Activity 9.3 which is in the style of an exam-based assessment question, albeit more comprehensive. Take your time over this activity and aim for a high degree of accuracy.

Activity 9.3

Extension Ltd is a large company based in Bolton selling DIY and home improvement products to wholesale and retail customers.

It is 30 June 20X4, the company's year end and the draft financial statements are to be prepared. Mr Pacioli, the bookkeeper, has produced an extended trial balance which is shown on the next page. The ETB includes some of the normal year end adjustments. Unfortunately, however, Mr Pacioli is not fully up to date with modern day financial reporting requirements.

You have therefore been asked to step in to assist him in drafting the company's year end financial statements

Your enquiries reveal the following additional information.

(i) Additions to fixed assets in the year were as follows.

	£
Fixtures and fittings	74,830
Motor vehicles	418,650
Office equipment	24,930

Disposals in the year were as follows.

	Cost £	Accumulated depreciation £
Fixtures and fittings	31,026	21,244
Motor vehicles	367,842	114,924
Office equipment	18,920	11,174

The additions and disposals have all been entered in the ledger accounts in the extended trial balance.

(ii) Audit fees of £73,146 relating to the audit of the year end accounts have yet to be provided for.

PART B LIMITED COMPANY ACCOUNTS

FOLIO	DESCRIPTION	TRIAL BALANCE		ADJUSTMENTS		ACCRUALS	PREPAY-MENTS	PROFIT AND LOSS ACCOUNT		BALANCE SHEET	
		£	£	DEBIT £	CREDIT £	£	£	DEBIT £	CREDIT £	DEBIT £	CREDIT £
A10	Advertising	1,130,988				55,442		1,186,430			
S10	Stock	2,973,910		4,018,960	4,018,960			2,973,910	4,018,960	4,018,960	
D10	Discounts allowed	148,374						148,374			
S20	Sales		30,368,730						30,368,730		
D20	Development costs	703,144								703,144	
L10	Land	1,200,000								1,200,000	
B10	Buildings	1,443,166								1,443,166	
F10	Fixtures & fittings	774,108								774,108	
M10	Motor vehicles	1,841,452								1,841,452	
E10	Office equipment	277,934								277,934	
D30	Accumulated depreciation										
	- Buildings		314,642		28,864						343,506
	- Fixtures and fittings		345,882		77,410						423,292
	- Motor vehicles		817,056		319,330						1,136,386
	- Office equipment		71,844		38,330						110,174
D40	Depreciation expense										
	- Buildings			28,864				28,864			
	- Fixtures and fittings			77,410				77,410			
	- Motor vehicles			319,330				319,330			
	- Office equipment			38,330				38,330			
P10	Purchases	16,402,622						16,402,622			
R10	Returns inwards	650,862						650,862			
R20	Returns outwards		373,306						373,306		
D50	12% Debentures		4,800,000								4,800,000
P20	Preference share capital		400,000								400,000
S40	Ordinary share capital		1,200,000								1,200,000
S50	Share premium		463,126								463,126
S60	Salaries and wages	3,670,616						3,670,616			
S70	Salesmen's commission	1,207,362						1,207,362			
I10	Insurance	43,874						43,874			
M20	Motor expenses	1,707,524						1,707,524			
R30	Rates	244,914					75,010	169,904			
C10	Carriage inwards	250,438						250,438			
L20	Light and heat	209,608				43,114		252,722			
B20	Bank	86,930									86,930
C20	Cash in hand	5,870								5,870	
P30	Profit and loss account		1,429,362								1,429,362
P60	Interim dividend	98,400						98,400			
G10	General expenses	173,028						173,028			
D80	Trade debtors	7,312,782								7,312,782	
P50	Bad debt provision		98,592		46,268						144,860
P60	Bad debt expense			46,268				46,268			
C30	Trade creditors		1,701,506								1,701,506
A20	Accruals					98,556					98,556
P90	Prepayments						75,010			75,010	
P100	Profit							5,314,728			5,314,728
		42,470,976	42,470,976	4,529,162	4,529,162	98,556	75,010	34,760,996	34,760,996	17,652,426	17,652,426

(iii) The debenture interest has not yet been paid or provided for in the trial balance. The debentures are secured against the land and buildings and are due for repayment in 20Y1.

(iv) The corporation tax charge for the year has been calculated as £1,470,314. The rate of corporation tax for the year is 33%.

(v) Stock which was valued at cost and included in the year end accounts at £294,426 was sold after the year end for £121,895. The auditors have asked that the stock be included in the year end accounts at a value of £121,896.

(vi) Directors' remuneration of £504,314 is included in the salaries and wages figure in the extended trial balance. The salary of the Sales Director is £173,042. The other directors work on general administration.

(vii) The land has been valued by a qualified chartered surveyor during the year. The market value of the land is £1,600,000. the revaluation is to be incorporated in the final financial statements.

(viii) It is proposed that the preference dividend should be provided for at the year end and that a final dividend of 6.5p per ordinary share relating to the current year should be provided for in the financial statements. An interim ordinary share dividend of 8.2p per share was paid in the year.

(ix) The authorised share capital of the company is as follows.

4,000,000 ordinary shares of £1 each
1,000,000 7.6% preference shares of £1 each

(x) For the purposes of published financial statements the following allocation of expenses is to be made.

	Distribution costs %	Administrative expenses %
Motor expenses	80	20
Motor depreciation	80	20
General expenses	80	20
Rates	75	25
Building depreciation	75	25
Light and heat	75	25
Insurance	75	25
Office equipment depreciation	60	40
Fixtures and fittings depreciation	100	–

The salaries and wages costs (excluding the Directors' remuneration) are made up of £2,184,270 relating to the sales department and £982,032 relating to other administrative staff.

(xi) The development costs included in the extended trial balance relate to costs sustained by the company in developing a new concept wallpaper product. The costs relate to the development costs specific to the product. The company are reasonably certain that the product will be viable given market research and projections of future revenue and expect to generate revenue from the project within two years. The company has sufficient resources to complete the project.

(xii) The company is currently engaged in a legal case involving some faulty paints sold to a customer. The customer is seeking damages for losses sustained as a result of the use of the defective paint amounting to £731,876. The

PART B LIMITED COMPANY ACCOUNTS

lawyers of Extension Ltd claim that the company has a very good defence against such a claim and that, in their opinion, it is unlikely that the damages will have to be paid.

(xiii) All operations of the company are continuing operations.

Tasks

(a) Taking each of the items of additional information in turn, make any adjustments necessary to the ETB and set out your adjustments in the form of journal entries. If no adjustment is required, this should be stated.

Note. You should assume that the adjustments do not affect the tax charge for the year as given above.

(b) Draft Extension Ltd's profit and loss account for the year ended 30 June 20X4 and a balance sheet as at that date in a form suitable for publication using Format 1 in accordance with the Companies Act 1985.

Note. In an exam question the formats would be given to you. For the purposes of this question you may need to refer to the formats in Chapter 4 of this Interactive Text.

(c) Draft a trading and profit and loss account for the year ended 30 June 20X4 for use by the management of Extension Ltd for internal purposes.

Now try the following activity, taken from a past AAT exam and therefore representative of the type of activity you are likely to come across.

Activity 9.4

You have been assigned to assist in the preparation of the financial statements of Spiraes Ltd for the year ended 30 November 20X6. The company is a trading company operating from freehold premises in a large industrial city. You have been provided with the extended trial balance of Spiraes Ltd on 30 November 20X6, which is set out on Page 190.

You have been given the following further information.

(a) The share capital of the business consists of ordinary shares with a nominal value of 25p.

(b) The company has paid no interim dividend this year but is proposing to provide a final dividend of 2 pence per share for the year.

(c) Depreciation has been calculated on all of the fixed assets of the business and has already been entered on a monthly basis into the distribution expenses and administration expenses ledger balances as shown on the extended trial balance.

(d) The tax charge for the year has been calculated as £1,356,000.

(e) Interest on the 9% debentures has been paid for the first six months of the year only. No adjustment has been made for the interest due for the final six months of the year.

(f) The land has been valued at market value at the end of the year by a professional valuer at £4,290,000. It is proposed that the valuation be incorporated into the financial statements of the company as at 30 November 20X6.

(g) The fixed asset investment consists of shares in a publicly quoted company and is shown in the extended trial balance at cost. The investment represents 7% of the total issued ordinary share capital of the quoted company and was purchased with the intention of investing in the company on a long-term basis.

(h) Some items of stock which were included in the stock balance in the extended trial balance at a cost of £405,000 were sold after the year end for £355,000.

Tasks

(a) Make any additional adjustments you feel to be necessary to the balances in the extended trial balance as a result of the matters set out in the further information above. Set out your adjustments in the form of journal entries.

Note

(1) Narratives are not required.
(2) Ignore any effect of these adjustments on the tax charge for the year as given above.

(b) Justify your treatment of items (f) and (h) in the further information above. Refer in your answer, where relevant, to company law, accounting concepts and applicable accounting standards.

(c) Draft a profit and loss account for the year ended 30 November 20X6 using Format 1 in accordance with the Companies Act 1985 as supplemented by FRS 3 *Reporting financial performance*.

Note

You are not required to prepare a balance sheet or the reconciliation of movements in shareholders' funds required under FRS 3.

(d) Prepare a statement of total recognised gains and losses for the year ended 30 November 20X6 for Spiraes Ltd as required by FRS 3.

PART B   LIMITED COMPANY ACCOUNTS

SPIRAES LIMITED
EXTENDED TRIAL BALANCE 30 NOVEMBER 20X6

	Trial balance Debit £'000	Trial balance Credit £'000	Adjustments Debit £'000	Adjustments Credit £'000	Profit and loss account Debit £'000	Profit and loss account Credit £'000	Balance sheet Debit £'000	Balance sheet Credit £'000
Trade creditors		2,653						2,653
Accruals				63				63
Cash at bank	375						375	
Interest charges	189				189			
Buildings - accumulated depreciation		810						810
Office equipment - accumulated depreciation		319						319
Motor vehicles - accumulated depreciation		1,912						1,912
Fixtures and fittings - accumulated depreciation		820						820
Sales		18,742				18,742		
Trade debtors	3,727						3,727	
Provision for doubtful debts		68						68
Dividends received		52				52		
Fixed asset investment	866						866	
Profit and loss account		6,192						6,192
9% debentures		4,200						4,200
Prepayments			31				31	
Land - cost	3,570						3,570	
Buildings - cost	2,933						2,933	
Office equipment - cost	882						882	
Motor vehicles - cost	3,485						3,485	
Fixtures and fittings - cost	2,071						2,071	
Purchases	10,776				10,776			
Administrative expenses	1,805			12	1,820			
Stock	3,871		27	4,153	3,871	4,153	4,153	
Returns inwards	595				595			
Returns outwards		314				314		
Ordinary share capital		1,000						1,000
Share premium		560						560
Distribution costs	2,497		36	19	2,514			
Profit					3,496			3,496
	37,642	37,642	4,247	4,247	23,261	23,261	22,093	22,093

Key learning points

- ☑ You should be aware that since many companies buy and sell goods overseas, the requirement to account for foreign currency transactions will arise regularly.

- ☑ Finance leases are like HP contracts. In both cases assets acquired should be capitalised and the interest element of instalments should be charged against profit. Operating leases are rental agreements and all instalments are charged against profit.

- ☑ FRS 17 *Retirement benefits* is a complicated standard, but for your purposes it is sufficient to be aware of the need to make provisions in accounts for pension costs.

- ☑ FRS 5 is likewise a complex standard. You do not have to know it in any detail, but you should be aware of the importance of recognising the substance of transactions.

- ☑ FRS 8 is primarily a disclosure statement. It is concerned to improve the quality of information provided by published accounts and also to strengthen their stewardship role.

- ☑ SSAP 25 is also a disclosure statement. You do not need to prepare a segmental analysis, but you need to understand why it is prepared.

- ☑ Exam questions on limited company accounts are likely to involve a trial balance or an extended trial balance.

PART B   LIMITED COMPANY ACCOUNTS

Quick quiz

1 Distinguish between the conversion and the translation of foreign currencies
2 What two categories of lease are identified in SSAP 21? What are the characteristics of each type?
3 Distinguish between a defined contribution and a defined benefit scheme.
4 What is the general principle of FRS 5?
5 What does FRS 8 require to be disclosed?
6 Are directors related parties?
7 What is SSAP 25's rule of thumb as to what constitutes a material segment for disclosure purposes?
8 How should common costs be allocated in segmental accounts?

Answers to quick quiz

1 Conversion is the process of exchanging amounts of one foreign currency for another. Translation does not involve exchanging one currency for another; it is required at the end of the accounting period where a company holds assets or liabilities denominated in foreign currency.

2 SSAP 21 identifies operating leases and finance leases. A finance lease transfers substantially all the risks and rewards of ownership to the lessee. An operating lease is any lease which is not a finance lease.

3 Under a defined contribution scheme, the employer makes an agreed contribution to a pension scheme. The amount of the pension ultimately payable to the employee is not guaranteed. Under a defined benefit scheme the eventual benefit payable to the employee is a predetermined amount, usually depending on the employee's salary immediately prior to retirement.

4 Financial statements should reflect the commercial substance of transactions rather than their legal form.

5 Disclosure is required of information on related party transactions and the name of the party controlling the reporting entity.

6 Yes

7 A segment's third party turnover should be $\geq$ 10% of the entity's total third party turnover or its profit should be $\geq$ 10% of the combined profit of all segments or its net assets should be $\geq$ of the total net assets of the entity.

8 In the manner thought most appropriate by the directors.

Activity checklist

This checklist shows which performance criteria, range statement or knowledge and understanding point is covered by each activity in this chapter. Tick off each activity as you complete it.

Activity

9.1 ☐ This activity deals with Performance Criteria 11.1.A regarding drafting financial statements from appropriate information.

9.2 ☐ This activity deals with Performance Criteria 11.1.C regarding compliance with relevant accounting standards.

9.3 ☐ This activity deals with Performance Criteria 11.1.A regarding drafting financial statements from appropriate information.

9.4 ☐ This activity deals with Performance Criteria 11.1.A regarding drafting financial statements from appropriate information.

PART B LIMITED COMPANY ACCOUNTS

PART C

Interpretation of accounts

chapter 10

Cash flow statements

Contents

1. The problem
2. The solution
3. FRS 1 *Cash flow statements* (revised)
4. Preparing a cash flow statement
5. Interpreting a cash flow statement

Performance criteria

11.1.D Prepare and interpret a limited company cash flow statement

Range statement

11.1.1 Limited company financial statements: cash flow statement (not consolidated)

Knowledge and understanding

3   The statutory form of accounting statements and disclosure requirements (Element 11.1)
4   The UK regulatory framework for financial reporting and the main requirements of relevant Financial Reporting Standards (Element 11.1)
8   Analysing and interpreting the information contained in financial statements (Element 11.2)

1 The problem

In the long run, a profit will result in an increase in the company's cash balance. In the short run, however, a profit will not necessarily result in an increased cash balance. The observation leads us to two questions.

- What is the **difference** between **cash** and **profit**?
- **How useful** are the **profit and loss account and balance sheet** in demonstrating whether a company has **sufficient cash** to finance its operations?

The importance of the distinction between cash and profit and the scant attention paid to this by the profit and loss account has resulted in the development of **cash flow statements**.

It has been argued that 'profit' does not always give a useful or meaningful picture of a company's operations. Readers of a company's financial statements might even be **misled by a reported profit figure**.

(a) Shareholders might believe that if a company makes a profit after tax, of say, £100,000 then this is the amount which it could afford to pay as a **dividend**. Unless the company has **sufficient cash** available to stay in business and also to pay a dividend, the shareholders' expectations would be wrong.

(b) Employees might believe that if a company makes profits, it can afford to pay **higher wages** next year. This opinion may not be correct: the ability to pay wages depends on the **availability of cash**.

(c) **Survival of a business** entity depends not so much on profits as on its ability to **pay its debts when they fall due**. Such payments might include 'profit and loss' items such as material purchases, wages, interest and taxation etc, but also capital payments for new fixed assets and the repayment of loan capital when this falls due (for example on the redemption of debentures).

2 The solution

From these examples, it may be apparent that a company's performance and prospects depend not so much on the 'profits' earned in a period, but more realistically on liquidity or **cash flows**.

A **cash flow statement** is unambiguous and provides information which is additional to that provided in the rest of the accounts. It also describes the cash flows of an organisation by activity and not by balance sheet classification.

3 FRS 1 *Cash flow statements*

3.1 Your approach

This chapter adopts a systematic approach to the preparation of cash flow statements in exams; you should learn this method and you will then be equipped for any problems in the exam itself.

Example: cash flow statement

Baldwin Ltd commenced trading on 1 January 20X1 with a medium-term loan of £21,000 and a share issue which raised £35,000. The company purchased fixed assets for £21,000 cash, and during the year to 31 December 20X1 entered into the following transactions.

(a) Purchases from suppliers were £19,500, of which £2,550 was unpaid at the year end.
(b) Wages and salaries amounted to £10,500, of which £750 was unpaid at the year end.
(c) Interest on the loan of £2,100 was fully paid in the year and a repayment of £5,250 was made.
(d) Sales turnover was £29,400, including £900 debtors at the year end.
(e) Interest on cash deposits at the bank amounted to £75.
(f) A dividend of £4,000 was proposed as at 31 December 20X1.

You are required to prepare a historical cash flow statement for the year ended 31 December 20X1.

Solution

BALDWIN LIMITED
STATEMENT OF CASH FLOWS FOR
THE YEAR ENDED 31 DECEMBER 20X1

	£	£
Operating activities		
Cash received from customers (£29,400 – £900)	28,500	
Cash paid to suppliers (£19,500 – £2,550)	(16,950)	
Cash paid to and on behalf of employees (£10,500 – £750)	(9,750)	
Cash flow from operating activities		1,800
Returns on investment and servicing of finance		
Interest paid	(2,100)	
Interest received	75	
		(2,025)
Capital expenditure		
Purchase of fixed assets	(21,000)	
Cash flow from investing activities		(21,000)
Financing		
Issue of shares	35,000	
Proceeds from medium-term loan	21,000	
Repayment of medium-term loan	(5,250)	
Cash flow from financing activities		50,750
Net increase in cash		29,525
Cash at 1 January 20X1		–
Cash at 31 December 20X1		29,525

Note that the dividend is only proposed and so there is no related cash flow in 20X1.

PART C   INTERPRETATION OF ACCOUNTS

Activity 10.1

The directors of Baldwin Ltd obtain the following information in respect of projected cash flows for the year to 31 December 20X2.

(a) Fixed asset purchases for cash will be £3,000.

(b) Further expenses will be:

    (i) Purchases from suppliers – £18,750 (£4,125 owed at the year end)
    (ii) Wages and salaries – £11,250 (£600 owed at the year end)
    (iii) Loan interest – £1,575

(c) Turnover will be £36,000 (£450 debtors at the year end).

(d) Interest on bank deposits will be £150.

(e) A further capital repayment of £5,250 will be made on the loan.

(f) A dividend of £5,000 will be proposed and last year's final dividend paid.

(g) Corporation tax of £2,300 will be paid in respect of 20X1.

Prepare the cash flow forecast for the year to 31 December 20X2.

3.2 Indirect method

Another way of arriving at net cash flows from operating activities is to start from operating profit and adjust for non-cash items, such as depreciation, debtors etc. This is known as the **indirect method**. A proforma calculation is given below.

FORMULA TO LEARN!

	£
Operating profit (P&L)	X
Add depreciation	X
Loss (profit) on sale of fixed assets	X
(Increase)/decrease in stocks	(X)/X
(Increase)/decrease in debtors	(X)/X
Increase/(decrease) in creditors	X/(X)
Net cash flow from operating activities	X

It is important to understand why certain items are added and others subtracted. Note the following points.

    (a) Depreciation is not a cash expense, but is deducted in arriving at the profit figure in the profit and loss account. It makes sense, therefore, to eliminate it by adding it back.

    (b) By the same logic, a loss on a disposal of a fixed asset (arising through underprovision of depreciation) needs to be added back and a profit deducted.

(c) An increase in stocks means less cash – you have spent cash on buying stock.

(d) An increase in debtors means debtors have not paid as much, therefore less cash.

(e) If we pay off creditors, causing the figure to decrease, again we have less cash.

> **Signpost**
>
> It is the indirect method which exam questions, based around FRS 1 (see below), will probably require you to use. This has been the case in all exams set so far.

3.3 FRS 1 *Cash flow statements* (revised)

FRS 1 sets out the structure of a cash flow statement and it also sets the minimum level of disclosure. Exam questions are likely to be computational, but some discussion and interpretation may be required.

3.3.1 Objective

The FRS requires companies to report their cash generation highlighting **key components**. The statement should provide information that assists in the assessment of the company's liquidity, solvency and financial adaptability.

3.3.2 Scope

The FRS applies to **all financial statements** intended to give a true and fair view of the financial position and profit or loss (or income and expenditure), except those of **various exempt bodies** in group accounts situations. In addition, **small entities are excluded** as defined by companies legislation.

3.3.3 Format of the cash flow statement

An example is given of the format of a cash flow statement for a single company and this is reproduced below.

A cash flow statement should list its cash flows for the period classified under the following **standard headings**:

- **Operating activities** (using either the direct or indirect method)
- Dividends from associates and joint ventures
- Returns on investments and servicing of finance
- Taxation
- Capital expenditure and financial investment
- Acquisitions and disposals
- Equity dividends paid
- Management of liquid resources
- Financing

The last two headings can be shown in a single section provided a subtotal is given for each heading. Acquisitions and disposals are not on your syllabus; the heading is included here for completeness.

Individual categories of inflows and outflows under the standard headings should be **disclosed separately** either in the cash flow statements or in a note to it unless they are allowed to be shown net.

Each cash flow should be classified according to the **substance of the transaction** giving rise to it.

3.3.4 Links to other primary statements

Because the information given by a cash flow statement is best appreciated in the context of the information given by the other primary statements, the FRS requires **two reconciliations**, between:

- Operating profit and the net cash flow from operating activities
- The movement in cash in the period and the movement in net debt

Neither reconciliation forms part of the cash flow statement but each may be given either adjoining the statement or in a separate note.

The **movement in net debt** should identify the following components and reconcile these to the opening and closing balance sheet amount:

(a) the cash flows of the entity;
(b) other non-cash changes;
(c) the recognition of changes in market value and exchange rate movements.

3.3.5 Definitions

The FRS includes the following important definitions (only those of direct concern to your exam are included here). Note particularly the definitions of cash and liquid resources.

> (a) An **active market** is a market of sufficient depth to absorb the investment held without a significant effect on the price. (This definition affects the definition of liquid resources below.)
>
> (b) **Cash** is cash in hand and deposits repayable on demand with any qualifying financial institution, less overdrafts from any qualifying financial institution repayable on demand. Deposits are repayable on demand if they can be withdrawn at any time without notice and without penalty or if a maturity or period of notice of not more than 24 hours or one working day has been agreed. Cash includes cash in hand and deposit denominated in foreign currencies.
>
> (c) **Cash flow** is an increase or decrease in an amount of cash.
>
> (d) **Liquid resources** are current asset investments held as readily disposable stores of value.
>
> (e) **Net debt** is the borrowings of the reporting entity less cash and liquid resources. Where cash and liquid resources exceed the borrowings of the entity reference should be to 'net funds' rather than to 'net debt'.
>
> (f) **Overdraft** is a borrowing facility repayable on demand that is used by drawing on a current account with a qualifying financial institution.

3.4 Classification of cash flows by standard heading

The FRS looks at each of the cash flow categories in turn.

3.4.1 Operating activities

Cash flows from operating activities are in general the **cash effects** of transactions and other events relating to **operating or trading activities, normally shown in the profit and loss account in arriving at operating profit**. They include cash flows in respect of operating items relating to provisions, whether or not the provision was included in operating profit.

A reconciliation between the **operating profit** reported in the profit and loss account and the **net cash flow from operating activities** should be given either adjoining the cash flow statement or as a note. The reconciliation is not part of the cash flow statement: if adjoining the cash flow statement, it should be clearly labelled and kept separate. The reconciliation should disclose separately the movements in stocks, debtors and creditors related to operating activities and other differences between cash flows and profits.

> **Signpost**
>
> A proforma will probably be given to you in the exam. Nevertheless, you should try and learn the FRS 1 format as doing so will speed you up and make you more confident.

3.4.2 Returns on investments and servicing of finance

These are receipts resulting from the **ownership of an investment** and payments to providers of finance and non-equity shareholders (eg the holders of preference shares).

Cash inflows from returns on investments and servicing of finance include:

- Interest received
- Dividends received

Cash outflows from returns on investments and servicing of finance include:

- Interest paid
- Cash flows that are treated as finance costs
- The interest element of finance lease rental payments
- Dividends paid on non-equity shares of the entity

3.4.3 Taxation

These are **cash flows to or from taxation authorities** in respect of the reporting entity's revenue and capital profits. VAT and other sales taxes are discussed below.

- Taxation cash inflows include cash receipts from the relevant tax authority
- Taxation cash outflows include cash payments to the relevant tax authority

3.4.4 Capital expenditure and financial investment

These cash flows are those related to the **acquisition or disposal of any fixed asset** other than one required to be classified under 'acquisitions and disposals' (discussed below), and any current asset investment not included in liquid resources (also dealt with below). If no cash flows relating to financial investment fall to be included under this heading the caption may be reduced to 'capital expenditure'.

The cash **inflows** here include:

- Receipts from sales or disposals of property, plant or equipment
- Receipts from the repayment of the reporting entity's loans to other entities

Cash outflows in this category include:

- Payments to acquire property, plant or equipment
- Loans made by the reporting entity

3.4.5 Acquisitions and disposals

These cash flows are related to the **acquisition or disposal of any trade or business, or of an investment** in an entity that is either an associate, a joint venture, or a subsidiary undertaking (these group matters are beyond the scope of your assessment).

(a) Cash **inflows** here include receipts from sales of trades or businesses
(b) Cash **outflows** here include payments to acquire trades or businesses

3.4.6 Equity dividends paid

The cash outflows are **dividends paid on the reporting entity's equity shares**.

3.4.7 Management of liquid resources

This section should include cash flows in respect of **liquid resources**. Each entity should explain what it includes as liquid resources and any changes in its policy. The cash flows in this section can be shown in a single section with those under 'financing' provided that separate subtotals for each are given.

Cash **inflows** include:

- Withdrawals from short-term deposits not qualifying as cash
- Inflows from disposal or redemption of any other investments held as liquid resources

Cash **outflows** include:

- Payments into short-term deposits not qualifying as cash
- Outflows to acquire any other investments held as liquid resources

3.4.8 Financing

Financing cash flows comprise **receipts or repayments of principal from or to external providers of finance**. The cash flows in this section can be shown in a single section with those under 'management of liquid resources' provided that separate subtotals for each are given.

Financing cash **inflows** include:

- Receipts from issuing shares or other equity instruments
- Receipts from issuing debentures and loans

Financing cash **outflows** include:

- Repayments of amounts borrowed (other than overdrafts)
- The capital element of finance lease rental payments
- Payments to reacquire or redeem the entity's shares
- Payments of expenses or commission on any issue of equity shares

Example: single company

The following example is provided by the standard for a single company.

XYZ LIMITED
CASH FLOW STATEMENT FOR THE YEAR ENDED 31 DECEMBER 20X1

Reconciliation of operating profit to net cash inflow from operating activities

	£'000
Operating profit	6,022
Depreciation charges	899
Increase in stocks	(194)
Increase in debtors	(72)
Increase in creditors	234
Net cash inflow from operating activities	6,899

CASH FLOW STATEMENT

	£'000
Net cash inflow from operating activities	6,889
Returns on investments and servicing of finance (note 1)	2,999
Taxation	(2,922)
Capital expenditure (note 1)	(1,525)
	5,441
Equity dividends paid	(2,417)
	3,024
Management of liquid resources (note 1)	(450)
Financing (note 1)	57
Increase in cash	2,631

PART C INTERPRETATION OF ACCOUNTS

Reconciliation of net cash flow to movement in net debt (note 2)

	£'000	£'000
Increase in cash in the period	2,631	
Cash to repurchase debenture	149	
Cash used to increase liquid resources	450	
Change in net debt*		3,230
Net debt at 1.1.X1		(2,903)
Net funds at 31.12.X1		327

*In this example all change in net debt are cash flows.

The reconciliation of operating profit to net cash flows from operating activities can be shown in a note.

NOTES TO THE CASH FLOW STATEMENT

1 Gross cash flows

	£'000	£'000
Returns on investments and servicing of finance		
Interest received	3,011	
Interest paid	(12)	
		2,999
Capital expenditure		
Payments to acquire intangible fixed assets	(71)	
Payments to acquire tangible fixed assets	(1,496)	
Receipts from sales of tangible fixed assets	42	
		(1,525)
Management of liquid resources		
Purchase of treasury bills	(650)	
Sale of treasury bills	200	
		(450)
Financing		
Issue of ordinary share capital	211	
Repurchase of debenture loan	(149)	
Expenses paid in connection with share issues	(5)	
		57

Note. These gross cash flows can be shown on the face of the cash flow statement, but it may sometimes be neater to show them as a note like this.

2 Analysis of changes in net debt

	As at 1 Jan 20X1 £'000	Cash flows £'000	Other changes £'000	At 31 Dec 20X1 £'000
Cash in hand, at bank	42	847		889
Overdrafts	(1,784)	1,784		
		2,631		
Debt due within 1 year	(149)	149	(230)	(230)
Debt due after 1 year	(1,262)		230	(1,032)
Current asset investments	250	450		700
Total	(2,903)	3,230	–	327

Activity 10.2

Close the book for a moment and jot down the format of the cash flow statement.

4 Preparing a cash flow statement

4.1 Getting started

In essence, preparing a cash flow statement is very straightforward. You should therefore simply learn the format given above and apply the steps noted in the example below. Note that the following items are treated in a way that might seem confusing, but the treatment is logical if you think in terms of **cash**.

(a) Increase in stock is treated as **negative** (in brackets). This is because it represents a cash **outflow**; cash is being spent on stock.

(b) An increase in debtors would be treated as **negative** for the same reasons; more debtors means less cash.

(c) By contrast an increase in creditors is **positive** because cash is being retained and not used to pay off creditors. There is therefore more of it.

Example: preparation of a cash flow statement

Tadman Ltd's profit and loss account for the year ended 31 December 20X2 and balance sheets at 31 December 20X1 and 31 December 20X2 were as follows.

PART C INTERPRETATION OF ACCOUNTS

TADMAN LIMITED
PROFIT AND LOSS ACCOUNT FOR THE YEAR ENDED 31 DECEMBER 20X2

	£'000	£'000
Sales		720
Raw materials consumed	70	
Staff costs	94	
Depreciation	118	
Loss on disposal	18	
		300
Operating profit		420
Interest payable		28
Profit before tax		392
Taxation		124
		268
Dividend		72
Profit retained for year		196
Balance brought forward		490
		686

TADMAN LIMITED
BALANCE SHEETS AS AT 31 DECEMBER

	20X2		20X1	
	£'000	£'000	£'000	£'000
Fixed assets				
Cost		1,596		1,560
Depreciation		318		224
		1,278		1,336
Current assets				
Stock	24		20	
Trade debtors	66		50	
Bank	58		64	
	148		134	
Current liabilities				
Trade creditors	12		6	
Taxation	102		86	
Proposed dividend	30		24	
	144		116	
Working capital		4		18
		1,282		1,354
Long-term liabilities				
Long-term loans		200		500
		1,082		854
Share capital		360		340
Share premium		36		24
Profit and loss account		686		490
		1,082		854

During the year, the company paid £90,000 for a new piece of machinery.

Task

Prepare a cash flow statement for Tadman Ltd for the year ended 31 December 20X2 in accordance with the requirements of FRS 1 (revised).

Solution

Step 1. Set out the proforma cash flow statement with all the headings required by FRS 1 (revised). You should leave plenty of space. Ideally, use three or more sheets of paper, one for the main statement, one for the notes (particularly if you have a separate note for the gross cash flows) and one for your workings. It is obviously essential to know the formats very well.

Step 2. Complete the reconciliation of operating profit to net cash inflow as far as possible. When preparing the statement from balance sheets, you will usually have to calculate such items as depreciation, loss on sale of fixed assets and profit for the year (see Step 4).

TADMAN LIMITED
CASH FLOW STATEMENT FOR THE YEAR ENDED 31 DECEMBER 20X2

Reconciliation of operating profit to net cash inflow

	£'000
Operating profit	420
Depreciation charges	118
Loss on sale of tangible fixed assets	18
Increase in stocks (24-20)	(4)
Increase in debtors (66-50)	(16)
Increase in creditors (12-6)	6
Net cash inflow from operating activities	542

Step 3. Calculate the figures for tax paid, dividends paid, purchase or sale of fixed assets, issue of shares and repayment of loans if these are not already given to you (as they may be). Note that you may not be given the tax charge in the profit and loss account. You will then have to assume that the tax paid in the year is last year's year-end provision and calculate the charge as the balancing figure.

Workings

1 *Corporation tax paid*

	£'000
Opening CT payable	86
Charge for year	124
Net CT payable at 31.12.X2	(102)
Paid	108

PART C INTERPRETATION OF ACCOUNTS

2   *Fixed asset disposals*

COST

	£'000		£'000
At 1.1.X2	1,560	At 31.12.X2	1,596
Purchases	90	Disposals	54
	1,650		1,650

ACCUMULATED DEPRECIATION

	£'000		£'000
At 31.1.X2	318	At 1.1.X2	224
Depreciation on disposals	24	Charge for year	118
	342		342

	£'000
NBV of disposals	30
Net loss reported	(18)
Proceeds of disposals	12

Step 4. If you are not given the profit figure, open up a working for the profit and loss account. Using the opening and closing balances, the taxation charge and dividends paid and proposed, you will be able to calculate profit for the year as the balancing figure to put in the statement.

Step 5. Complete Note 1, the gross cash flows, if asked for it. Alternatively, the information may go straight into the statement.

Step 6. You will now be able to complete the statement by slotting in the figures given or calculated.

CASH FLOW STATEMENT

	£'000	£'000
Net cash flows from operating activities		542
Returns on investment and servicing of finance		
Interest paid		(28)
Taxation		
Corporation tax paid (W1)		(108)
Capital expenditure		
Payments to acquire tangible fixed assets	(90)	
Receipts from sales of tangible fixed assets	12	
Net cash outflow from capital expenditure		(78)
		328
Equity dividends paid (72 – 30 + 24)		(66)
		262
Financing		
Issues of share capital (360 + 36 – 340 – 24)	32	
Long-term loans repaid (500 – 200)	(300)	
Net cash outflow from financing		(268)
Decrease in cash		(6)

Step 7. Complete Note 2, the analysis of changes in net debt, if asked.

NOTES TO THE CASH FLOW STATEMENT

Analysis of changes in net debt

	At 1 Jan 20X2 £'000	Cash flows £'000	At 31 Dec 20X2 £'000
Cash in hand, at bank	64	(6)	58
Debt due after 1 year	(500)	300	(200)
Total	(436)	294	(142)

Activity 10.3

The summarised accounts of Seager plc for the year ended 31 December 20X8 are as follows.

SEAGER PLC
BALANCE SHEET AS AT 31 DECEMBER 20X8

	20X8 £'000	20X8 £'000	20X7 £'000	20X7 £'000
Fixed assets				
Tangible assets		628		514
Current assets				
Stocks	214		210	
Debtors	168		147	
Cash	7		–	
	389		357	
Creditors: amounts falling due within one year				
Trade creditors	136		121	
Tax payable	39		28	
Dividends payable	18		16	
Overdraft	–		14	
	193		179	
Net current assets		196		178
Total assets less current liabilities		824		692
Creditors: amounts falling due after more than one year				
10% debentures		(80)		(50)
		744		642
Capital and reserves				
Share capital (£1 ords)		250		200
Share premium account		70		60
Revaluation reserve		110		100
Profit and loss account		314		282
		744		642

PART C INTERPRETATION OF ACCOUNTS

SEAGER PLC
PROFIT AND LOSS ACCOUNT
FOR THE YEAR ENDED 31 DECEMBER 20X8

	£'000
Sales	600
Cost of sales	(319)
Gross profit	281
Other expenses (including depreciation of £42,000)	(194)
Profit before tax	87
Tax	(31)
Profit after tax	56
Dividends	(24)
Retained profit for the year	32

You are additionally informed that there have been no disposals of fixed assets during the year. New debentures were issued on 1 January 20X8. Wages for the year amounted to £86,000.

Task

Produce a cash flow statement using the direct method suitable for inclusion in the financial statements, as per FRS 1.

> **Signpost**
> You could be asked for a full cash flow statement, or alternatively just for the reconciliation to net cash inflow from operating activities.

Try the Activities below, both from past exams.

Activity 10.4

The bookkeeper of Cashedin Ltd has asked for your assistance in producing a cash flow statement for the company for the year ended 30 September 20X5 in accordance with FRS 1. He has derived the information which is required to be included in the cash flow statement, but is not sure of the format in which it should be presented. The information is set out below.

	£'000
Operating profit before tax	24
Depreciation charge for the year	318
Proceeds from sale of fixed assets	132
Issue of shares for cash	150
Cash received from new loan	200
Purchase of fixed assets for cash	358
Interest paid	218
Taxation paid	75
Dividends paid	280

	£'000
Increase in stocks	251
Increase in debtors	152
Increase in creditors	165
Decrease in cash	345

Using the information provided by the bookkeeper given above, prepare a cash flow statement for Cashedin Ltd for the year ended 30 September 20X5 in accordance with the requirements of FRS 1. Show clearly your reconciliation between operating profit and net cash inflow from operating activities.

Activity 10.5

You have been asked to assist in the production of a reconciliation between cash flows from operating activities and operating profit for the year ended 31 July 20X6 for Poised Ltd. The financial statements of the company drafted for internal purposes are set out below, along with some further information relating to the reporting year.

POISED LIMITED
PROFIT AND LOSS ACCOUNT FOR THE YEAR ENDED 31 JULY 20X6

		20X6
		£'000
Turnover		12,482
Opening stock	2,138	
Purchases	8,530	
Closing stock	(2,473)	
Cost of sales		8,195
Gross profit		4,287
Depreciation		1,347
Other expenses		841
Operating profit for the year		2,099
Interest paid		392
Profit before tax		1,707
Taxation on profit		562
Profit after tax		1,145
Ordinary dividend		360
Retained profit		785

PART C INTERPRETATION OF ACCOUNTS

POISED LIMITED
BALANCE SHEET AS AT 31 JULY 20X6

	20X6 £'000	20X5 £'000
Fixed assets	6,867	6,739
Current assets		
Stocks	2,473	2,138
Trade debtors	1,872	1,653
Cash	1,853	149
	6,198	3,940
Current liabilities		
Trade creditors	1,579	1,238
Dividends payable	240	265
Taxation	562	477
	2,381	1,980
Net current assets	3,817	1,960
Long term loan	4,200	3,800
	6,484	4,899
Capital and reserves		
Called up share capital	3,000	2,500
Share premium	400	100
Profit and loss account	3,084	2,299
	6,484	4,899

Further information

(a) No fixed assets were sold during the year.
(b) All sales and purchases were on credit. Other expenses were paid for in cash.

Provide a reconciliation between cash flows from operating activities and operating profit for the year ended 31 July 20X6.

Note. You are *not* required to prepare a cash flow statement.

4.2 Advantages of cash flow accounting

(a) **Survival in business depends on the ability to generate cash**. Cash flow accounting directs attention towards this critical issue.

(b) Cash flow is **more comprehensive** than 'profit' which is dependent on accounting conventions and concepts.

(c) **Creditors** (long and short-term) are more interested in an **entity's ability to repay them** than in its profitability. Whereas 'profits' might indicate that cash is likely to be available, cash flow accounting is more direct with its message.

(d) Cash flow reporting provides a better means of **comparing the results** of different companies than traditional profit reporting.

(e) Cash flow reporting **satisfies the needs of all users** better.

   (i) For management, it provides the sort of information on which decisions should be taken: (in management accounting, 'relevant costs' to a decision are future cash flows); traditional profit accounting does not help with decision-making.

   (ii) For shareholders and auditors, cash flow accounting can provide a satisfactory basis for stewardship accounting.

   (iii) As described previously, the information needs of creditors and employees will be better served by cash flow accounting.

(f) **Cash flow forecasts are easier to prepare**, as well as more useful, than profit forecasts.

(g) They **can** in some respects **be audited more easily** than accounts based on the accruals concept.

(h) The accruals concept is confusing, and cash flows are **more easily understood**.

(i) Cash flow accounting should be both **retrospective, and also include a forecast** for the future. This is of great information value to all users of accounting information.

(j) **Forecasts can subsequently be monitored** by the publication of variance statements which compare actual cash flows against the forecast.

Activity 10.6

Can you think of some possible disadvantages of cash flow accounting?

PART C INTERPRETATION OF ACCOUNTS

Activity 10.7

The balance sheet of Cat plc for the year ended 31 December 20X7, together with comparative figures for the previous year, is shown below (all figures £'000).

	20X7		20X6	
Fixed assets		540		360
Less depreciation		(180)		(112)
		360		248
Current assets				
Stock	100		84	
Debtors	80		66	
Cash	–		22	
	180		172	
Current liabilities				
Trade and operating creditors	66		48	
Taxation	38		34	
Dividend	56		52	
Bank overdraft	20		–	
	(180)		(134)	
Net current assets		–		38
Net assets		360		286

	20X7	20X6
Represented by		
Ordinary share capital (£1 shares)	50	40
Share premium	20	16
Profit and loss account	130	110
Shareholders' funds	200	166
15% debentures, repayable 20X1	160	120
Capital employed	360	286

(a) There were no sales of fixed assets during 20X7
(b) The company does not pay interim dividends
(c) New debentures and shares issued in 20X7 were issued on 1 January

Task

(a) Show your calculation of the operating profit of Cat plc for the year ended 31 December 20X7.

(b) Prepare a cash flow statement for the year, in accordance with FRS 1 *Cash flow statements* including the reconciliation of operating profit to net cash inflow from operating activities and Note 1 as required by the standard, ie the 'gross cash flows'.

(c) State the headings of the other reconciliation and note which you would be required to include in practice under FRS 1.

5 Interpreting a cash flow statement

FRS 1 *Cash flow statements* was introduced on the basis that it would provide better, more comprehensive and more useful information than its predecessor standard. So what kind of information does the cash flow statement, along with its notes, provide?

Some of the main areas where FRS 1 should provide information not found elsewhere in the accounts are as follows.

(a) The **relationships between profit and cash** can be seen clearly and analysed accordingly.
(b) **Management of liquid resources** is highlighted, giving a better picture of the liquidity of the company.
(c) **Financing inflows** and outflows must be **shown, rather than simply passed through reserves**.

It is wrong to try to assess the health or predict the death of a reporting entity solely on the basis of a single indicator. When analysing cash flow data, the **comparison should not just be between cash flows and profit, but also between cash flows over a period of time** (say three to five years).

The **behaviour** of profit and cash flows will be very different. **Profit is smoothed out** through accruals, prepayments, provisions and other accounting conventions. This does not apply to cash, so the **cash flow figures** are likely to be **'lumpy'** in comparison. You must distinguish between this 'lumpiness' and the trends which will appear over time.

The **relationship between profit and cash flows will vary constantly**. Healthy companies do not always have reported profits exceeding operating cash flows. Similarly, unhealthy companies can have operating cash flows well in excess of reported profit. The value of comparing them is in determining the extent to which earned profits are being converted into the necessary cash flows.

Profit is not as important as the extent to which a company can **convert its profits into cash on a continuing basis**. This process should be judged over a period longer than one year. The cash flows should be compared with profits over the same periods to decide how successfully the reporting entity has converted earnings into cash.

Cash flow figures should also be considered in terms of their specific relationships with each other over time. A form of **'cash flow gearing'** can be determined by comparing operating cash flows and financing flows, particularly borrowing, to establish the extent of dependence of the reporting entity on external funding.

Other relationships can be examined.

(a) Operating cash flows and investment flows can be related to match cash recovery from investment to investment.
(b) Investment can be compared to distribution to indicate the proportion of total cash outflow designated specifically to investor return and reinstatement.
(c) A comparison of tax outflow to operating cash flow minus investment flow will establish a 'cash basis tax rate'.

Try the Activity below, which asks you to comment on a cash flow statement as well as preparing one.

PART C INTERPRETATION OF ACCOUNTS

Activity 10.8

You are presented with Ealing Ltd's summary profit and loss account for the year ended 31 December 20X9 and the balance sheet at the beginning and end of the year.

EALING LIMITED
PROFIT AND LOSS ACCOUNT FOR THE YEAR ENDED 31 DECEMBER 20X9

	£'000
Profit on ordinary activities before taxation	2,440
Tax on profit on ordinary activities	895
Profit on ordinary activities after taxation	1,545
Less proposed dividends	80
Retained profit for the financial year	1,465
Profit and loss account at 1 January 20X9	1,090
Profit and loss account at 31 December 20X9	2,555

EALING LIMITED
BALANCE SHEETS AS AT

	1 January 20X9		31 December 20X9	
	£'000	£'000	£'000	£'000
Fixed assets				
Cost		6,545		9,563
Depreciation		5,120		6,010
		1,425		3,553
Current assets				
Stock	2,695		4,217	
Debtors	1,740		2,500	
	4,435		6,717	
Current liabilities				
Creditors	2,065		3,290	
Bank overdraft	110		420	
Taxation	400		895	
Proposed dividends	30		80	
	2,605		4,685	
Net current assets		1,830		2,032
		3,255		5,585
Long-term loans		875		1,145
		2,380		4,440
Capital and reserves				
Ordinary share capital		795		1,235
Share premium		495		650
Profit and loss account		1,090		2,555
		2,380		4,440

Notes

(a) During the year fixed assets were sold for £500,000. They cost £2,500,000 and had a net book value of £750,000.

(b) Interest paid during the year was £235,000.

(c) There was no under or over provision for corporation tax in the previous year.

Task

(a) Prepare a cash flow statement for Ealing Ltd for the year ended 31 December 20X9 in accordance with recognised accounting standards. Present any additional notes or reconciliations required by the accounting standard adopted.

(b) Comment on the cash flows of Ealing Ltd.

PART C INTERPRETATION OF ACCOUNTS

Key learning points

- ☑ **Cash flow statements** were made compulsory for companies because it was recognised that accounting profit is not the only indicator of a company's performance.
- ☑ Cash flow statements concentrate on the **sources** and **uses of cash** and are a useful indicator of a company's liquidity and solvency.
- ☑ You need to learn the **format** of the statement; setting out the format is an essential first stage in preparing the statement but it will only really sink in with more question practice.
- ☑ Remember the **step-by-step** preparation procedure and use it for all the questions you practise.
- ☑ Cash flow statements provide **useful information** about a company which is not provided elsewhere in the accounts.
- ☑ Note that you may be expected to **analyse** or **interpret** a cash flow statement.

Quick quiz

1. What are the aims of a cash flow statement?
2. 'Equity dividends paid' is one of the standard headings required by FRS 1. True or false?
3. What are the two reconciliations required by FRS 1 (revised)?
4. Define cash according to FRS 1 (revised).
5. Define 'liquid resources'.
6. Cash flow information is of more use to creditors than the profit figure. Why?
7. Which of the following headings is not a classification of cash flows in FRS 1?

    A   Operating activities
    B   Financial investment
    C   Administration
    D   Financing

Answers to quick quiz

1. (a) To ensure that reporting entities report cash generation and absorption by highlighting key, comparable components of cash flow.

    (b) To ensure such entities provide information that assists in the assessment of their liquidity, solvency and financial adaptability.

2. True

3. (a) A reconciliation of operating profit to net cash inflow from operating activities
   (b) A reconciliation of movement in cash and movement in net debt

4. Cash in hand and deposits repayable on demand with any qualifying financial institution less overdrafts from any qualifying financial institution repayable on demand

5. Current asset investments held as readily disposable stores of value.

6. While profits might point to a healthy cash flow, the cash flow statement is a more direct indicator of a company's ability to repay a debt.

7. C   Administration costs are a classification in the profit and loss account, not the cash flow statement.

PART C INTERPRETATION OF ACCOUNTS

Activity checklist

This checklist shows which performance criteria, range statement or knowledge and understanding point is covered by each activity in this chapter. Tick off each activity as you complete it.

Activity

10.1 ☐ This activity deals with Performance Criteria 11.1.D: prepare a limited company cash flow statement.

10.2 ☐ This activity deals with Knowledge & Understanding point 3: preparing financial statements in proper form.

10.3 ☐ This activity deals with Performance Criteria 11.1.D: prepare a limited company cash flow statement.

10.4 ☐ This activity deals with Performance Criteria 11.1.D: prepare a limited company cash flow statement.

10.5 ☐ This activity deals with Performance Criteria 11.1.D: prepare a limited company cash flow statement.

10.6 ☐ This activity deals with Knowledge & Understanding point 8: analysing the information contained in financial statements.

10.7 ☐ This activity deals with Performance Criteria 11.1.D prepare a limited company cash flow statement.

10.8 ☐ This activity deals with Performance Criteria 11.1.D prepare and interpret a limited company cash flow statement.

chapter 11

Ratio analysis

Contents

1. The problem
2. The solution
3. The broad categories of ratios
4. Profitability and return on capital
5. Liquidity, gearing and working capital
6. Presentation of a ratio analysis report
7. Limitations of ratio analysis
8. Guidance from the Chief Assessor

Performance criteria

11.2.D Interpret the relationship between elements of limited company financial statements using ratio analysis

11.2.E Identify unusual features or significant issues within financial statements of limited companies

11.2.F Draw valid conclusions from the information contained within financial statements of limited companies

11.2.G Present issues, interpretations and conclusions clearly to the appropriate people

Range statement

11.2.1 Financial statements: income statement; balance sheet

11.2.2 Elements: assets; liabilities; ownership interest; gains; losses; contributions from owners; distributions to owners

11.2.3 Relationships between elements: profitability, liquidity, efficient use of resources, financial position

Knowledge and understanding

1. The elements and purposes of financial statements of limited companies as set out in the conceptual framework for financial reporting (Element 11.2)

8. Analysing and interpreting the information contained in financial statements (Element 11.2)

Knowledge and understanding (cont'd)

9   Computing and interpreting accounting ratios (Element 11.2)

12   How the accounting systems of an organisation are affected by its roles, organisational structure, its administrative systems and procedures and the nature of its business transactions (Element 11.2)

1 The problem

If you were to look at a balance sheet or P & L account, how would you decide whether the company was doing well or badly? Or whether it was financially strong or financially vulnerable? And what would you be looking at in the figures to help you to make your judgement?

2 The solution

Your exam requires you to appraise and communicate the position and prospects of a business based on given and prepared statements and **ratios**.

Ratio analysis involves comparing one figure against another to produce a ratio, and assessing whether the ratio indicates a weakness or strength in the company's affairs.

3 The broad categories of ratios

Broadly speaking, basic ratios can be grouped into five categories.

(a) Profitability and return
(b) Long-term solvency and stability
(c) Short-term solvency and liquidity
(d) Efficiency (turnover ratios)
(e) Shareholders' investment ratios

Within each heading we will identify a number of standard measures or ratios that are normally calculated and generally accepted as meaningful indicators. One must stress however that each individual business must be considered separately, and a ratio that is meaningful for a manufacturing company may be completely meaningless for a financial institution. Try not to be too mechanical when working out ratios and constantly think about what you are trying to achieve.

The key to obtaining meaningful information from ratio analysis is **comparison**. This may involve comparing ratios over time within the same business to establish whether things are improving or declining, and comparing ratios between similar businesses to see whether the company you are analysing is better or worse than average within its specific business sector.

It must be stressed that ratio analysis **on its own is not sufficient for interpreting** company accounts, and that there are other items of information which should be looked at, for example:

(a) Comments in the Chairman's report and directors' report

(b) The age and nature of the company's assets

(c) Current and future developments in the company's markets, at home and overseas

(d) Any other noticeable features of the report and accounts, such as post balance sheet events, contingent liabilities, a qualified auditors' report, the company's taxation position, and so on

Scenario

To illustrate the calculation of ratios, the following balance sheet and P & L account figures will be used.

BETATEC PLC PROFIT AND LOSS ACCOUNT
FOR THE YEAR ENDED 31 DECEMBER 20X8

	Notes	20X8 £	20X7 £
Turnover	1	3,095,576	1,909,051
Operating profit	1	359,501	244,229
Interest	2	17,371	19,127
Profit on ordinary activities before taxation		342,130	225,102
Taxation on ordinary activities		74,200	31,272
Profit on ordinary activities after taxation		267,930	193,830
Dividend		41,000	16,800
Retained profit for the year		226,930	177,030
Earnings per share		12.8p	9.3p

BETATEC PLC BALANCE SHEET
AS AT 31 DECEMBER 20X8

	Notes	20X8 £	20X7 £
Fixed assets			
Tangible fixed assets		802,180	656,071
Current assets			
Stocks and work in progress		64,422	86,550
Debtors	3	1,002,701	853,441
Cash at bank and in hand		1,327	68,363
		1,068,450	1,008,354
Creditors: amounts falling due within one year	4	881,731	912,456
Net current assets		186,719	95,898
Total assets less current liabilities		988,899	751,969
Creditors: amounts falling due after more than one year			
10% first mortgage debenture stock 20Y4/20Y9		(100,000)	(100,000)
Provision for liabilities and charges		(20,000)	(10,000)
		868,899	641,969
Capital and reserves			
Called up share capital	5	210,000	210,000
Share premium account		48,178	48,178
Profit and loss account		610,721	383,791
		868,899	641,969

PART C INTERPRETATION OF ACCOUNTS

NOTES TO THE ACCOUNTS

1 Turnover and profit

		20X8 £	20X7 £
(i)	Turnover	3,095,576	1,909,051
	Cost of sales	2,402,609	1,441,950
	Gross profit	692,967	467,101
	Administration expenses	333,466	222,872
	Operating profit	359,501	244,229
(ii)	Operating profit is stated after charging:		
	Depreciation	151,107	120,147
	Auditors' remuneration	6,500	5,000
	Leasing charges	47,636	46,336
	Directors' emoluments	94,945	66,675

2 Interest

	20X8 £	20X7 £
Payable on bank overdrafts and other loans	8,115	11,909
Payable on debenture stock	10,000	10,000
	18,115	21,909
Receivable on short-term deposits	744	2,782
Net payable	17,371	19,127

3 Debtors

	20X8	20X7
Amounts falling due within one year		
Trade debtors	884,559	760,252
Prepayments and accrued income	97,022	45,729
	981,581	805,981
Amounts falling due after more than one year		
Trade debtors	21,120	47,460
Total debtors	1,002,701	853,441

4 Creditors: amounts falling due within one year

	20X8	20X7
Trade creditors	627,018	545,340
Accruals and deferred income	81,279	280,464
Corporation tax	108,000	37,200
Other taxes and social security costs	44,434	32,652
Dividend	21,000	16,800
	881,731	912,456

5 Called up share capital

	20X8	20X7
Authorised ordinary shares of 10p each	1,000,000	1,000,000
Issued and fully paid ordinary shares of 10p each	210,000	210,00

4 Profitability and return on capital

4.1 PBIT

In our example, the company made a profit in both 20X8 and 20X7, and there was an increase in profit on ordinary activities between one year and the next:

- Of 52% before taxation
- Of 39% after taxation

Profit on ordinary activities *before* **taxation** is generally thought to be a **better** figure to use **than profit after taxation**, because there might be unusual variations in the tax charge from year to year which would not affect the underlying profitability of the company's operations.

Another profit figure that should be calculated is **PBIT, profit before interest** and tax. This is the amount of profit which the company earned before having to pay interest to the providers of loan capital. By providers of loan capital, we usually mean longer-term loan capital, such as debentures and medium-term bank loans, which will be shown in the balance sheet as 'creditors: amounts falling due after more than one year'.

Profit before interest and tax is therefore:

- Profit on ordinary activities before taxation; PLUS
- Interest charges on long-term loan capital

Published accounts do not always give sufficient detail on interest payable to determine how much is interest on long-term finance. We will assume in our example that the whole of the interest payable (£18,115, note 2) relates to long-term finance.

PBIT in our example is therefore:

	20X8 £	20X7 £
Profit on ordinary activities before tax	342,130	225,102
Interest payable	18,115	21,909
PBIT	360,245	247,011

This shows a 46% growth between 20X7 and 20X8.

4.2 Return on capital employed (ROCE)

It is impossible to assess profits or profit growth properly without relating them to the amount of funds (capital) that were employed in making the profits. The most important profitability ratio is therefore return on capital employed (ROCE), which states the profit as a percentage of the amount of capital employed.

FORMULA TO LEARN!

$$\text{ROCE} = \frac{\text{Profit on ordinary activities before interest and taxation}}{\text{Capital employed}}$$

PART C INTERPRETATION OF ACCOUNTS

Capital employed = Shareholders' funds plus 'creditors: amounts falling due after more than one year' plus any long-term provision for liabilities and charges (*or* total assets less current liabilities).

The underlying principle is that we must compare like with like, and so if capital means share capital and reserves plus long-term liabilities and debt capital, profit must mean the profit earned by all this capital together. This is PBIT, since interest is the return for loan capital.

Example: ROCE

In our example, capital employed = 20X8 868,899 + 100,000 + 20,000 = £988,899
                                   20X7 641,969 + 100,000 + 10,000 = £751,969

These total figures are the total assets less current liabilities figures for 20X8 and 20X7 in the balance sheet.

	20X8	20X7
ROCE =	$\dfrac{360,245}{988,899} = 36.4\%$	$\dfrac{247,011}{751,969} = 32.8\%$

What does a company's ROCE tell us? What should we be looking for? There are three comparisons that can be made.

(a) The change in ROCE from one year to the next can be examined. In this example, there has been an increase in ROCE by about 10% or 11% from its 20X7 level.

(b) The ROCE being earned by other companies, if this information is available, can be compared with the ROCE of this company. Here the information is not available.

(c) A **comparison** of the ROCE with **current market borrowing** rates may be made.

   (i) What would be the cost of extra borrowing to the company if it needed more loans, and is it earning a ROCE that suggests it could make profits to make such borrowing worthwhile?

   (ii) Is the company making a ROCE which suggests that it is getting value for money from its current borrowing?

   (iii) Companies are in a risk business and commercial borrowing rates are a good independent yardstick against which company performance can be judged.

In this example, if we suppose that current market interest rates, say, for medium-term borrowing from banks, is around 10%, then the company's actual ROCE of 36% in 20X8 would not seem low. On the contrary, it might seem high.

However, it is **easier to spot a low ROCE than a high one**, because there is always a chance that the company's **fixed assets**, especially property, **are undervalued** in its balance sheet, and so the capital employed figure might be unrealistically low. If the company had earned a ROCE, not of 36%, but of, say only 6%, then its return would have been below current borrowing rates and so disappointingly low.

> **Signpost**
> There are different ways of calculating ROCE, and the assessor will give you credit for them. If he tells you how to calculate it you should, of course, follow his instructions.

4.3 Return on shareholders' capital (ROSC)

Another measure of profitability and return is the return on shareholders' capital (ROSC):

FORMULA TO LEARN!

$$\text{ROSC} = \frac{\text{Profit on ordinary activities before tax}}{\text{Share capital and reserves}}$$

It is intended to focus on the return being made by the company for the benefit of its shareholders, and in our example, the figures are:

20X8	20X7
$\frac{342{,}130}{868{,}899} = 39.4\%$	$\frac{225{,}102}{641{,}969} = 35.1\%$

These figures show an improvement between 20X7 and 20X8, and a return which is clearly in excess of current borrowing rates.

ROSC is not a widely-used ratio, however, because there are more useful ratios that give an indication of the return to shareholders, such as earnings per share, dividend per share, dividend yield and earnings yield, which are described later.

4.4 Analysing profitability and return in more detail: the secondary ratios

We often sub-analyse ROCE, to find out more about why the ROCE is high or low, or better or worse than last year. There are two factors that contribute towards a return on capital employed, both related to sales turnover.

(a) **Profit margin**. A company might make a high or low profit margin on its sales. For example, a company that makes a profit of 25p per £1 of sales is making a bigger return on its turnover than another company making a profit of only 10p per £1 of sales.

(b) **Asset turnover**. Asset turnover is a measure of how well the assets of a business are being used to generate sales. For example, if two companies each have capital employed of £100,000 and Company A makes sales of £400,000 per annum whereas Company B makes sales of only £200,000 per annum, Company A is making a higher turnover from the same amount of assets (twice as much asset turnover as Company B) and this will help A to make a higher return on capital employed than B. Asset turnover is expressed as 'x times' so that assets generate x times their value in annual turnover. Here, Company A's asset turnover is 4 times and B's is 2 times.

Profit margin and asset turnover together explain the ROCE and if the ROCE is the primary profitability ratio, these other two are the secondary ratios. The relationship between the three ratios can be shown mathematically.

FORMULA TO LEARN!

Profit margin × Asset turnover = ROCE

$$\therefore \quad \frac{\text{PBIT}}{\text{Sales}} \times \frac{\text{Sales}}{\text{Capital employed}} = \frac{\text{PBIT}}{\text{Capital employed}}$$

PART C INTERPRETATION OF ACCOUNTS

In our example:

		Profit margin		Asset turnover		ROCE
(a)	20X8	360,245 / 3,095,576	×	3,095,576 / 988,899	=	360,245 / 988,899
		11.64%	×	3.13 times	=	36.4%
(b)	20X7	247,011 / 1,909,051	×	1,909,051 / 751,969	=	247,011 / 751,969
		12.94%	×	2.54 times	=	32.8%

In this example, the company's improvement in ROCE between 20X7 and 20X8 is attributable to a higher asset turnover. Indeed the profit margin has fallen a little, but the higher asset turnover has more than compensated for this.

It is also worth commenting on the change in sales turnover from one year to the next. You may already have noticed that Betatec plc achieved sales growth of over 60% from £1.9 million to £3.1 million between 20X7 and 20X8. This is very strong growth, and this is certainly one of the most significant items in the P & L account and balance sheet.

4.5 A warning about comments on profit margin and asset turnover

It might be tempting to think that a high profit margin is good, and a low asset turnover means sluggish trading. In broad terms, this is so. But there is a **trade-off between profit margin and asset turnover**, and you cannot look at one without allowing for the other.

(a) A high profit margin means a high profit per £1 of sales, but if this also means that sales prices are high, there is a strong possibility that sales turnover will be depressed, and so asset turnover lower.

(b) A high asset turnover means that the company is generating a lot of sales, but to do this it might have to keep its prices down and so accept a low profit margin per £1 of sales.

Consider the following.

Company A		Company B	
Sales	£1,000,000	Sales	£4,000,000
Capital employed	£1,000,000	Capital employed	£1,000,000
PBIT	£200,000	PBIT	£200,000

These figures would give the following ratios.

	Company A			Company B	
ROCE	= 200,000 / 1,000,000	= 20%	ROCE	= 200,000 / 1,000,000	= 20%
Profit margin	= 200,000 / 1,000,000	= 20%	Profit margin	= 200,000 / 4,000,000	= 5%
Asset turnover	= 1,000,000 / 1,000,000	= 1	Asset turnover	= 4,000,000 / 1,000,000	= 4

The companies have the same ROCE, but it is arrived at in a very different fashion. Company A operates with a low asset turnover and a comparatively high profit margin whereas company B carries out much more business, but on a lower profit margin. Company A could be operating at the luxury end of the market, whilst company B is operating at the popular end of the market (Fortnum and Masons v Sainsbury's).

Activity 11.1

Which one of the following formulae correctly expresses the relationship between return on capital employed (ROCE), profit margin (PM) and asset turnover (AT)?

A $PM = \dfrac{AT}{ROCE}$

B $ROCE = \dfrac{PM}{AT}$

C $AT = PM \times ROCE$

D $PM = \dfrac{ROCE}{AT}$

4.6 Gross profit margin, net profit margin and profit analysis

Depending on the format of the P & L account, you may be able to calculate the gross profit margin as well as the net profit margin. Looking at the two together can be quite informative.

For example, suppose that a company has the following summarised profit and loss accounts for two consecutive years.

	Year 1 £	Year 2 £
Turnover	70,000	100,000
Cost of sales	42,000	55,000
Gross profit	28,000	45,000
Expenses	21,000	35,000
Net profit	7,000	10,000

Although the net profit margin is the same for both years at 10%, the gross profit margin is not.

In year 1 it is: $\dfrac{28,000}{70,000} = 40\%$

and in year 2 it is: $\dfrac{45,000}{100,000} = 45\%$

The improved gross profit margin has not led to an improvement in the net profit margin. This is because expenses as a percentage of sales have risen from 30% in year 1 to 35% in year 2.

PART C INTERPRETATION OF ACCOUNTS

5 Liquidity, gearing and working capital

5.1 Long-term solvency: debt and gearing ratios

Debt ratios are concerned with **how much the company owes in relation to its size**, whether it is getting into heavier debt or improving its situation, and whether its debt burden seems heavy or light.

(a) When a company is heavily in debt banks and other potential lenders may be unwilling to advance further funds.

(b) When a company is earning only a modest profit before interest and tax, and has a heavy debt burden, there will be very little profit left over for shareholders after the interest charges have been paid. And so if interest rates were to go up (on bank overdrafts and so on) or the company were to borrow even more, it might soon be incurring interest charges in excess of PBIT. This might eventually lead to the liquidation of the company.

These are two big reasons why companies should keep their debt burden under control. There are four ratios that are particularly worth looking at, the **debt** ratio, **gearing** ratio, **interest cover** and **cash flow** ratio.

5.2 Debt ratio

The **debt ratio** is the ratio of a **company's total debts to its total assets**.

Assets consist of fixed assets at their balance sheet value, plus current assets. Debts consist of all creditors, whether amounts falling due within one year or after more than one year.

You can ignore long-term provisions and liabilities, such as deferred taxation.

There is no absolute guide to the maximum safe debt ratio, but as a **very general guide**, you might regard **50% as a safe limit** to debt. In practice, many companies operate successfully with a higher debt ratio than this, but 50% is nonetheless a helpful benchmark. In addition, if the debt ratio is over 50% and getting worse, the company's debt position will be worth looking at more carefully.

In the case of Betatec plc the debt ratio is as follows.

	20X8	20X7
Total debts	(881,731 + 100,000)	(912,456 + 100,000)
Total assets	(802,180 + 1,068,450)	(656,071 + 1,008,354)
	= 52%	= 61%

In this case, the debt ratio is quite high, mainly because of the large amount of current liabilities. However, the debt ratio has fallen from 61% to 52% between 20X7 and 20X8, and so the company appears to be improving its debt position.

5.3 Gearing ratio

Capital gearing is concerned with a company's **long-term capital structure**. We can think of a company as consisting of fixed assets and net current assets (ie working capital, which is current assets minus current liabilities). These assets must be financed by **long-term capital** of the company, which is **one of two** things.

(a) **Share capital and reserves** (shareholders' funds) which can be divided into:
   (i) Ordinary shares plus reserves
   (ii) Preference shares

(b) **Long-term debt capital**: 'creditors: amounts falling due after more than one year'

Preference share capital is not debt. It would certainly not be included as debt in the debt ratio. However, like loan capital, preference share capital **has a prior claim over profits** before interest and tax, ahead of ordinary shareholders. Preference dividends must be paid out of profits before ordinary shareholders are entitled to an ordinary dividend, and so we refer to preference share capital and loan capital as prior charge capital.

The **capital gearing ratio** is a measure of the proportion of a company's capital that is prior charge capital. It is measured as follows:

FORMULA TO LEARN!

$$\text{Capital gearing ratio} = \frac{\text{prior charge capital}}{\text{total capital}}$$

(a) **Prior charge capital** is capital carrying a right to a fixed return. It will include preference shares and debentures.

(b) **Total capital** is ordinary share capital and reserves plus prior charge capital plus any long-term liabilities or provisions. In group accounts we would also include minority interests. It is easier to identify the same figure for total capital as total assets less current liabilities, which you will find given to you in the balance sheet.

As with the debt ratio, there is no absolute limit to what a gearing ratio ought to be. A company with a gearing ratio of **more than 50%** is said to be **high-geared** (whereas low gearing means a gearing ratio of less than 50%). Many companies are high geared, but if a high geared company is becoming increasingly high geared, it is likely to have difficulty in the future when it wants to borrow even more, unless it can also boost its shareholders' capital, either with retained profits or by a new share issue.

A similar ratio to the gearing ratio is the **debt/equity ratio**, which is calculated as follows.

FORMULA TO LEARN!

$$\text{Debt/equity ratio} = \frac{\text{prior charge capital}}{\text{ordinary share capital and reserves}}$$

This gives us the same sort of information as the gearing ratio, and a ratio of 100% or more would indicate high gearing.

In the example of Betatec plc, we find that the company, although having a high debt ratio because of its current liabilities, has a low gearing ratio. It has no preference share capital and its only long-term debt is the 10% debenture stock.

PART C INTERPRETATION OF ACCOUNTS

	20X8	20X7
Gearing ratio	$\frac{100{,}000}{988{,}899} = 10\%$	$\frac{100{,}000}{751{,}969} = 13\%$
Debt/equity ratio	$\frac{100{,}000}{868{,}899} = 12\%$	$\frac{100{,}000}{641{,}969} = 16\%$

5.4 The implications of high or low gearing

We mentioned earlier that gearing is, amongst other things, an attempt to quantify the **degree of risk** involved in holding equity shares in a company, risk both in terms of the company's ability to remain in business and in terms of expected ordinary dividends from the company. The problem with a high geared company is that by definition there is a lot of debt. Debt generally carries a fixed rate of interest (or fixed rate of dividend if in the form of preference shares), hence there is a given (and large) amount to be paid out from profits to holders of debt before arriving at a residue available for distribution to the holders of equity. The riskiness will perhaps become clearer with the aid of an example.

	Company A £'000	Company B £'000	Company C £'000
Ordinary share capital	600	400	300
Profit and loss account	200	200	200
Revaluation reserve	100	100	100
	900	700	600
6% preference shares	-	-	100
10% loan stock	100	300	300
Capital employed	1,000	1,000	1,000
Gearing ratio	10%	30%	40%

Now suppose that each company makes a profit before interest and tax of £50,000, and the rate of corporation tax is 30%. Amounts available for distribution to equity shareholders will be as follows:

	Company A £'000	Company B £'000	Company C £'000
Profit before interest and tax	50	50	50
Interest	10	30	30
Profit before tax	40	20	20
Taxation at 30%	12	6	6
Profit after tax	28	14	14
Preference dividend	-	-	6
Available for ordinary shareholders	28	14	8

If in the subsequent year profit before interest and tax falls to £40,000, the amounts available to ordinary shareholders will become:

	Company A £'000	Company B £'000	Company C £'000
Profit before interest and tax	40	40	40
Interest	10	30	30
Profit before tax	30	10	10
Taxation at 30%	9	3	3
Profit after tax	21	7	7
Preference dividend	-	-	6
Available for ordinary shareholders	21	7	1
Note the following.			
Gearing ratio	10%	30%	40%
Change in PBIT	– 20%	– 20%	– 20%
Change in profit available for ordinary shareholders	– 25%	– 50%	– 87.5%

The more highly geared the company, the greater the risk that little (if anything) will be available to distribute by way of dividend to the ordinary shareholders.

(a) The example clearly displays this fact in so far as the more highly geared the company, the greater the percentage change in profit available for ordinary shareholders for any given percentage change in profit before interest and tax.

(b) The relationship similarly holds when profits increase, and if PBIT had risen by 20% rather than fallen, you would find that once again the largest percentage change in profit available for ordinary shareholders (this means an increase) will be for the highly geared company.

(c) This means that there will be greater volatility of amounts available for ordinary shareholders, and presumably therefore greater volatility in dividends paid to those shareholders, where a company is highly geared. That is the risk: you may do extremely well or extremely badly without a particularly large movement in the PBIT of the company.

The risk of a company's ability to remain in business was referred to earlier. Gearing is relevant to this. A high geared company has a large amount of interest to pay annually (assuming that the debt is external borrowing rather than preference shares). If those borrowings are 'secured' in any way (and debentures in particular are secured), then the holders of the debt are perfectly entitled to force the company to realise assets to pay their interest if funds are not available from other sources. Clearly the more highly geared a company the more likely this is to occur when and if profits fall. **Higher gearing may mean higher returns, but also higher risk.**

5.5 Interest cover

The interest cover ratio shows whether a company is earning enough profits before interest and tax to pay its interest costs comfortably, or whether its interest costs are high in relation to the size of its profits, so that a fall in PBIT would then have a significant effect on profits available for ordinary shareholders.

PART C INTERPRETATION OF ACCOUNTS

FORMULA TO LEARN!

$$\text{Interest cover} = \frac{\text{profit before interest and tax}}{\text{interest charges}}$$

An interest cover of 2 times or less would be low, and should really exceed 3 times before the company's interest costs are to be considered within acceptable limits.

Returning first to the example of Companies A, B and C, the interest cover was as follows.

		Company A	Company B	Company C
(a)	When PBIT was £50,000 =	50,000 / 10,000	50,000 / 30,000	50,000 / 30,000
		5 times	1.67 times	1.67 times
(b)	When PBIT was £40,000 =	40,000 / 10,000	40,000 / 30,000	40,000 / 30,000
		4 times	1.33 times	1.33 times

Note. Although preference share capital is included as prior charge capital for the gearing ratio, it is usual to exclude preference dividends from 'interest' charges. We also look at all interest payments, even interest charges on short-term debt, and so interest cover and gearing do not quite look at the same thing.

Both B and C have a low interest cover, which is a warning to ordinary shareholders that their profits are highly vulnerable, in percentage terms, to even small changes in PBIT.

Activity 11.2

Returning to the example of Betatec plc above, what is the company's interest cover?

5.6 Cash flow ratio

The **cash flow ratio** is the ratio of a company's net cash inflow to its total debts.

(a) Net cash inflow is the amount of cash which the company has coming into the business from its operations. A suitable figure for net cash inflow can be obtained from the cash flow statement.

(b) Total debts are short-term and long-term creditors, together with provisions for liabilities and charges. A distinction can be made between debts payable within one year and other debts and provisions.

Obviously, a company needs to be earning enough cash from operations to be able to meet its foreseeable debts and future commitments, and the cash flow ratio, and changes in the cash flow ratio from one year to the next, provide a useful indicator of a company's cash position.

5.7 Short-term solvency and liquidity

Profitability is of course an important aspect of a company's performance and debt or gearing is another. Neither, however, addresses directly the key issue of **liquidity**.

Liquidity is the amount of cash a company can put its hands on quickly to settle its debts (and possibly to meet other unforeseen demands for cash payments too).

Liquid funds consist of:

(a) Cash

(b) Short-term investments for which there is a ready market

(c) Fixed-term deposits with a bank or building society, for example, a six month high-interest deposit with a bank

(d) Trade debtors (because they will pay what they owe within a reasonably short period of time)

(e) Bills of exchange receivable (because like ordinary trade debtors, these represent amounts of cash due to be received within a relatively short period of time)

In summary, **liquid assets** are current asset items that will or could soon be **converted into cash, and cash itself**. Two common definitions of liquid assets are:

(a) All current assets without exception
(b) All current assets with the exception of stocks

A company can obtain liquid assets from sources other than sales, such as the issue of shares for cash, a new loan or the sale of fixed assets. But a company cannot rely on these at all times, and in general, obtaining liquid funds depends on making sales and profits. Even so, profits do not always lead to increases in liquidity. This is mainly because funds generated from trading may be immediately invested in fixed assets or paid out as dividends. You should refer back to the chapter on cash flow statements to examine this issue.

The reason why a company needs liquid assets is so that it can meet its debts when they fall due. Payments are continually made for operating expenses and other costs, and so there is a cash cycle from trading activities of cash coming in from sales and cash going out for expenses. This is illustrated by the diagram below.

5.8 The cash cycle

To help you to understand liquidity ratios, it is useful to begin with a brief explanation of the cash cycle. The cash cycle describes the flow of cash out of a business and back into it again as a result of normal trading operations.

Cash goes out to pay for supplies, wages and salaries and other expenses, although payments can be delayed by taking some credit. A business might hold stock for a while and then sell it. Cash will come back into the business from the sales, although customers might delay payment by themselves taking some credit.

PART C INTERPRETATION OF ACCOUNTS

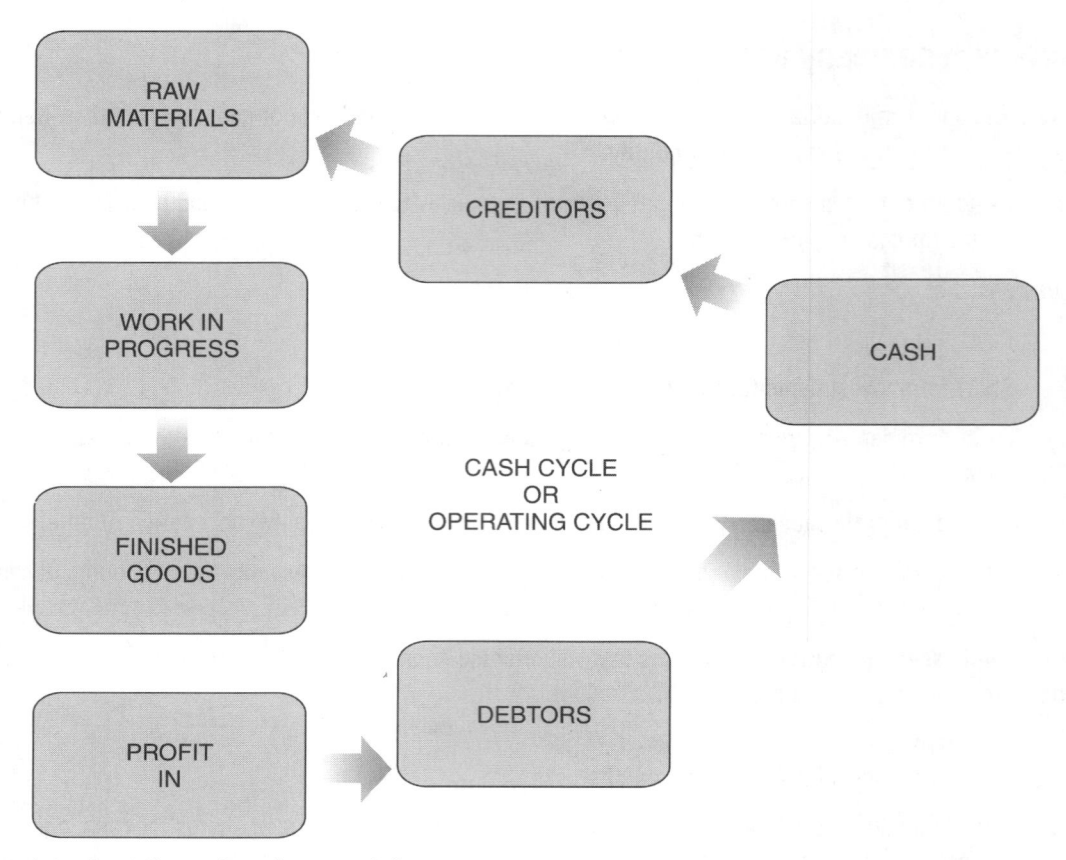

```
RAW MATERIALS → WORK IN PROGRESS → FINISHED GOODS → PROFIT IN → DEBTORS → CASH → CREDITORS → RAW MATERIALS

CASH CYCLE OR OPERATING CYCLE
```

The main points about the cash cycle are as follows.

(a) The **timing of cash flows in and out of a business does not coincide with the time when sales and costs of sales occur**. Cash flows out can be postponed by taking credit. Cash flows in can be delayed by having debtors.

(b) **The time between making a purchase and making a sale also affects cash flows**. If stocks are held for a long time, the delay between the cash payment for stocks and cash receipts from selling them will also be a long one.

(c) Holding stocks and having debtors can therefore be seen as two reasons why cash receipts are delayed. Another way of saying this is that **if a company invests in working capital, its cash position will show a corresponding decrease**.

(d) Similarly, **taking credit from creditors can be seen as a reason why cash payments are delayed**. The company's liquidity position will worsen when it has to pay the creditors, unless it can get more cash in from sales and debtors in the meantime.

The liquidity ratios and working capital turnover ratios are used to test a company's liquidity, length of cash cycle, and investment in working capital.

5.9 Liquidity ratios: current ratio and quick ratio

The 'standard' test of liquidity is the **current ratio**. It can be obtained from the balance sheet, and is calculated as follows.

FORMULA TO LEARN!

Current ratio = $\dfrac{\text{current assets}}{\text{current liabilities}}$

The idea behind this is that a company should have enough current assets that give a promise of 'cash to come' to meet its future commitments to pay off its current liabilities. Obviously, a **ratio in excess of 1** should be expected. Otherwise, there would be the prospect that the company might be unable to pay its debts on time. In practice, a ratio comfortably in excess of 1 should be expected, but what is 'comfortable' varies between different types of businesses.

Companies are not able to convert all their current assets into cash very quickly. In particular, some manufacturing companies might hold large quantities of raw material stocks, which must be used in production to create finished goods stocks. Finished goods stocks might be warehoused for a long time, or sold on lengthy credit. In such businesses, where stock turnover is slow, most stocks are not very 'liquid' assets, because the cash cycle is so long. For these reasons, we calculate an additional liquidity ratio, known as the **quick ratio** or **acid test** ratio.

FORMULA TO LEARN!

The **quick ratio**, or **acid test ratio** is: $\dfrac{\text{current assets less stocks}}{\text{current liabilities}}$

This ratio should ideally be at least 1 for companies with a slow stock turnover. For companies with a fast stock turnover, a quick ratio can be comfortably less than 1 without suggesting that the company should be in cash flow trouble.

Both the current ratio and the quick ratio offer an indication of the company's liquidity position, but the absolute figures should not be interpreted too literally. It is often theorised that an acceptable current ratio is 1.5 and an acceptable quick ratio is 0.8, but these should only be used as a guide.

Example

Different businesses operate in very different ways. Budgens (the supermarket group) for example had (as at 30 April 1993) a current ratio of 0.52 and a quick ratio of 0.17. Budgens has low debtors (people do not buy groceries on credit), low cash (good cash management), medium stocks (high stocks but quick turnover, particularly in view of perishability) and very high creditors (Budgens buys its supplies of groceries on credit).

Compare the Budgens ratios with the Tomkins group which had a current ratio of 1.44 and a quick ratio of 1.03 (as at 1 May 1993). Tomkins is a manufacturing and retail organisation and operates with liquidity ratios closer to the standard. At 25 September 1993, Tate & Lyle's figures gave a current ratio of 1.18 and a quick ratio of 0.80.

What is important is the **trend** of these ratios. From this, one can easily ascertain whether liquidity is improving or deteriorating. If Budgens has traded for the last 10 years (very successfully) with current ratios of 0.52 and quick ratios of 0.17 then it should be supposed that the company can continue in business with those levels of liquidity. If in the following year the current ratio were to fall to 0.38 and the quick ratio to 0.09, then further investigation into the liquidity situation would be appropriate. It is the relative position that is far more important than the absolute figures.

Don't forget the other side of the coin either. **A current ratio and a quick ratio can get bigger than they need to be**. A company that has large volumes of stocks and debtors might be over-investing in working capital, and so tying up more funds in the business than it needs to. This would suggest poor management of debtors (credit) or stocks by the company.

5.10 Efficiency ratios: control of debtors and stock

A rough measure of the average length of time it takes for a company's debtors to pay what they owe is the 'debtor days' ratio, or **average debtors' payment period**.

FORMULA TO LEARN!

$$\text{Debtors payment period} = \frac{\text{trade debtors}}{\text{sales}} \times 365 \text{ days}$$

The estimated average **debtors' payment period** is calculated as follows.

The figure for sales should be taken as the turnover figure in the P & L account. The trade debtors are not the total figure for debtors in the balance sheet, which includes prepayments and non-trade debtors. The trade debtors figure will be itemised in an analysis of the debtors total, in a note to the accounts.

The estimate of debtor days is only approximate.

(a) The balance sheet value of debtors might be abnormally high or low compared with the 'normal' level the company usually has.

(b) Turnover in the P & L account is exclusive of VAT, but debtors in the balance sheet are inclusive of VAT. **We are not strictly comparing like with like**. (Some companies show turnover inclusive of VAT as well as turnover exclusive of VAT, and the 'inclusive' figure should be used in these cases.)

Sales are usually made on 'normal credit terms' of payment within 30 days. Debtor days significantly in excess of this might be representative of poor management of funds of a business. However, **some companies must allow generous credit terms to win customers**. Exporting companies in particular may have to carry large amounts of debtors, and so their average collection period might be well in excess of 30 days.

The **trend** of the collection period (debtor days) **over time is probably the best guide**. If debtor days are increasing year on year, this is indicative of a poorly managed credit control function (and potentially therefore a poorly managed company).

Example: debtor days

Using the same examples as before, the debtor days of those companies were as follows.

Company	Date	Trade debtors / turnover	Debtor days (× 365)	Previous year	Debtor days (× 365)
Budgens	30.4.93	£5,016k / £284,986k =	6.4 days	3,977K / £290,668K =	5.0 days
Tomkins	1.5.93	£458.3m / £2,059.5m =	81.2 days	£272.4m / £1,274.2m =	78.0 days
Tate & Lyle	25.9.93	£304.4m / £3,817.3m =	29.3 days	£287.0m / £3,366.3m =	31.1 days

The differences in debtor days reflect the differences between the types of business. Budgen's has hardly any trade debtors at all, whereas the manufacturing companies have far more. The debtor days are fairly constant from the previous year for all three companies.

5.11 Stock turnover period

Another ratio worth calculating is the **stock turnover period**, or **stock days**. This is another estimated figure, obtainable from published accounts, which indicates the average number of days that items of stock are held for. As with the average debt collection period, however, it is only an approximate estimated figure, but one which should be reliable enough for comparing changes year on year.

FORMULA TO LEARN!

The number of **stock days** is calculated as:

$$\frac{\text{Stock}}{\text{Cost of sales}} \times 365$$

The reciprocal of the fraction:

$$\frac{\text{cost of sales}}{\text{stock}}$$

is termed the stock turnover, and is another measure of how vigorously a business is trading. A lengthening stock turnover period from one year to the next indicates one of two things:

(a) A slowdown in trading
(b) A build-up in stock levels, perhaps suggesting that the investment in stocks is becoming excessive

Presumably if we add together the stock days and the debtor days, this should give us an indication of how soon stock is convertible into cash. Both debtor days and stock days therefore give us a further indication of the company's liquidity.

PART C INTERPRETATION OF ACCOUNTS

Example: stock turnover

Returning once more to our first example, the estimated stock turnover periods for Budgens were as follows.

Company	Date	Stock / Cost of sales	Stock turnover period (days × 365)	Previous year		
Budgens	30.4.92	£15,554K / £254,571K	22.3 days	£14,094K / £261,368K	× 365	= 19.7 days

The figures for cost of sales were not shown in the accounts of either Tate & Lyle or Tomkins.

Activity 11.3

Butthead Ltd buys raw materials on six weeks credit, holds them in store for three weeks and then issues them to the production department. The production process takes two weeks on average, and finished goods are held in store for an average of four weeks before being sold. Debtors take five weeks credit on average.

Calculate the length of the cash cycle.

Activity 11.4

During a year a business sold stock which had cost £60,000. The stock held at the beginning of the year was £6,000 and at the end of the year £10,000.

What was the annual rate of stock turnover?

Activity 11.5

Calculate liquidity and working capital ratios from the accounts of the BET Group, a business which provides service support (cleaning etc) to customers worldwide.

	20X7	20X6
	£'000	£'000
Turnover	2,176.2	2,344.8
Cost of sales	1,659.0	1,731.5
Gross profit	517.2	613.3
Current assets		
Stocks	42.7	78.0
Debtors (note 1)	378.9	431.4
Short-term deposits and cash	205.2	145.0
	626.8	654.4
Creditors: amounts falling due within one year		
Loans and overdrafts	32.4	81.1
Corporation taxes	67.8	76.7
Dividend	11.7	17.2
Creditors (note 2)	487.2	467.2
	599.1	642.2
Net current assets	27.7	12.2
Notes		
1 Trade debtors	295.2	335.5
2 Trade creditors	190.8	188.1

BET Group is a service company and hence it would be expected to have very low stock and a very short stock turnover period. The similarity of debtors' and creditors' turnover periods means that the group is passing on most of the delay in receiving payment to its suppliers.

Creditors' turnover is ideally calculated by the formula:

$$\frac{\text{Trade creditors}}{\text{Purchases}} \times 365$$

However, it is rare to find purchases disclosed in published accounts and so cost of sales serves as an approximation. The creditors' turnover ratio often helps to assess a company's liquidity; an increase in creditor days is often a sign of lack of long-term finance or poor management of current assets, resulting in the use of extended credit from suppliers, increased bank overdraft and so on.

BET's current ratio is a little lower than average but its quick ratio is better than average and very little less than the current ratio. This suggests that stock levels are strictly controlled, which is reinforced by the low stock turnover period. It would seem that working capital is tightly managed, to avoid the poor liquidity which could be caused by a high debtors' turnover period and comparatively high creditors.

PART C INTERPRETATION OF ACCOUNTS

6 Presentation of a ratio analysis report

6.1 Basic approach

Exam questions on ratio analysis may try to **simulate a real life situation**. A set of accounts could be presented and you may be asked to prepare a report on them, addressed to a specific interested party, such as a bank. You should begin your report with a heading showing who it is from, the name of the addressee, the subject of the report and a suitable date.

A good approach is often to head up a **schedule of ratios** which will form an **appendix to the main report**. Calculate the ratios in a logical sequence, dealing in turn with operating and profitability ratios, use of assets (eg turnover periods for stocks and debtors), liquidity and gearing.

As you calculate the ratios you are likely to be struck by **significant fluctuations and trends**. These will form the basis of your comments in the body of the report. The report should begin with some introductory **comments**, setting out the scope of your analysis and mentioning that detailed figures have been included in an appendix. You should then go on to present your analysis under any categories called for by the question (eg separate sections for management, shareholders and creditors, or separate sections for profitability and liquidity).

Finally, look out for opportunities to **suggest remedial action** where trends appear to be unfavourable. Questions sometimes require you specifically to set out your advice and recommendations.

You may be asked to prepare a report on ratios which have already been calculated. Alternatively you may be given a full set of accounts and asked to calculate, evaluate and comment on the ratios. The AAT's Guidance for Unit 11 states that it is not enough simply to be able to calculate the ratios. Unusual or significant issues must be identified and there results of the analysis must be interpreted and valid conclusions clearly presented.

6.2 Planning your answers

This is as good a place as any to stress the importance of planning your answers. This is particularly important for 'wordy' questions. While you may feel like breathing a sigh of relief after all that number crunching, you should not be tempted to 'waffle'. The best way to avoid going off the point is to prepare an answer plan. This has the advantage of making you think before you write and structure your answer logically.

The following approach may be adopted when preparing an answer plan.

(a) Read the question requirements.
(b) Skim through the question to see roughly what it is about.
(c) Read through the question carefully, underlining any key words.
(d) Set out the headings for the main parts of your answer. Leave space to insert points within the headings.
(e) Jot down points to make within the main sections, underlining points on which you wish to expand.
(f) Write your full answer.

You should allow yourself the full time allocation for written answers. If, however, you run out of time, a clear answer plan with points in note form will earn you more credit than an introductory paragraph written out in full.

7 Limitations of ratio analysis

Ratio analysis is not foolproof. There are many problems in trying to identify trends and make comparisons. Below are just a few.

(a) **Information problems**

　(i)　The base information is often out of date, so timeliness of information leads to problems of interpretation

　(ii)　Historical cost information may not be the most appropriate information for the decision for which the analysis is being undertaken

　(iii)　Information in published accounts is generally summarised information and detailed information may be needed

　(iv)　Analysis of accounting information only identifies symptoms not causes and thus is of limited use

(b) **Comparison problems: inter-temporal**

　(i)　Effects of price changes make comparisons difficult unless adjustments are made
　(ii)　Impacts of changes in technology on the price of assets, the likely return and the future markets
　(iii)　Impacts of a changing environment on the results reflected in the accounting information
　(iv)　Potential effects of changes in accounting policies on the reported results
　(v)　Problems associated with establishing a normal base year to compare other years with

(c) **Comparison problems: inter-firm**

　(i)　Selection of industry norms and the usefulness of norms based on averages
　(ii)　Different firms having different financial and business risk profiles and the impact on analysis
　(iii)　Different firms using different accounting policies
　(iv)　Impacts of the size of the business and its comparators on risk, structure and returns
　(v)　Impacts of different environments on results, eg different countries or home-based versus multinational firms

8 Guidance from the Chief Assessor

At a recent seminar, the Chief Assessor for Unit 11 had various comments to make about this topic.

8.1 Required approach

Students need to:

(a) Calculate the ratio correctly

(b) Explain:

　(i)　The meaning of the ratio

PART C INTERPRETATION OF ACCOUNTS

      (ii)   How the ratio has changed
      (iii)   The meaning of the change

(c)   Draw conclusions on the basis of the analysis

Generally the ratios are calculated accurately and the explanations of the meaning of the ratios are good.

8.2 Problems

(a)   Some ratios are incorrectly calculated (eg ROCE, gearing, interest cover)

(b)   The weaker students merely say that a ratio is 'better' or 'worse', without providing any further explanation.

(c)   Candidates have difficulty in applying a general meaning to an interpretation of specific results of a calculation.

(d)   The ratios are often left to speak for themselves.

(e)   Candidates sometimes fail to **argue** for a conclusion.

(f)   The report format is not always observed, and presentation is sometimes poor.

(g)   Sometimes the better students assume that everything is obvious or come up with arguments that are speculative.

Try the Activity below. It is from a past exam and therefore a good example of what might come up.

Activity 11.6

Bimbridge Hospitals Trust has just lost its supplier of bandages. The company that has been supplying it for the last five years has gone into liquidation. The Trust is concerned to select a new supplier which it can rely on to supply it with its needs for the foreseeable future. You have been asked by the Trust managers to analyse the financial statements of a potential supplier of bandages. You have obtained the latest financial statements of the company, in summary, form which are set out below.

PATCH LIMITED
SUMMARY PROFIT AND LOSS ACCOUNTS
FOR THE YEAR ENDED 30 SEPTEMBER 20X8

	20X8	20X7
	£'000	£'000
Turnover	2,300	2,100
Cost of sales	1,035	945
Gross profit	1,265	1,155
Expenses	713	693
Net profit before interest and tax	552	462

PATCH LIMITED
SUMMARY BALANCE SHEETS
AS AT 30 SEPTEMBER 20X8

	20X8		20X7	
	£'000	£'000	£'000	£'000
Fixed assets		4,764		5,418
Current assets				
Stocks	522		419	
Debtors	406		356	
Cash	117		62	
	1,045		837	
Current liabilities				
Trade creditors	305		254	
Taxation	170		211	
	475		465	
Net current assets		570		372
Long-term loan		(1,654)		(2,490)
		3,680		3,300
Share capital		1,100		1,000
Share premium		282		227
Profit and loss account		2,298		2,073
		3,680		3,300

You have also obtained the relevant industry average ratios which are as follows:

	20X8	20X7
Return on capital employed	9.6%	9.4%
Net profit percentage	21.4%	21.3%
Quick ratio/acid test	1.0:1	0.9:1
Gearing (debt/capital employed)	36%	37%

Task

Prepare a report for the managers of Bimbridge Hospitals Trust recommending whether or not to use Patch Ltd as a supplier of bandages. Use the information contained in the financial statements of Patch Ltd and the industry averages supplied.

Your answer should:

(a) Comment on the company's profitability, liquidity and financial position
(b) Consider how the company has changed over the two years
(c) Include a comparison with the industry as a whole

The report should include calculation of the following ratios for the two years.

(a) Return on capital employed
(b) Net profit percentage
(c) Quick ratio/acid test
(d) Gearing

PART C INTERPRETATION OF ACCOUNTS

Key learning points

- ☑ This lengthy chapter has gone into quite a lot of detail about basic **ratio analysis**. The ratios you should be able to calculate and/or comment on are as follows.

    - **Profitability ratios**

        return on capital employed
        net profit as a percentage of sales
        asset turnover ratio
        gross profit as a percentage of sales

    - **Debt and gearing ratios**

        debt ratio
        gearing ratio
        interest cover
        cash flow ratio

    - **Liquidity and working capital ratios**

        current ratio
        quick ratio (acid test ratio)
        debtor days (average debt collection period)
        average stock turnover period

- ☑ With the exception of the last three ratios, where the share's market price is required, all of these ratios can be calculated from information in a company's **published accounts**.

- ☑ Ratios provide information through comparison:

    - **trends** in a company's ratios from one year to the next, indicating an improving or worsening position;

    - in some cases, against a **'norm'** or 'standard';

    - in some cases, against the **ratios of other companies**, although differences between one company and another should often be expected.

- ☑ Ratio analysis is not foolproof. There are several **problems** inherent in making comparisons over time and between organisations.

Quick quiz

1. Apart from ratio analysis, what other information might be helpful in interpreting a company's accounts?
2. What is the usual formula for ROCE?
3. ROCE can be calculated as the product of two other ratios. What are they?
4. Define the 'debt ratio'.
5. Give two formulae for calculating gearing.
6. In a period when profits are fluctuating, what effect does a company's level of gearing have on the profits available for ordinary shareholders?
7. What are the formulae for:

    (a) The current ratio?
    (b) The quick ratio?
    (c) The debtors payment period?
    (d) The stock turnover period?

8. Company Q has a profit margin of 7%. Briefly comment on this.
9. The debt ratio is a company's long term debt over its net assets.

    True [ ]

    False [ ]

10. Cash flow ratio is the ratio of:

    A   Gross cash inflow to total debt
    B   Gross cash inflow to net debt
    C   Net cash inflow to total debt
    D   Net cash inflow to net debt

Answers to quick quiz

1. (a) Comments in the Chairman's report and directors' report.
   (b) The age and nature of the company's assets.
   (c) Current and future developments in the company's markets.
   (d) Post balance sheet events, contingencies, qualified audit report and so on.

2. $$\frac{\text{Profit on ordinary activities before interest and tax}}{\text{Capital employed}}$$

3. Asset turnover and profit margin.

4. The ratio of a company's total debts to its total assets.

PART C INTERPRETATION OF ACCOUNTS

5   (a)   Capital gearing ratio $= \dfrac{\text{Prior charge capital}}{\text{Total capital}}$

      (b)   Debt/equity ratio $= \dfrac{\text{Prior charge capital}}{\text{Ordinary share capital and reserves}}$

6   The more highly geared a company, the greater the percentage change in profit available for ordinary shareholders for any given percentage change in profit before interest and tax.

7   (a) $\dfrac{\text{Current assets}}{\text{Current liabilities}}$

      (b) $\dfrac{\text{Current assets less stock}}{\text{Current liabilities}}$

      (c) $\dfrac{\text{Trade debtors}}{\text{Sales}} \times 365$

      (d) $\dfrac{\text{Stock}}{\text{Cost of sales}} \times 365$

8   You should be careful here. You have very little information. This is a low margin, but you need to know what industry the company operates in. 7% may be good for a major retailer.

9   False

10   C

11: RATIO ANALYSIS

Activity checklist

This checklist shows which performance criteria, range statement or knowledge and understanding point is covered by each activity in this chapter. Tick off each activity as you complete it.

Activity

11.1	☐	This activity deals with Knowledge & Understanding point 9: computing accounting ratios.
11.2	☐	This activity deals with Range Statement 11.2.3: relationships between elements: financial position.
11.3	☐	This activity deals with Performance Criteria 11.2.D: interpret relationships between elements of financial statements.
11.4	☐	This activity deals with Performance Criteria 11.2.D: interpret relationships between elements of financial statements.
11.5	☐	This activity deals with Knowledge & Understanding point 9: computing accounting ratios.
11.6	☐	This activity deals with Performance Criteria 11.2.E to G regarding unusual features, conclusions and presentation.

PART C INTERPRETATION OF ACCOUNTS

PART D

Simple consolidated accounts

chapter 12

Introduction to group accounts

Contents

1. Introduction
2. Groups and consolidation: an overview
3. Definitions
4. Exclusion of subsidiary undertakings from group accounts
5. Exemption from the requirement to prepare group accounts

Performance criteria

11.1.A Draft limited company financial statements from the appropriate information

11.1.B Correctly identify and implement subsequent adjustments and ensure that discrepancies, unusual features or queries are identified and either resolved or referred to the appropriate person

11.1.C Ensure that limited company financial statements comply with relevant accounting standards and domestic legislation and with the organisation's policies, regulations and procedures

Range statement

11.1.1 Limited company financial statements: income statement; balance sheet; consolidated

11.1.2 Domestic legislation: Companies Act

11.1.3 Relevant accounting standards

Knowledge and understanding

2. The general legal framework of limited companies and the obligations of directors in respect of the financial statements (Element 11.1)

3. The statutory form of accounting statements and disclosure requirements (Element 11.1)

Knowledge and understanding (cont'd)

4   The UK regulatory framework for financial reporting and the main requirements of relevant Financial Reporting Standards
7   Preparing financial statements in proper form (Element 11.1)
11 The general principles of consolidation (Element 11.1)
12 How the accounting systems of an organisation are affected by its roles, organisational structure, its administrative systems and procedures and the nature of its business transactions (Elements 11.1 & 11.2)

1 Introduction

You will probably know that many large companies actually consist of several companies controlled by one central or administrative company. Together, these companies are called a **group**.

2 Groups and consolidation: an overview

2.1 How does a group arise?

The central company, called a **parent**, generally owns most or all of the shares in the other companies, which are called **subsidiaries**.

The parent company usually **controls** the subsidiary by owning most of the shares, but share ownership is not always the same as control, which can arise in other ways.

Businesses may operate as a group for all sorts of practical reasons. If you were going out for a pizza, you might go to Pizza Hut; if you wanted some fried chicken you might go to KFC. Both sound more appetising than 'Tricon', the parent company of these subsidiaries.

However, from the legal point of view, the **results of a group must be presented as a whole**. In other words, they need to be **consolidated**. Consolidation will be defined more formally later in the chapter. Basically, it means **presenting the results of a group of companies as if they were a single company**.

2.2 What does consolidation involve?

Before moving on to the formal definitions, think about what consolidation involves.

BASIC PRINCIPLES

- Consolidation means **adding together**.
- Consolidation means **cancellation of like items** internal to the group.
- Consolidate as if you **owned everything** then **show** the **extent to which you do not** own everything.

What does this mean? Consider the following example.

12: INTRODUCTION TO GROUP ACCOUNTS

Example to show basic principles

There are two companies, Pleasant Ltd and Sweet Ltd. Pleasant owns 80% of the shares in Sweet. Pleasant has a head office building worth £100,000. Sweet has a factory worth £80,000. Remember that consolidation means presenting the results of two companies as if they were one.

Solution

You add together the values of the head office building and the factory to get an asset, land and buildings, in the group accounts of £100,000 + £80,000 = £180,000. So far so good; this is what you would expect consolidation to mean.

Example continued

Suppose Pleasant has debtors of £40,000 and Sweet has debtors of £30,000. Included in the debtors of Pleasant is £5,000 owed by Sweet. Remember again that consolidation means presenting the results of the two companies as if they were one.

Do we then simply add together £40,000 and £30,000 to arrive at the figure for consolidated debtors? We cannot simply do this, because £5,000 of the debtors is owed within the group. This amount is irrelevant when we consider what the group as a whole is owed.

Suppose further that Pleasant has creditors of £50,000 and Sweet has creditors of £45,000. We already know that £5,000 of Sweet's creditors is a balance owed to Pleasant. If we just added the figures together, we would not reflect fairly the amount the group owes to the outside world. The outside world does not care what these companies owe to each other – that is an internal matter for the group.

Solution

To arrive at a fair picture we eliminate both the debtor of £5,000 in Pleasant's books and the creditor of £5,000 in Sweet's books. Only then do we consolidate by adding together.

Consolidated debtors = £40,000 + £30,000 − £5,000
 = £65,000

Consolidated creditors = £50,000 + £45,000 − £5,000
 = £90,000

Example continued

So far we have established that consolidation means adding together any items that are not eliminated as internal to the group. Going back to the example, however, we see that Pleasant only owns 80% of Sweet. Should we not then add Pleasant's assets and liabilities to 80% of Sweet's?

PART D   SIMPLE CONSOLIDATED ACCOUNTS

Solution

The answer is no. Pleasant **controls** Sweet, its subsidiary. The directors of Pleasant can visit **all** of Sweet's factory, if they wish, not just 80% of it. So the figure for consolidated land and buildings is £100,000 plus £80,000 as stated above.

However, if we just add the figures together, we are not telling the whole story. There may well be one or more shareholders who own the remaining 20% of the shares in Sweet Ltd. These shareholders cannot visit 20% of the factory or tell 20% of the workforce what to do, but they do have an **interest** in 20% of the net assets of Sweet. The answer is to show this **minority interest** separately in the bottom half of the consolidated balance sheet.

2.3 To sum up

- Consolidation means adding together (uncancelled items).
- Consolidation means cancellation of like items internal to the group.
- Consolidate as if you owned everything then show the extent to which you do not.

IMPORTANT!
Keep these basic principles in mind as you work through the detailed techniques of group accounts.

3 Definitions

Now you know what a group is in general terms and what consolidation means in principle, you are ready to learn some more formal definitions.

These definitions have come up in exams, so you need to know them.

3.1 Parent and subsidiary undertakings: definition

Group accounts are governed by FRS 2 *Accounting for subsidiary undertakings*. FRS 2 states that an undertaking is the **parent undertaking** of another undertaking (**a subsidiary undertaking**) if any of the following apply.

> **PARENT UNDERTAKING**
>
> (a)   It holds a majority of the voting rights in the undertaking.
>
> (b)   It is a member of the undertaking and has the right to appoint or remove directors holding a majority of the voting rights at meetings of the board on all, or substantially all, matters.
>
> (c)   It has the right to exercise a dominant influence over the undertaking:
>
>   (i)   by virtue of provisions contained in the undertaking's memorandum or articles; or

> (ii) by virtue of a control contract (in writing, authorised by the memorandum or articles of the controlled undertaking, permitted by law).
>
> (d) It is a member of the undertaking and controls alone, under an agreement with other shareholders or members, a majority of the voting rights in the undertaking.
>
> (e) It has a participating interest in the undertaking and:
>
>   (i) it actually exercises a dominant influence over the undertaking; or
>   (ii) it and the undertaking are managed on a unified basis.
>
> (f) A parent undertaking is also treated as the parent undertaking of the subsidiary undertakings of its subsidiary undertakings (a sub-subsidiary).

3.2 Other definitions

The above definition is extremely important and you may be asked to apply it to a given situation in an exam. It depends in turn, however, on the definition of various terms which are included in the definition.

3.2.1 Participating interest

FRS 2 states that a **participating** interest is an interest held by an undertaking in the shares of another undertaking which it holds on a **long-term basis** for the purpose of securing a contribution to its activities by the exercise of control or influence arising from or related to that interest.

(a) A holding of **20% or more** of the shares of an undertaking is **presumed** to be a participating interest unless the contrary is shown.

(b) An interest in shares includes an interest which is convertible into an interest in shares, and includes an option to acquire shares or any interest which is convertible into shares.

(c) An interest held on behalf of an undertaking shall be treated as held by that undertaking (ie all group holdings must be aggregated to determine if a subsidiary exists).

A 'participating interest', like an investment in a 'subsidiary undertaking', **need not be in a company**, because an 'undertaking' means one of three things.

(a) A body corporate
(b) A partnership
(c) An unincorporated association carrying on a trade or business, with or without a view to profit

3.2.2 Dominant influence

> **Dominant influence** is influence that can be exercised to achieve the operating and financial policies desired by the holder of the influence, notwithstanding the rights or influence of any other party. *(FRS 2)*

The standard then distinguishes between the two different situations involving dominant influence.

(a) In the context of the definition above, **the right to exercise a dominant influence** means that the holder has a right to give directions regarding the operating and financial policies of another undertaking with which its directors are obliged to comply, whether or not they are for the benefit of that undertaking.

(b) **The actual exercise of dominant influence** means that the operating and financial policies of the undertaking influenced are set in accordance with the wishes of the holder of the influence and for the holder's benefit whether or not those wishes are explicit. The actual exercise of dominant influence is identified by its effect in practice rather than by the way in which it is exercised.

There are four other important definitions.

> (a) **Control** is the ability of an undertaking to direct the financial and operating policies of another undertaking with a view to gaining economic benefits from its activities.
>
> (b) An **interest held on a long-term basis** is an interest which is held other than exclusively with a view to subsequent resale.
>
> (c) An **interest held exclusively with a view to subsequent resale** is either:
>
> (i) an interest for which a purchaser has been identified or is being sought, and which is reasonably expected to be disposed of within approximately one year of its date of acquisition; or
>
> (ii) an interest that was acquired as a result of the enforcement of a security, unless the interest has become part of the continuing activities of the group or the holder acts as if it intends the interest to become so.
>
> (d) **Managed on a unified basis:** two or more undertakings are managed on a unified basis if the whole of the operations of the undertakings are integrated and they are managed as a single unit. Unified management does not arise solely because one undertaking manages another.

Other definitions from the standard will be introduced where relevant over the next two chapters.

3.3 The requirement to consolidate

FRS 2 requires a parent undertaking to prepare consolidated financial statements for its group unless it uses one of the exemptions available in the standard (see Section 4).

> **Consolidation** is defined as: 'The process of adjusting and combining financial information from the individual financial statements of a parent undertaking and its subsidiary undertaking to prepare consolidated financial statements that present financial information for the group as a single economic entity.'
>
> **Consolidated accounts** are one form of group accounts which combines the information contained in the separate accounts of a holding company and its subsidiaries as if they were the accounts of a single entity.

In simple terms a set of consolidated accounts is prepared by **adding together** the assets and liabilities of the holding company and each subsidiary.

(a) The **whole** of the assets and liabilities of each company are included, even though some subsidiaries may be only partly owned.

(b) The 'capital and reserves' side of the balance sheet will indicate how much of the net assets are attributable to the group and how much to outside investors in partly owned subsidiaries. These **outside investors** are known as **minority interests**.

Most parent companies present their own individual accounts and their group accounts in a single **package**. The package typically comprises:

(a) **Parent company balance sheet**, which will include 'investments in subsidiary undertakings' as an asset
(b) Consolidated balance sheet
(c) Consolidated profit and loss account
(d) Consolidated cash flow statement

It is not necessary to publish a parent company profit and loss account (s 230 CA 1985), provided the consolidated profit and loss account contains a note stating the profit or loss for the financial year dealt with in the accounts of the parent company and the fact that the statutory exemption is being relied on.

4 Exclusion of subsidiary undertakings from group accounts

S 229 CA 1985 (as amended by the CA 1989) provides that a **subsidiary may be omitted** from the consolidated accounts of a group in **any** of these cases.

(a) In the opinion of the directors, its inclusion 'is **not material** for the purpose of giving a true and fair view; but two or more undertakings may be excluded only if they are not material taken together'.

(b) There are **severe long-term restrictions** in exercising the parent company's rights.

(c) The holding is **exclusively for resale**.

(d) The information cannot be obtained 'without **disproportionate expense** or undue delay'.

If in the opinion of the directors, a subsidiary undertaking's consolidation is undesirable because the **business of the holding company and subsidiary are so different that they cannot reasonably be treated as a single undertaking, then that undertaking** *must* **be excluded.**

> This .... does not apply merely because some of the undertakings are industrial, some commercial and some provide services, or because they carry on industrial or commercial activities involving different products or provide different services.

FRS 2 states that a **subsidiary must be excluded** from consolidation in some cases.

(a) Severe long-term restrictions are **substantially hindering the exercise** of the **parent's rights** over the subsidiary's assets or management.

(b) The group's interest in the subsidiary undertaking is held **exclusively with a view to subsequent resale** *and* the subsidiary has **not been consolidated previously**.

(c) The subsidiary undertaking's **activities are so different** from those of other undertakings to be included in the consolidation that its inclusion would be incompatible with the obligation to give a true and fair view.

The FRS requires the circumstances in which subsidiary undertakings are to be excluded from consolidation to be interpreted **strictly**.

Where a subsidiary is excluded from group accounts, FRS 2 lays down **supplementary provisions** on the disclosures and accounting treatment required.

5 Exemption from the requirement to prepare group accounts

The CA 1989 introduced a completely new provision **exempting some groups** from preparing consolidated accounts. There are two grounds.

(a) **Smaller groups** can claim exemptions on grounds of size (see below).

(b) **Parent companies** (*except* for listed companies) **whose immediate parent is established in an EU member country** need not prepare consolidated accounts. The accounts must give the name and country of incorporation of the parent and state the fact of the exemption. In addition, a copy of the audited consolidated accounts of the parent must be filed with the UK company's accounts. Minority shareholders can, however, require that consolidated accounts are prepared.

FRS 2 adds that exemption may be gained if all of the parent's subsidiary undertakings gain exemption under s 229 CA 1985.

The **exemption** from preparing consolidated accounts is **not available** to:

- Public companies
- Banking and insurance companies
- Authorised persons under the Financial Services Act 1986
- Companies belonging to a group containing a member of the above

Any two of the following **size criteria** for small and medium-sized groups must be met.

	Small	Medium-sized
Aggregate turnover	$\leq$ £2.8 million net/ £3.36 million gross	$\leq$ £11.2 million net/ £13.44 million gross
Aggregate gross assets	$\leq$ £1.4 million net/ £1.68 million gross	$\leq$ £5.6 million net/ £6.72 million gross
Aggregate number of employees (average monthly)	$\leq$ 50	$\leq$ 250

The aggregates can be calculated either before (gross) or after (net) consolidation adjustments for intra-group sales, unrealised profit on stock and so on (see following chapters). The qualifying conditions must be met in the **present and previous financial year**.

When the exemption is claimed, but the auditors believe that the company is not entitled to it, then they must state in their report that the company is in their opinion not entitled to the exemption and this report must be attached to the individual accounts of the company (ie no report is required when the company *is* entitled to the exemption).

Activity 12.1

Apple Ltd owns 60% of Pear Ltd. Apple has creditors of £120,000. Pear has creditors of £90,000 of which £10,000 is owed to Apple. Apple has debtors of £60,000 and Pear has debtors of £40,000. Apple has fixed assets of £80,000 and Pear has fixed assets of £50,000.

(a) Consolidated fixed assets is calculated as

	£
Apple	80,000
Pear 60% × £50,000	30,000
	110,000

True or false? Explain your answer.

(b) Calculate

  (i) Consolidated debtors
  (ii) Consolidated creditors

PART D SIMPLE CONSOLIDATED ACCOUNTS

Key learning points

- ☑ This chapter has explained the concept of a **group** and introduced several important principles and definitions.
- ☑ Consolidation means presenting the results, assets and liabilities of a group of companies as if they were one company.
- ☑ Consolidation means adding together non-cancelled items.
- ☑ Intra-group items should be cancelled.
- ☑ Consolidate as if you owned everything, and then show the extent to which you do not.
- ☑ The principal **regulations** governing the preparation of group accounts have been explained. Many of these are hard to understand and you should re-read this chapter after you have completed your study of this section of the text.

Quick quiz

1. Company A holds 45% of the shares of Company B. Company B cannot, therefore, be a subsidiary of Company A. True or false?

2. Company A holds 25% of the shares of Company B. Does it therefore hold a participating interest?

3. What is dominant influence?

4. A group's interest in a subsidiary undertaking is held exclusively with a view to resale. The subsidiary has not been consolidated previously. Consolidation of the subsidiary is therefore optional. True or false?

5. What are the grounds on which some groups may be exempted from preparing consolidated accounts?

6. **Fill in the blanks** in the statements below, using the words in the box.

    Per FRS 2, A is a parent of B if:

    (a) A holds (1) .... in B
    (b) A can appoint or remove (2) ....
    (c) A has the right to exercise (3) .... over B
    (d) B is a (4) .... of A

• Sub-subsidiary	• Dominant influence
• Directors holding a majority of the voting rights	• A majority of the voting rights

Answers to quick quiz

1. False. There are five other criteria (see Paragraph 2.2) which determine whether or not Company B is a subsidiary of Company A.

2. Company A will be presumed to hold a participating interest unless the contrary is shown.

3. The influence that can be exercised to achieve the operating and financial policies desired by the holder of the influence notwithstanding the rights or influences of any other party (FRS 2).

4. False. The subsidiary **must** be excluded from consolidation (FRS 2).

5. (a) Smaller groups may claim exemption on grounds of size.

    (b) Parent companies (other than listed companies) whose immediate parent is established in an EU member country need not prepare consolidated accounts.

6. (a) A majority of the voting rights
    (b) Directors holding a majority of the voting rights
    (c) Dominant influence
    (d) Sub-subsidiary

PART D SIMPLE CONSOLIDATED ACCOUNTS

Activity checklist

This checklist shows which performance criteria, range statement or knowledge and understanding point is covered by each activity in this chapter. Tick off each activity as you complete it.

Activity

12.1 ☐ This activity deals with Knowledge & Understanding point 11: general principles of consolidation.

chapter 13

The consolidated balance sheet

Contents

1. Introduction
2. Cancellation and part cancellation
3. Minority interests
4. Dividends payable by a subsidiary
5. Goodwill arising on consolidation
6. A technique of consolidation
7. Inter-company trading
8. Overview: consolidated balance sheet

Performance criteria

11.1.A Draft limited company financial statements from the appropriate information

11.1.B Correctly identify and implement subsequent adjustments and ensure that discrepancies, unusual features or queries are identified and either resolved or referred to the appropriate person

11.1.C Ensure that limited company financial statements comply with relevant accounting standards and domestic legislation and with the organisation's policies, regulations and procedures

Range statement

11.1.1 Limited company financial statements: income statement; balance sheet; consolidated

11.1.2 Domestic legislation: Companies Act

11.1.3 Relevant accounting standards

Knowledge and understanding

2. The general legal framework of limited companies and the obligations of Directors in respect of the financial statements (Element 11.1)

3. The statutory form of accounting statements and disclosure requirements (Element 11.1)

Knowledge and understanding (continued)

4　The UK regulatory framework for financial reporting and the main requirements of relevant Financial Reporting Standards (Element 11.1)

7　Preparing financial statements in proper form (Element 11.1)

11　The general principles of consolidation (Element 11.1)

12　How the accounting systems of an organisation are affected by its roles, organisational structure, its administrative systems and procedures and the nature of its business transactions (Elements 11.1 & 11.2)

1 Introduction

We looked at consolidation in Chapter 12. Now we will look in detail at the mechanics of producing a consolidated balance sheet.

2 Cancellation and part cancellation

> **Signpost**
> The AAT's Guidance for Unit 11 states that **only simple consolidations will be assessed**.

2.1 What needs to be cancelled?

As indicated in Chapter 12, the preparation of a consolidated balance sheet, in a very simple form, consists of two procedures.

(a) Take the individual accounts of the holding company and each subsidiary and **cancel out items** which appear as an asset in one company and a liability in another.

(b) **Add together all the uncancelled assets** and liabilities throughout the group.

Items requiring cancellation may include the following.

(a) There may be **inter-company trading** within the group. For example, S Ltd may sell goods to H Ltd. H Ltd would then be a debtor in the accounts of S Ltd, while S Ltd would be a creditor in the accounts of H Ltd. You covered this briefly in Chapter 12.

(b) The asset **'shares in subsidiary companies'** which appears in the parent company's accounts will be matched with the liability 'share capital' in the subsidiaries' accounts.

This second item requires explanation. A shareholder in a parent company, looking at the parent company's accounts, will see an asset 'investment in subsidiary' shown at cost. However, a shareholder in a parent company is also a shareholder in the group. Showing the investment at cost does not give a true picture of the assets and liabilities which the parent company controls. This is achieved by consolidating, ie cancelling like items and adding together uncancelled items.

So what is the item in the subsidiary's account that corresponds to the figure 'investment in subsidiary' in the accounts of the parent company? The answer is the subsidiary has issued share capital which the parent has purchased.

Example: cancellation

Parent Ltd has just bought 100% of the shares of Subsidiary Ltd. Below are the balance sheets of both companies just before consolidation.

PARENT LIMITED BALANCE SHEET	£'000	SUBSIDIARY LIMITED BALANCE SHEET	£'000
Assets			
Investment in subsidiary*	50	Debtors	20
Debtors	30	Cash	30
	80		50
Share capital	80	Share capital*	50
	80		50

* Cancelling items

The consolidated balance sheet will appear as follows.

PARENT AND SUBSIDIARY
CONSOLIDATED BALANCE SHEET

	£'000
Debtors (30 + 20)	50
Cash	30
	80
Share capital**	80
	80

**Note. This is the parent company's share capital only. The subsidiary's has been cancelled.

PART D   SIMPLE CONSOLIDATED ACCOUNTS

Example: cancellation with intercompany trading

P Ltd regularly sells goods to its one subsidiary company, S Ltd. The balance sheets of the two companies on 31 December 20X6 are given below.

P LIMITED
BALANCE SHEET AS AT 31 DECEMBER 20X6

	£	£	£
Fixed assets			
Tangible assets			35,000
40,000 £1 shares in S Ltd at cost			40,000
			75,000
Current assets			
Stocks		16,000	
Debtors: S Ltd	2,000		
Other	6,000		
		8,000	
Cash at bank		1,000	
		25,000	
Current liabilities			
Creditors		14,000	
			11,000
			86,000
Capital and reserves			
70,000 £1 ordinary shares			70,000
Reserves			16,000
			86,000

S LIMITED
BALANCE SHEET AS AT 31 DECEMBER 20X6

	£	£	£
Fixed assets			
Tangible assets			45,000
Current assets			
Stocks		12,000	
Debtors		9,000	
		21,000	
Current liabilities			
Bank overdraft		3,000	
Creditors: P Ltd	2,000		
Other	2,000		
		4,000	
		7,000	
			14,000
			59,000
Capital and reserves			
40,000 £1 ordinary shares			40,000
Reserves			19,000
			59,000

Prepare the consolidated balance sheet of P Ltd.

Solution

The cancelling items are:

(a) P Ltd's asset 'investment in shares of S Ltd' (£40,000) cancels with S Ltd's liability 'share capital' (£40,000);

(b) P Ltd's asset 'debtors: S Ltd' (£2,000) cancels with S Ltd's liability 'creditors: P Ltd' (£2,000).

The remaining assets and liabilities are added together to produce the following consolidated balance sheet.

P LIMITED
CONSOLIDATED BALANCE SHEET AS AT 31 DECEMBER 20X6

	£	£
Fixed assets		
Tangible assets		80,000
Current assets		
Stocks		28,000
Debtors		15,000
Cash at bank	1,000	
	44,000	
Current liabilities		
Bank overdraft	3,000	
Creditors	16,000	
	19,000	
		25,000
		105,000
Capital and reserves		
70,000 £1 ordinary shares		70,000
Reserves		35,000
		105,000

2.1.1 Notes on the example

(a) P Ltd's bank balance is not netted off with S Ltd's bank overdraft. To offset one against the other would be less informative and would conflict with the statutory principle that assets and liabilities should not be netted off.

(b) The share capital in the consolidated balance sheet is the share capital of the parent company alone. This must *always* be the case, no matter how complex the consolidation, because the share capital of subsidiary companies must *always* be a wholly cancelling item.

2.2 Part cancellation

An item may appear in the balance sheets of a parent company and its subsidiary, but not at the same amounts.

(a) The parent company may have acquired **shares in the subsidiary** at a price **greater or less than their nominal value**. The asset will appear in the parent company's accounts at cost, while the liability will appear in the subsidiary's accounts at nominal value. This raises the issue of **goodwill**, which is dealt with later in this chapter.

(b) Even if the parent company acquired shares at nominal value, it **may not** have **acquired all the shares of the subsidiary** (so the subsidiary may be only partly owned). This raises the issue of **minority interests**, which you touched on in Chapter 12 and which are also dealt with later in this chapter.

The Chief Assessor has commented that some candidates show a lack of awareness of what consolidation is doing. For example, the investment in the subsidiary is shown in the consolidated balance sheet.

3 Minority interests

Let's recap on the general principles covered in the previous chapter.

- Consolidation means adding together of uncancelled items.
- Consolidation means adding together of like items.
- Consolidate as if you owned everything and then show the extent to which you do not.

It is this third concept of minority interest with which we are now concerned.

Following the above principle, the total assets and liabilities of subsidiary companies are included in the consolidated balance sheet, even in the case of subsidiaries which are only partly owned. A proportion of the net assets of such subsidiaries in fact belongs to investors from outside the group (minority interests).

> FRS 2 defines **minority interest** in a subsidiary undertaking as the 'interest in a subsidiary undertaking included in the consolidation that is attributable to the shares held by or on behalf of persons other than the parent undertaking and its subsidiary undertakings'.

In the consolidated balance sheet it is necessary to distinguish this proportion from those assets attributable to the group and financed by shareholders' funds.

The net assets of a company are financed by share capital and reserves. The consolidation procedure for dealing with partly owned subsidiaries is to **calculate the proportion of ordinary shares and reserves attributable to minority interests.**

Example: minority interests

P Ltd has owned 75% of the share capital of S Ltd since the date of S Ltd's incorporation. Their latest balance sheets are given below.

P LIMITED
BALANCE SHEET

	£
Fixed assets	
Tangible assets	50,000
30,000 £1 ordinary shares in S Ltd at cost → *Does not appear on CBS*	30,000
	80,000
Net current assets	25,000
	105,000
Capital and reserves	
80,000 £1 ordinary shares	80,000
Reserves	25,000
	105,000

S LIMITED
BALANCE SHEET

	£
Tangible fixed assets	35,000
Net current assets	15,000
	50,000
Capital and reserves	
40,000 £1 ordinary shares	40,000
Reserves	10,000
	50,000

Prepare the consolidated balance sheet.

Solution

All of S Ltd's net assets are consolidated despite the fact that the company is only 75% owned. The amount of net assets attributable to minority interests is calculated as follows.

	£
Minority share of share capital (25% × £40,000)	10,000
Minority share of reserves (25% × £10,000)	2,500
	12,500

Of S Ltd's share capital of £40,000, £10,000 is included in the figure for minority interest, while £30,000 is cancelled with P Ltd's asset 'investment in S Ltd'.

The consolidated balance sheet can now be prepared.

P GROUP
CONSOLIDATED BALANCE SHEET

	£
Tangible fixed assets	85,000
Net current assets	40,000
	125,000
Share capital	80,000
Reserves £(25,000 + (75% × 10,000))	32,500
Shareholders' funds	112,500
Minority interest	12,500
	125,000

In this example we have shown minority interest on the 'capital and reserves' side of the balance sheet to illustrate how some of S Ltd's net assets are financed by shareholders' funds, while some are financed by outside investors. You may see minority interest as a deduction from the other side of the balance sheet. The second half of the balance sheet will then consist entirely of shareholders' funds.

In more complicated examples the following technique is recommended for dealing with minority interests.

Step 1. Cancel common items in the draft balance sheets. If there is a minority interest, the subsidiary company's share capital will be a partly cancelled item. Ascertain the proportion of ordinary shares held by the minority.

Step 2. Produce a working for the minority interest. Add in the amounts of ordinary share capital calculated in step 1: this completes the cancellation of the subsidiary's share capital.

Add also the minority's share of reserves in the subsidiary company.

Step 3. Produce a separate working for each reserve (capital, revenue etc) found in the subsidiary company's balance sheet. The initial balances on these accounts will be taken straight from the draft balance sheets of the parent and subsidiary company.

Step 4. The closing balances in these workings can be entered directly onto the consolidated balance sheet.

Activity 13.1

Set out below are the draft balance sheets of P Ltd and its subsidiary S Ltd. You are required to prepare the consolidated balance sheet.

P LIMITED

	£
Fixed assets	
Tangible assets	31,000
Investment in S Ltd	
12,000 £1 ordinary shares at cost	12,000
	43,000
Net current assets	11,000
	54,000
Capital and reserves	
Ordinary shares of £1 each	40,000
Reserves	14,000
	54,000

S LIMITED

	£
Tangible fixed assets	25,000
Net current assets	5,000
	30,000
Capital and reserves	
Ordinary shares of £1 each	20,000
Reserves	10,000
	30,000

4 Dividends payable by a subsidiary

4.1 Paid and proposed dividends

When a subsidiary company pays a dividend during the year the accounting treatment is not difficult. Suppose S Ltd, a 60% subsidiary of H Ltd, pays a dividend of £1,000 on the last day of its accounting period. Its total reserves before paying the dividend stood at £5,000.

(a) £400 of the dividend is paid to minority shareholders. The cash leaves the group and will not appear anywhere in the consolidated balance sheet.

(b) The holding company receives £600 of the dividend, debiting cash and crediting profit and loss account.

(c) The remaining balance of reserves in S Ltd's balance sheet (£4,000) will be consolidated in the normal way. The group's share (60% × £4,000 = £2,400) will be included in group reserves in the balance sheet; the minority share (40% × £4,000 = £1,600) is credited to the minority interest account.

More care is needed when dealing with **proposed dividends** not yet paid by a subsidiary. The first step must be to ensure that the draft accounts of both subsidiary and parent company are up-to-date and reflect the proposed dividend.

PART D SIMPLE CONSOLIDATED ACCOUNTS

A question may state that both companies have accrued for the proposed dividend; alternatively you may be presented with draft balance sheets in which one or other company, or possibly both companies, have omitted to make the necessary entries.

If neither company has accrued for the proposed dividend you will need to make appropriate adjustments to the draft balance sheets.

(a) If the subsidiary has not yet accrued for the proposed dividend, the adjustment is:

DEBIT Revenue reserves
CREDIT Dividends payable

with the full amount of the dividend payable in the subsidiary's books, whether it is due to the parent company or to minority shareholders.

(b) If the parent company has not yet accrued for its share of the proposed dividend, the adjustment is:

DEBIT Debtors (dividend receivable)
CREDIT Revenue reserves

with the *parent company's share* of the dividend receivable in the parent's books.

On consolidation, the **dividend payable** in S Ltd's accounts will **cancel with the dividend receivable** in H Ltd's accounts. If S Ltd is a wholly owned subsidiary, there will be complete cancellation; if S Ltd is only partly owned, there will be only part cancellation. The uncancelled portion will be the amount of dividend payable to minority shareholders and this will appear in the consolidated balance sheet as a current liability.

When preparing the workings for reserves and minority interest, the relevant reserves figures for both companies are the figures *after* adjusting for the proposed dividend.

Example: dividends

Set out below are the draft balance sheets of Hug Ltd and its subsidiary Bug Ltd. Hug Ltd has not yet taken account of the dividend proposed by Bug Ltd.

You are required to prepare the consolidated balance sheet.

HUG LIMITED

	£	£
Fixed assets		
Tangible assets		1,350
Investment in Bug Ltd: 1,500 shares at cost		1,500
		2,850
Current assets	700	
Current liabilities		
Creditors	400	
		300
		3,150
Capital and reserves		
Ordinary shares of £1 each		1,000
Revenue reserves		2,150
		3,150

BUG LIMITED

	£	£
Tangible fixed assets		2,500
Current assets	900	
Current liabilities		
Creditors	200	
Proposed dividend	200	
	500	500
		3,000
Capital and reserves		
Ordinary shares of £1 each		2,000
Revenue reserves		1,000
		3,000

Solution

The first step is to bring Hug Ltd's balance sheet up to date by accruing for its share of the dividend receivable from Bug Ltd. Hug Ltd owns 75% (1,500/2,000) of the shares in Bug Ltd. Its share of the proposed dividend is therefore 75% × £200 = £150. Hug Ltd's draft balance sheet should be adjusted as follows.

DEBIT	Debtors: dividend receivable	£150	
CREDIT	Revenue reserves		£150

Next deal with cancellation. There are two part-cancelling items, the shares of Bug Ltd and the dividend receivable/payable.

The workings may now be produced. Notice how the relevant reserves figures are the figures after adjusting for the proposed dividend. Because Bug Ltd's accounts are up-to-date, and reflect the proposed figure, the correct reserves figure (£1,000) can be taken straight from the draft balance sheet. In the case of Hug Ltd, it is the adjusted reserves figure (£2,150 + £150 = £2,300) which is used.

Workings

1   Minority interests

	£
Share capital (25% × 2,000)	500
Revenue reserves (25% × 1,000)	250
	750

2   Revenue reserves

	£
Hug Ltd (as adjusted)	2,300
Share of Bug Ltd's revenue reserves (1,000 × 75%)	750
	3,050

HUG GROUP
CONSOLIDATED BALANCE SHEET

	£	£
Tangible fixed assets		3,850
Current assets	1,600	
Current liabilities		
Creditors	600	
Minority proposed dividend	50	
		950
		4,800
Capital and reserves		
Ordinary shares of £1 each		1,000
Revenue reserves		3,050
Shareholders' funds		4,050
Minority interests		750
		4,800

5 Goodwill arising on consolidation

5.1 Introduction to goodwill

In the examples we have looked at so far the cost of shares acquired by the parent company has always been equal to the nominal value of those shares. This is seldom the case in practice and we must now consider some more complicated examples. To begin with, **we will examine the entries made by the parent company in its own balance sheet when it acquires shares.**

When a company P Ltd wishes to **purchase shares** in a company S Ltd it must pay the previous owners of those shares. The most obvious form of payment would be in **cash**. Suppose P Ltd purchases all 40,000 £1 shares in S Ltd and pays £60,000 cash to the previous shareholders in consideration. The entries in P Ltd's books would be:

DEBIT	Investment in S Ltd at cost	£60,000	
CREDIT	Bank		£60,000

However, the previous shareholders might be prepared to accept some other form of consideration. For example, they might accept an agreed number of **shares** in P Ltd. P Ltd would then issue new shares in the agreed number and allot them to the former shareholders of S Ltd. This kind of deal might be attractive to P Ltd since it avoids the need for a heavy cash outlay. The former shareholders of S Ltd would retain an indirect interest in that company's profitability via their new holding in its parent company.

Continuing the example, suppose the shareholders of S Ltd agreed to accept one £1 ordinary share in P Ltd for every two £1 ordinary shares in S Ltd. P Ltd would then need to issue and allot 20,000 new £1 shares. How would this transaction be recorded in the books of P Ltd?

The simplest method would be as follows.

DEBIT	Investment in S Ltd	£20,000	
CREDIT	Share capital		£20,000

However, if the 40,000 £1 shares acquired in S Ltd are thought to have a value of £60,000 this would be misleading. The former shareholders of S Ltd have presumably agreed to accept 20,000 shares in P Ltd because they consider each of those shares to have a value of £3. This view of the matter suggests the following method of recording the transaction in P Ltd's books.

DEBIT	Investment in S Ltd	£60,000	
CREDIT	Share capital		£20,000
	Share premium account		£40,000

The second method is the one which the Companies Act 1985 requires should normally be used in preparing consolidated accounts.

The amount which P Ltd records in its books as the cost of its investment in S Ltd may be more or less than the book value of the assets it acquires. Suppose that S Ltd in the previous example has nil reserves, so that its share capital of £40,000 is balanced by net assets with a book value of £40,000. For simplicity, assume that the book value of S Ltd's assets is the same as their market or fair value.

Now when the directors of P Ltd agree to pay £60,000 for a 100% investment in S Ltd they must believe that, in addition to its tangible assets of £40,000, S Ltd must also have intangible assets worth £20,000. This amount of £20,000 paid over and above the value of the tangible assets acquired is called **goodwill arising on consolidation** (sometimes **premium on acquisition**).

Following the normal cancellation procedure the £40,000 share capital in S Ltd's balance sheet could be cancelled against £40,000 of the 'investment in S Limited' in the balance sheet of P Ltd. This would leave a £20,000 debit uncancelled in the parent company's accounts and this £20,000 would appear in the consolidated balance sheet under the caption 'Intangible fixed assets. Goodwill arising on consolidation' (although see below for FRS 10's requirements on this type of goodwill).

5.2 Goodwill and pre-acquisition profits

Up to now we have assumed that S Ltd had nil reserves when its shares were purchased by P Ltd. Assuming instead that S Ltd had earned profits of £8,000 in the period before acquisition, its balance sheet just before the purchase would look as follows.

	£
Net tangible assets	48,000
Share capital	40,000
Reserves	8,000
	48,000

If P Ltd now purchases all the shares in S Ltd it will acquire net tangible assets worth £48,000 at a cost of £60,000. Clearly in this case S Ltd's intangible assets (goodwill) are being valued at £12,000. It should be apparent that any **reserves** earned by the subsidiary **prior to its acquisition** by the parent company must be **incorporated in the cancellation** process so as to arrive at a figure for goodwill arising on consolidation. In other words, not only S Ltd's share capital, but also its pre-acquisition reserves, must be cancelled against the asset 'investment in S Ltd' in the accounts of the parent company. The uncancelled balance of £12,000 appears in the consolidated balance sheet.

The consequence of this is that **any pre-acquisition reserves of a subsidiary company are not aggregated with the parent company's reserves** in the consolidated balance sheet. The figure of consolidated reserves comprises the

PART D SIMPLE CONSOLIDATED ACCOUNTS

reserves of the parent company plus the post-acquisition reserves only of subsidiary companies. The post-acquisition reserves are simply reserves now less reserves at acquisition.

POINT TO NOTE!

If you're confused by this, think of it another way, from the point of view of group reserves. Only the profits earned by the group should be consolidated. Profits earned by the subsidiary before it became part of the group are not group profits; they reflect what the parent company is getting for its money on acquisition.

Example: goodwill and pre-acquisition profits

Sing Ltd acquired the ordinary shares of Wing Ltd on 31 March when the draft balance sheets of each company were as follows.

SING LIMITED
BALANCE SHEET AS AT 31 MARCH

	£
Fixed assets	
Investment in 50,000 shares of Wing Ltd at cost	80,000
Net current assets	40,000
	120,000
Capital and reserves	
Ordinary shares	75,000
Revenue reserves	45,000
	120,000

WING LIMITED
BALANCE SHEET AS AT 31 MARCH

	£
Net current assets	60,000
Share capital and reserves	
50,000 ordinary shares of £1 each	50,000
Revenue reserves	10,000
	60,000

Prepare the consolidated balance sheet as at 31 March.

Solution

The technique to adopt here is to produce a new working: 'Goodwill'. A proforma working is set out below.

Goodwill

	£	£
Cost of investment		X
Share of net assets acquired as represented by:		
Ordinary share capital	X	
Share premium	X	
Reserves on acquisition	X	
Group share	%	(X)
Goodwill		X

Applying this to our example the working will look like this.

	£	£
Cost of investment		80,000
Share of net assets acquired as represented by:		
Ordinary share capital	50,000	
Revenue reserves on acquisition	10,000	
	60,000	
Group share 100%		60,000
Goodwill		20,000

SING LIMITED
CONSOLIDATED BALANCE SHEET AS AT 31 MARCH

	£
Fixed assets	
Goodwill arising on consolidation	20,000
Net current assets	100,000
	120,000
Capital and reserves	
Ordinary shares	75,000
Revenue reserves	45,000
	120,000

5.3 Revaluation reserves

The assets of the subsidiary may be worth more than their book value. They may therefore be **revalued** on acquisition. You have met the idea of revaluations before in connection with companies and partnerships.

The assets need to be consolidated at their **fair value**. There will be a revaluation reserve representing the difference between fair and book value. This is consolidated in the same manner as a revenue reserve. The goodwill calculation will appear as follows.

PART D   SIMPLE CONSOLIDATED ACCOUNTS

Goodwill

	£	£
Cost of investment		X
Share of net assets acquired as represented by		
Ordinary share capital	X	
Reserves on acquisition	X	
Revaluation reserve*	X	
	X	
Group share (%)		(X)
Goodwill		X

*Fair value of revalued assets less book value

5.4 FRS 10 *Goodwill and intangible assets*

Goodwill arising on consolidation is one form of **purchased goodwill** and is therefore governed by FRS 10. As explained in Chapter 5, goodwill should be **capitalised in the balance sheet** and should normally be **amortised over its useful economic life.**

The **consolidation adjustment** required each year is then as follows.

    DEBIT   Consolidated profit and loss account
    CREDIT   Provision for amortisation of goodwill

The **unamortised portion** will be included in the consolidated balance sheet under **fixed assets**.

The standard contains a presumption that the useful life of the goodwill is less than 20 years. The presumption may be rebutted. If it is greater than 20 years, goodwill must still be amortised. If it is indefinite, goodwill should not be amortised, but a full impairment review should be performed each year. (Impairment means that the recoverable amount of an asset has fallen below the carrying amount.) An impairment review should, in any case, be performed at the end of the first full year after acquisition. The impairment review should be performed in accordance with FRS 11 *Impairment of fixed assets and goodwill*.

> **Signpost**
>
> Do not worry too much about this. The question will tell you the period over which to amortise any goodwill, and past exams have generally advised you to leave it unamortised.

Goodwill arising on consolidation is the difference between the cost of an acquisition and the value of the subsidiary's net assets acquired. This difference can be **negative**: the aggregate of the fair values of the separate net assets acquired may exceed what the holding company paid for them. This 'negative goodwill', also sometimes called 'discount arising on consolidation' is required by FRS 10 to be shown as a **negative asset** in the 'assets' section of the balance sheet just below any positive goodwill. It should be released to the profit and loss account in line with the depreciation or sale of non-monetary assets acquired. (Non-monetary assets normally consist of fixed assets and stocks.)

6 A technique of consolidation

We have now looked at the topics of cancellation, minority interests and goodwill arising on consolidation. It is time to set out an approach to be used in tackling consolidated balance sheets. The approach we recommend consists of five stages.

Stage 1. Update the draft balance sheets of subsidiaries and parent company to take account of any proposed dividends not yet accrued for.

Stage 2. Agree inter-company current accounts by adjusting for items in transit.

Stage 3. Cancel items common to both balance sheets.

Stage 4. Produce working for minority interests.

Stage 5. Produce a goodwill working. Then produce a working for capital and revenue reserves, making sure to deduct from revenue reserves any pre-acquisition profits.

You should now attempt to apply this technique to the following Activity. It is taken from a past AAT exam and is about **as difficult as it gets** (not very difficult!)

Activity 13.2

You have been asked to assist in the preparation of the consolidated accounts of the Thomas group. Set out below are the balance sheets of Thomas Ltd and James Ltd for the year ended 30 September 20X6.

BALANCE SHEET AS AT 30 SEPTEMBER 20X6

	Thomas Ltd £'000	James Ltd £'000
Fixed assets	13,022	3,410
Investment in James Ltd	3,760	–
Current assets		
Stocks	6,682	2,020
Debtors	5,526	852
Cash	273	58
	12,481	2,930
Current liabilities		
Trade creditors	3,987	507
Taxation	834	173
	4,821	680
Net current assets	7,660	2,250
Total assets less current liabilities	24,442	5,660
Long-term loan	8,000	1,500
	16,442	4,160

PART D SIMPLE CONSOLIDATED ACCOUNTS

	Thomas Ltd £'000	James Ltd £'000
Capital and reserves		
Called up share capital	5,000	1,000
Share premium	2,500	400
Profit and loss account	8,942	2,760
	16,442	4,160

You have been given the following further information.

(a) The share capital of both Thomas Ltd and James Ltd consists of ordinary shares of £1 each. There have been no changes to the balances during the year.

(b) Thomas Ltd acquired 800,000 shares in James Ltd on 30 September 20X5 at a cost of £3,760,000.

(c) At 30 September 20X5 the balance on the profit and loss account of James Ltd was £2,000,000.

(d) The fair value of the fixed assets of James Ltd at 30 September 20X5 was £3,910,000. The revaluation has not been reflected in the books of James Ltd.

(e) Goodwill arising on consolidation is considered to have an indefinite life and is to remain in the balance sheet.

Task

Prepare a consolidated balance sheet for Thomas Ltd and its subsidiary undertaking as at 30 September 20X6.

7 Inter-company trading

We have already come across cases where one company in a group engages in trading with another group company. Any debtor/creditor balances outstanding between the companies are cancelled on consolidation. No further problem arises if all such intra-group transactions are undertaken at cost, without any mark-up for profit.

However, each company in a group is a separate trading entity and may wish to treat other group companies in the same way as any other customer. In this case, a company (say A Ltd) may buy goods at one price and sell them at a higher price to another group company (B Ltd). The accounts of A Ltd will quite properly include the profit earned on sales to B Ltd; and similarly B Ltd's balance sheet will include stocks at their cost to B Ltd at the amount at which they were purchased from A Ltd.

This gives rise to two problems.

(a) Although A Ltd makes a profit as soon as it sells goods to B Ltd, the group does not make a sale or achieve a profit until an outside customer buys the goods from B Ltd.

(b) Any purchases from A Ltd which remain unsold by B Ltd at the year end will be included in B Ltd's stock. Their balance sheet value will be their cost to B Ltd, which is not the same as their cost to the group.

The objective of consolidated accounts is to present the financial position of several connected companies as that of a single entity, the group. This means that **in a consolidated balance sheet the only profits recognised should be those**

earned by the group in providing goods or services to outsiders; and similarly, stock in the consolidated balance sheet should be valued at cost to the group.

Suppose that a holding company H Ltd buys goods for £1,600 and sells them to a wholly owned subsidiary S Ltd for £2,000. The goods are in S Ltd's stock at the year end and appear in S Ltd's balance sheet at £2,000. In this case, H Ltd will record a profit of £400 in its individual accounts, but from the group's point of view the figures are:

Cost	£1,600
External sales	nil
Closing stock at cost	£1,600
Profit/loss	nil

If we add together the figures for retained reserves and stock in the individual balance sheets of H Ltd and S Ltd the resulting figures for consolidated reserves and consolidated stock will each be overstated by £400. A **consolidation adjustment** is therefore necessary as follows.

DEBIT   Group reserves
CREDIT   Group stock (balance sheet)

with the amount of **profit unrealised** by the group.

Activity 13.3

H Ltd acquired all the shares in S Ltd when the reserves of S Ltd stood at £10,000. Draft balance sheets for each company are as follows.

	H Ltd		S Ltd	
	£	£	£	£
Fixed assets				
Tangible assets		80,000		40,000
Investment in S Ltd at cost		46,000		
		126,000		
Current assets	40,000		30,000	
Current liabilities	21,000		18,000	
		19,000		12,000
		145,000		52,000
Capital and reserves				
Ordinary shares of £1 each		100,000		30,000
Reserves		45,000		22,000
		145,000		52,000

During the year S Ltd sold goods to H Ltd for £50,000, the profit to S Ltd being 20% of selling price. At the balance sheet date, £15,000 of these goods remained unsold in the stocks of H Ltd. At the same date, H Ltd owed S Ltd £12,000 for goods bought and this debt is included in the creditors of H Ltd and the debtors of S Ltd.

Task

Prepare a draft consolidated balance sheet for H Ltd. Assume that the goodwill has an indefinite useful economic life.

PART D SIMPLE CONSOLIDATED ACCOUNTS

Now try some more consolidated balance sheet activities. With practice you'll soon get the hang of it.

Activity 13.4

The draft balance sheets of Oak plc and its subsidiary Chestnut Ltd at 30 September 20X8 are as follows.

	Oak plc		Chestnut Limited	
	£	£	£	£
Fixed assets				
Tangible assets, net book value				
Land and buildings		225,000		270,000
Plant		202,500		157,500
		427,500		427,500
Investment				
Shares in Chestnut Ltd at cost		562,500		
Current assets				
Stock	255,000		180,000	
Debtors	375,000		90,000	
Bank	112,500		22,500	
	742,500		292,500	
Creditors: amounts falling due within				
one year	157,500		67,500	
Net current assets		585,000		225,000
		1,575,000		652,500
Capital and reserves				
Called up share capital – issued and fully paid				
£1 ordinary shares		1,125,000		450,000
Reserves		450,000		202,500
		1,575,000		652,500

The following information is also available.

(a) Oak plc purchased 360,000 shares in Chestnut Ltd some years ago when that company had a credit balance of £105,000 in reserves. The goodwill was fully amortised through the profit and loss account by 30 September 20X7.

(b) For the purpose of the takeover, the land of Chestnut Ltd was revalued at £120,000 in excess of its book value. This was not reflected in the accounts of Chestnut Ltd. Land is not depreciated.

(c) At 30 September 20X8 Chestnut Ltd owed Oak plc £15,000 for goods purchased.

(d) The stock of Chestnut Ltd includes goods purchased from Oak plc at a price which includes a profit to Oak plc of £10,500.

Tasks

(a) Prepare the consolidated balance sheet for Oak plc as at 30 September 20X8.

(b) Explain the accounting treatment of inter-company trading transactions and balances when consolidating accounts. Use the data for the companies in this question to illustrate your answer.

Activity 13.5

You are provided with the following balance sheets for Shark plc and Minnow Ltd.

BALANCE SHEETS AS AT 31 OCTOBER 20X0

	Shark plc		Minnow Limited	
	£'000	£'000	£'000	£'000
Fixed assets, at net book value				
Land		325		70
Fixtures		200		50
		525		120
Investment				
Shares in Minnow Ltd at cost		200		
Current assets				
Stock at cost	220		70	
Debtors	145		105	
Bank	100		0	
	465		175	
Creditors: amounts falling due within one year				
Creditors	275		55	
Bank overdraft	0		20	
	275		75	
Net current assets		190		100
		915		220
Capital and reserves				
£1 Ordinary shares		700		170
Reserves		215		50
		915		220

The following information is also available.

(a) Shark plc purchased 70% of the issued ordinary share capital of Minnow Ltd on 1 November 20W0 when the reserves of Minnow Ltd were £20,000. Goodwill was fully amortised through the profit and loss account by 31 October 20W9.

(b) For the purposes of the acquisition, land in Minnow Ltd with a book value of £50,000 was revalued to its fair value of £60,000. The revaluation was not recorded in the accounts of Minnow Ltd. Land is not depreciated.

(c) Shark plc sells goods to Minnow Ltd at a mark up of 25%. At 31 October 20X0, the stocks of Minnow Ltd included £45,000 of goods purchased from Shark plc.

PART D   SIMPLE CONSOLIDATED ACCOUNTS

(d) Minnow Ltd owes Shark plc £35,000 for goods purchased and Shark Ltd owes Minnow Ltd £15,000.

Task

Prepare the consolidated balance sheet of Shark plc as at 31 October 20X0.

8 Overview: consolidated balance sheet

Purpose	To show the net assets which P controls and the ownership of those assets.
Net assets	Always 100% P plus 100% S providing P holds a majority of voting rights.
Share capital	P only.
Reason	Simply reporting to the holding company's shareholders in another form.
Reserves	100% P plus group share of post-acquisition retained reserves of S less consolidation adjustments.
Reason	To show the extent to which the group actually owns net assets included in the top half of the balance sheet.
Minority interest	MI share of S's consolidated net assets.
Reason	To show the extent to which other parties own net assets that are under the control of the holding company.

Signpost

The Chief Assessor has commented that the weaker students do not show a clear technique for consolidation. It is very important to show detailed workings to gain credit for what you get right.

13: THE CONSOLIDATED BALANCE SHEET

Key learning points

- ☑ This chapter has covered the mechanics of preparing simple **consolidated balance sheets**. In particular, procedures have been described for dealing with
    - Cancellation
    - Calculation of minority interests
    - Calculation of goodwill arising on consolidation

- ☑ A five-stage drill has been described and exemplified in a comprehensive example.

- ☑ The stages are as follows.
    - Update the draft balance sheets to take account of proposed dividends not accrued for
    - Agree intercompany current accounts by adjusting for items in transit
    - Cancel items common to both balance sheets
    - Minority interests
    - Goodwill

- ☑ We have examined the consolidation adjustments necessary when group companies **trade with each other**.
    - Any profit arising on intra-group transactions must be eliminated from the group accounts unless and until it is realised by a sale outside the group.

PART D   SIMPLE CONSOLIDATED ACCOUNTS

Quick quiz

1   What are the components making up the figure of minority interest in a consolidated balance sheet?

2   What adjustment is necessary before consolidation in cases where a holding company has not accrued for dividends receivable from a subsidiary?

3   What is 'goodwill arising on consolidation'?

4   How should 'negative goodwill' be disclosed in the consolidated balance sheet?

5   What is the basic principle of consolidation that determines the accounting treatment of inter-company trading?

Answers to quick quiz

1   Interest in a subsidiary undertaking included in the consolidation that is attributable to the shares held by or on behalf of persons other than the parent undertaking and its subsidiary undertakings. (In practice, minority interest consists of the minority's share of the subsidiary's share capital and reserves.)

2   DEBIT   Debtors (dividend receivable)
    CREDIT   Revenue reserves

3   The amount paid over and above the fair value of the net assets acquired.

4   It should appear as a credit in the balance sheet just below positive goodwill.

5   The only profits recognised should be those earned by the group.

Activity checklist

This checklist shows which performance criteria, range statement or knowledge and understanding point is covered by each activity in this chapter. Tick off each activity as you complete it.

Activity

13.1	☐	This activity deals with Knowledge & Understanding point 11: general principles of consolidation.
13.2	☐	This activity deals with Performance Criteria 11.1.A: draft financial statements from the appropriate information.
13.3	☐	This activity deals with Range Statement 11.1.1: limited company financial statements: consolidated.
13.4	☐	This activity deals with Range Statement 11.1.1: limited company financial statements: consolidated.
13.5	☐	This activity deals with Range Statement 11.1.1: limited company financial statements: consolidated.

chapter 14

Further aspects of group accounting

Contents

1. Introduction to consolidated P&L account
2. Inter-company trading
3. Inter-company dividends
4. Overview: consolidated P&L account
5. Acquisition and merger accounting
6. Accounting for associated undertakings

Performance criteria

11.1.A Draft limited company financial statements from the appropriate information

11.1.B Correctly identify and implement subsequent adjustments and ensure that discrepancies, unusual features or queries are identified and either resolved or referred to the appropriate person

11.1.C Ensure that limited company financial statements comply with relevant accounting standards and domestic legislation and with the organisation's policies, regulations and procedures

Range statement

11.1.1 Limited company financial statements: income statement; balance sheet; consolidated

11.1.2 Domestic legislation: Companies Act

11.1.3 Relevant accounting standards

Knowledge and understanding

2. The general legal framework of limited companies and the obligations of directors in respect of the financial statements (Element 11.1)

3. The statutory form of accounting statements and disclosure requirements (Element 11.1)

Knowledge and understanding (cont'd)

4 The UK regulatory framework for financial reporting and the main requirements of relevant Financial Reporting Standards
7 Preparing financial statements in proper form (Element 11.1)
11 The general principles of consolidation (Element 11.1)
12 How the accounting systems of an organisation are affected by its roles, organisational structure, its administrative systems and procedures and the nature of its business transactions (Elements 11.1 & 11.2)

1 Introduction to consolidated P&L account

As with the balance sheet, the source of the consolidated profit and loss account is the individual accounts of the separate companies in the group. You combine the individual companies' accounts largely by adding the amounts together.

Use workings to show the calculation of complex figures such as the minority interest and show the derivation of others on the face of the profit and loss account, as shown in our examples.

1.1 Consolidated profit and loss account: simple example

P Ltd acquired 75% of the ordinary shares of S Ltd on that company's incorporation in 20X3. The summarised profit and loss accounts of the two companies for the year ending 31 December 20X6 are set out below.

	P Limited £	S Limited £
Turnover	75,000	38,000
Cost of sales	30,000	20,000
Gross profit	45,000	18,000
Administrative expenses	14,000	8,000
Profit before taxation	31,000	10,000
Taxation	10,000	2,000
Retained profit for the year	21,000	8,000
Retained profits brought forward	87,000	17,000
Retained profits carried forward	108,000	25,000

Task

Prepare the consolidated profit and loss account.

Solution

P LIMITED
CONSOLIDATED PROFIT AND LOSS ACCOUNT
FOR THE YEAR ENDED 31 DECEMBER 20X6

	£
Turnover (75 + 38)	113,000
Cost of sales (30 + 20)	50,000
Gross profit	63,000
Administrative expenses (14 + 8)	22,000
Profit before taxation	41,000
Taxation (10 + 2)	12,000
Profit after taxation	29,000
Minority interest (25% × £8,000)	2,000
Group retained profit for the year	27,000
Retained profits brought forward	
(group share only: 87 + (17 × 75%))	99,750
Retained profits carried forward	126,750

Notice how the minority interest is dealt with.

(a) Down to the line **'profit after taxation'** the **whole** of S Ltd's results is included without reference to group share or minority share. A **one-line adjustment** is then inserted to deduct the minority's share of S Ltd's profit after taxation.

(b) The minority's share (£4,250) of S Ltd's retained profits brought forward is excluded. This means that the carried forward figure of £126,750 is the figure which would appear in the balance sheet for group retained reserves.

This last point may be clearer if we revert to our balance sheet technique and construct the working for group reserves.

Group reserves

	£
P Ltd	108,000
Share of S Ltd's PARR (75% × £25,000)	18,750
	126,750

The minority share of S Ltd's reserves comprises the minority interest in the £17,000 profits brought forward plus the minority interest (£2,000) in £8,000 retained profits for the year. (*Note.* PARR = Post acquisition retained reserves.)

Notice that a consolidated profit and loss account links up with a consolidated balance sheet exactly as in the case of an individual company's accounts: the figure of retained profits carried forward at the bottom of the profit and loss account appears as the figure for retained profits in the balance sheet.

We will now look at the complications introduced by **inter-company trading**, **inter-company dividends** and **pre-acquisition profits** in the subsidiary.

Cancelling items
Dividends: Ignore dividend Received from Subsidiary - "P" only.

2 Inter-company trading

2.1 Basic principles

Like the consolidated balance sheet, the consolidated profit and loss account should deal with the results of the group as those of a single entity. When one company in a group sells goods to another an identical amount is added to the turnover of the first company and to the cost of sales of the second. Yet as far as the entity's dealings with outsiders are concerned no sale has taken place.

The consolidated figures for turnover and cost of sales should represent sales to, and purchases from, outsiders. An adjustment is therefore necessary to reduce the turnover and cost of sales figures by the value of inter-company sales during the year.

We have also seen in an earlier chapter that any unrealised profits on inter-company trading should be excluded from the figure of group profits. This will occur whenever goods sold at a profit within the group remain in the stock of the purchasing company at the year end. The best way to deal with this is to **calculate the unrealised profit** on **unsold stocks at the year end and reduce consolidated gross profit by this amount**. Cost of sales will be the balancing figure

Example: inter-company trading

Suppose in our earlier example that S Ltd had recorded sales of £5,000 to P Ltd during 20X6. S Ltd had purchased these goods from outside suppliers at a cost of £3,000. One half of the goods remained in P Ltd's stock at 31 December 20X6.

Solution

The consolidated profit and loss account for the year ended 31 December 20X6 would now be as follows.

	Group £
Turnover (75 + 38 − 5)	108,000
Cost of sales (balancing figure)	46,000
Gross profit (45 + 18 − 1*)	62,000
Administrative expenses	(22,000)
Profit before taxation	40,000
Taxation	(12,000)
	28,000
Minority interest (25% × (£8,000 − £1,000*))	1,750
Group retained profit for the year	26,250
Retained profits brought forward	99,750
Retained profits carried forward	126,000

*Provision for unrealised profit: ½ × (£5,000 − £3,000)

A provision will be made for the unrealised profit against the stock figure in the consolidated balance sheet, as explained in Chapter 13.

3 Inter-company dividends

3.1 Basic principles

In our example so far we have assumed that S Ltd retains all of its after-tax profit. It may be, however, that S Ltd distributes some of its profits as dividends. As before, the minority interest in the subsidiary's profit should be calculated immediately after the figure of after-tax profit. For this purpose, no account need be taken of how much of the minority interest is to be distributed by S Ltd as dividend.

A complication may arise if the subsidiary has **preference shares** and wishes to pay a **preference dividend** as well as an ordinary dividend. In such a case great care is needed in calculating the minority interest in S Ltd's after-tax profit.

Example: inter-company dividends

Sam Ltd's capital consists of 10,000 6% £1 preference shares and 10,000 £1 ordinary shares. On 1 January 20X3, the date of Sam Ltd's incorporation, Ham Ltd acquired 3,000 of the preference shares and 7,500 of the ordinary shares. The profit and loss accounts of the two companies for the year ended 31 December 20X6 are set out below.

	Ham Ltd £	Sam Ltd £
Turnover	200,000	98,000
Cost of sales	90,000	40,000
Gross profit	110,000	58,000
Administrative expenses	35,000	19,000
Profit before tax	75,000	39,000
Taxation	23,000	18,000
Profit after tax	52,000	21,000
Dividends proposed: preference	–	600
Ordinary	14,000	2,000
Retained profit for the year	38,000	18,400
Retained profits brought forward	79,000	23,000
	117,000	41,400

Ham Ltd has not yet accounted for its share of the dividends receivable from Sam Ltd.

Prepare Ham Ltd's consolidated profit and loss account.

Solution

To calculate the minority interest in Sam Ltd's after-tax profit it is necessary to remember that the first £600 of such profits goes to pay the preference dividend. The balance of after-tax profits belongs to the equity shareholders. The calculation is as follows.

PART D SIMPLE CONSOLIDATED ACCOUNTS

	Total £		Minority share £
Profits earned for preference shareholders	600	(70%)	420
Balance earned for equity shareholders	20,400	(25%)	5,100
Total profits after tax	21,000		5,520

It is irrelevant how much of this is distributed to the minority as dividends: the whole £5,520 must be deducted in arriving at the figure for group profit. The dividends receivable by Ham Ltd, calculated below would cancel with the dividends payable by Sam Ltd to its holding company.

	£
Preference dividend (30% × £600)	180
Ordinary dividend (75% × £2,000)	1,500
	1,680

HAM LIMITED
CONSOLIDATED PROFIT AND LOSS ACCOUNT
FOR THE YEAR ENDED 31 DECEMBER 20X5

	Group £
Turnover (200 + 98)	298,000
Cost of sales (90 + 40)	130,000
Gross profit	168,000
Administrative expenses (35 + 19)	54,000
Profit before tax	114,000
Taxation (23 + 18)	41,000
Profit after tax	73,000
Minority interest (as above)	5,520
Group profit for the year	67,480
Dividend proposed (parent company only)	14,000
Retained profit for the year	53,480
Retained profits brought forward (group share only: 79 + (23 × 75%))	96,250
Retained profits carried forward	149,730

4 Overview: consolidated P&L account

The table below summaries the main points about the consolidated profit and loss account.

Purpose	To show the results of the group for an accounting period as if it were a single entity.
Turnover to profit after tax	100% P + 100% S (excluding dividend receivable from subsidiary and adjustments for inter-company transactions).
Reason	To show the results of the group which were controlled by the holding company.
Inter-company sales	Strip out inter-company activity from both turnover and cost of sales.
Unrealised profit on inter-company sales	Increase cost of sales by unrealised profit.
Minority interests	S's profit after tax (PAT) X MI% X
Reason	To show the extent to which profits generated through P's control are in fact owned by other parties.
Dividends	**P's only.**
Reason	S's dividend is due (a) to P; and (b) to MI. P has taken in its share by including the results of S in the consolidated P & L a/c. The MI have taken their share by being given a proportion of S's PAT. Remember: PAT = dividends + retained profit.
Retained reserves	As per the balance sheet calculations.

Now try the Activity below. It is as hard as you are likely to get in an exam. Note that this activity asks for a consolidated balance sheet as well as a profit and loss account. In an exam you'll probably get one or the other.

PART D SIMPLE CONSOLIDATED ACCOUNTS

Activity 14.1

You are provided with the following summarised financial information for Bamber Ltd and Renshaw Ltd.

PROFIT AND LOSS ACCOUNT FOR THE YEAR ENDED 31 OCTOBER 20X9

	Bamber Limited £'000	Renshaw Limited £'000
Turnover	1,000	250
Cost of sales	650	180
Gross profit	350	70
Distribution costs	75	15
Administrative expenses	60	20
Operating profit	215	35
Investment income	14	0
Profit on ordinary activities before tax	229	35
Tax on profit on ordinary activities	70	10
Profit on ordinary activities after taxation	159	25
Proposed ordinary dividends	80	15
Retained profit for the year	79	10

BALANCE SHEET AS AT 31 OCTOBER 20X9

	Bamber Limited £'000	Bamber Limited £'000	Renshaw Limited £'000	Renshaw Limited £'000
Fixed assets				
Tangible assets at net book value		350		75
Investment				
Shares in Renshaw Ltd at cost		100		
Current assets				
Stock at cost	180		45	
Debtors	145		55	
Bank	70		20	
	395		120	
Creditors: amounts falling due within one year				
Creditors	50		30	
Proposed dividends	80		15	
Corporation tax	70		10	
	200		55	
Net current assets		195		65
		645		140
Capital and reserves				
Called up share capital – issued and fully paid				
£1 ordinary shares		500		100
Profit and loss account		145		40
		645		140

The following information is also available.

(a) Bamber Ltd purchased 80% of the issued ordinary share capital of Renshaw Ltd on 1 November 20X7 when the profit and loss account of Renshaw Ltd was £20,000. Goodwill is amortised over its estimated useful life of four years.

(b) Bamber Ltd sold goods costing £100,000 to Renshaw Ltd for £160,000 during the year ended 31 October 20X9. At 31 October 20X9, 25% of these goods remained in Renshaw Ltd's stocks.

(c) Bamber Ltd has recognised the dividends proposed by Renshaw Ltd in its profit and loss account.

Tasks

(a) Prepare the following statements for Bamber Ltd.

   (i) The consolidated profit and loss account for the year ended 31 October 20X9. Disclosure notes are not required.

   (ii) The consolidated balance sheet as at 31 October 20X9.

(b) Explain the circumstances in which the accounts of a subsidiary company need not be consolidated into the group accounts.

5 Acquisition and merger accounting

Signpost
You need to know the criteria for treating a business combination as an acquisition or merger, but preparation of merger accounts is not required.

5.1 Acquisition or merger accounting?

FRS 6 *Acquisitions and mergers* deals with the accounting treatment of business combinations which arise when one or more companies become subsidiaries of another company. Two different methods of accounting for such combinations have evolved in practice.

(a) **Acquisition accounting** is the traditional method of accounting for business combinations and is the method which has been described in the previous chapters of this section. A company acquires shares in another company (or companies) and either pays for them in cash or issues its own shares or loan stock in exchange for them. If much of the purchase price is paid in cash, there may be a significant outflow of assets from the group.

(b) **Merger accounting** is a method of preparing consolidated accounts which may be regarded as appropriate in cases where a business combination is brought about without any significant outflow of funds from the group. This might happen, for example, where one company acquires shares in another company and issues its own shares as consideration for the purchase, rather than paying cash.

PART D SIMPLE CONSOLIDATED ACCOUNTS

You should be clear in your mind that the term **merger accounting refers to a method of preparing consolidated accounts**. FRS 6 does not mention (except briefly in an appendix) the problems of how to account for share acquisitions in the individual accounts of the acquiring company.

The main problem with using the acquisition method concerns the **effect on the holding company's distributable profits**. Suppose that P Ltd acquires all the shares of S Ltd on day 1 and on day 2 S Ltd pays a dividend equal to the entire amount of its distributable profits. Using the conventional techniques of acquisition accounting described in earlier chapters, P Ltd would not credit the dividend received to its own profit and loss account, so as to increase its own distributable profits; instead, the dividend would be applied to reduce the cost of the investment in S Ltd. The profits available for distribution to members of P Ltd would be unchanged from what they were before the combination.

If the shares in S Ltd were purchased for cash, this might seem reasonable: cash has been paid out as well as received and so net assets have not increased. The amount of profits available to distribute to the original shareholders of P Ltd remains unchanged, being the distributable profits shown in P Ltd's own individual accounts. On this assumption, conventional acquisition accounting seems to achieve a fair result.

But what happens if the shareholders in S Ltd are not bought out for cash? This would be the case if P Ltd paid for the shares in S Ltd by, say, an issue of new shares in P Ltd. This would mean that members of S Ltd would exchange their shares in that company for a share of the newly-formed group. The number of shareholders of P Ltd would now be greatly increased. But using acquisition accounting there would be no corresponding increase in the distributable profits of P Ltd.

This result can be avoided if merger accounting principles are used. Broadly speaking **a business combination may be accounted for as a merger if payment for the shares acquired is by means of a share exchange**; if payment is by cash, conventional acquisition accounting must be used.

Merger accounting differs from acquisition accounting in a number of ways.

(a) **Assets** can be recorded at their **previous values**, as there is no obligation to record them at fair value.

(b) **No share premium account** will arise in the books of the holding company, as shares issued are recorded at their nominal value only.

(c) A **premium on acquisition (goodwill) will never arise** under merger accounting.

(d) Previously **distributable reserves** of the individual companies may **remain distributable** as there is no enforced freezing of pre-acquisition reserves.

(e) It is **simpler** than acquisition accounting.

5.2 Use of merger accounting

Merger accounting should be used when the use of merger accounting is not prohibited by companies legislation and the **five specific criteria for a merger laid out in FRS 6** are satisfied by the combination.

The criteria for determining whether the definition of a merger is met are as follows. (Note that convertible share or loan stock should be regarded as equity to the extent that it is converted into equity **as a result of the business combination.**)

Criterion 1

Neither party is portrayed, by either its management or any other party, as either acquirer or acquired.

Criterion 2

All parties take part in setting up a management structure and selecting personnel for the combined entity on the basis of consensus rather than purely by exercise of voting rights.

Criterion 3

The relative sizes of the parties are not so disparate that one party dominates the combined entity by virtue of its relative size.

Criterion 4

A substantial part of the consideration for equity shareholdings in each party will comprise equity shares; conversely, non-equity shares or equity shares with reduced voting rights will comprise only an 'immaterial' part of the consideration. This criterion also covers existing shareholdings.

Criterion 5

No equity shareholders of any of the combining entities retain any material interest in the future performance of only part of the combined entity.

6 Accounting for associated undertakings

6.1 What are associated undertakings?

Certain substantial investments are known as 'associated undertakings' for the purpose of consolidated accounts. These are holdings too significant to be treated simply as trade investments but not qualifying as investments in subsidiaries. To cater for this situation a form of accounting known as **equity accounting** has developed. FRS 9 *Associates and joint ventures* requires that X Ltd should adopt equity accounting principles if its investment in Y Ltd is such that Y Ltd has the status of an **associated company**.

> An **associate** is a long term investment where the investor holds a 'participating interest' and exercises 'significant influence'.

A **participating interest** is deemed to be a shareholding of over 20%. This holding, however, must be one held for the purpose of contributing to the associate's activities in order to generate financial benefits for the investor. The exercise of significant influence means that the investor is actively involved in influencing the associate's strategic decisions – the holding company should influence decisions such as changes in the associate's products, markets, direction and general activities. The investor's percentage holding on its own is not enough to give associate status.

Signpost

In an exam testing of FRS 9 will be restricted to the definition of associates and the application of equity accounting to simple examples. You are most likely to get a written question asking when to equity account and why.

6.2 Equity accounting

(a) The investor should **include its associates** in its consolidated financial statements using the **equity method.**

(b) In the investor's consolidated profit and loss account the **investor's share** of its **associates' operating** results should be included immediately after group operating results.

(c) **From the level of profit before tax**, the **investor's share of the relevant amounts for associates** should be included within the amounts for the group.

(d) In the consolidated statement of total recognised gains and losses the **investor's** share of the **total recognised gains and losses** of its associates should be included, shown separately under each heading, if material.

(e) In the **balance sheet** the **investor's share** of the **net assets of its associate** should be **included and separately disclosed**.

(f) The **cash flow statement** should include the **cash flows between the investor and its associates**.

(g) **Goodwill** arising on the investor's acquisition of its associates, less any amortisation or write-down, should be **included** in the carrying amount for the associates but should be **disclosed separately**.

(h) In the **profit and loss account** the amortisation or write-down of such goodwill should be **separately disclosed as part of the investor's share of its associates' results**.

6.2.1 The investor's own financial statements

In the investor's own financial statements associates should be treated as fixed asset investments, at cost less any amounts written off, or at a valuation.

Example: associated company

Tornado plc is a long established business in office supplies. The nature of its business has expanded and diversified to take account of technological changes which have taken place in recent years. Now in addition to stationery and office furniture, it also supplies photocopiers, fax machines and more recently new computer based technologies. Tornado has a 40% interest in the issued share capital of Whirlpool Ltd and representation on the board. Whirlpool Ltd manufactures office furniture and a large proportion of what it produces is sold to Tornado. Tornado is therefore actively involved in decisions regarding product ranges, designs and pricing to ensure they get the products they want.

The following is an extract from the financial statements of Whirlpool for the year ended 31 March 20X8.

14: FURTHER ASPECTS OF GROUP ACCOUNTING

PROFIT AND LOSS ACCOUNT

	£'000
Turnover	2,034
Operating costs	1,936
Operating profit	98
Interest payable	–
Profit before tax	98
Tax	20
Profit after tax	78

BALANCE SHEET

	£'000
Fixed assets	180
Current assets	1,470
Creditors falling due within one year	(1,107)
Creditors falling due after more than one year	(13)
	530

Cost of investment

Task

Produce extracts from the consolidated profit and loss account and balance sheet of Tornado for the year ended 31 March 20X8 indicating clearly the treatment for Whirlpool and where each item would appear. Ignore goodwill.

Solution

EXTRACTS FROM THE CONSOLIDATED PROFIT AND LOSS ACCOUNT FOR THE YEAR ENDED 31 MARCH 20X8

	£'000
Turnover	X
Group operating profit	X
Share of operating profit in associates (W1)	39
Interest payable	X
Profit before tax	X
Tax (see below)	X
Profit after tax	X
Tax relates to	
Parent and subsidiary	X
Associates (40% × 20)	8

EXTRACTS FROM THE CONSOLIDATED BALANCE SHEET AS AT 31 MARCH 20X8

	£'000
Fixed assets	
Investment in associate (W2)	212

Workings

1   *Share of associate company profit*

	£'000
Profit of Whirlpool per question	98
Group share (40%) (rounded)	39

2   *Investment in associates*

	£'000
Net assets per question	530
Group share (40%)	212

Activity 14.2

Big Ltd is a holding company with subsidiaries. It also has 25% of Small Ltd, representation on the board and is actively involved in the decision-making process of the board.

The following is an extract from Small Ltd's financial statements for the year ended 31 December 20X1.

PROFIT AND LOSS ACCOUNT

	£'000
Turnover	2,000
Operating costs	1,000
Operating profit	1,000
Interest payable	100
Profit before tax	900
Tax	300
Profit after tax	600

BALANCE SHEET

	£'000
Fixed assets	2,000
Current assets	1,000
Creditors falling due within one year	(500)
Creditors falling due after more than one year	(500)
Profit before tax	2,000

Task

Produce extracts from the consolidated profit and loss account and balance sheet of Big Ltd for the year ended 31 December 20X1 indicating clearly the treatment for Small and where each item would appear. Ignore goodwill.

Activity 14.3

Tutorial note. This is mainly a revision activity covering material from Chapter 13. Remember, control is not just about ownership of shares. The activity will also test whether you have understood the section of the chapter you have just been reading.

You have been told that your employer Port plc acquired 45,000 ordinary shares of Starboard Ltd on 31 December 20X5 when the balance on Starboard's profit and loss account was £250,000. In addition Port plc is able to appoint four of the five directors of Starboard Ltd thus exercising control over their activities.

The balance sheets of Port plc and Starboard Ltd for the year ended 31 December 20X6 are shown below.

	Port plc		Starboard Limited	
	£'000	£'000	£'000	£'000
Fixed assets				
Freehold properties		400		300
Plant and machinery		200		150
Investments: Starboard Ltd		450		
		1,050		450
Current assets				
Stock	150		100	
Debtors	170		80	
Bank	40		20	
	360		200	
Less current liabilities				
Creditors	120		100	
Proposed dividend	50		20	
	170		120	
Working capital		190		80
		1,240		530
Share capital		500		100
Profit and loss account		740		430
		1,240		530

You are given the following additional information.

(a) Share capital of Port plc is 500,000 shares of £1 each and the share capital of Starboard is 100,000 ordinary shares of £1 each.

(b) Goodwill is assumed to have an indefinite useful life and is to be carried in the balance sheet indefinitely.

(c) Port plc has not accounted for its share of Starboard Ltd's proposed dividend.

Tasks

(a) Prepare the draft consolidated balance sheet of Port plc as at 31 December 20X6.

(b) Explain why you have consolidated Starboard Ltd when Port plc owns less than 50% of the ordinary shares of Starboard Ltd and in what circumstances consolidation would not have been appropriate.

PART D   SIMPLE CONSOLIDATED ACCOUNTS

Key learning points

- ☑ This chapter has explained how to prepare a **consolidated profit and loss account** by combining the profit and loss accounts of each group company.

- ☑ **Adjustments** must be made:
    - To reduce turnover by the amount of any **intra-group trading**, and to deduct from consolidated gross profit any unrealised profit on stocks thus acquired which are held at the year end. Cost of sales will be the balancing figure
    - To reduce stock values by the amount of any **unrealised profit** on intra-group trading
    - To calculate the **minority interest** in subsidiary companies' results for the year
    - To account for **intra-group dividends**
    - To **eliminate pre-acquisition** profits

- ☑ You should know the basic ways in which **merger accounting** differs from acquisition accounting.

- ☑ FRS 9 and CA 95 require that, in consolidated accounts, investments in **associated companies** should be accounted for using **equity accounting** principles.

14: FURTHER ASPECTS OF GROUP ACCOUNTING

Quick quiz

1 Describe the preparation of a consolidated profit and loss account in its simplest form.
2 At what stage in the consolidated profit and loss account does the figure for minority interests appear?
3 What adjustments are made to the consolidated profit and loss account in respect of inter-company trading?
4 What dispensation is granted to a parent company by s 230 CA 1985?
5 Does goodwill arise in merger accounting?
6 A shareholding of 25% is always a participating interest. True or false?
7 The following figures relate to Sanderstead plc and its subsidiary Croydon Ltd for the year ended 31 December 20X9.

	Sanderstead plc £	Croydon Limited £
Turnover	600,000	300,000
Cost of sales	(400,000)	(200,000)
Gross profit	200,000	100,000

During the year, Sanderstead plc sold goods to Croydon Ltd for £20,000 making a profit of £5,000. These goods were all sold by Croydon Ltd before the year end.

What are the amounts for turnover and gross profit in the consolidated profit and loss accounts of Sanderstead plc for the year ended 31 December 20X9?

Answers to quick quiz

1 The individual profit and loss accounts are totalled and certain adjustments made.
2 After 'profit after tax'.
3 An adjustment is made to reduce the turnover and cost of sales figures by the value of inter-company sales during the year. Thus the consolidated figures for turnover and cost of sales should represent sales to and purchases from outsiders.
4 A parent company may dispense with the need to publish its own profit and loss account.
5 No. A premium on acquisition will never arise.
6 False. Significant influence must be exercised.
7

	£
Turnover (600 + 300 – 20)	880
Cost of sales (400 + 200 – 20)	580
Gross profit	300

PART D SIMPLE CONSOLIDATED ACCOUNTS

Activity checklist

This checklist shows which performance criteria, range statement or knowledge and understanding point is covered by each activity in this chapter. Tick off each activity as you complete it.

Activity

14.1	☐	This activity deals with Range Statement 11.1.1: limited company financial statements: consolidated.
14.2	☐	This activity deals with Performance Criteria: 11.1.A: draft limited company accounts from appropriate information.
14.3	☐	This activity deals with Knowledge & Understanding point 11: principles of consolidation.

Answers to Activities

Answers to activities

Chapter 1

Answer 1.1

The answer is that limited companies (though not other forms of business such as partnerships) are required to make certain accounting information public. They do so by sending copies of the required information to the Registrar of Companies at Companies House. The information filed at Companies House is available, at a fee, to any member of the public who asks for it. Other sources include financial comment in the press and company brochures.

Answer 1.2

Assets less **liabilities** = ownership interest

Answer 1.3

(a) This is an asset, albeit an intangible one. There is a past event, control and future economic benefit (through cost savings).

(b) This cannot be classified as an asset. Baldwin Ltd has no control over the car repair shop and it is difficult to argue that there are 'future economic benefits'.

(c) This is a liability; the business has taken on an obligation. It would be recognised when the warranty is issued rather than when a claim is made.

(d) As a firm financial commitment, this has all the appearance of a liability. However, as the consultant has not done any work yet, there has been no past event which could give rise to a liability. Similarly, because there has been no past event there is no asset.

(e) The situation is not clear cut. It could be argued that there is a liability, depending on the whether the potential danger to the public arising from the building creates a legal obligation to do the repairs. If there is such a liability, it might be possible to set off the sale proceeds of £100,000 against the cost of essential repairs of £200,000, giving a net obligation to transfer economic benefits of £100,000.

The building is clearly not an asset, because although there is control and there has been a past event, there is no expected access to economic benefit.

ANSWERS TO ACTIVITIES

Answer 1.4

Here are the main reasons why the ASB developed the *Statement of Principles*.

(a) To assist the ASB by providing a basis for reducing the number of alternative accounting treatments permitted by accounting standards and company law

(b) To provide a framework for the future development of accounting standards

(c) To assist auditors in forming an opinion as to whether financial statements conform with accounting standards

(d) To assist users of accounts in interpreting the information contained in them

(e) To provide guidance in applying accounting standards

(f) To give guidance on areas which are not yet covered by accounting standards

(g) To inform interested parties of the approach taken by the ASB in formulating accounting standards

The role of the *Statement* can thus be summed up as being to provide consistency, clarity and information.

Answer 1.5

Tutorial note. You were asked for only one example – our answer gives three for completeness. Other reasonable types of organisation and user would also be acceptable.

(a) (i) (1) Supplier
       (2) Bank
       (3) Shareholders

   (ii)

User	Possible decisions
Supplier	Whether to carry on supplying goods on credit (eg by looking at liquidity position)
Bank	Whether to continue an overdraft facility (by assessing profitability and liquidity)
Shareholders	Whether to increase or decrease holding or whether to remove directors. They will assess liquidity, profitability, gearing and the stewardship of management.

(b) Each of the items in the accounting equation is defined in the ASB's *Statement of Principles*.

   (i) *Assets* are 'rights or other access to future economic benefits controlled by an entity as a result of past transactions or events'.

   (ii) *Liabilities* are 'obligations of an entity to transfer economic benefits as a result of past transactions or events'.

(iii) *Ownership interest* is the residual amount found by deducting all of the entity's liabilities from all of the entity's assets.

More simply, assets are owned by an entity, liabilities are owed by an entity and ownership interest is capital, which is owed to the owner.

Chapter 2

Answer 2.1

(a) If the business is to be closed down, the remaining three machines must be valued at the amount they will realise in a forced sale, ie 3 × £60 = £180.

(b) If the business is regarded as a going concern, the stock unsold at 31 December will be carried forward into the following year, when the cost of the three machines will be matched against the eventual sale proceeds in computing that year's profits. The three machines will therefore appear in the balance sheet at 31 December at cost, 3 × £100 = £300.

Answer 2.2

(a) No. You would write it off to the profit and loss account as an expense.

(b) Yes. You would capitalise the computer and charge depreciation on it.

(c) Your answer depends on the size of the company and whether writing off the item has a material effect on its profits. A larger organisation might well write this item off under the heading of advertising expenses, while a small one would capitalise it and depreciate it over time. This is because the item would be material to the small company but not to the large company.

Answer 2.3

No. This is a change to the **estimation technique**. The same measurement basis is used. The historical cost is allocated over the asset's estimated useful life.

Answer 2.4

Yes. This is a change to the **measurement basis**.

Answer 2.5

Yes. (The choice to capitalise or not is given in SSAP 13). The criteria affected by this decision are **recognition and presentation**.

Answer 2.6

Yes. Beelzebub would be changing the way they **presented** the depreciation figure.

Chapter 3

Answer 3.1

False. Limited liability means that shareholders are not personally liable for the company's debt.

Answer 3.2

800,000 × 50p × 5% = £20,000.

Answer 3.3

		£	£
DEBIT	Bank (200,000 × £1.30)	260,000	
CREDIT	Share capital (200,000 × £1)		200,000
CREDIT	Share premium (200,000 × 30p)		60,000

Answer 3.4

HANOI LIMITED
TRADING, PROFIT AND LOSS ACCOUNT
FOR THE YEAR ENDED 31 MARCH 20X4

	£'000	£'000
Turnover		305
Cost of sales		
Opening stock	62	
Purchases	108	
	170	
Closing stock	45	
		125
Gross profit		180
Operating expenses (W4)	63	
Plant depreciation (W5)	31	
Freehold premises depreciation (W7)	3	
Bad debt expense	12	
		109
Operating profit		71
Debenture interest		11
		60
Dividends: ordinary		25
preference		8
Retained profit for the year		27

HANOI LIMITED
BALANCE SHEET AS AT 31 MARCH 20X4

	Cost £'000	Depn £'000	NBV £'000
Fixed assets			
Freehold land	200	–	200
Freehold premises (W7)	150	9	141
Plant and equipment (W5) (W6)	120	79	41
	470	88	382
Current assets			
Stocks		45	
Debtors (96 – 2)		94	
Bank (W1)		164	
		303	
Current liabilities			
Trade creditors		58	
Accrual		15	
		73	
Net current assets			230
			612
10% debentures			110
			502
Capital and reserves			
Ordinary £1 shares (200 + 50)			250
Share premium			25
8% preference shares			100
Profit and loss a/c (100 + 27)			127
			502

Workings

1　Bank balance

BANK A/C

	£'000		£'000
Balance b/d	20	Creditors (W3)	101
Debtors (W2)	272	Dividends: ordinary	25
Share capital	50	preference	8
Share premium	25	Debenture interest	11
		Operating expenses	58
		Balance c/d	164
	367		367

ANSWERS TO ACTIVITIES

2   Receipts from debtors

DEBTORS CONTROL A/C

	£'000		£'000
Balance b/d	100	Contra with CCA	25
Sales	305	Bad debts written off	12
		Bank (bal fig)	272
		Balance c/d	96
	405		405

3   Payments to creditors

CREDITORS CONTROL A/C

	£'000		£'000
Contras with DCA	25	Balance b/d	76
Bank (bal fig)	101	Purchases	108
Balance c/d	58		
	184		184

4   Operating expenses

	£'000
Accrual at 1.4.X3	(10)
Paid during year	58
Accrued 31.3.X4	15
P & L charge	63

5   Plant cost and depreciation

	£'000
Plant at cost b/d	120
Less fully depreciated item	40
Depreciable amount	80

Depreciation charge £80,000 × 20% = £16,000

Write down on machine (20 − 5) = £15,000.

∴ Total depreciation charge on plant (16 + 15) = £31,000.

6   Plant: accumulated depreciation

	£'000
B/d	48
Add charge for year	31
	79

7   Freehold premises depreciation

	£'000
B/d	6
Charge for year (150/50)	3
	9

ANSWERS TO ACTIVITIES

Chapter 4

Answer 4.1

	£
Audit of accounts	10,000
Expenses	1,100
Taxation computation and advice	1,500
	12,600

The consultancy fees are not received by the auditors.

Answer 4.2

See Section 4 of this chapter.

Answer 4.3

Your table should look like this.

Type of Business	Companies Act	FRSs/SSAPs	IASs	Stock Exchange Listing Rules
Public Listed Company	YES	YES	NO	YES
Private Limited Company	YES	YES	NO	NO
Sole Tradership	NO	NO	NO	NO

Answer 4.4

The going concern concept is that an enterprise will continue in operational existence for the foreseeable future. This means that the financial statements of an enterprise are prepared on the assumption that the enterprise will continue trading. If this were not the case, various adjustments would have to be made to the accounts: provisions for losses; revaluation of assets to their possible market value and so forth.

Unless it can be assumed that the business is a going concern, the other three fundamental accounting concepts cannot apply. This can be seen by considering each concept in turn as follows.

Consistency

It is meaningless to speak of consistency from one accounting period to the next when this is the final accounting period.

Accruals

The accruals or matching concept states that revenue and expenses which are related to each other are matched, so as to be dealt with in the same accounting period, without regard to when the cash is actually paid or received. This is particularly relevant to the purchase of fixed assets. The cost of a fixed asset is spread over the accounting periods expected to benefit from it, thus matching costs and revenues. In the absence of the going concern convention, this cannot happen, as an example will illustrate.

Suppose a company has a machine which cost £10,000 two years ago and now has a net book value of £6,000. The machine can be used for another three years, but as it is obsolete, there is no possibility of selling it, and so it has no market value.

If the going concern concept applies, the machine will be shown at cost less depreciation in the accounts, as it still has a part to play in the continued life of the enterprise. However, if the assumption cannot be applied the machine will be given a nil value and other assets and liabilities will be revalued on the basis of winding down the company's operations.

Prudence

The prudence concept as we normally understand it cannot apply if the business is no longer a going concern. A more drastic approach than mere caution is required when it is known that the business must cease trading.

Chapter 5

Answer 5.1

(b) A factory building may require a new roof every 10 years, whereas the factory itself may have a useful economic life of 50 years. In this case the roof will be treated as a separate asset and depreciated over 10 years and the expenditure incurred in replacing the roof will be accounted for as an addition and the carrying amount of the replaced asset removed from the balance sheet.

(c) An aircraft may be required by law to be overhauled every three years. Unless the overhaul is carried out the aircraft will not be licensed to fly. The entity will reflect the need to overhaul the aircraft by depreciating an amount equivalent to the estimated cost of the overhaul over the three year period. The cost of the overhaul will then be capitalised because it restores the economic value of the aircraft.

Answer 5.2

(a) Revaluation reserve = Valuation – net book value

= £250,000 – £125,000

= £125,000

(b) Depreciation $= \dfrac{\text{revalued amount}}{\text{remaining useful life}}$

$= \dfrac{£250,000}{25}$

= £10,000 pa

Answer 5.3

SSAP 19 recognises that there is a conceptual difference between *investment properties* and other fixed assets. Such properties are not depreciated and are carried in the balance sheet at open market value, re-assessed every year. An external valuation should be made at least once every five years.

Changes in the value of an investment property should not be taken to the profit and loss account. In other words, a company cannot claim profit on the unrealised gains on revaluation of such properties. The revaluation should be disclosed as a movement on an 'investment revaluation reserve'. Should this reserve show a debit balance (a loss) the full amount of the balance should be removed by charging it to the profit and loss account.

SSAP 19 acknowledges that there is a difference between investment properties and other fixed assets, including non-investment properties. Investment properties are held 'not for consumption in the business operations but as investments, the disposal of which would not materially affect any manufacturing or trading operations of the enterprise'.

It follows from this that the item of prime importance is the current value of the investment properties and changes in their current value rather than a calculation of systematic annual depreciation.

Answer 5.4

JOURNAL ENTRIES

		£	£
DEBIT	Plant and machinery	126,580	
	Motor lorries	42,520	
	Motor cars	12,259	
	VAT	29,593	
CREDIT	Suspense		210,952

Being extraction of asset costs from suspense account.

Note. You should remember the VAT rules from your Unit 7 studies. VAT can not be reclaimed on motor cars used as fixed assets.

		£	£
DEBIT	Suspense	40,916	
CREDIT	Government grants		25,316
	Profit and loss		15,600

Being the extraction and capitalisation of capital-based grants, and the crediting to profit and loss of revenue-based grant from suspense account.

DEBIT	Profit and loss	36,272	
CREDIT	Plant and machinery acc. depreciation		25,316
	Motor lorries accumulated depreciation		8,504
	Motor cars accumulated depreciation		2,452

Being the provision for depreciation of assets at 20% on cost for the year.

Depreciation of a full 20% on cost has been charged on the assumption that the assets have been held for the whole year.

DEBIT	Government grants (20% × £25,316)	5,063	
CREDIT	Profit and loss		5,063

Being the amortisation of capital-based government grants for the year.

Answer 5.5

SSAP 13 states that expenditure on tangible fixed assets acquired or constructed to provide facilities for research and/or development activities should be capitalised and depreciated over their useful lives in the usual way. The depreciation may be capitalised as part of deferred development expenditure if the development work for which the assets are used meets the criteria given in the SSAP. However, since the tank is for pure research, this does not apply.

Answer 5.6

Project A

This project meets the SECTOR criteria for SSAP 13 for development expenditure to be recognised as an asset. These are as follows.

(a) The product or process is clearly defined and the costs attributable to the product or process can be separately identified and measured reliably.

(b) The project is commercially feasible.

(c) The technical feasibility of the product or process can be demonstrated.

(d) An overall profit is expected.

(e) Adequate resources exist, or their availability can be demonstrated, to complete the project and market or use the product or process.

The capitalisation development costs in a company which is a going concern means that these are accrued in order that they can be matched against the income they are expected to generate.

Hence the costs of £280,000 incurred to date should be transferred from research and development costs to capitalised development expenditure and carried forward until revenues are generated; they should then be matched with those revenues.

Project B

Whilst this project meets most of the criteria discussed above which would enable the costs to be carried forward it fails on the requirements that 'adequate resources exist, or their availability can be demonstrated, to complete the project.

Hence it would be prudent to write off these costs. Once funding is obtained the situation can then be reassessed and these and future costs may be capitalised. In this case the prudence concept overrides the accruals assumption.

Project C

This is a research project according to SSAP 13, ie original and planned investigation undertaken with the prospect of gaining new scientific or technical knowledge or understanding.

There is no certainty as to its ultimate success or commercial viability and therefore it cannot be considered to be a development project. SSAP 13 therefore requires that costs be written off as incurred. Once again, prudence overrides the accruals assumption.

Chapter 6

Answer 6.1

	£
Corporation tax on profits	45,000
Deferred taxation	16,000
Underprovision of tax in previous year £(40,500 – 38,000)	2,500
Tax on profits for 20X3	63,500

Answer 6.2

CORPORATION TAX

20X3		£	20X3		£
1 October	Cash	40,500	1 January	Bal b/f	38,000
31 December	Bal c/f	45,000	31 December	Provision for tax on 2003 profits	45,000
				P&L a/c – under-provision for 2002	2,500
		85,500			85,500

DEFERRED TAX

20X3		£	20X3		£
31 December	Bal c/f	28,000	1 January	Bal b/f	12,000
			31 December	P&L a/c	16,000
		28,000			28,000

Extract from balance sheet:

Creditors due within one year
Corporation tax   45,000

Provision for liabilities and charges
Deferred tax   28,000

Chapter 7

Answer 7.1

(b), (e) and (f) are adjusting; the others are non-adjusting.

Answer 7.2

(a)   C   Quack was dismissed the day after the balance sheet date and his lawsuit throws no light on conditions existing at the balance sheet date – accounting conditions, anyway! This is not, therefore, an adjusting post balance sheet event, nor is it a contingency.

(b)   B   Although the loss on disposal sustained after the year end will probably be material, it does not relate to the year ended 31 March 20X8 unless it renders the going concern basis inappropriate, which seems unlikely. However, the discovery that the accounts are fundamentally incorrect would result in adjustment, as the misappropriations would have to be reclassified and there might be tax effects.

Answer 7.3

The treatment of the events arising in the case of Fabricators Ltd would be as follows.

(a) The fall in value of the investment in Patchup Ltd has arisen over the previous year and that company's financial accounts for the year to 28 February 20X1 provide additional evidence of conditions that existed at the balance sheet date. The loss of £50,000 is material in terms of the trading profit figure and, as an adjusting event, should be reflected in the financial statements of Fabricators Ltd.

(b) The destruction of stock by fire on 30 April (one month after the balance sheet date) must be considered to be a non-adjusting event (ie this is 'a new condition which did not exist at the balance sheet date'). Since the loss is material, being £250,000, it should be disclosed by way of a note to the accounts. The note should describe the nature of the event and an estimate of its financial effect. Non-reporting of this event would prevent users of the financial statements from reaching a proper understanding of the financial position.

(c) The approval on 1 June of the company's design for tank cleaning equipment creates a new condition which did not exist at the balance sheet date. This is, therefore, a non-adjusting event and if it is of such material significance that non-reporting would prevent a proper understanding of the financial position it should be disclosed by way of note. In this instance non-disclosure should not prevent a proper understanding of the financial position and disclosure by note may be unnecessary.

Answer 7.4

(a) No provision would be recognised as the decision has not been communicated.

(b) A provision would be made in the 20X9 financial statements.

(c) A provision for such costs is appropriate.

(d) No present obligation exists and under FRS 12 no provision would be appropriate. This is because the entity could avoid the future expenditure by its future actions, maybe by changing its method of operation.

Answer 7.5

(a) *At 31 December 20X1*

There is a present obligation as a result of a past obligating event. The obligating event is the giving of the guarantee, which gives rise to a legal obligation. However, at 31 December 20X1 no transfer of economic benefits is probable in settlement of the obligation.

No provision is recognised. The guarantee is disclosed as a contingent liability unless the probability of any transfer is regarded as remote.

(b) *At 31 December 20X2*

As above, there is a present obligation as a result of a past obligating event, namely the giving of the guarantee.

At 31 December 20X2 it is probable that a transfer of economic benefits will be required to settle the obligation. A provision is therefore recognised for the best estimate of the obligation.

Chapter 8

Answer 8.1

	20X2		20X1	
	£'000	£'000	£'000	£'000
Turnover				
Continuing operations (200 – 22 – 7)/(180 – 26)		171		154
Acquisitions		7		–
		178		154
Discontinued		22		26
		200		180
Cost of sales		(60)		(80)
Gross profit		140		100
Distribution costs		(25)		(20)
Administration expenses (50 – 2)		(48)		(45)
Operating profit				
Continuing operations* (bal)	73		41	
Acquisitions	1		–	
	74		41	
Discontinued	(7)		(6)	
		67		35
Exceptional item		(2)		–
		65		35

* ie 65 + 2 + 7 – 1 = 73; 35 + 6 = 41

Answer 8.2

(a) Gains or losses arising on the translation of foreign currency, for example with overseas investments
(b) Gains or losses on long-term trade investments

Answer 8.3

STATEMENT OF RECOGNISED GAINS AND LOSSES

	£'000
Profit after tax	512
Asset revaluation	110
	622

RECONCILIATION OF MOVEMENTS IN SHAREHOLDERS' FUNDS

	£'000
Profit after tax	512
Dividend	(120)
	392
Other recognised gains and losses (622 – 512)	110
New share capital	300
Net addition to shareholders' funds	802
Opening shareholders' funds	3,100
Closing shareholders' funds	3,902

The write down of the stock items will be included in the P&L a/c and so is already included in the profit after tax figure.

Answer 8.4

RECONCILIATION OF PROFIT TO HISTORICAL COST PROFIT
FOR THE YEAR ENDED 31 DECEMBER 20X1

	£'000
Reported profit on ordinary activities before taxation	162
Realisation of property revaluation gains	20
Difference between historical cost depreciation charge and the Actual depreciation charge of the year calculated on the revalued amount (75,000 – 40,000)/5	7
	189

Answer 8.5

Earnings = 134,000 – 2,000 = 132,000

No of shares = 100,000

EPS = $\dfrac{132,000}{100,000}$ = £1.32

Note. This exercise (and perhaps an exam question you might meet) contains an extraordinary item to test whether you know you should deduct it for the EPS calculation. In practice, FRS 3 has made such items more or less redundant.

Answer 8.6

If the new accounting policy had been adopted since the company was incorporated, the additional profit and loss account charges for development expenditure would have been:

	£'000
20X0	525
20X1 (780 – 215)	565
	1,090
20X2 (995 – 360)	635
	1,725

ANSWERS TO ACTIVITIES

This means that the reserves brought forward at 1 January 20X3 would have been £1,725,000 less than the reported figure of £4,780,000; while the reserves brought forward at 1 January 20X2 would have been £1,090,000 less than the reported figure of £2,955,000.

The statement of reserves in Wick Ltd's 20X3 accounts should, therefore, appear as follows.

STATEMENT OF RESERVES (EXTRACT)

	20X3 £'000	Comparative (previous year) figures 20X2 £'000	
Retained profits at the beginning of year			
Previously reported	4,780	2,955	
Prior year adjustment (note 1)	1,725	1,090	
Restated	3,055	1,865	
Retained profits for the year	2,030	1,190	(note 2)
Retained profits at the end of the year	5,085	3,055	

Notes

1 The accounts should include a note explaining the reasons for and consequences of the changes in accounting policy. (See above workings for 20X3 and 20X2.)

2 The retained profit shown for 20X2 is after charging the additional development expenditure of £635,000.

Answer 8.7

(a) STUD-U-LIKE LIMITED
PROFIT AND LOSS ACCOUNT FOR THE YEAR ENDED 30 JUNE 20X7

	£'000	£'000
Turnover (W1)		292
Cost of sales (W2)		72
Gross profit		220
Operating expenses	18	
Decrease in doubtful debt provision (W3)	(1)	
Depreciation (10% × 100)	10	
		27
Net operating profit		193
Closure and redundancy costs	75	
Debenture interest (10% × 60)	6	
		81
Net profit before tax		112
Tax		30
Net profit after tax		82
Preference dividend (10% × 20,000)		2
Profit for the year available to ordinary shareholders		80

Workings

1   Turnover

	£'000
Sales per trial balance	300
Less returns incorrectly included	2
	298
Sales returns per trial balance	4
Add returns incorrectly excluded	2
	6

Turnover = sales less returns = 298 – 6 = 292

2   Cost of sales

	£'000
Opening stock	30
Purchases less returns (85 – 8)	77
	107
Closing stock	35
	72

3   Decrease in doubtful debt provision

	£'000
Provision as at 1 July 20X6	2
Provision required: 2½% × 40	1
∴ Decrease needed	1

(b) (i) The major change to the profit and loss account brought in by FRS 3 *Reporting financial performance* was to highlight certain key aspects of financial performance. It does this by requiring the following.

(1) All statutory headings from turnover to operating profit must be subdivided between that arising from continuing operations and that arising from discontinued operations.

(2) The following categories of exceptional items must be shown separately on the face of the profit and loss account after operating profit and before interest and allocated appropriately to discontinued and continued activities.

- Profit or loss on the sale or termination of an operation.
- Costs of a fundamental re-organisation or restructuring that has a material effect on the nature and focus of the reporting entity's operations.
- Profit or loss on disposal of a fixed asset.

The item to which FRS 3 could apply in the profit and loss account of Stud-U-Like is the closure/redundancy costs. The figure of £75,000 is material in the context of the accounts. If the factory making the ring binders is to be regarded as a discontinued operation, it will be necessary to separate out revenues and expenses associated with it from other revenues and expenses and show them separately as required by FRS 3. It will, in any case, be necessary to separate the profit or loss on the sale of fixed assets from the other costs as, if material, this is required to be shown separately as an exceptional item.

(ii) It is not clear, however, whether the manufacture of the special ring binders can be regarded as a separate operation which has now been discontinued. It appears that the ring binders were not sold separately, giving rise to separate revenues and costs, but were part of the cost of the Study Pack products. Further information on this point would be needed to determine exactly how FRS 3 should be applied.

Chapter 9

Answer 9.1

BUTTHEAD LIMITED
TRADING, PROFIT AND LOSS ACCOUNT
FOR THE YEAR ENDED 31 DECEMBER 20X7

	£	£
Sales (160,800 – 1,600)		159,200
Cost of goods sold		
Opening stock	10,800	
Purchases	82,400	
	93,200	
Closing stock	(13,600)	
		(79,600)
Gross profit		79,600
Sundry expenses (W1)		(46,400)
Operating profit		33,200
Debenture interest		(1,600)
Net profit		31,600
Dividends: preference	400	
ordinary (92,000 × 0.20)	18,400	
		(18,800)
Retained profit for the year		12,800
Retained profit brought forward		15,200
Retained profit carried forward		28,000

ANSWERS TO ACTIVITIES

BUTTHEAD LIMITED
BALANCE SHEET AS AT 31 DECEMBER 20X7

	£	£
Fixed assets		
Freehold building		60,000
Fixtures and fittings: cost	52,000	
depreciation	18,800	
		33,200
		93,200
Current assets		
Stock	13,600	
Debtors	17,600	
Cash in hand	1,200	
	32,400	
Current liabilities		
Creditors	16,000	
Debenture interest ($^6/_{12} \times 1,600$)	800	
Dividends	18,800	
Bank overdraft	2,000	
	37,600	
Net current liabilities		(5,200)
Total assets less current liabilities		88,000
10% debentures		(16,000)
		72,000
Share capital and reserves		
Ordinary shares of 25p		23,000
5% preference shares of 25p		8,000
Share premium		9,000
Revaluation reserve		4,000
Profit and loss reserve		28,000
		72,000

Workings

1   Sundry expenses

	£
Per trial balance	37,600
Less debenture interest ($16,000 \times 10\% \times ^6/_{12}$)	(800)
Suspense account (W4)	6,400
Bank (2,800 + 400)	3,200
	46,400

ANSWERS TO ACTIVITIES

2 *Debtors control account and debtors ledger*

DEBTORS CONTROL ACCOUNT

	£		£
Balance b/d	21,200	Sales	1,600
Suspense	1,200	Contra	1,600
		Suspense	1,600
		Balance c/d	17,600
	22,400		22,400

Debtors ledger

	Dr	Cr
	£	£
Balances b/d	20,000	1,200
Understatement	400	
Sales		1,600
	20,400	2,800

Net corrected balance: £17,600

3 *Creditors control account and creditors ledger*

CREDITORS CONTROL ACCOUNT

	£		£
Contra	1,600	Balance b/d	14,400
Balance c/d	16,000	Suspense a/c	3,200
	17,600		17,600

Creditors ledger

	Dr	Cr
	£	£
Balance b/d	800	16,000
Beavis plc		800
	800	16,800

Net credit balances: £16,000

4 *Suspense account*

SUSPENSE ACCOUNT

	£		£
Balance b/d	2,800	Debtors control	1,200
Creditors control	3,200	Sundry expenses (bal fig)	6,400
Debtors control	1,600		
	7,600		7,600

ANSWERS TO ACTIVITIES

5   Bank

	£	
Balance per bank statement	(1,200)	o/d
Unpresented cheques	(800)	
	(2,000)	o/d
Cash book balance per t/b	1,200	
Cheque difference (to sundry expenses)	(400)	
Bank charges (bal fig)	(2,800)	
	(2,000)	

Answer 9.2

(a) *Statement of total recognised gains and losses*

	£'000
Profit for the financial year	566
Surplus on revaluation of freehold land and buildings (500 – 375 – 5 (see below))	120
Deficit on revaluation of investment properties	(60)
	626

(b) *Reconciliation of movements in shareholders' funds*

	£'000
Profit for the financial year	566
Revaluation surplus	120
Dividend	(200)
	486
Other recognised losses (temporary write down to IRR)	(60)
New share capital subscribed	600
Net addition to shareholders' funds	1,026
Opening shareholders' funds	6,820
Closing shareholders' funds	7,846

(c) *Note of historical cost profits for the period*

	£'000
Reported profit before tax	806
Realisation of property revaluation gains of previous years $\left(50,000 - \left(\frac{50,000}{10} \times 3\right)\right)$	35
Difference between an historical cost depreciation charge and the actual depreciation charge of the year calculated on the revalued amount ((500,000 – 375,000)/25)	5
	846
Historical cost retained profit for the year (366 + 35 + 5)	406

Answer 9.3

(a) (i) No adjustment is required

				£	£
(ii)	DEBIT	Audit fees (P&L)		73,146	
	CREDIT	Accruals			73,146

Being provision of audit fees

(iii)	DEBIT	Debenture interest (P&L)	576,000*	
	CREDIT	Interest payable		576,000

Being provision for debenture interest payable
*(4,800,000 × 12% = £576,000)

(iv)	DEBIT	Tax charge (P&L)	1,470,314	
	CREDIT	Tax payable		1,470,314

Being provision of corporation tax payable

(v)	DEBIT	Cost of sales (closing stock)	172,530**	
	CREDIT	Stock		172,530

Being write down of stock to net realisable value
**(£294,426 – £121,896)

(vi) No adjustment is required

(vii)	DEBIT	Land	400,000	
	CREDIT	Revaluation reserve		400,000

Being revaluation of land

(viii)	DEBIT	Ordinary dividends (P&L)	78,000***	
	DEBIT	Preference dividends (P&L)	30,400***	
	CREDIT	Proposed dividend		108,400

Being provision of ordinary and preference dividends

***Note   Ordinary dividend: 1,200,000 × 6.5p per share = £78,000
         Preference dividend: £400,000 × 7.6% = £30,400

(ix) – (xiii) No adjustment required

(b) **EXTENSION LIMITED**
PROFIT AND LOSS ACCOUNT FOR THE YEAR ENDED 30 JUNE 20X4

	£
Turnover (W1)	
Continuing operations	29,717,868
Cost of sales (W2)	15,407,234
Gross profit	14,310,634
Distribution costs (W3)	6,982,942
Administrative expenses (W3)	2,160,240
Operating profit	
Continuing operations	5,167,452
Interest payable and similar charges	576,000
Profit on ordinary activities before taxation	4,591,452
Tax on profit on ordinary activities	1,470,314
Profit on ordinary activities after taxation	3,121,138
Dividends (W4)	206,800
Retained profit for the financial year	2,914,338
Retained profit b/fwd	1,429,362
Retained profit c/fwd	4,343,700

EXTENSION LIMITED
BALANCE SHEET AS AT 30 JUNE 20X4

	£	£
Fixed assets		
Tangible assets	3,923,302	
Intangible assets	703,144	
		4,626,446
Current assets		
Stocks	3,846,430	
Debtors	7,242,932	
Cash at bank and in hand	5,870	
	11,095,232	
Creditors: amounts falling due within one year (W5)	4,114,852	
		6,980,380
Total assets less current liabilities		11,606,826
Creditors: amounts falling due after more than one year		4,800,000
		6,806,826
Capital and reserves		
Called up share capital		1,600,000
Share premium		463,126
Revaluation reserve		400,000
Profit and loss account		4,343,700
		6,806,826

ANSWERS TO ACTIVITIES

Workings

1   *Turnover*

	£
Sales	30,368,730
Less returns inwards	(650,862)
Turnover	29,717,868

2   *Cost of sales*

	£
Opening stock	2,973,910
Purchases	16,402,622
Plus carriage inwards	250,438
Less returns outwards	(373,306)
	19,253,664
Less closing stock	(3,846,430)
Cost of sales	15,407,234

3   *Distribution costs and administrative expenses*

	Distribution costs £	Administrative expenses £
Advertising	1,186,430	
Salaries and wages	2,184,270	982,032
Increase in provision for doubtful debts		46,268
Discounts allowed		148,374
Motor expense (80/20)	1,366,020	341,504
Salesmen's commission	1,207,362	
Rates (75/25)	127,428	42,476
Light and heat (75/25)	189,542	63,180
Insurance (75/25)	32,906	10,968
Audit		73,146
General expenses (80/20)	138,422	34,606
Directors' remuneration	173,042	331,272
Depreciation: Motor vehicles (80/20)	255,464	63,866
Fixtures and fittings	77,410	
Office equipment (60/40)	22,998	15,332
Buildings (75/25)	21,648	7,216
	6,982,942	2,160,240

4   *Dividends*

	£
Preference dividends	30,400
Interim dividend paid	98,400
Final dividend proposed	78,000
	206,800

ANSWERS TO ACTIVITIES

5 *Creditors: amounts falling due within one year*

		£
From ETB:	Trade creditors	1,701,506
	Accruals	98,556
	Bank overdraft	86,930
Journals:	Audit fees	73,146
	Interest payable	576,000
	Tax payable	1,470,314
	Proposed dividend	108,400
		4,114,852

(c) **EXTENSION LIMITED**
TRADING, PROFIT AND LOSS ACCOUNT
FOR THE YEAR ENDED 30 JUNE 20X4

	£	£
Sales		30,368,730
Less returns inwards		(650,862)
		29,717,868
Opening stock	2,973,910	
Purchases	16,402,622	
Plus carriage inwards	250,438	
Less returns outwards	(373,306)	
	19,253,664	
Less closing stock	(3,846,430)	
		(15,407,234)
Gross profit		14,310,634
Less expenses		
Advertising	1,186,430	
Salaries and wages	3,166,302	
Discount allowed	148,374	
Motor expenses	1,707,524	
Salesmen's commission	1,207,362	
Rates	169,904	
Light and heat	252,722	
Insurance	43,874	
Audit fees	73,146	
General expenses	173,028	
Increase in provision for doubtful debts	46,268	
Directors' remuneration	504,314	
Debenture interest	576,000	
Depreciation: motor vehicles	319,330	
fixtures and fittings	77,410	
office equipment	38,330	
buildings	28,864	
		9,719,182
Profit for the year before taxation		4,591,452
Corporation tax		1,470,314
Profit for the year after taxation		3,121,138
Retained profits brought forward		1,429,362
		4,550,500
Preference dividends	30,400	
Interim dividend paid	98,400	
Final dividend proposed	78,000	
		206,800
Retained profits carried forward		4,343,700

Answer 9.4

(a)

				£'000	£'000
	(i)	DEBIT	Dividends P&L	80	
		CREDIT	Dividends payable (b/s)		80
			£(1,000,000 × 4 × 0.02)		
	(ii)	DEBIT	Tax charge (P&L)	1,356	
		CREDIT	Corporation tax payable (b/s)		1,356
	(iii)	DEBIT	Interest payable (P&L)	189	
		CREDIT	Interest payable (b/s)		189
			£4,200,000 × 9% × 6/12		
	(iv)	DEBIT	Land	720	
		CREDIT	Revaluation reserve		720
			£(4,290,000 – 3,570,000)		
	(v)	DEBIT	Stock (P&L)	50	
		CREDIT	Stock (b/s)		50

(b) **Item (f) – revaluation of land**

Although the Companies Act 1985 states that the normal basis for the preparation of financial statements should be historical cost principles, under the alternative accounting rules, assets may be revalued.

Where the value of any fixed asset is determined by using the alternative accounting rules, the amount of profit or loss arising must be credited to a separate reserve, the revaluation reserve. The calculation of the relevant amounts should be based on the written down values of the assets prior to revaluation. The year of valuation and the name of the valuer must be disclosed. Spiraes Ltd has adopted the alternative accounting rules and intends to show the land at valuation rather than at historical cost.

Item (h) – stock

The stock figure has been written down to reflect the fall in value. The main principle being applied here derives from SSAP 9 *Accounting for stocks and long-term contracts*. The SSAP states that stocks must be shown at the lower of cost and net realisable value. The stocks were sold for £355,000 after the year end, which provides evidence of their net realisable value at the year end.

The other relevant accounting standard is SSAP 17 *Accounting for post balance sheet events*. According to SSAP 17 this is an adjusting event, so the accounts must be adjusted to reflect the fall in value.

(c) SPIRAES LIMITED
PROFIT AND LOSS ACCOUNT
FOR THE YEAR ENDED 30 NOVEMBER 20X6

	£'000
Turnover (W1)	
Continuing operations	18,147
Cost of sales (W2)	10,230
Gross profit	7,917
Distribution costs	2,514
Administrative expenses	1,820
Operating profit	
Continuing operations	3,583
Income from other fixed asset investments	52
	3,635
Interest payable and similar charges (189 × 2)	378
Profit on ordinary activities before taxation	3,257
Tax on profit on ordinary activities	1,356
Profit for the financial year	1,901
Dividends (Task 1)	80
Retained profit for the financial year	1,821

Workings

1   *Turnover*

	£'000
Sales per ETB	18,742
Returns inwards	595
	18,147

2   *Cost of sales*

	£'000	£'000
Opening stock		3,871
Purchases	10,776	
Less returns outwards	314	
		10,462
		14,333
Less closing stock		4,103
		10,230

(d) STATEMENT OF TOTAL RECOGNISED GAINS AND LOSSES

	£'000
Profit for the financial year	1,901
Unrealised surplus on revaluation of properties	720
	2,621

Chapter 10

Answer 10.1

BALDWIN LIMITED
STATEMENT OF FORECAST CASH FLOWS FOR
THE YEAR ENDING 31 DECEMBER 20X2

	£	£
Operating activities		
Cash received from customers	36,450	
(£36,000 + £900 – £450)		
Cash paid to suppliers (£18,750 + £2,550 – £4,125)	(17,175)	
Cash paid to and on behalf of employees		
(£11,250 + £750 – £600)	(11,400)	
Net cash flow from operating activities		7,875
Returns on investments and servicing of finance		
Interest paid	(1,575)	
Interest received	150	
		(1,425)
Taxation		(2,300)
Capital expenditure		
Purchase of fixed assets		(3,000)
		1,150
Equity dividends paid		(4,000)
Financing		
Repayment of medium-term loan		(5,250)
Forecast net decrease in cash at 31 December 20X2		(8,100)
Cash as at 31 December 20X1		29,525
Forecast cash as at 31 December 20X2		21,425

Answer 10.3

SEAGER PLC
CASH FLOW STATEMENT
FOR THE YEAR ENDED 31 DECEMBER 20X8

	£'000	£'000
Operating activities		
Cash received from customers (W1)	579	
Cash payments to suppliers (W2)	(366)	
Cash payments to and on behalf of employees	(86)	
		127
Returns on investments and servicing of finance		
Interest paid		(8)
Taxation		
UK corporation tax paid (W5)		(20)
Capital expenditure		
Purchase of tangible fixed assets (W6)	(146)	
Net cash outflow from capital expenditure		(146)
		(47)
Equity dividends paid (W4)		(22)
Financing		
Issue of share capital	60	
Issue of debentures	30	
Net cash inflow from financing		90
Increase in cash		21

NOTES TO THE CASHFLOW STATEMENT

1 *Reconciliation of operating profit to net cash inflow from operating activities*

	£'000
Operating profit (87 + 8)*	95
Depreciation	42
Increase in stock	(4)
Increase in debtors	(21)
Increase in creditors	15
	127

Operating profit is adjusted for debenture interest (10% × £80,000 = £8,000). The reason for this is that debenture interest is a cost of servicing of finance, not part of operating profit.

ANSWERS TO ACTIVITIES

2   *Reconciliation of net cash flow to movement in net debt*

	£'000
Net cash inflow for the period	21
Cash received from debenture issue	(30)
Change in net debt	(9)
Net debt at 1 January 20X8	(64)
Net debt at 31 December 20X8	(73)

3   *Analysis of changes in net debt*

	At 1 January 20X8 £'000	Cash flows £'000	At 31 December 20X8 £'000
Cash at bank	–	7	7
Overdrafts	(14)	14	–
		21	
Debt due after 1 year	(50)	(30)	(80)
Total	(64)	(9)	(73)

Workings

1   *Cash received from customers*

DEBTORS CONTROL ACCOUNT

	£'000		£'000
B/f	147	Cash received (bal)	579
Sales	600	C/f	168
	747		747

2   *Cash paid to suppliers*

CREDITORS CONTROL ACCOUNT

	£'000		£'000
Cash paid (bal)	366	B/f	121
C/f	136	Purchases (W3)	381
	502		502

3   *Purchases*

	£'000
Cost of sales	319
Opening stock	(210)
Closing stock	214
Expenses (194 – 42 – 86 – 8 debenture interest)	58
	381

4   *Dividends*

DIVIDENDS

	£'000		£'000
∴ Dividends paid	22	Balance b/f	16
Balance c/f	18	Dividend for year	24
	40		40

5   *Taxation*

TAXATION

	£'000		£'000
∴ Tax paid	20	Balance b/f	28
Balance c/f	39	Charge for year	31
	59		59

6   *Purchase of fixed assets*

	£'000
Opening fixed assets	514
Less depreciation	(42)
Add revaluation (110 – 100)	10
	482
Closing fixed assets	628
Difference = additions	146

Answer 10.4

CASHEDIN LIMITED
CASH FLOW STATEMENT FOR THE YEAR ENDED 30 SEPTEMBER 20X5

	£'000	£'000
Net cash inflow from operating activities		104
Returns on investments and servicing of finance		
Interest paid		(218)
Taxation		(75)
		(189)
Capital expenditure		
Payments to acquire tangible fixed assets	(358)	
Proceeds from sale of fixed assets	132	
		(226)
		(415)
Equity dividends paid		(280)
		(695)
Financing		
Loans	200	
Issue of ordinary share capital	150	
		350
Decrease in cash		(345)

Reconciliation of operating profit and net cash inflow from operating activities

	£'000
Operating profit	24
Depreciation	318
Increase in stock	(251)
Increase in debtors	(152)
Increase in creditors	165
Net cash inflow from operating activities	104

Answer 10.5

POISED LIMITED
RECONCILIATION OF OPERATING PROFIT
TO NET CASH INFLOW FROM OPERATING ACTIVITIES

	£'000
Operating profit	2,099
Depreciation	1,347
Increase in stocks (2,473 – 2,138)	(335)
Increase in debtors (1,872 – 1,653)	(219)
Increase in creditors (1,579 – 1,238)	341
Net cash inflow from operating activities	3,233

Answer 10.6

The main disadvantages of cash accounting are essentially the advantages of accruals accounting (proper matching of related items). There is also the practical problem that few businesses keep historical cash flow information in the form needed to prepare a historical cash flow statement and so extra record keeping is likely to be necessary.

Answer 10.7

(a) *Calculation of operating profit*

PROFIT AND LOSS ACCOUNT

	£'000		£'000
Taxation*	38	Balance at 1.1.X7	110
Dividends	56	Profit for the year (bal fig)	138
Debenture interest (160 × 15%)	24		
Balance at 31.12.X7	130		
	248		248

* Last year's year end provision

ANSWERS TO ACTIVITIES

(b) CAT PLC
CASH FLOW STATEMENT
FOR THE YEAR ENDED 31 DECEMBER 20X7

Reconciliation of operating profit to net cash inflow from operating activities

	£'000
Operating profit (part (a))	138
Depreciation (180 – 112)	68
Increase in stocks	(16)
Increase in debtors	(14)
Increase in creditors	18
Net cash inflow from operating activities	194

CASH FLOW STATEMENT

	£'000
Net cash inflow from operating activities	194
Returns on investments and servicing of finance (note 1)	(24)
Taxation	(34)
Capital expenditure (note 1)	(180)
	(44)
Equity dividends paid	(52)
	(96)
Financing (note 1)	54
Decrease in cash	(42)

Note 1 – Gross cash flows

	£'000	£'000
Returns on investments and servicing of finance		
Interest paid	(24)	
		(24)
Capital expenditure		
Purchase of fixed assets (270 – 180)	(180)	
		(180)
Financing		
Issue of share capital	10	
Share premium	4	
Issue of debentures	40	
		54

(c) Attached to the cash flow statement is a reconciliation of net cash flow to movement in net debt. Note 2 to the cash flow statement is an analysis of changes in net debt.

Answer 10.8

(a) EALING LIMITED
CASH FLOW STATEMENT
FOR THE YEAR ENDED 31 DECEMBER 20X9

Reconciliation of operating profit to net cash flows from operating activities

	£'000
Profit before interest and tax (2,440 + 235)	2,675
Depreciation (W1)	2,640
Loss on disposal	250
Increase in stock (4,217 – 2,695)	(1,522)
Increase in debtors (2,500 – 1,740)	(760)
Increase in creditors (3,290 – 2,065)	1,225
Net cash inflow from operating activities	4,508

Cash flow statement

	£'000	£'000
Net cash inflow from operating activities		4,508
Returns on investments and servicing of finance		
Interest paid		(235)
Taxation		
Corporation tax paid		(400)
Capital expenditure		
Payments to acquire fixed assets (W)	(5,518)	
Proceeds from sale of fixed assets	500	
		(5,018)
		(1,145)
Equity dividends paid		(30)
Financing		
Issue of share capital (1,235 – 795)	440	
Share premium (650 – 495)	155	
Long term loans (1,145 – 875)	270	
		865
Decrease in cash		(310)

Notes to the cash flow statement

1 Reconciliation of net cash flow to movement in net debt

	£'000
Net cash outflow for the period	(310)
Increase in long term loans	(270)
Change in net debt	(580)
Net debt at 1 January 20X9	(985)
Net debt at 31 December 20X9	(1,565)

ANSWERS TO ACTIVITIES

2 *Analysis of changes in net debt*

	At 1 Jan 20X9 £'000	Cash flows £'000	At 31 Dec 20X9 £'000
Bank overdraft	(110)	(310)	(420)
Debt due after 1 year	(875)	(270)	(1,145)
	(985)	(580)	(1,565)

Working: fixed assets and depreciation

FIXED ASSETS: COST

	£'000		£'000
Balance b/f	6,545	Disposals	2,500
Additions	5,518	Balance c/f	9,563
	12,063		12,063

FIXED ASSETS: ACCUMULATED DEPRECIATION

	£'000		£'000
Disposals	1,750	Balance b/f	5,120
Balance c/f	6,010	P & L a/c (bal. fig.)	2,640
	7,760		7,760

FIXED ASSETS: DISPOSALS

	£'000		£'000
Disposals	2,500	Accumulated depn.	1,750
		Sale proceeds	500
		Loss on disposal	250
	2,500		2,500

(b) Ealing Ltd is showing a **net decrease in cash** for the year ended 31 December 20X9 of £310,000. This is not good news. The net cash inflow from operating activities is impressive at £4,508,000, but this is offset by the factors that are putting the company's working capital under strain.

The main cash outflow is the **purchase of fixed assets** for £5,518,000. This suggests that the company is **expanding, perhaps too rapidly**, although it is to be hoped that the fixed assets would generate profits in future years.

Ealing Ltd has **borrowed heavily** to finance this expansion – the overdraft has increased and there are new long-term loans of £270,000. These incurred high interest costs. The company's gearing will be prevented from going too high by the issue of ordinary share capital of £595,000.

Stocks, debtors and creditors have all increased, again showing that the company's **working capital is under strain**.

Chapter 11

Answer 11.1

ROCE = $\dfrac{\text{Profit}}{\text{Capital employed}}$

PM = $\dfrac{\text{Profit}}{\text{Sales}}$

AT = $\dfrac{\text{Sales}}{\text{Capital employed}}$

It follows that ROCE = PM x AT, which can be re-arranged to the form given in option D.

Answer 11.2

Interest payments should be taken gross, from the note to the accounts, and not net of interest receipts as shown in the P & L account.

	20X8	20X7
PBIT	360,245	247,011
Interest payable	18,115	21,909
	= 20 times	= 11 times

Betatec plc has more than sufficient interest cover. In view of the company's low gearing, this is not too surprising and so we finally obtain a picture of Betatec plc as a company that does not seem to have a debt problem, in spite of its high (although declining) debt ratio.

Answer 11.3

The cash cycle is the length of time between paying for raw materials and receiving cash from the sale of finished goods. In this case Butthead Ltd stores raw materials for three weeks, spends two weeks producing finished goods, four weeks storing the goods before sale and five weeks collecting the money from debtors: a total of 14 weeks. However, six weeks of this period is effectively financed by the company's creditors so that the length of the cash cycle is eight weeks.

Answer 11.4

Stock turnover = $\dfrac{\text{Cost of goods sold}}{\text{Average stock}}$ = $\dfrac{£60,000}{£8,000}$

= 7.5 times

Answer 11.5

	20X7	20X6
Current ratio	$\dfrac{626.8}{599.1} = 1.05$	$\dfrac{654.4}{642.2} = 1.02$
Quick ratio	$\dfrac{584.1}{599.1} = 0.97$	$\dfrac{576.4}{642.2} = 0.90$
Debtors' payment period	$\dfrac{295.2}{2{,}176.2} \times 365 = 49.5$ days	$\dfrac{335.5}{2{,}344.8} \times 365 = 52.2$ days
Stock turnover period	$\dfrac{42.7}{1{,}659.0} \times 365 = 9.4$ days	$\dfrac{78.0}{1{,}731.5} \times 365 = 16.4$ days
Creditors' turnover period	$\dfrac{190.8}{1{,}659.0} \times 365 = 42.0$ days	$\dfrac{188.1}{1{,}731.5} \times 365 = 40.0$ days

Answer 11.6

> **Tutorial note.** Do not be put off by the fact that you are writing to the managers of a hospitals trust – this is ratio analysis in its normal form. Don't forget – you need to *comment* on the ratios as well as calculating them correctly.

REPORT

To: The Managers, Bimbridge Hospitals Trust
From: A Technician
Date: 20 November 20X8

Performance and position of Patch Ltd

As requested, I have analysed the performance and position of Patch Ltd with special reference to selected accounting ratios. The calculation of the ratios is shown in the Appendix attached to this report. The purpose of the analysis is to determine whether we should use Patch Ltd as a supplier of bandages.

General comments

Both turnover and profits have increased over the two years. The company is clearly expanding, although not at an exceptionally fast rate. The growth seems to have been achieved without investing heavily in fixed assets, the fall in this figure presumably being due to depreciation. Shares were issued in 20X8 at a premium, while a sizeable portion of the long-term loan has been paid off. Expansion appears to be financed by share capital and profits.

Return on capital employed

This has increased from 8% in 20X7 to 10.3% in 20X8. It had also gone from being below the industry average in 20X7 to above it in 20X8. These are encouraging signs. As indicated above, the company has not invested significantly in fixed assets to finance its expansion – the assets/capital employed is simply working harder.

Net profit percentage

This has also increased from 22% in 20X7 to 24% in 20X8. In both years it was higher than the industry average. This is obviously good news. Sometimes when a company grows, it is at the expense of lower margins, but this is clearly not the case for Patch Ltd.

Quick ratio or acid test

The quick ratio shows how many assets, excluding stock, are available to meet the current liabilities. Stock is excluded because it is not always readily convertible into cash. The quick ratio or acid test is therefore a better indicator of a company's true liquidity than the current ratio which does not exclude stock. Patch Ltd's quick ratio is healthy (around 1) in both years, and has in fact improved from) 0.9:1 to 1.1:1. While Patch's quick ratio was the same as the industry average in 20X7, it was better than average in 20X8.

These are encouraging signs. Sometimes growth can lead to overtrading to the detriment of liquidity, but Patch Ltd has not fallen into this trap.

Gearing

The gearing ratio is also favourable. This can be calculated in two ways: debt/capital employed and debt/equity. Debt/capital employed shows a fall from 43% in 20X7 to 31% in 20X8. In 20X7 it was higher than the industry average, but in 20X8 it is lower. Calculated as debt/equity, the ratio shows an even more significant decline.

This is reassuring. A high geared company is more risky than a low geared one in that, if profits are falling, it is more difficult for a high geared company to meet interest payments. A high geared company is therefore more likely to go into liquidation, as our last supplier of bandages did.

Conclusion

On the basis of the above analysis, I see every reason to use Patch Ltd as our supplier. The company's profitability and liquidity are improving and the gearing is at a lower level than last year. In addition the company compares favourably with other companies operating in the same sector.

APPENDIX – CALCULATION OF RATIOS

	20X8	Industry average 20X8	20X7	Industry average 20X7
Return on capital employed	$\frac{552}{5,334} = 10.3\%$	9.6%	$\frac{462}{5,790} = 8.0\%$	9.4%
Net profit percentage	$\frac{552}{2,300} = 24\%$	21.4%	$\frac{462}{2,100} = 22\%$	21.3%
Quick ratio/acid test	$\frac{1,045 - 522}{475} = 1.1:1$	1.0:1	$\frac{837 - 419}{465} = 0.9:1$	0.9:1
Gearing:				
Debt/capital employed	$\frac{1,654}{5,334} = 31\%$	36%	$\frac{2,490}{5,790} = 43\%$	37%
Debt/equity	$\frac{1,654}{3,680} = 45\%$		$\frac{2,490}{3,300} = 75\%$	

ANSWERS TO ACTIVITIES

Chapter 12

Answer 12.1

(a) False. The correct calculation is

	£
Apple	80,000
Pear	50,000
	130,000

Pear is a subsidiary of Apple, who controls **all** its fixed assets not just 60%. The 40% minority interest is accounted for separately.

(b) (i) *Consolidated debtors*

	£
Apple	60,000
Less inter-company	(10,000)
	50,000
Pear	40,000
Consolidated	90,000

(ii) *Consolidated creditors*

	£	£
Apple		120,000
Pear	90,000	
Less inter-company	(10,000)	
		80,000
		200,000

Chapter 13

Answer 13.1

The partly cancelling item is P Ltd's investment in S Ltd, ie ordinary shares. Minorities have an interest in 40% (8,000/20,000) of S Ltd's equity, including reserves.

You should now produce workings for minority interests and reserves as follows.

Workings

1 *Minority interests*

	£
Ordinary share capital: 40% of 20,000	8,000
Reserves: 40% of 10,000	4,000
	12,000

2 *Reserves*

	£
P Ltd	14,000
Share of S Ltd's reserves (60% × 10,000)	6,000
	20,000

The results of the workings are now used to construct the consolidated balance sheet (CBS).

P GROUP
CONSOLIDATED BALANCE SHEET

	£
Tangible fixed assets (31,000 + 25,000)	56,000
Net current assets (11,000 + 5,000)	16,000
	72,000
Capital and reserves	
Ordinary shares of £1 each	40,000
Reserves	20,000
Shareholders' funds	60,000
Minority interests	12,000
	72,000

Notes

1 S Ltd is a subsidiary of P Ltd because P Ltd owns 60% of its equity capital.

2 As always, the share capital in the consolidated balance sheet is that of the parent company alone. The share capital in S Ltd's balance sheet was partly cancelled against the investment shown in P Ltd's balance sheet, while the uncancelled portion was credited to minority interest.

3 The figure for minority interest comprises the interest of outside investors in the share capital and reserves of the subsidiary.

Answer 13.2

THOMAS LIMITED
CONSOLIDATED BALANCE SHEET AS AT 30 SEPTEMBER 20X6

	£'000	£'000
Fixed assets		
Intangible: goodwill		640
Tangible		16,932
Current assets		
Stocks	8,702	
Debtors	6,378	
Cash	331	
	15,411	
Current liabilities		
Trade creditors	4,494	
Taxation	1,007	
	5,501	
Net current assets		9,910
Total assets less current liabilities		27,482
Long-term loan		9,500
		17,982
Capital and reserves		
Called up share capital		5,000
Share premium		2,500
Profit and loss account		9,550
		17,050
Minority interest		932
		17,982

Workings

1 Group structure

$$\frac{800,000}{1,000,000}$$

Thomas Ltd
|
80%
|
James Ltd

2   Goodwill

	£'000	£'000
Cost of investment		3,760
Net assets acquired		
Share capital	1,000	
Share premium	400	
Revaluation reserve (3,910 – 3,410)	500	
Profit and loss account	2,000	
	3,900	
Group share × 80%		3,120
Goodwill		640

3   Minority interest

	£'000
Net assets at 30 September 20X6	
Share capital	1,000
Share premium	400
Revaluation reserve	500
Profit and loss account	2,760
	4,660

Minority interest = £4,660,000 × 20% = £932,000.

4   Profit and loss account

	£'000
Thomas Ltd	8,942
James Ltd 80% × (2,760 – 2,000)	608
	9,550

Answer 13.3

1   Goodwill

	£	£
Cost of investment		46,000
Share of net assets acquired as represented by		
Share capital	30,000	
Reserves	10,000	
	40,000	
Group share (100%)		40,000
Goodwill		6,000

ANSWERS TO ACTIVITIES

2 *Reserves*

	£
H Ltd	45,000
Share of S Ltd's post acquisition retained reserves £(22,000 – 10,000)	12,000
	57,000
Stock: unrealised profit (20% × £15,000)	3,000
Group reserves	54,000

H LIMITED
CONSOLIDATED BALANCE SHEET

	£	£
Intangible fixed asset: goodwill		6,000
Tangible fixed assets		120,000
Current assets (W1)	55,000	
Current liabilities (W2)	27,000	
		28,000
		154,000
Capital and reserves		
Ordinary shares of £1 each		100,000
Reserves		54,000
		154,000

Workings

1 *Current assets*

	£	£
In H Ltd's balance sheet		40,000
In S Ltd's balance sheet	30,000	
Less S Ltd's current account with H Ltd cancelled	12,000	
		18,000
		58,000
Less unrealised profit excluded from stock valuation		3,000
		55,000

2 *Current liabilities*

	£
In H Ltd's balance sheet	21,000
Less H Ltd's current account with S Ltd cancelled	12,000
	9,000
In S Ltd's balance sheet	18,000
	27,000

Answer 13.4

(a) OAK PLC
CONSOLIDATED BALANCE SHEET AS AT 30 SEPTEMBER 20X8

	£	£
Fixed assets		
Land and buildings (W3)		615,000
Plant		360,000
		975,000
Current assets		
Stock (W6)	424,500	
Debtors (W7)	450,000	
Bank	135,000	
	1,009,500	
Creditors: amounts falling due within one year (W8)	(210,000)	
		799,500
		1,774,500
Capital and reserves		
Ordinary £1 shares		1,125,000
Reserves (W5)		495,000
		1,620,000
Minority interest (W4)		154,500
		1,774,500

Workings

1 Group structure

$$\frac{360,000}{450,000} = 80\%$$

2 Goodwill

	£	£
Cost of investment		562,500
Net assets acquired		
Share capital	450,000	
Reserves	105,000	
Revaluation reserve	120,000	
	675,000	
× 80%		540,000
Goodwill		22,500

ANSWERS TO ACTIVITIES

3   *Land and buildings*

		£	£
Oak plc			225,000
Chestnut Ltd:			
Net book value		270,000	
Revaluation		120,000	
			390,000
			615,000

4   *Minority interests*

	£
Share capital	450,000
Revaluation	120,000
Reserves	202,500
	772,500
20% × £772,500 =	£154,500

5   *Reserves*

	£
Oak plc	450,000
Chestnut Ltd (202,500 – 105,000) × 80%	78,000
Goodwill	(22,500)
Unrealised profit	(10,500)
	495,000

6   *Stock*

	£
Oak	255,000
Chestnut	180,000
Less unrealised profit	10,500
	424,500

7   *Debtors*

	£
Oak	375,000
Chestnut	90,000
Less intercompany	(15,000)
	450,000

8   *Creditors: amounts falling due within one year*

	£
Oak	157,500
Chestnut	67,500
Less intercompany	(15,000)
	210,000

(b)   We prepare group accounts to reflect the group's trading as if it were a **single** entity. Companies within a group may trade with each other, and any profit made on such trading must be shown in the individual company accounts.

For example, Oak plc has sold goods to Chestnut plc at a profit. The individual accounts of Oak plc rightly show this profit. However, the group does not make a sale or achieve a profit until the goods are sold outside the group. Similarly, any goods that Chestnut Ltd has not sold by the end of the year will be included in Chestnut Ltd's stock at cost plus profit. In terms of the group's position, stock could be overvalued, because the actual cost to the group at the start will be what it cost Oak plc.

This anomaly is dealt with by **eliminating the unrealised profit** from stock in the consolidated balance sheet and from consolidated reserves.

The same reasoning can be applied to intercompany debtors and creditors. Chestnut Ltd owes £15,000 to Oak plc which is included in the creditors of Chestnut Ltd and the debtors of Oak plc. However, the group does not owe this amount to any outsiders and is not owed the money by outsiders. The balances should therefore be eliminated on consolidation.

Answer 13.5

SHARK PLC
CONSOLIDATED BALANCE SHEET AS AT 31 OCTOBER 20X0

	£'000	£'000
Fixed assets		
Land (W2)		405
Fixtures (200 + 50)		250
		655
Current assets		
Stock (W3)	281	
Debtors (W4)	200	
Bank	100	
	581	
Creditors: amounts falling due within one year		
Creditors (W5)	280	
Bank overdraft	20	
	300	
Net current assets		281
		936
Capital and reserves		
Share capital		700
Reserves (W6)		167
		867
Minority interests (W7)		69
		936

ANSWERS TO ACTIVITIES

Workings

1. *Goodwill*

	£'000	£'000
Cost of investment		200
Net assets acquired		
Share capital	170	
Reserves	20	
Revaluation reserve (60 – 50)	10	
	200	
Group share: 70%		140
Goodwill		60

2. *Land*

	£'000	£'000
Shark		325
Minnow		
Per question	70	
Revalued (60 – 50)	10	
		80
		405

3. *Stock*

	£'000	£'000
Shark		220
Minnow	70	
Less PUP ($45 \times {}^{25}/_{125}$)	(9)	
		61
		281

4. *Debtors*

	£'000	£'000
Shark		145
Less intercompany		35
		110
Minnow	105	
Less intercompany	15	
		90
		200

ANSWERS TO ACTIVITIES

5 *Creditors*

	£'000	£'000
Shark		275
Less intercompany		15
		260
Minnow	55	
Less intercompany	35	
		20
		280

6 *Reserves*

	£'000	£'000
Shark		215
Less goodwill fully amortised (W1)	60.0	
PUP (W3)	9.0	
	5.6	
		69
		146
Minnow: 70% × (50 − 20)		21
		167

7 *Minority interests*

	£'000
Share capital	170
Revaluation	10
Reserves	50
	230

∴ Minority interests: 30% × £230,000 = £69,000.

Chapter 14
Answer 14.1

(a) (i) BAMBER LIMITED
CONSOLIDATED PROFIT AND LOSS ACCOUNT
FOR THE YEAR ENDED 31 OCTOBER 20X9

	£'000
Turnover (1,000 + 250 – 160)	1,090
Cost of sales (bal. fig.)	685
Gross profit (350 + 70 – 15 (W3))	405
Distribution costs (75 + 15)	90
Administrative expenses (W5)	81
Operating profit	234
Investment income (W4)	2
Profit on ordinary attributes before tax	236
Tax on profit on ordinary activities (70 + 10)	80
Profit on ordinary activities after tax	156
Minority interests (25 × 20%)	5
Group profit for the year	151
Dividends	80
Group retained profit for the year	71

(ii) BAMBER LIMITED
CONSOLIDATED BALANCE SHEET AS AT 31 OCTOBER 20X9

	£'000	£'000
Fixed assets		
Goodwill (W2) 4 – 2		2
Tangible fixed assets (350 + 75)		425
Current assets		
Stock (180 + 45 – 15(W3))	210	
Debtors (145 + 55 – 12*)	188	
Bank (70 + 20)	90	
	488	
Creditors: amounts falling due within one year		
Creditors (50 + 30)	80	
Proposed dividends (80 + 3**)	83	
Corporation tax (70 + 10)	80	
	243	
Net current assets		245
		672

ANSWERS TO ACTIVITIES

	£'000
Capital and reserves	
£1 ordinary shares	500
Profit and loss account (W7)	144
	644
Minority interests (W6)	28
	672

*Exclusion of intragroup dividends from debtors
**Dividends to minority included in creditors

Workings

1   Group structure

```
        Bamber
          │ 80%
        Renshaw
```

2   Goodwill

	£'000	£'000
Cost of acquisition		100
Share of net assets acquired		
Share capital	100	
Profit and loss account	20	
	120	
Group share: 80%		96
Goodwill		4

Amortised over 4 years = £1,000 per year

3   Provision for unrealised profit

(160,000 − 100,000) × 25% = £15,000

Because the sale was made by the holding company, the whole of this unrealised profit must be eliminated.

4   Investment income

Dividends receivable from Renshaw Ltd = £15,000 × 80% = £12,000

These will cancel on consolidation, leaving £14,000 − £12,000 = £2,000 investment income due to the group.

5   Administrative expenses

	£'000
Bamber	60
Renshaw	20
Goodwill amortised	1
	81

ANSWERS TO ACTIVITIES

      6   *Minority interest (b/s)*

           Net assets of Renshaw at 31 October 20X9 = £140,000

           ∴ Minority interest = 20% × £140,000 = £28,000

      7   *Group reserves at 31 October 20X9*

	£	£
Bamber Ltd		145
Less goodwill amortisation		
£4,000 × $^2/_4$		(2)
		143
Less PUP (W3)		(15)
		128
Renshaw Ltd		
Per 31.10.X9 b/s	40	
Less pre-acquisition	(20)	
	20	
Group share: 80%		16
		144

(b) The circumstances under which a subsidiary *may be* excluded from consolidation are set out in the **Companies Act 1985**. They should be distinguished from those circumstances under which a subsidiary *must be* excluded, which are set out in **FRS 2**.

    (i)   In the opinion of the directors it is **not material** for the purpose of giving a true and fair view, but two or more undertakings may be excluded only if they are not material taken together.

    (ii)   There are **severe long-term restrictions** in exercising the parent company's rights, eg civil war in the country of an overseas subsidiary.

    (iii)   The holding is **exclusively for resale**.

    (iv)   The information cannot be obtained without **disproportionate expense or undue delay**.

FRS 2 states that a subsidiary **must** be excluded from consolidation in the following cases.

    (i)   Severe long term restrictions are **substantially hindering the exercise of the parent's rights** over the subsidiary's assets or management.

    (ii)   The interest in the subsidiary undertaking is held **exclusively with a right to subsequent resale** and has not been previously consolidated.

    (iii)   The activities of the subsidiary undertaking are so **different** from those of other undertakings to be consolidated that its inclusion should **not give a true and fair view**.

Answer 14.2

EXTRACTS FROM THE CONSOLIDATED PROFIT AND LOSS ACCOUNT
FOR THE YEAR ENDED 31 DECEMBER 20X1

	£'000
Turnover	X
Group operating profit	X
Share of operating profit in associate (25% × 1,000)	250
Interest payable (see below)	X
Profit before tax	X
Tax (see below)	X
Profit after tax	X
Interest payable relates to	
Parent and subsidiaries	X
Associate (25% × 100)	25
Tax relates to	
Parent and subsidiaries	X
Associate (25% × 300)	75

EXTRACTS FROM THE CONSOLIDATED BALANCE SHEET
AS AT 31 DECEMBER 20X1

	£'000
Fixed assets	
Investment in associate (25% × 2,000)	500

Answer 14.3

(a) PORT PLC
CONSOLIDATED BALANCE SHEET AS AT 31 DECEMBER 20X6

	£'000	£'000
Fixed assets		
Goodwill		293
Freehold properties (400 + 300)		700
Plant and machinery (200 + 150)		350
		1,343
Current assets		
Stock (150 + 100)	250	
Debtors (170 + 80)	250	
Bank (40 + 20)	60	
	560	
Current liabilities		
Creditors (W5)	231	
Proposed dividend	50	
	281	
Net current assets		279
		1,622
Capital and reserves		
Share capital		500
Profit and loss account (W3)		830
		1,330
Minority interests (W2)		292
		1,622

Workings

1 Goodwill

	£'000
Cost of investment	450
Net assets acquired: 45% × (100 + 250)	157
	293

2 Minority interests

	£'000
55% × 530	292

3 Profit and loss account

	£'000
Port plc	740
Starboard Ltd (200 (W4) × 45%)	90
	830

4   *Post acquisition reserves of Starboard plc*

	£'000
Profit and loss reserve at 31.12.20X6	430
Add back dividend	20
	450
Less profit and loss reserve on acquisition	250
	200

5   *Creditors*

	£'000
Port plc	120
Starboard Ltd	100
Dividend to minority interests (55% × 20)	11
	231

(b) Port plc holds **less than 50%** of the ordinary shares of Starboard Ltd. Nevertheless, Starboard Ltd is a **subsidiary** of Port plc because its status is determined by a number of factors other than percentage of shares held. The key point is **control** rather than share ownership.

The requirement for Starboard Ltd to be treated as a subsidiary is determined by the Companies Act 1985 as amended by the Companies Act 1989 and by FRS 2 *Accounting for subsidiary undertakings*. FRS 2 states that an undertaking is the parent of another undertaking (a subsidiary undertaking) if any of the following apply.

(i)   It holds a majority of the voting rights.

(ii) It is a member of the undertaking and has the right to appoint or remove directors holding the majority of the voting rights at meetings of the board on all or all substantial matters.

(iii) It has a right to exercise a dominant influence over the undertaking by virtue of a contract or provisions in the memorandum and articles.

(iv) It has the right to control alone, under an agreement with other shareholders, a majority of the voting rights.

(v)   It has a participating interest and actually exercises a dominant influence over operating and financial policies or it and the undertakings are managed on a unified basis.

Starboard Ltd falls to be treated as a **subsidiary** on the grounds that Port plc is able to appoint four out of the five directors (criterion (ii)). Assuming that the other criteria do not apply, if Port plc did not have such a power, consolidation would not be appropriate because Starboard Ltd would not be a subsidiary.

ANSWERS TO ACTIVITIES

Index

INDEX

Accounting information, 4
Accounting policies, 33
Accounting Standards Board (ASB), 74, 75
Accounting standard, 74
Acid test ratio, 239
Accruals
   basis, 12
   concept, 12, 28
Accruals, 12
Acquisition accounting, 299
Adjusting events, 139
Alternative accounting, 93
Analysis of cash flow statements, 217
ASB, 161
Asset turnover, 229
Assets, 11, 17
Associate, 301
Associated undertakings, 301
Authorised (nominal) capital, 47
Average cost, 121

Balance sheet, 11, 19, 80
Big GAAP/little GAAP, 86
Bonus issues, 59

Calculating ratios, 225
Called-up capital, 47
Capital, 9, 13
Capital gearing ratio, 233
Capital grants, 108
Capitalisation of finance costs, 95
Cash cycle, 237
Cash flow ratio, 236
Cash flow statement, 19
Chairman's report, 224
Change in accounting policy, 165
Closing rate method, 174
Companies Act 1985, 51, 83, 107, 301
Companies Act 1989 (CA 1989), 74, 262
Company law, 74
Consolidated accounts, 260
Consolidated balance, 268
Consolidation, 260
Constructive obligation, 145
Consultative Committee of Accountancy Bodies (CCAB), 75

Contingent asset, 148
Contingent liabilities, 148
Continuing operating, 154
Control, 179, 260
Conversion, 172
Corporation tax, 130
Cost, 95
Creditors' turnover, 243
Current ratio, 239

Debenture loans, 54
Debt ratio, 232
Debt/equity ratio, 234
Debtor days, 241
Debtor days ratio, 240
Debtors payment period, 240
Deferred income, 109
Deferred taxation, 131
Defined benefit scheme, 175
Defined contribution scheme, 175
Depreciation, 96
Derecognition, 17
Directly attributable finance costs, 95
Directors' report, 83, 224
Disclosure requirements of FRS 15, 100
Discontinued operations, 154, 159
Dividends payable by a subsidiary, 275
Dominant influence, 259

Earnings per share (EPS), 155, 163, 164
Efficiency ratios, 240
Elements of financial statements, 14, 17
Equity accounting, 301
Estimation technique, 34
ETB, 185
European Union, 74
Exceptional items, 155, 156
Exemption of subsidiary undertakings from preparing group account, 262
Extended trial balance, 182
Extraordinary items, 155, 157

Factors affecting depreciation, 97
FIFO (first in, first out), 121
Finance lease, 174
Financial adaptability, 15
Financial Reporting Council (FRC), 75

Financial Reporting Exposure Draft (FRED), 77
Financial Reporting Standards (FRSs), 74, 77
Financial Reporting Standard for Smaller Entities (FRSSE), 86
Financial statements, 11
Fixed assets, 92
Fixed assets valuation: alternative accounting rules, 93
Fixed assets: disclosure, 94
Foreign currency translation, 173
FRS 1 Cash flow statements, 201, 217
FRS 2, 261
FRS 3 Reporting financial performance, 98, 155, 154
FRS 5 Reporting the substance of transactions, 176, 179
FRS 6 Acquisitions and mergers deals with the accounting treatment of business combinations which arise when, 299, 300
FRS 9 Associates and joint ventures, 301
FRS 10 Goodwill and intangible assets, 117, 282
FRS 11 Impairment of fixed assets and goodwill, 99, 118
FRS 12 Provisions, contingent liabilities and contingent assets, 95, 144
FRS 14 Earnings per share, 164
FRS 15 Tangible fixed assets, 93, 96
FRS 17 Retirement benefits, 175
FRS 18 Accounting policies, 26, 177
FRSSE, 86, 87
Fundamental errors, 165

Gains, 17
Gearing ratio, 232
Generally Accepted Accounting Practice (GAAP), 86
Goodwill, 305
Goodwill and pre-acquisition profits, 279
Goodwill arising on consolidation, 278
Government grants, 108
Gross profit margin, 231

HM Customs & Excise, 128
HP agreement, 174
Historical cost, 32

Implications of high or low gearing, 234
Indirect method, 200
Inherent goodwill, 116

Initial recognition, 17
Intangible assets, 92
Intangible fixed assets, 54, 81
Inter-company trading, 294
Interest cover, 235, 236
Interest held on a long-term basis, 260
International Accounting Standards, 76
International Accounting Standards Committee (IASC), 76
Investment properties, 106
Investments, 54, 92, 118
Issued capital, 47

Liabilities, 11, 17
Liability, 144
LIFO (last in, first out), 121
Limited companies, 6, 52, 78
Limited company accounts, 51
Limited liability, 45, 44
Liquidity, 232, 237, 239
Long-term solvency, 232

Machine hour method, 99
Making of accounting standards, 75
Market value of shares, 50
Measurement in financial statements, 14, 18
Medium-sized company, 85
Merger accounting, 299
Methods of calculating, 98
Methods of depreciation, 98
Minority interest, 272, 293

Need for accounts, 7
Negative goodwill, 117
Net book value (NBV), 97
Net investment method, 174
Net profit margin, 231
Net Realisable Value (NRV), 119
New acquisitions, 154
Nominal value, 56
Non-adjusting events, 140
Notes to the accounts, 80

Objective of financial statements, 14
Operating lease, 175
Operating profit, 80

Ordinary activities, 156
Ownership interest, 17

Paid-up capital, 48
Parent undertaking, 258
Participating interest, 259
PBIT, profit before interest and tax, 227
Permanent differences, 131
Post balance sheet, 138
Presentation of financial information, 14, 19
Primary profitability ratio, 229
Primary statement, 161
Prior period adjustments, 165
Private companies, 45
Profit, 10
Profit analysis, 231
Profit and loss account, 11, 19, 79
Profit and loss reserve, 57
Profit before interest and tax, 227
Profit margin, 229
Profit smoothing, 144
Profitability, 227
Provision, 144
Provisions, 144
Prudence concept, 29
Public companies, 45
Published accounts, 78
Purchased goodwill, 116

Qualitative characteristics of financial information, 14, 16
Quick ratio, 239

Ratio analysis, 224
Realised profits, 161
Recognition in financial statements, 14, 17
Reconciliation of movements in shareholders' funds, 162
Reducing balance method, 98
Related parties, 180
Related party transactions, 179
Replacement cost, 121
Reporting entity, 14
Research and development, 111
Reserves, 56, 82
Restructuring, 146

Return on capital employed (ROCE), 227
Return on shareholders' capital (ROSC), 229
Revaluation reserve, 93, 102
Revaluations, 100
Revenue grants, 108
Review Panel, 75
Rights issues, 60
ROCE, 227
ROSC, 229

Secondary ratios, 229
Share capital, 56
Share premium account, 58
Short-term solvency, 237
Small and medium-sized groups, 262
Small company, 84
SSAP 1 Accounting for associated companies, 301
SSAP 2 Disclosure of accounting policies, 26
SSAP 3 Earnings per share, 164
SSAP 4 Accounting for government grants, 108, 109, 110
SSAP 5 Accounting for value added tax, 128
SSAP 6 Extraordinary items and prior year adjustment, 155
SSAP 12, 97, 100, 106
SSAP 13 Accounting for research and development, 111
SSAP 15, 131
SSAP 15 Accounting for deferred tax, 131
SSAP 17, 141
SSAP 17 Accounting for post balance sheet events, 138
SSAP 19 accounting for investment properties, 105
SSAP 20 Foreign currency translation, 172
SSAP 21 Accounting for leases and hire purchase contracts, 174
SSAP 22, 117
SSAP 23 Accounting for acquisitions and mergers, 299
SSAP 25 Segmental reporting, 180
Standard cost, 121
Statement of principles, 30
Statement of Principles for Financial Reporting, 14
Statement of total recognised gains and losses, 19, 155, 161
Statements of Standard Accounting Practice (SSAPs), 74
Statutory accounts, 78

Statutory books, 46
Statutory provisions relating to all fixed assets, 92
Stock days, 241
Stock Exchange, 76, 85
Stock turnover period, 241
Stock valuation, 119
Straight line method, 98
Subsequent expenditure, 96
Subsequent remeasurement, 17
Subsidiary undertaking, 258
Substance over form, 33
Sum of digits method, 99

Tangible assets, 92
Tangible fixed assets, 54
Taxation, 55, 132
Temporal (or 'historical') method, 174
Timing differences, 131
Translation, 173

Unlimited liability, 44
Unrealised profits, 161
Urgent Issues Task Force (UITF), 75
Users of accounting information, 7
Users of financial statements, 15

Valuation of fixed assets, 92
VAT, 128

Yellow Book, 76

See overleaf for information on other
BPP products and how to order

AAT Order

To BPP Professional Education, Aldine Place, London W12 8AW
Tel: 020 8740 2211. Fax: 020 8740 1184
E-mail: Publishing@bpp.com Web:www.bpp.com

Mr/Mrs/Ms (Full name) _____

Daytime delivery address _____

_____ Postcode _____

Daytime Tel _____ E-mail _____

	5/04 Texts	5/04 Kits	Special offer	8/04 Passcards	Success CDs
FOUNDATION (£14.95 except as indicated)				Foundation	
Units 1 & 2 Receipts and Payments	☐	☐	Foundation Sage Bookeeping and Excel Spreadsheets CD-ROM free if ordering all Foundation Text and Kits, including Units 21 and 22/23	£6.95 ☐	£14.95 ☐
Unit 3 Ledger Balances and Initial Trial Balance	☐ (Combined Text & Kit)				
Unit 4 Supplying Information for Mgmt Control	☐ (Combined Text & Kit)				
Unit 21 Working with Computers (£9.95)	☐				
Unit 22/23 Healthy Workplace/Personal Effectiveness (£9.95)	☐				
Sage and Excel for Foundation (Workbook with CD-ROM £9.95)	☐				
INTERMEDIATE (£9.95 except as indicated)			☐		
Unit 5 Financial Records and Accounts	☐	☐		£5.95 ☐	£14.95 ☐
Unit 6/7 Costs and Reports (Combined Text £14.95)	☐			£5.95 ☐	
Unit 6 Costs and Revenues	☐	☐			
Unit 7 Reports and Returns	☐	☐			
TECHNICIAN (£9.95 except as indicated)					
Unit 8/9 Core Managing Performance and Controlling Resources	☐	☐		£5.95 ☐	£14.95 ☐
Spreadsheets for Technician (Workbook with CD-ROM)	☐		Spreadsheets for Technicians CD-ROM free if take Unit 8/9 Text and Kit ☐		
Unit 10 Core Managing Systems and People (£14.95)	☐ (Combined Text & Kit)			£5.95 ☐	£14.95 ☐
Unit 11 Option Financial Statements (A/c Practice)	☐	☐		£5.95 ☐	
Unit 12 Option Financial Statements (Central Govnmt)	☐	☐		£5.95 ☐	
Unit 15 Option Cash Management and Credit Control	☐	☐		£5.95 ☐	
Unit 17 Option Implementing Audit Procedures	☐	☐		£5.95 ☐	
Unit 18 Option Business Tax FA04 (8/04) (£14.95)	☐ (Combined Text & Kit)			£5.95 ☐	
Unit 19 Option Personal Tax FA04 (8/04) (£14.95)	☐ (Combined Text & Kit)			£5.95 ☐	
TECHNICIAN 2003 (£9.95)					
Unit 18 Option Business Tax FA03 (8/03 Text & Kit)	☐				
Unit 19 Option Personal Tax FA03 (8/03 Text & Kit)	☐				
SUBTOTAL	£	£		£	£

TOTAL FOR PRODUCTS £ ☐

POSTAGE & PACKING

Texts/Kits	First	Each extra
UK	£3.00	£3.00
Europe*	£6.00	£4.00
Rest of world	£20.00	£10.00
Passcards		
UK	£2.00	£1.00
Europe*	£3.00	£2.00
Rest of world	£8.00	£8.00
Success CDs		
UK	£2.00	£1.00
Europe*	£3.00	£2.00
Rest of world	£8.00	£8.00

TOTAL FOR POSTAGE & PACKING £ ☐
(Max £12 Texts/Kits/Passcards - deliveries in UK)

Grand Total (Cheques to *BPP Professional Education*) £ ☐
I enclose a cheque for (incl. Postage)

Or charge to Access/Visa/Switch

Card Number ☐☐☐☐ ☐☐☐☐ ☐☐☐☐ ☐☐☐☐ CV2 No ☐☐☐ last 3 digits on signature strip

Expiry date ☐☐/☐☐ Start Date ☐☐/☐☐

Issue Number (Switch Only) ☐☐

Signature _____

We aim to deliver to all UK addresses inside 5 working days; a signature will be required. Orders to all EU addresses should be delivered within 6 working days. All other orders to overseas addresses should be delivered within 8 working days. * Europe includes the Republic of Ireland and the Channel Islands.

See overleaf for information on other
BPP products and how to order

AAT Order

To BPP Professional Education, Aldine Place, London W12 8AW
Tel: 020 8740 2211. Fax: 020 8740 1184
E-mail: Publishing@bpp.com Web:www.bpp.com

Mr/Mrs/Ms (Full name) _____
Daytime delivery address _____
_____ Postcode _____
Daytime Tel _____ E-mail _____

OTHER MATERIAL FOR AAT STUDENTS	8/04 Texts	3/03 Text	3/04 Text
FOUNDATION (£5.95)			
Basic Maths and English	☐		
INTERMEDIATE (£5.95)			
Basic Bookkeeping (for students exempt from Foundation)	☐		
FOR ALL STUDENTS (£5.95)			
Building Your Portfolio (old standards)		☐	
Building Your Portfolio (new standards)	☐		
Basic Costing			☐

AAT PAYROLL

	Finance Act 2004	Finance Act 2003
	8/04	9/03
	December 2004 and June 2005 assessments	June 2004 exams only

Special offer Take Text and Kit together £44.95 ☐ | **Special offer** Take Text and Kit together £44.95 ☐

LEVEL 2 Text (£29.95)	☐	☐
LEVEL 2 Kit (£19.95)	☐ For assessments in 2005 £44.95 ☐	☐ For assessments in 2004 £44.95 ☐
LEVEL 3 Text (£29.95)	☐	☐
LEVEL 3 Kit (£19.95)	☐	☐

SUBTOTAL £ _____   £ _____   £ _____

TOTAL FOR PRODUCTS £ _____

POSTAGE & PACKING

	First	Each extra
Texts/Kits		
UK	£3.00	£3.00
Europe*	£6.00	£4.00
Rest of world	£20.00	£10.00
Passcards		
UK	£2.00	£1.00
Europe*	£3.00	£2.00
Rest of world	£8.00	£8.00
Tapes		
UK	£2.00	£1.00
Europe*	£3.00	£2.00
Rest of world	£8.00	£8.00

TOTAL FOR POSTAGE & PACKING £ _____
(Max £12 Texts/Kits/Passcards - deliveries in UK)

Grand Total (Cheques to *BPP Professional Education*) £ _____

I enclose a cheque for (incl. Postage) ☐
Or charge to Access/Visa/Switch

Card Number ☐☐☐☐ ☐☐☐☐ ☐☐☐☐ ☐☐☐☐   CV2 No ☐☐☐ last 3 digits on signature strip

Expiry date _____   Start Date _____

Issue Number (Switch Only) _____

Signature _____

We aim to deliver to all UK addresses inside 5 working days; a signature will be required. Orders to all EU addresses should be delivered within 6 working days. All other orders to overseas addresses should be delivered within 8 working days. * Europe includes the Republic of Ireland and the Channel Islands.

Review Form & Free Prize Draw – Unit 11 Drafting Financial Statements (5/04)

All original review forms from the entire BPP range, completed with genuine comments, will be entered into one of two draws on 31 January 2005 and 31 July 2005. The names on the first four forms picked out on each occasion will be sent a cheque for £50.

Name: _____   Address: _____

How have you used this Interactive Text?
(Tick one box only)
☐ Home study (book only)
☐ On a course: college _____
☐ With 'correspondence' package
☐ Other _____

Why did you decide to purchase this Interactive Text? *(Tick one box only)*
☐ Have used BPP Texts in the past
☐ Recommendation by friend/colleague
☐ Recommendation by a lecturer at college
☐ Saw advertising
☐ Other _____

During the past six months do you recall seeing/receiving any of the following?
(Tick as many boxes as are relevant)
☐ Our advertisement in *Accounting Technician* magazine
☐ Our advertisement in *Pass*
☐ Our brochure with a letter through the post

Which (if any) aspects of our advertising do you find useful?
(Tick as many boxes as are relevant)
☐ Prices and publication dates of new editions
☐ Information on Interactive Text content
☐ Facility to order books off-the-page
☐ None of the above

Have you used the companion Assessment Kit for this subject?   ☐ Yes   ☐ No

Your ratings, comments and suggestions would be appreciated on the following areas

	Very useful	Useful	Not useful
Introduction	☐	☐	☐
Chapter contents lists	☐	☐	☐
Examples	☐	☐	☐
Activities and answers	☐	☐	☐
Key learning points	☐	☐	☐
Quick quizzes and answers	☐	☐	☐
Activity checklist	☐	☐	☐

	Excellent	Good	Adequate	Poor
Overall opinion of this Text	☐	☐	☐	☐

Do you intend to continue using BPP Interactive Texts/Assessment Kits?   ☐ Yes   ☐ No

Please note any further comments and suggestions/errors on the reverse of this page.

The BPP author of this edition can be e-mailed at: janiceross@bpp.com

Please return this form to: Janice Ross, BPP Professional Education, FREEPOST, London, W12 8BR

Review Form & Free Prize Draw (continued)

Please note any further comments and suggestions/errors below

Free Prize Draw Rules

1. Closing date for 31 January 2005 draw is 31 December 2004. Closing date for 31 July 2005 draw is 30 June 2005.
2. Restricted to entries with UK and Eire addresses only. BPP employees, their families and business associates are excluded.
3. No purchase necessary. Entry forms are available upon request from BPP Professional Education. No more than one entry per title, per person. Draw restricted to persons aged 16 and over.
4. Winners will be notified by post and receive their cheques not later than 6 weeks after the relevant draw date.
5. The decision of the promoter in all matters is final and binding. No correspondence will be entered into.